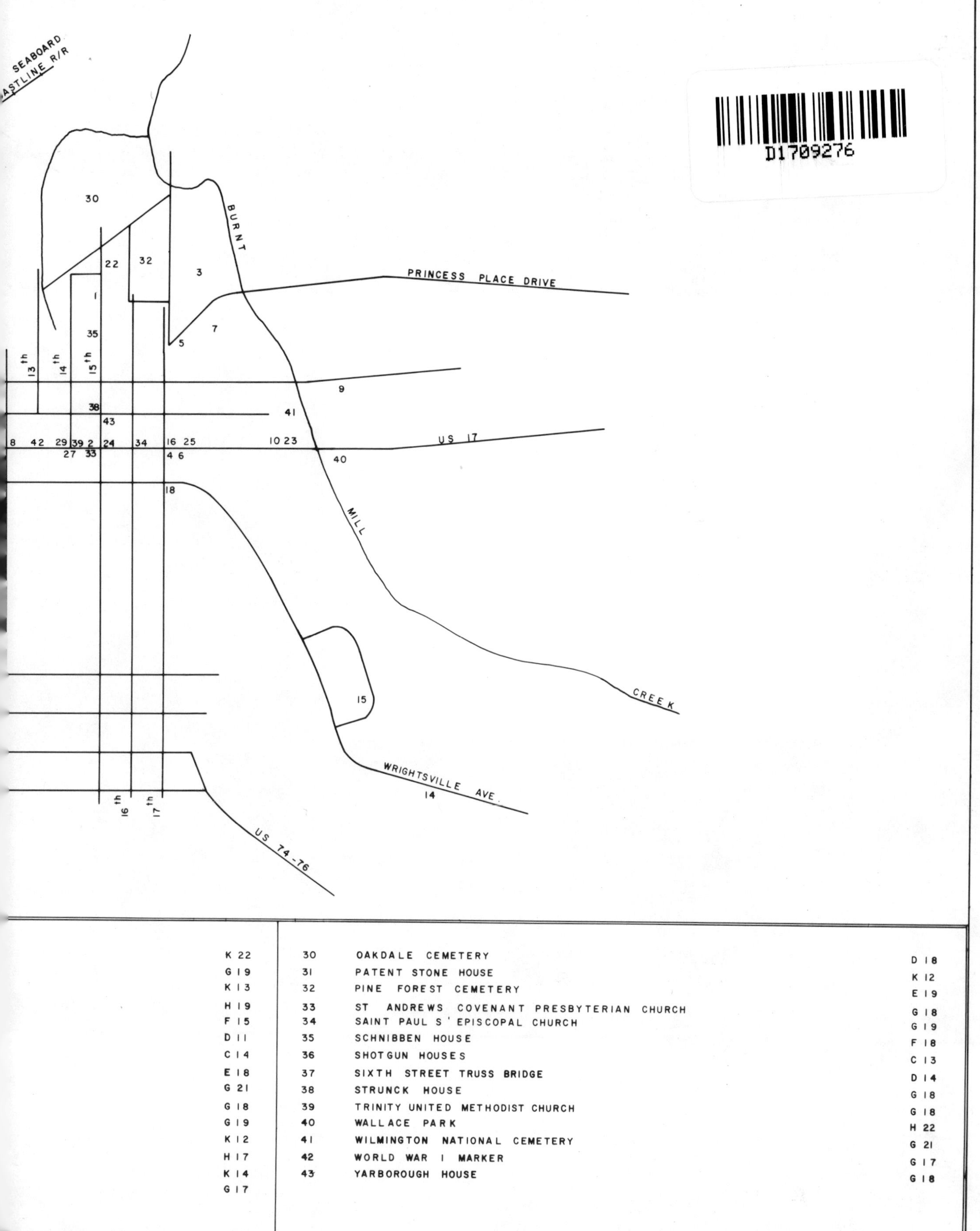

K 22	30	OAKDALE CEMETERY	D 18
G 19	31	PATENT STONE HOUSE	K 12
K 13	32	PINE FOREST CEMETERY	E 19
H 19	33	ST ANDREWS COVENANT PRESBYTERIAN CHURCH	G 18
F 15	34	SAINT PAUL S' EPISCOPAL CHURCH	G 19
D 11	35	SCHNIBBEN HOUSE	F 18
C 14	36	SHOTGUN HOUSES	C 13
E 18	37	SIXTH STREET TRUSS BRIDGE	D 14
G 21	38	STRUNCK HOUSE	G 18
G 18	39	TRINITY UNITED METHODIST CHURCH	G 18
G 19	40	WALLACE PARK	H 22
K 12	41	WILMINGTON NATIONAL CEMETERY	G 21
H 17	42	WORLD WAR I MARKER	G 17
K 14	43	YARBOROUGH HOUSE	G 18
G 17			

The rich history of Wilmington, North Carolina, is preserved in its commercial, governmental, ecclesiastical, and domestic structures. Its past is also reflected in early paving materials, landscaped areas, ironwork, and statuary. This architecture is characterized by a boldness and directness that emphasizes the energy, forcefulness, and taste of the citizens of the bustling port city. Settled in the early eighteenth century, the city's shipbuilding and lumber mills helped North Carolina become the world leader in the production of naval stores. Wilmington was a political center during the American Revolution when violent demonstrations against the Stamp Act occurred, and it was the most important Southern port during the Civil War.

The volume covers all of Wilmington's architecture, from the mid-eighteenth century to the present, from high style to simple vernacular buildings. It also covers structures built or occupied by all of Wilmington's society, from the financial elite to alley dwellers. The significant architectural and historical heritage of Wilmington's minority black community is included.

Clear, concise, architectural description and historical narrative combined with over 180 photographs make this book an exceptionally attractive one for architects, historians, and others. The city of Wilmington is history and architecture that one can see and touch and walk through. Beginning on the waterfront, with some of the earliest buildings, the author leads us through the city street-by-street. This is at once a useful guidebook and a dependable volume for reference.

Here is a portrait of Wilmington, a city notable for its unique historical character and its architectural distinction.

WILMINGTON, NORTH CAROLINA

An Architectural and Historical Portrait

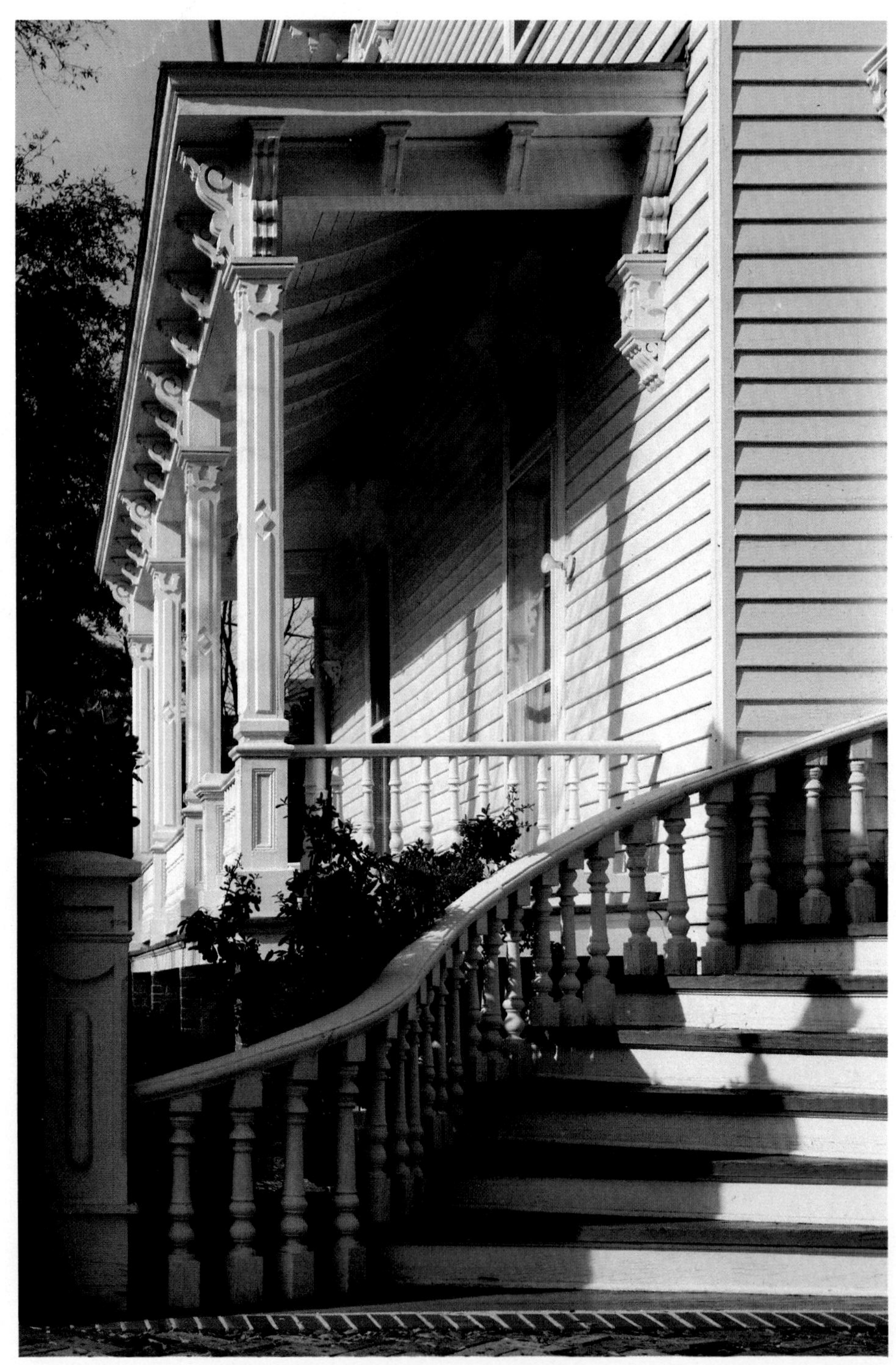

Costin House porch, 20 South Fifth Avenue.

WILMINGTON NORTH CAROLINA

An Architectural and Historical Portrait

by

Tony P. Wrenn

with photographs by

Wm. Edmund Barrett

Published for the

Junior League of Wilmington, N.C., Inc.

by the University Press of Virginia

Charlottesville

THE UNIVERSITY PRESS OF VIRGINIA

Library of Congress Cataloging in Publication Data

Wrenn, Tony P.
Wilmington, North Carolina : an architectural and historical portrait.

Bibliography: p.
Includes index.
1. Wilmington (N.C.)—Buildings. 2. Wilmington (N.C.)—Parks. 3. Architecture—North Carolina—Wilmington. 4. Wilmington (N.C.)—History. I. Barrett, William Edmund. II. Title.
NA735.W52W73 1984 720′.9756′27 83-16932
ISBN 0-8139-0959-7

First published 1984

Printed in the United States of America

Ida Brooks Kellam, 1895–1981

DEDICATION There are three people without whom this work could not have been produced. It is their volume, and the author's debt to Ida Brooks Kellam, Bill Reaves, and Ann Scott is readily acknowledged. A good many other people accomplished herculean research tasks and provided unexcelled information and assistance.

The Junior League of Wilmington, Inc., and the Archives and History Division, North Carolina Department of Cultural Resources, and the individuals from both who helped, also deserve this dedication, for without them there would have been no publication.

Contents

Illustrations

Preface

Though I had been to Wilmington before 1973 and recognized that it had architectural charm and historical importance, I had never actually *seen* the city. That year I spent the summer in Wilmington. Along with Ruth Selden-Sturgill and Claire Fahnenstock, who worked with me, I walked the streets of the city, evaluating buildings, marking maps, taking photographs, making architectural notes. Early and late we transcribed notes, identified photographs, or read whatever we could find about the city.

We were frequently excited with what we saw, asking questions locally about what this or that was. Often we were excited enough to call our fellow workers at the Division of Archives and History, Department of Cultural Resources in Raleigh, to share with them the city we were discovering. And throughout we talked with people, asked questions, and made notes. Frequently, in response to one of our questions, Ida Brooks Kellam would pull out a file to share with us her own excitement and love for the city.

Later Bill Reaves would do the same, as would Ann Scott, Ann Cook, "Billie" McEachern, and a host of other people. It is still a puzzle to me that they never complained about my steady stream of questions and requests for information, or that they never thought my liking for certain buildings misplaced.

I do not know how many trips I have made to Wilmington since 1973, or how many months altogether I have spent there. Each time, however, I spent as much time as possible in the streets, or at least outside, for many hours were also spent in the city's cemeteries and parks.

In this work I have tried to show the reader what Wilmington meant to me. The failure is that so little of the city is actually covered here. Some of my favorite sites were torn down during the years between 1973 and the present: the Victoria Theater; the Seaboard Air Line Train Station; the Hotel Wilmington; James Walker Memorial Hospital, and more that I liked have disappeared, and space does not permit their inclusion in this volume. Nonetheless, others I like as well remain, from mansions to shotgun houses, from icehouses to manufactories, from saloons to massive hotels, and many of those are also not covered.

At various times I walked to, looked at, and made notes on some 1,400 sites, buildings, and objects in Wilmington. In the Wilmington cemeteries I made notes on several hundred more monuments, vistas, plans, etc. Yet I only walked through part of the city.

I hope that the result of this volume, with Wm. Edmund Barrett's photographs, will be to inspire additional volumes by others until the city has been covered, sites have been at least recognized, and an *Encyclopedia Wilmingtoniana* has at last been produced. Even then there should be plans for regular supplements.

Acknowledgments

No matter how carefully records are kept, it is inevitable that someone who has given assistance in a work of this type will fail to be acknowledged. The author apologizes beforehand and confesses his indebtedness to all the Wilmingtonians who offered hospitality, information, leads, and good will.

Ruth Selden-Sturgill and Claire Fahnenstock, who worked with me in the summer of 1973 in accomplishing a Wilmington architectural survey for the Division of Archives and History, Department of Cultural Resources, Raleigh, had much to do with my involvement in Wilmington. During that same summer Ida Brooks Kellam and Henry J. MacMillan provided space, information, and ready assistance.

As the present volume evolved, it was Janet Seapker who talked me into taking on the task of getting this work together and who later provided much valuable material. Mrs. Neill Laney, as the first of several committee chairpersons representing the Junior League of Wilmington, N.C., Inc., the organization that sponsored this project, was also most persuasive. Mrs. Robert Daniell Cook, also committee chairperson and major helper throughout, and Mrs. Richard Franklin Bryan, who was the last chairperson with whom I worked, are owed a major debt of gratitude. Mrs. Donald M. Reid, Jr., Mrs. Margaret Faw Fonvielle, Mrs. S. Clayton Callaway, Jr., and Mrs. R. Edward Kizer, Jr., also served as representatives of the League in working with the author.

Mrs. Herbert Pearce Scott directed local research efforts and accomplished major research throughout the period of the project. Ida Brooks Kellam, whose own files and those of the Lower Cape Fear Historical Society (of which she was archivist) were major sources, cooperated with Mrs. Scott and with William M. Reaves, whose newspaper and other files were another major source. The three provided a steady stream of information and support throughout the project. Their proofreading and checking of the manuscript saved the author many errors, and he takes the blame for those that crept in despite their efforts.

In Vienna, Virginia, Mayo Stuntz, who lived in Wilmington in the 1930s, made available his newspaper and manuscript files, especially on the Hotel Cape Fear and the U.S. Post Office and Federal Building. Architectural historian Gale Alder of Washington, D.C., also provided much information on Wilmington public buildings, while architectural historian Ruth Selden-Sturgill of New York provided information on Henry Bacon.

In Wilmington, architects Charles and Leslie N. Boney provided constant information on architects of contemporary buildings as well as information on their own firm; Leora H. McEachern provided material on Episcopal churches and on cemeteries; Isabel M. Williams provided material on Thalian Hall–City Hall; James Robert Warren provided material on schools, especially Tileston, and on other topics; James D. Carr provided material on several houses and a taped commentary on the initial drafts of this work; Henry J. MacMillan provided material on the Williams and MacMillan families and the sites associated with them; Katherine Howell provided material on the John Taylor House and access to other material in the Wilmington files of the local library; and R. V. Asbury provided material on structures granted markers by the Historic Wilmington Foundation. Architect Edward F. Turberg also provided advice and valuable information.

On each structure included in this work, we attempted to put together a chain of title, and to check city directories, the Sanborn Insurance map and other maps, family records, newspapers, and other primary and secondary sources. Due to the wealth of material gathered, we decided to limit the facts in the book to information concerning the original owners of each structure, also mentioning any other important occupants or notable events. We also chose structures representative of different architectural styles, omitting some significant buildings if a similar one had previously been described. Mrs. Herbert Pearce Scott was chairperson and coordinator, for this effort, accomplishing research, assigning research, and coordinating material in files for the author. She worked with Ida Brooks Kellam and William M. Reaves, who provided endless material from their own files. Others who did major research included Sue Bayrd; Mrs. William Benjamin Beery, III; Charles Boney; Mrs. William G. Broadfoot, Jr.; Mrs. Lawrence Dawson Bullard; Mrs. Algernon Lee Butler, Jr.; Mrs. Lawrence G. Calhoun; Mrs. S. Clayton Callaway, Jr.; Mrs. Robert Daniell Cook; Mrs. Harold Cobb Ernst; Mrs. William T. Francis; Mrs. G. Deanes Gornto; Mrs. George Everard Kidder; Mrs. Alton Yates Lennon; Mrs. Edward F. Mintz; Mrs. Ralph Bryan Moore, Jr.; Mrs. James C. Muller; Mr. and Mrs. Wallace Carmichael Murchison; Mrs. James Frederick Murray, II; Mrs. Ernst Tilgham Poole, Jr.; Mrs. James Fulton Smith, Jr.; Mrs. Laurence Gray Sprunt; Mrs. James Steadman; Mrs. Harry Wylie Stovall, III; Mrs. Alan Taylor Strange; Mrs. Stuart D. Sundquist; Mrs. Wade Hampton Tillery, Jr.; Mrs. Raiford Graham Trask, Jr.; Mrs. Sam Walker; James Robert Warren; Mrs. Martin Stevenson Willard; Mrs. L. E. Woodbury III; Mrs. Lionel Leon Yow.

The following also assisted: Mrs. William Paul Allen; Mrs. Raymond Lacy Ballard, Jr.; Mrs. Ralph Buckner Barden; James R. Beeler; Mrs. James R. Beeler; Mrs. Charles E. Bergamini; Mrs. R. D. Conrad; Mrs. Tom L. Crittenden; Dottie Crouch; Mrs. G. LaRue Downing; Mrs. Alonzo Dumay Gorham, Jr.; Mrs. Benjamin Robinson Graham; Mrs. Frederick Bolles Graham, Jr.; Margaret Hall; Mrs. Richard Vollers Hanson; Mrs. Miles Higgins; Mrs. J. Howard Highsmith; Mrs. Spotswood Hathaway Huntt; Mrs. F. D. Ingram; Mrs. Paul Jennewein; Mrs. C. B. Jennings; Mrs. Robert Boyd Jones; Mrs. William Talmage Jones; Mrs. Donald B. Koonce; Mrs. Rufus L. Legrand; Mrs. E. Emory Lewallen III; Mrs. William Louis Mabry; Mrs. William Carter Mebane III; Col. Robert S. Milner; Mrs. Howell Anderson Nicholson III; Mrs. J. B. Patrick; Mrs. T. A. Price; Mrs. James Adkins Price; Mrs. Burk Rehder; Mrs. James Fred Rippy III; Mrs. Junius Calvin Smith; Mickey Southerland; Mrs. Emmet Crow Stovall; Mrs. Ivey Sutton, Jr.; Mrs. David Pryse Thomas; Mrs. Virginia F. Van Velsor; Mrs. Calvin Fleming Wells; Mrs. Joseph Willard Whitted, Jr.; Mrs. Frederick Willetts III; Mrs. William J. Wolff; Thomas H. Wright, Jr.; Mrs. Richard Youngblood; Lesi Ann Wright.

In the final stages of the project, Mrs. Richard F. Bryan and Mrs. Herbert P. Scott worked tirelessly to see the project through. Mrs. Rhoderick C. Hawk, Mrs. George William Jones, Jr., Mrs. G. Deanes Gornto, Mrs. Llewellyn E. Woodbury III, and Mrs. John Lynn Leonard III, presidents of the League, were most helpful and supportive. Among others in Wilmington who worked on the project during this period were Mrs. Richard C. Andrews, Jr., Mr. and Mrs. William J. Boney, Jr., Miss Catharine Drewry, Miss Constance Hobbs, Mrs. Crayne Howes, Miss Ann Conner, Mrs. James O. Carter, Mr. Joe Holman, Mrs. Kay G. McGhee, Mrs. John A. Messick, Mr. and Mrs. Wallace C. Murchison, Mrs. Allen J. Pennington, Mrs. Fred A. Rogers III, Miss Mary Scott, Ms. Julie Shields, Mrs. Mickey G. Southerland, Mrs. Heide Trask, Mrs. Martin S. Willard, Mrs. Ronald Woodruff, and Mrs. Lionel L. Yow.

Photographer Wm. Edmund Barrett and his wife, Mary Barrett, were major sources of support. Their inspiration and point of view were invaluable. Mr. Gary L. Johnson and Ms. Ruth Coder Fitzgerald, who assisted with proofreading and other drudgeries, and Ms. Una Crist and Ms. Georgia Hening, who typed the final product, are also owed a great debt. The endpaper maps were designed by T. Richard Ponnell.

WILMINGTON, NORTH CAROLINA

An Architectural and Historical Portrait

1. A New Map of Carolina, By Philip Lea, London. (Lower Cape Fear Historical Society Archives. Copy by William J. Boney, Jr.)

Wilmington Historic District Introduction

A Wilmington Historic District, larger than the area covered in this text, has been entered in the National Register of Historic Places. The nomination to the National Register contains the following summation of reasons for listing the district:

Wilmington, long North Carolina's chief port, is the most distinctively urban of the state's towns; in a state historically rural, only Wilmington exhibits the character of a nineteenth-century city. *The grid of streets extending back from the waterfront is densely filled with commercial, governmental, ecclesiastical, and domestic buildings of consistent scale; the townscape is enhanced by the retention of early paving materials, large trees, and street furniture including ironwork and statuary. The architecture of nearly every period is characterized by a boldness and directness that place grand effect over precision of detail, seeming to express the energy and forcefulness of the merchants, shippers, and politicians of the bustling port city. There are a number of structures of outstanding merit, including works by Samuel Sloan and Thomas U. Walter, but the architectural fabric is dominated and unified by an apparently indigenous bracketed, vented Italianate idiom that was popular throughout much of the nineteenth century, especially during the antebellum boom period. As a major center of political, cultural, and commercial activity and as the most significant concentration of urban architectural fabric, Wilmington is of prime importance to North Carolina. It is nationally significant as a major Southern port—the last Atlantic Coast port open to support the Confederacy—and a city where local efforts are actively preserving a townscape notable for its unique character and architectural distinction.*

There is indeed an allure to Wilmington that sets it apart from other coastal settlements. As the register nomination also notes, "In the midst of pine barrens and swamps which surround the city, Wilmington has an oasis quality about it."

Wilmington began, as did several other North Carolina coastal settlements, in the eighteenth century. Though Verrazanno explored the Cape Fear area in 1524 and was followed by Spanish adventurers before the end of the sixteenth century, English explorers did not arrive until the seventeenth, and there was no permanent settlement along the Cape Fear River until the eighteenth century. (See fig. 1.)

The town of Brunswick, just below Wilmington, was founded in 1725. Church and government followed in 1729, the year New Hanover Precinct was established. By 1731, land on a river bluff northeast of Brunswick was being bought and sold as a suggested town site. In April 1731 Governor George Burrington asked the general assembly to pass an act "for building a Town on Cape Fear [River] and appointing commissioners for that purpose." The assembly noted that there was already a town on the Cape Fear—Brunswick—and the act failed, but proponents continued planning. They wanted a new town on the eastern bluffs of the Cape Fear River, just south of the junction of its northeast and northwest branches. A town was actually laid off by April 1733.

The settlement was first called New Carthage, then New Liverpool, and by 1735, New Town or Newton. That year, Newton residents petitioned for formal establishment. Formation of a town was held up until February 1739, when the general assembly passed a bill creating, not Newton, but Wilmington—assigning the name to honor Spencer Compton, Earl of Wilmington, sponsor and mentor of then-Governor Gabriel Johnston.

After the establishment of Wilmington, government functions moved there from Brunswick, and the Episcopal parish of St. James was established to serve the new town. Wilmington almost immediately became the state's most important port, partly because of the fine safe harbor, partly because of settlement nearby and upriver in the present Fayetteville

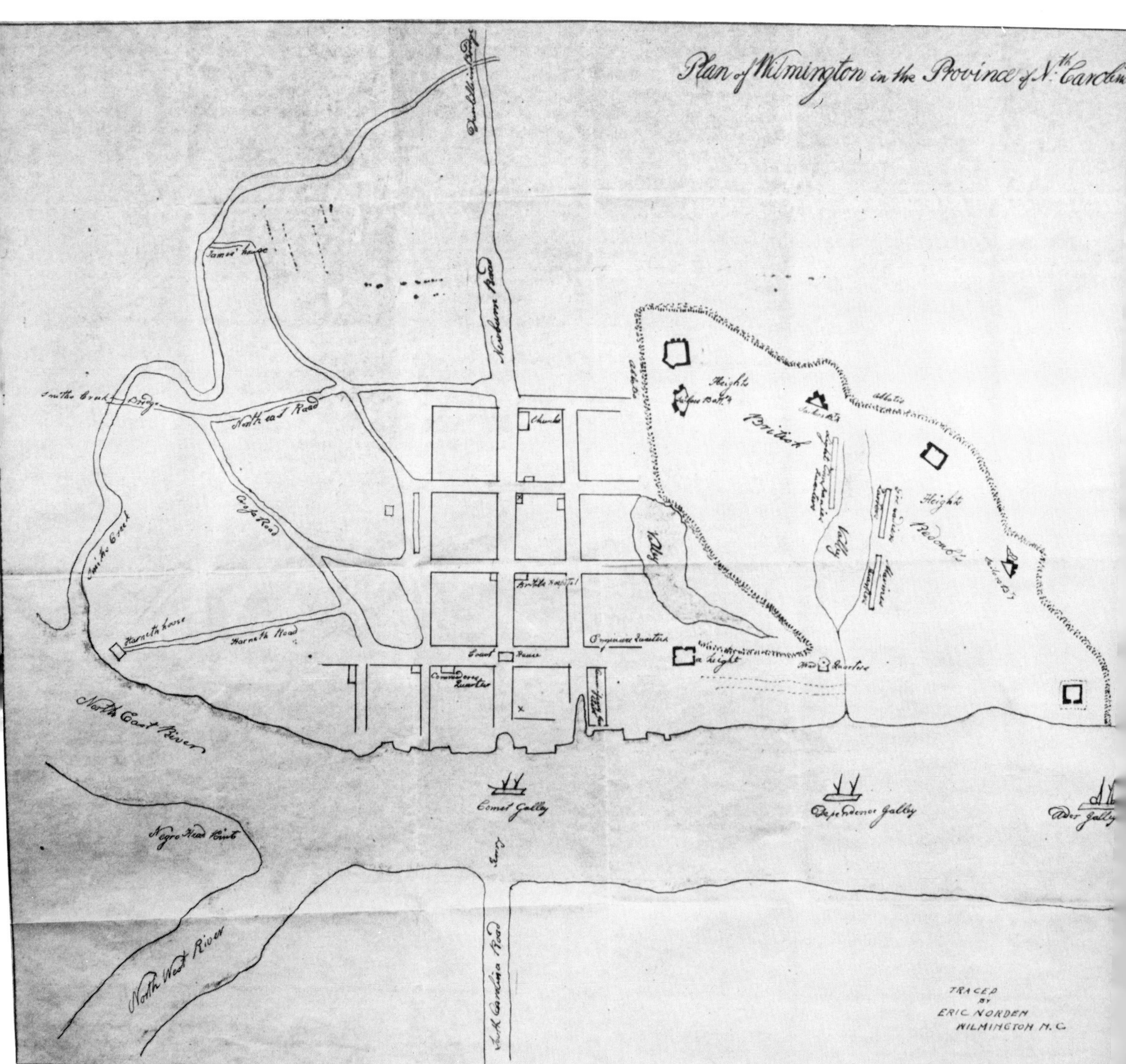

2. Plan of Wilmington in the Province of Nth Carolina. (Clinton map 286, courtesy William L. Clements Library, University of Michigan, Ann Arbor. Copy by William J. Boney, Jr.)

area, but mainly because of the products of surrounding pine forests. They provided tar, pitch, and turpentine, along with rosin—naval stores of primary importance to Britain's fleet. North Carolina led the world in production of naval stores from approximately 1720 to 1870. Lumber mills, shipbuilding and repair yards, tar and turpentine distilleries were established as important industries.

Around this industry and commerce grew a rich plantation area and town. Settlers arrived from other American cities—Boston, New York, Philadelphia, Charleston—as well as from the West Indies, England, Ireland, Scotland, France, and later, and in great numbers, from Germany. In 1759 Thomas Godfrey came from Philadelphia to Wilmington, where he completed his dramatic work *The Prince of Parthia,* said to have been the first American attempt at dramatic composition. It was not performed until 1767, four years after Godfrey died in Wilmington. By that time the *North Carolina Gazette and Weekly Post Boy* was being published. The *Cape Fear Mercury* came in 1769, and other newspapers followed. A classical school was established by Presbyterian minister James Tate in 1760, the same year that the Cape Fear Library Society was founded. Before the eighteenth century ended, the Thalian Society had been formed to promote amateur theater and drama. The small town had become a cultural as well as a commercial center.

With the approach of the American Revolution, the town also became a political center. Large, violent demonstrations against the Stamp Act occurred in October 1765, and on November 16 the visiting stamp master was forced by several hundred Sons of Liberty to resign his office. The local publisher agreed to produce his news on unstamped paper. In February 1766, after a Wilmington meeting to plan resistance to the Stamp Act, Governor William Tryon in Brunswick was forced to give up the colony's comptroller and the papers for several ships that the British had seized for Stamp Act violations. On February 16 they forced release of the vessels as well, and gained assurance, though not from the governor, that they would not have to comply with the hated act.

Cornelius Harnett, one of the protesters, became a leading revolutionist in North Carolina. Harnett, whose home was on the northern outskirts of the city, served as a member of the Continental Congress and was presiding officer of the North Carolina Provincial Council after October 18, 1775, making him, for a time, acting governor. He died in 1781 after being captured by British soldiers, who did not provide adequate medical care for an already ill man.

William Hooper was also a resident of the town and another of the state's chief revolutionists. A lawyer, he too served in the Continental Congress and was one of the North Carolina signers of the Declaration of Independence. He moved to Hillsborough in 1782, and his Wilmington dwelling was destroyed before 1900.

During the revolutionary era, Wilmington troops battled the British at Moore's Creek on February 27, 1776. The city remained relatively peaceful from then until January 1781, when the British, commanded by Major Craig, seized the city. After the battle of Guilford Court House on April 12, the forces under command of General Cornwallis arrived in the Wilmington area, where they remained eleven days. The rest of the British occupation forces departed in November. By that time Cornwallis had already surrendered at Yorktown.

The end of the conflict brought new trade and prosperity to the growing city. Naval stores continued to be the mainstay, but the area became a regional trading center as well. Improvements in roads and in railroads later added measurably to the status of the city in this regard. The Wilmington and Raleigh Railroad was chartered in 1834, begun in 1836, and completed to Weldon in 1840. It was the first in North Carolina and at that time had the longest track in the world. The line became the Wilmington and Weldon Railroad in 1855. Edward B. Dudley, a Wilmingtonian and president of the railroad, became the first North Carolina governor to be popularly elected, when he was chosen for the office in 1836.

Before the end of the nineteenth century, several other railroads had joined the Wilmington and Weldon in providing rail access to and from Wilmington. The Atlantic Coast Line, which incorporated the Wilmington and Weldon, maintained headquarters in the city until after World War II. The Seaboard Air Line also maintained large and important facilities in Wilmington for passengers and freight. By the end of the nineteenth century, a series of street railways offered fast and efficient transportation within the city and to beach areas.

From a population of 1,000 in 1790, the city had grown to 10,000 by 1860, and there was a corresponding growth in architectural achievement at that time. Its city theater, largest in the south and one of the largest in the country, seated 1,500 people. Using designs by John Trimble of New York, the theater, Thalian Hall, was connected to the major City Hall building. The Greek Revival Custom House was designed by John Norris of New York; the Marine Hospital was by Ammi B. Young. Saint James Episcopal Church, by Thomas U. Walter, had been in use for two decades in 1860. Major new Baptist and Presbyterian churches, both designed by Samuel Sloan of Philadelphia, were under construction. Local craftsmen James F. Post, James Walker, George Rose, John and R. B. Wood, and others were designing their own buildings or supervising construction by architects from other areas. The city already contained an impressive collection of buildings by important architects.

The city was the victim of two recurring prob-

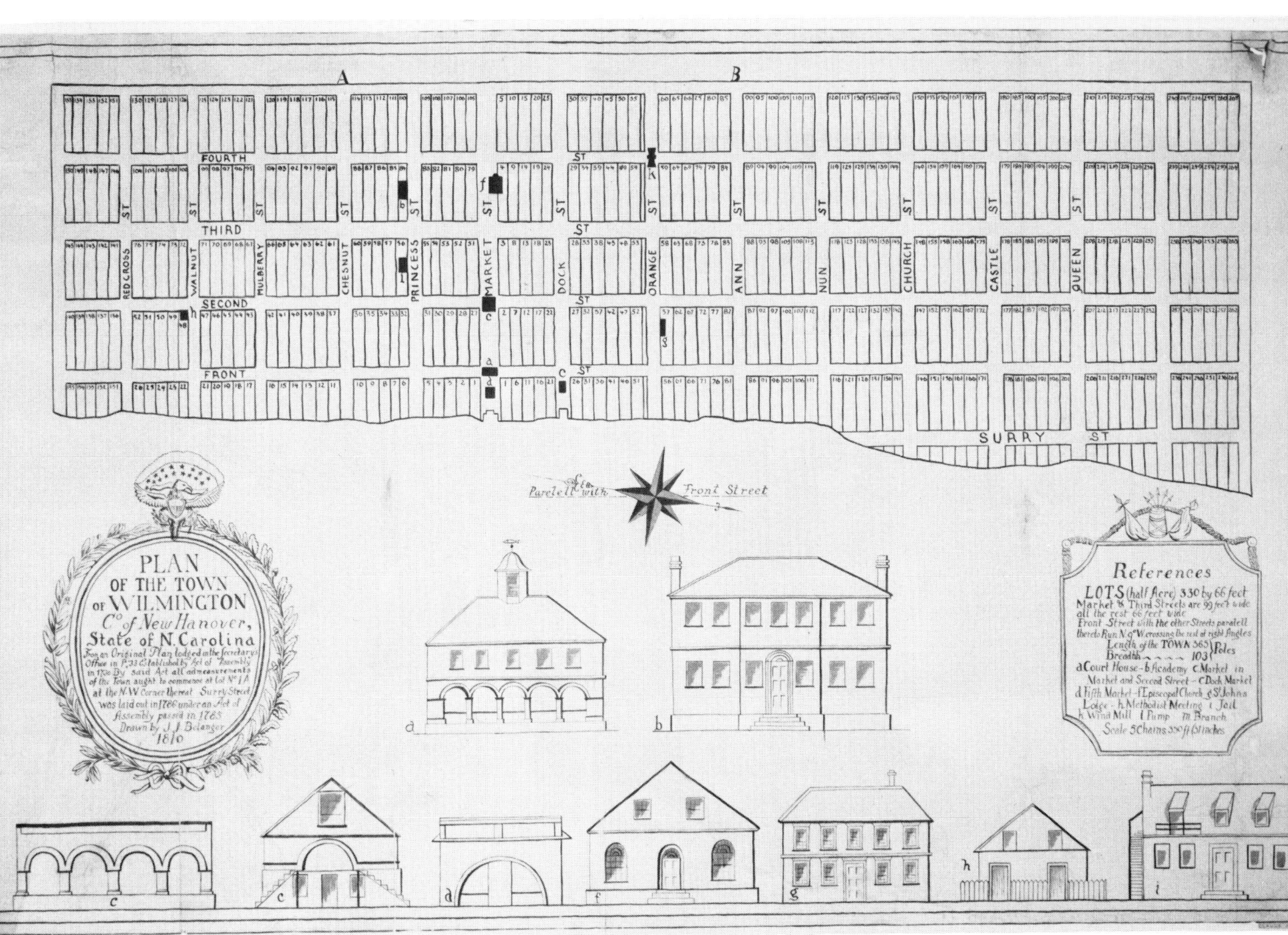

3. Plan Of The Town of Wilmington. Drawn by J. J. Belanger, 1810. (Copy by Claude Howell; St. John's Museum of Art, Inc.)

lems—fire and yellow fever. As early as 1745, city commissioners were authorized to eliminate such fire hazards as wooden chimneys and trash in the streets. In 1791 the general assembly incorporated a fire company in Wilmington, but disastrous fires continued, often burning entire sections of town. They were especially virulent in areas along the waterfront where naval stores, cotton, and other flammable materials made fire control chancy and the frequent devastating blazes inevitable. Yellow fever seems to have been a frequent city visitor as well, culminating in the 1862 attack. Those who could deserted the city that year, and a distressing number of those who couldn't leave died. A sizable section in Oakdale Cemetery holds hundreds of graves of fever victims who were white. Among blacks, the disease was also virulent, and Pine Forest Cemetery contains hundreds of black victims of the 1862 outbreak.

During the Civil War, the city—upriver from the ocean, protected by strong forts, with natural shoals, and with easy access by its roads and railroads to Lee's armies in Virginia—became the most important Confederate port. The geography of the area made the port difficult to blockade, and the sleek and fast Confederate blockade-runners, which plied between Wilmington and foreign ports, swept regularly back and forth beneath the dangerous guns of the Union blockaders or the protection of Confederate guns at Fort Fisher. Fisher, begun in April of 1861 to supplement existing forts, was later de-

Wilmington, N. C. View of the City and Cape Fear River, looking South, from Chestnut Street

4. North Front Street, looking south from Chestnut Street, c. 1901. (Wm. Edmund Barrett collection.)

scribed as the Gibraltar of America.

Cotton became a major war-era export, replacing naval stores, and cotton presses worked around the clock. By mid-1864 Wilmington was the preeminent Southern port, its cotton providing major money for the Confederate cause. In addition, Lee's armies were then receiving at least half of their supplies through the port. The fall of the city, the last remaining Atlantic-coast port open to Confederate ships, doomed Lee's southern forces.

After failing to take Fort Fisher in December 1864, Union forces renewed the battle on January 12, 1865. On January 15 the fort surrendered, after being subjected to naval bombardment said to have been the most intensive ever to that time. After securing nearby forts, Union forces occupied Wilmington on February 22, 1865. With the fall of Wilmington, Lee's Army of Northern Virginia no longer had access to European markets and supplies.

The Reconstruction era in Wilmington was a turbulent one. Blacks gained many city and county offices and became a strong political force, though there was substantial opposition. Control of local government changed several times, and tensions were often high. The culmination of the era came on November 10, 1898, when, during the Wilmington Riot, there was destructive fighting and intimidation of black and some white leaders and the local black newspaper office was destroyed.

Though politics may have been less than settled in the post–Civil War era, the cultural and commercial life of the city expanded. Cotton, which had come to the city in quantity during the war, remained a major product shipped through the port. Rice produced below Wilmington was another major export to northern and other markets. Iron foundries were established, as were fertilizer mills. Railroads operating out of Wilmington maintained headquarters and repair shops within the city, as did several shipping lines. Great Britain, Norway, Swe-

5. North Front Street, looking north from Market Street. Left center, Masonic Temple, Charles McMillen, architect, 1899.

den, and other nations maintained Wilmington consulates, and foreign trade was extensive. The lumber industry remained a force and, beginning in the 1880s, truck farming became an important industry. Crops raised during the mild and long coastal growing seasons could provide early produce for northern markets, and fields that formerly contained timber, rice, or cotton were changed to lettuce, corn, and other vegetable crops. Wholesale grocers became important merchants.

Luckily, as the pine forests were depleted, tar, pitch, turpentine, and rosin became less important to the port, just as cotton diminished as an export item at the same time that growth of North Carolina textile mills began to demand the local cotton.

In the twentieth century the world wars brought increased military shipping to the harbor, and area military bases provided considerable prosperity for Wilmington merchants. The city remains the chief port of North Carolina, even though in the decades since World War II several industries have moved inland, railroads have moved their headquarters elsewhere, and trucks have provided strong competition to the once-successful Wilmington combination of train and ship.

What remains in Wilmington is a three-dimen-

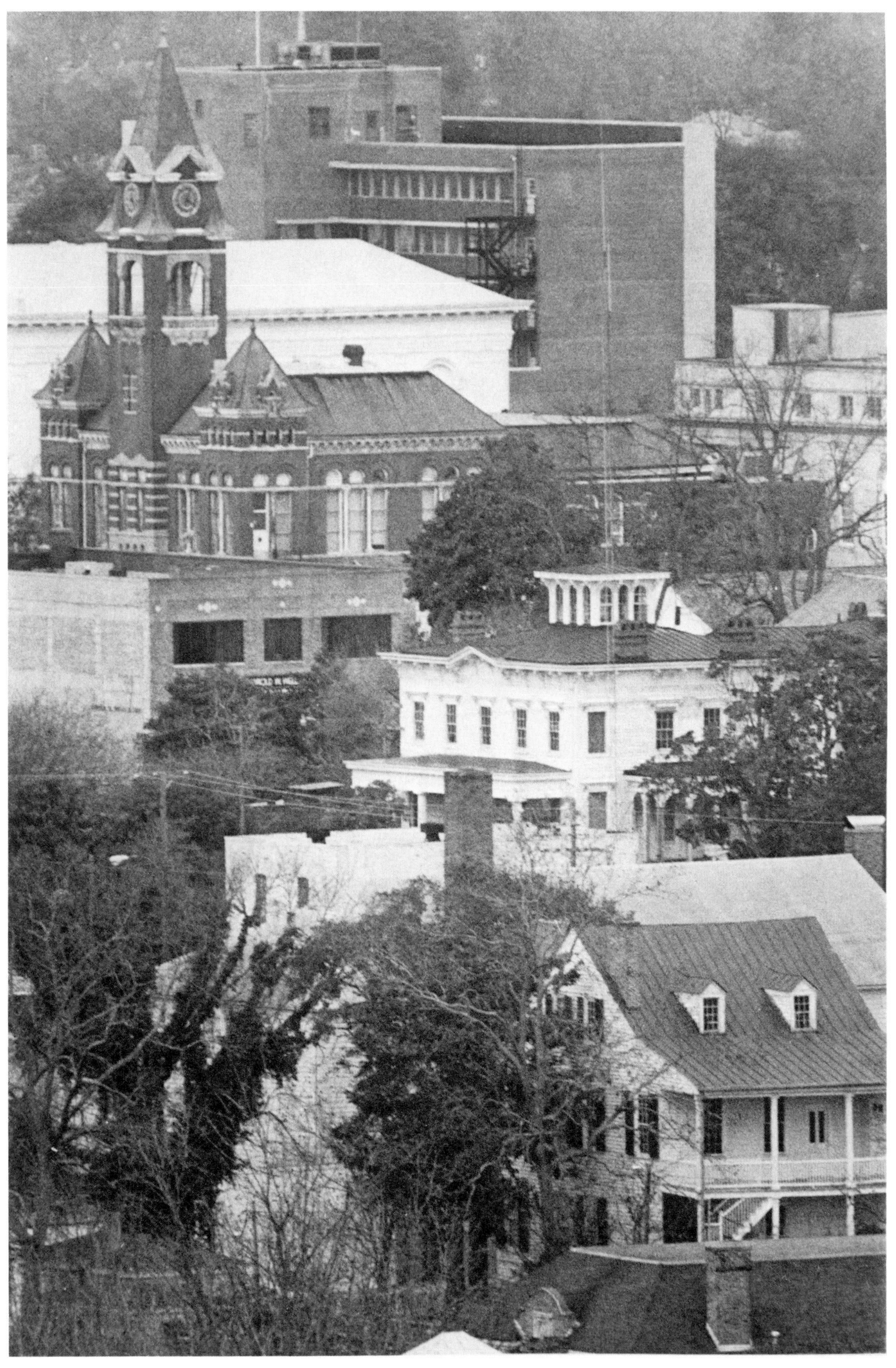

6. View of the city, looking northeast from the Cape Fear River Lift Bridge, 1979. Right bottom, Hogg-Anderson House, c. 1825.

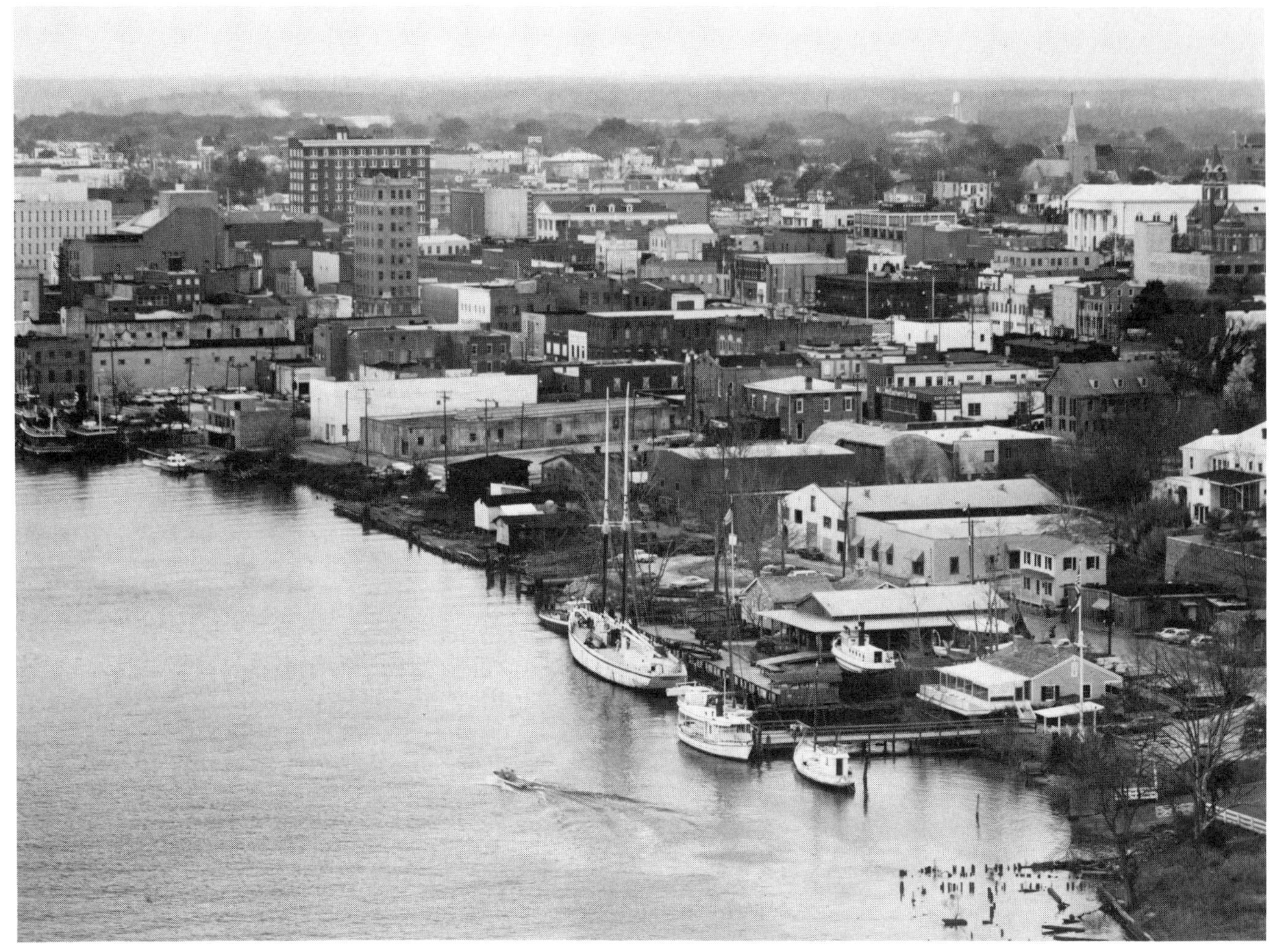

7. View from the Cape Fear River Lift Bridge of the waterfront and downtown Wilmington, looking northeast.

sional nineteenth-century city. It is a rare survival that one can see and touch and walk through. This study attempts to show the depth of what survives, concentrating not on the well-known buildings, but on lesser-known ones, and on streetscapes of paving material, houses, stores, and other types of structures.

As one wanders through city streets, the influence of local artisans is obvious. The architecture of James F. Post, H. E. Bonitz, Burett Stephens, and others is a strong heritage, comparing favorably with the local works of such nationally known architects as Thomas U. Walter, Samuel Sloan, Carrere and Hastings, Henry Bacon, Hobart Upjohn, and others, also represented here. The collection of outstanding buildings, whether in style and finish or in the reputation of designer or other artisan, is larger than that in any other North Carolina city of the eighteenth and nineteenth centuries. Indeed, one of the great treasures of the state is the manner in which no one North Carolina coastal city duplicates another. Each maintains an individual character and identity—Beaufort, Edenton, New Bern, and Wilmington are hardly recognizable as having a close common architectural and geographic heritage. Each of the North Carolina coastal cities is unique, with Wilmington, because of its size, having the largest collection of turn-of-the-century buildings and amenities.

The size and importance of the city kept Wilmington in the mainstream, bringing trade, culture, and important visitors. Politicians such as George Washington, James K. Polk, William Howard Taft, Daniel Webster, Ulysses S. Grant, and William Jennings Bryan visited Wilmington. Persons of literature, drama, and music visited and performed here—Edward Everett, Oscar Wilde, Marion Anderson, John Philip Sousa, Sybil Thorndyke. Thomas Edison, Lajos Kossuth, Mary Baker Eddy, and a great many more found their way to Wilmington for one

8. Looking southwest on Market Street from the corner of North Front Street.

9. 100 and 200 blocks of Princess Street, looking west from the tower of the Court House on North Third Street.

10. Looking south on Third Street from Chestnut Street: (left to right) City Hall, New Hanover County Courthouse, St. James Episcopal Church, and First Presbyterian Church.

11. South Front Street looking north from Nun Street: (left to right) 315 (not discussed), 319 (c. 1835; c. 1851; c. 1857; c. 1942), and 323 (c. 1843; after 1862).

12. Looking west on Nun Street from just above South Second Street, with 202 Nun Street in foreground.

reason or another. Woodrow Wilson spent part of his youth here. Henry Bacon graduated from high school here, as did Robert Ruark. James Cardinal Gibbons served the St. Thomas the Apostle Church as vicar apostolic of North Carolina at the beginning of his rise to international fame. It was in that little church that he began writing his *Faith of our Fathers.* In no way comparable, but still memorable, the song *Don't Bring Lulu* is said to have been first sung in Wilmington's Victoria Theatre (now demolished.) This work is a narrative of places associated with these and other people and events.

In Wilmington as in other historic areas the challenge of the present is, to a large extent, how to maintain traditional amenities and conveniences in a downtown commercial and residential setting while still providing sufficient monetary returns. If in Wilmington the effort is succeeding, it is because local residents have realized the unique quality of what they have, and they have gone about the business of devising means for preservation.

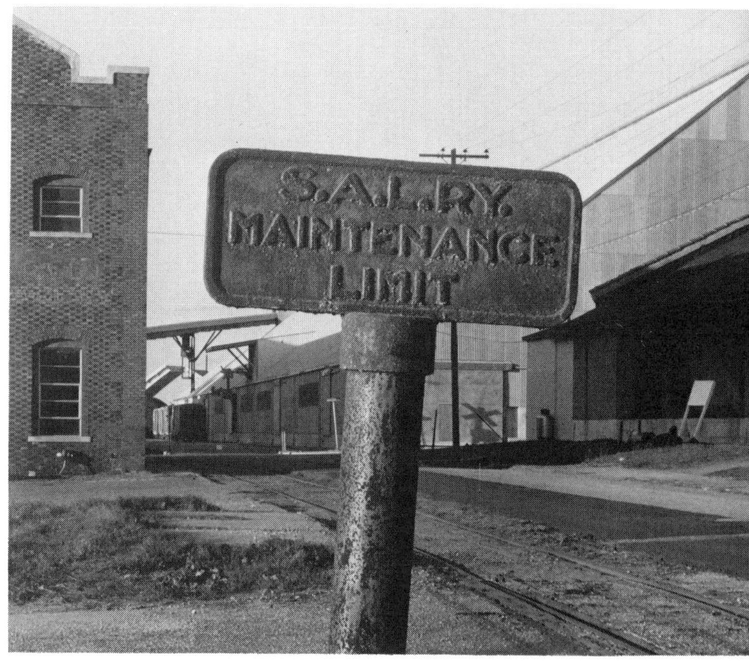

13. Nutt Street looking north toward Bladen Street, with Seaboard Air Line Railway sign in foreground.

Cape Fear River

Wilmington's western border, the river is the city's reason for existence. (See color plate 1.) It provided both the site for the city and a roadway to and from that site. The first settlers sailed up the Cape Fear. In January 1781 the British arrived by ship to occupy the town during the waning days of the American Revolution. Union forces steamed and sailed upriver in February 1865 to take the city from Confederate control. During that war and later ones, ships were manufactured in Wilmington and launched into Cape Fear waters.

Wilmington's success as a trading center was dependent on its location on the river. Traffic in naval stores and later in cotton had much to do with the ability of Wilmington merchants to get products out to Europe by water. Railroads found the port a ready destination because they could meet there with boats and transload.

The Wilmington and Southport Boat Line docks and the steamer *Wilmington* were a feature of the river and waterfront during the late nineteenth century, as were ships of the Clyde Steamship Company, which plied trade in passengers and freight between New York and Wilmington.

A great number of vessels have used this river. Freight and passenger ships were regular nineteenth-century visitors, crowding the city's moorings. The wharves in town were heavily used by ships through the World War I era and into World War II. Fireboats and Coast Guard cutters were at regular mooring, ferryboats operated to bridge the river, and tugs massed at several company docks on the downtown waterfront.

Before its destruction, the presidential yacht *Mayflower* was moored on this waterfront. The Coast Guard cutter *Modoc,* involved in one of the most famous engagements in naval history, was also a regular at the Coast Guard moorings at the foot of Market Street. The *Modoc* and crew, on patrol in the north Atlantic, were the sole Americans (this was in mid-1941 before the United States entered World War II) involved in the battle in which the British navy sank the German warship *Bismarck.*

Though the *Modoc,* the *Mayflower,* the *Wilmington,* and other ships are gone from the downtown waterfront, the battleship U.S.S. *North Carolina* (fig. 14) remains a dominant feature, as do Coast Guard ships, tugs, and the vessels at Chandler's Wharf.

U.S.S. NORTH CAROLINA "THE SHOWBOAT"

Cape Fear River mooring, opposite Chestnut and North Front streets
1936: Construction authorized; October 27, 1937: keel laid; June 13, 1940: launched at Navy Yard, Brooklyn, New York; April 9, 1941: joined fleet

The fourth vessel to bear the name *North Carolina,* this battleship is one of three U.S. Navy ships with that designation.

When the keel of the present U.S.S. *North Carolina* was laid on Navy Day, October 27, 1937, as BB 55—the fifty-fifth battleship keel laid—it was the first of a new class of battleships. At 728 feet 8⅝ inches overall length, 108 feet 3⅞ inches wide at the maximum, and a tower reaching some 125 feet above mean waterline, the ship required new facilities for construction. The keel was completed and the ship launched from the Brooklyn Navy Yard on June 13, 1940. It was commissioned on April 9, 1941. On June 27, 1947, it was decommissioned and assigned to the mothball fleet at Bayonne, New Jersey. In 1960 the vessel was sentenced to salvage for scrap.

Governor Luther Hodges appointed a commission to study the ship's acquisition by the state and its preservation as a memorial to North Carolinians killed during World War II. North Carolina schoolchildren and others raised money, and the ship was purchased on September 6, 1961. Later that month

14. U.S.S. North Carolina *(1940), looking west from North Water Street.*

she began a last trip, to Wilmington and permanent mooring beside a reflecting pool and in a dominant position on the Wilmington skyline. The battleship entered the Cape Fear River in late September, and on October 2 it was moved into permanent berth. Opened to the public just twelve days later, the U.S.S. *North Carolina Battleship Memorial* was dedicated on April 29, 1962, by Admiral Arleigh Burke, with then Secretary of Commerce Luther Hodges and Governor Terry Sanford participating. At the time it was the largest vessel ever dedicated as an historical and commemorative memorial.

At its commissioning on April 9, 1941, Secretary of the Navy Frank Knox had said, "The *North Carolina* is one of a new line of ships that will give the United States unchallenged supremacy on the seas." During the shakedown period that followed commissioning, while the ship was being tested and its crew trained in the vessel's peculiarities, the ship steamed in and out of New York harbor so frequently and became so well known that it earned the name "The Showboat."

The ship traveled through the Panama Canal to the Pacific, arriving in Honolulu on July 11, 1942. Admiral Chester W. Nimitz, the Naval commander in the Pacific, later recalled: "I well remember the great thrill when she arrived in Pearl Harbor during the early stages of the war—at a time when our strength and fortunes were at low ebb. She was the first of the great new battleships to join the Pacific Fleet, and her mere presence in a task force was enough to keep morale at a peak. Before the war's end she built for herself a magnificent record of accomplishment."

One of the items of equipment on the *North Carolina* was the OS2U Vought Kingfisher aircraft. The ship carried three of these, which were catapult-launched and landed in the water, regaining the deck by crane hoist. Of some fifteen hundred of the aircraft built during World War II, the one now displayed on the deck of the *North Carolina* is a rare survivor. Discovered in Alaska, where it had crashed in 1942, the plane's wreckage was recovered by the Royal Canadian Air Force. Eventually it was shipped to Dallas, where it was restored by retired workers of the Vought Aeronautical Company. In 1971 it was brought by truck to Wilmington and reassembled on deck. The plane predated radar, and was used for spotting in long-range gunfire.

In 1966 a sound-and-light production was added as a nightly attraction at the battleship during the summer season. Entitled "The Immortal Showboat," the show is said to be the world's largest automated sound-and-light spectacular.

The centerpiece of the U.S.S. *North Carolina* Battleship Memorial is the Roll of Honor Room. There the names of some ten thousand North Carolinians who died while in the military in World War II are recorded. Though the saving of the battleship and the Kingfisher aircraft was surely justified on the basis of their historical importance, this Roll of Honor is the legal and real reason for the battleship memorial.

North Water Street

Market Street northward to Red Cross

In Wilmington's original plan, the street at the water's edge became Front Street rather than First Street. In 1785 the North Carolina legislature authorized cutting another street between Front Street and the waters of the Cape Fear River. This street took a name as logical as Front; it became Water Street.

Once one of the proudest and most intensely developed of the waterfront industrial and commercial streets, North Water Street initially stretched only three blocks, from Market to Grace. Early in the twentieth century it was cut through from Grace to Walnut, following railroad tracks already in place. The tracks ran the full length of North and South Water, from Walnut to Surry. In the 1960s another block was added to North Water, so that the street now runs from Market to Red Cross.

Parsley's Wharf, DeRosset's Wharf, London Wharf, the Springer Coal Company, Navassa Guano Company, and others operated from the west, or water, side of North Water in the nineteenth century. The U.S. Custom House was located in the first block on the east side of North Water Street at least as early as 1819. At various times, the post office, courthouse, appraisals store, and other uses were combined with customs within this building, thus making the street one of the most important ones in the port city.

Wilmington and Southport Boat Line steamers operated from docks at the base either of Princess Street or of Market Street at Water, depending on the era. A ferry crossed the Cape Fear River from Water and Market, a major route to the south and west. One of the ferry boats used in crossings like this one is at North Water and Red Cross and is now used as the Alton F. Lennon Oceanographic Laboratory of Cape Fear Technical Institute.

North Water is now bare of nineteenth century buildings. In fact, there are only two buildings on the street between Market and Grace. The present U.S. Custom House, in the first block, was constructed in the second decade of the twentieth century; the hotel at the foot of Grace was constructed in the sixth decade of this century.

To the west in the first block is the U.S. Coast Guard dock, used for mooring Coast Guard cutters and other craft. The Wilmington fireboat, *Atlantic IV*, and various fishing or other boats tie up here. Freighters and tankers going upriver to the wharves at Brunswick and Bladen streets also pass, but generally the river is quiet. The U.S.S. *North Carolina*, the battleship moored across the river, can be seen

15. U.S. Custom House, between Market and Princess streets on North Water Street. James A. Wetmore, architect, 1916–19. (1930 photograph courtesy New Hanover County Public Library, Louis T. Moore Collection.)

from any of the first three blocks of North Water Street.

U.S. CUSTOM HOUSE–ALTON F. LENNON FEDERAL BUILDING

North Water Street between Market and Princess
1916–19: James A. Wetmore, acting supervising architect, U.S. Treasury; W. C. Watson, construction supervisor

A U.S. custom house operated within this block as early as 1819, when property was purchased for custom-house use. The earliest structure burned in the 1840s, and New York architect John Norris, who had come to Wilmington to supervise construction of Saint James Episcopal Church, was commissioned to design a new structure. He designed a three-story, pedimented Greek Revival building that was demolished in 1915. The present building was designed by James A. Wetmore while he was acting supervising architect of the U.S. Treasury.

The cornerstone was laid December 9, 1916. The building was to have been completed in 1918; however the work was delayed during World War I and was not completed until 1919. Court was first held in the building in May of that year, and on July 19 the building was opened to the public. At the present time, the building no longer houses customs, but serves instead as the federal courthouse and provides office space for the Corps of Engineers and other federal agencies.

A three-story Neoclassical Revival stone building with projecting wings balanced on either side of a long central block featuring Doric pilasters and Temple of the Winds engaged columns, the building (figs. 15 and 16) has a massive rusticated stone base as its first floor and a solid stone balustrade atop the third floor. A continuous molded cornice with running frieze marks the roof line. Second- and third-story surfaces alternate between recessed areas with bays flanked by columns and flush areas with bays flanked by pilasters.

John Norris's design for the 1849 building, with its temple-form and cast-iron balustrades decorated with eagles, was retained and used in the wings of the 1916–19 structure. It appears as the engaged pedimented porticos of each of the flanking wings. The balustrade design was copied for the railings of the French windows, which open onto flush balconies.

It has been claimed that Woodrow Wilson, then president of the United States, was responsible for the size and finish of the Wilmington structure. Wilson may or may not have been interested in the project, though it is certain that the construction was not harmed by the fact that Wilmington was one of the president's hometowns.

16. U.S. Custom House, now Alton F. Lennon Federal Building, from the Cape Fear River.

The entrance has a bronze frieze decorated with triglyphs and rondelles and a ten-light panel above tinted glass doors. On the interior, wall surfaces are of rusticated white marble and plaster. Floors are black and white marble. Ceilings and arched hallway openings are decorated with Neoclassical motifs. Other interiors are considerably more changed.

A recessed courtyard elevated above North Water Street is landscaped with a central fountain and entrance stairs flanked by walls topped with balustrades.

The building is listed in the National Register of Historic Places as the United States Federal Building and Courthouse.

Princess Street enters North Water from the east

Though no buildings survive here, the retaining wall and buttresses to the east are handsome, as is the landscaping of a small area before the walls. The nineteenth century walls of stone and/or brick supported North Front Street buildings. Wall sections retained here originally served as part of the foundation of The Orton Hotel built in 1886. One of Wilmington's most famous hostelries, The Orton burned in 1949.

South Water Street

Market Street southward to Ann

Though the blocks created by Water Street to the north of Market Street were of normal Wilmington block size, those created to the south of Market Street, between Front and Water streets, were small and, on their western, or Water Street side, irregularly shaped. South Water Street really was on the water, with very little land for development between it and the river. Nevertheless, South Water developed almost as intensely as North Water, and fortuitously much of the nineteenth- and early twentieth-century development of South Water survives in 1982—street, waterfront, and buildings.

In 1881 Turner's Wood Wharf and Hall & Pearsall's Wharf were on the waterfront between Market and Dock streets, and the Ice House Wharf and Lippitt's Wharf were on South Water between Dock and Orange streets. The first three blocks from Market to Ann were intensely developed in 1880, while the blocks between Ann and Church streets were less densely developed. The street was not cut through from Nun to Church, though the waterfront was developed and a right-of-way existed. South of Church Street, Water Street became Surry Street. In the late nineteenth century a railroad line was opened down Water Street from the Wilmington and Weldon tracks at Nutt and Red Cross streets to Surry Street and on south to connect with other tracks.

By the turn of the century, the major downtown market was located between South Water and South Front streets, near Orange. Since 1910 the Wilmington Iron Works, probably Wilmington's oldest continuously operating business, has occupied its present site on South Water, between Orange and Ann streets.

Market Street

Within the first block, only those buildings on the waterfront side of the street have South Water Street addresses. To the east there is a maze of alleys—Quince Alley, Henderson Alley, Wilkinson Alley, Muter's Alley—running through the block to South Front Street. Most of the buildings on this side of South Water are the rear of South Front Street buildings and are numbered on South Front. One of these structures between Quince and Henderson alleys is worth notice. It is a three-story brick building, marked "N. Jacobi Hdw Co., Warehouse, 1856/1913"—the 1913 showing the date of construction of the building. (See Fig. 17)

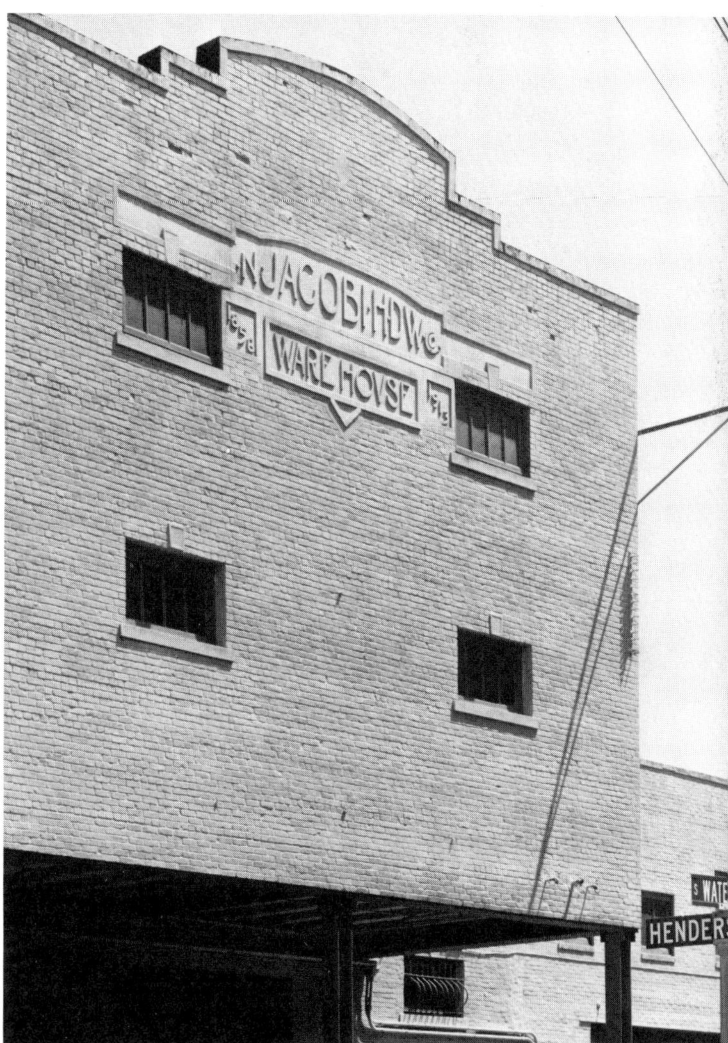

17. N. Jacobi Hardware Co. warehouse, South Water Street, 1913.

18. J. W. Brooks Wholesale Grocer and Commission Merchant, office and warehouse, 10–18 South Water Street, 1920.

J. W. BROOKS WHOLESALE GROCER AND COMMISSION MERCHANT, OFFICE AND WAREHOUSE

10–18 South Water Street
1920

A handsome structure constructed partially over the water, the Brooks building (Fig.18) is a three-story structure of six-to-one common-bond brick on a stone base and concrete piers. Courses and corners of stretchers flanked by headers outline the structure. The South Water Street facade is twenty-one bays of alternating paired and single segmental-arch windows with twelve-light sash, with a six-light center section on a swing bar. Each of three loading entrances on the first floor has a triple row of headers forming arches that rest on impost blocks.

The main-office entrance is in the southern end of the building, reached through a vestibule recess. In the frieze of the surmounting entablature is "J. W. Brooks," and the capitals of the pilasters contain "1899" to the left and "1920" to the right—the dates of the founding of the business and the construction of this office/warehouse.

The firm succeeded the original firm of Brooks & Taylor, founded January 1, 1899, when it became J. W. Brooks on September 1, 1907. The company occupied extensive premises on three corners of Dock Street at this location before purchasing the site of this building in 1918. By occupying the building then there, they utilized all four street corners. The 1912 chamber of commerce publication *The City of Wilmington* described the Brooks stock as consisting of:

everything comprised under the general term of heavy groceries and among these the house makes a specialty of its own brand of flour "Belle of Wilmington," a high grade fancy patent, manufactured expressely for this concern. All supplies are obtained direct from manufacturers and original sources in very large quantities and are sold to merchants at lowest current rates. The house also transacts a commission business receiving consignments of cotton, spirits of turpentine, rosin, etc., and advances are made if desired and the interests of consignors are well looked after in every available manner. Mr. Brooks is also the owner of a number of schooners and steamers which ply principally on the Cape Fear and Black rivers between Wilmington and Seaside, N.C.

The location of the warehouse was such that it was able to load and unload from its own and other ships on the water side of the building and to do the same from freight trains on the land side, since track ran by its door with a siding in front of the warehouse.

The building is part of a streetscape that evidences the relation of the town to the water and is particularly important. That relationship was once embodied in other busy industrial and commercial uses of the street and adjacent areas and riverside. The three-dimensional remnants that still stand are particularly important in giving us a feeling of the importance and vitality of the area's water-oriented past.

Dock Street crosses South Water; begin 100 street numbers

Josephus Daniels reported in his *Life of Woodrow Wilson* that in Wilmington the young Wilson swam in the Cape Fear River at the base of Dock Street. The ragged riverfront contains a variety of wharves and docks where tugs and various fishing boats tie up.

Orange Street crosses South Water; begin 200 street numbers

ROBINSON & KING; WILMINGTON IRON WORKS

201–3 South Water Street (at Orange Street),
southeast and southwest corners,
pre 1884 and later

It is difficult to date utilitarian complexes such as this one, which have seen multiple industrial uses. Certainly the stone wall constructed of ballast and cobblestone is old, possibly late eighteenth or early nineteenth century. The wall seems to have been built to enclose a space at the southeast corner of Orange and South Water Streets, though why it was built or by whom is not known. The site would have been a natural one for the gathering and use of ships' ballast stone since major docks and the riverside were quite near. As shown on the 1884 Sanborn map, the wall is 104 feet west of Front Street and parallel to it. It ran south for 132 feet, made a ninety degree turn and ran west parallel to Orange Street for 96 feet to Water Street. Though now interrupted at several places, the stone wall is still visually exciting and a fine example of craftsmanship in stone construction. It is best viewed from the south side of Orange Street, along Stonewall Alley.

The two-story brick-and-tin covered former office building (see fig. 153) on South Water displays a bronze plaque cast by the Wilmington Iron Works with the following legend:

Wilmington Iron Works
The Iron Men
G. E. Kidder, Pres. W. W. Storm, V. Pres.
E. Z. King, Secy.-Treas.
C. C. Wilson, Supt. D. C. King, Asst. Treas.
Founded 1838.

The building does not appear on the 1884 Sanborn map; it is on the 1899 map, though only one story tall. It is likely that the first story was built c. 1885 by Robinson & King. The second story was added c. 1910 by the Wilmington Iron Works after their move to this site. Since 1970 the offices have been located at 208 South Front Street.

Robinson & King was a predecessor firm on the street corners now occupied by the iron works. They are listed on Gray's 1881 map as there and are there on the Sanborn Map of 1884. The company seems to have been involved in production of naval stores with a turpentine warehouse and storage facilities for rosin. They maintained their own cooper shed for manufacture of the barrels used in the business. Fowler and Morrison operated a woodyard adjacent to Robinson & King on the south.

Just after the Wilmington Iron Works moved to the site, the 1910 Sanborn map shows the firm on the southeast and southwest, or water, side of South Water at Orange Street, the same premises occupied earlier by Robinson & King. A machine shop was at the southeast corner of the block, the office slightly to the south, and the foundry to its rear. Across the street at the water side was a warehouse used for machine storage on the first level and for pattern storage on the second. All the buildings now in use were standing when the iron works moved to the site.

In 1910 The Brunswick Wood & Coal Co. operated a planing mill and sash and door factory immediately to the south of the iron works. By the time Sanborn issued a 1915 map, that company had disappeared, perhaps burned.

Business at the iron works was good enough so that the warehouse was no longer used just for storage, but for another machine shop on the first level and for a pattern shop on the second. Though the firm no longer does its own foundry work (that is contracted out), it engages in essentially the same business that it always has, except that there is little copper work being ordered.

Levi A. Hart is credited with founding the company in 1838, first doing business in tin under the name of "Hart and Porter" or "Porter and Hart." By 1840 the name seems to have changed to "Polley and Hart," and the company was also making turpentine stills. By 1851 they are said to have been manufacturing more turpentine stills than any other American manufacturer.

John C. Bailey arrived in Wilmington in 1852 and, evidently an experienced patternmaker, found work with the Clarendon Iron Works. By 1857 he was working with Polley and Hart. Polley withdrew from the firm, and in 1859 Bailey and Hart entered partnership under the firm name of "Hart and Bailey." In 1868 Henry A. Burr married Hart's daughter, and in 1879 the firm became "Burr and Bailey," though it was shown as "Hart, Bailey & Co." on the 1884 Sanborn map. John C. Bailey died in 1880; Levi Hart, in 1882. In 1892 the firm became the "Wilmington Iron Works." Edward P. Bailey, nephew of the elder Bailey, became the president of the firm. He was followed by his son Edward P. Bailey, Jr. For a period of time near the end of the century, the firm seems to have been known as "Wilmington Iron & Copper Works" or "Wilmington Copper and Iron Works," but after 1900 the name remained "Wilmington Iron Works."

The iron works, at least by 1866, was located on South Front, between Market and Dock streets along Bettencourt Alley. By the time of Sanborn's 1893 map the company had moved to the other end of the alley, along South Second. Evidently the iron works also had shops at other locations, at least at the foot of Nun. The *Morning Star* for January 22, 1898, reported the Nun Street shops destroyed by fire—a total loss and only partially covered by insurance. In 1909 the offices, foundry, and machine shops of the company moved from the South Second Street site to South Water, the present location.

Products of the iron works have been diverse, to say the least. In addition to turpentine stills, they are said to have manufactured cannonballs and cannon shot for Confederate forces during the Civil War and to have worked on Confederate ironclads. They were into boat building—launching, among others, the yacht *Rosa,* as reported in the *Star* for June 28, 1878. In 1886 they built and operated the plant that brought electricity to Wilmington, providing power for experimental street lights. The *Star* for December 1, 1891, noted that "The Raleigh Chronicle mentions that Messrs. Burr & Bailey are placing steam heating apparatus in the Executive Mansion."

For the architectural historian, however, the firm is important because of its involvement in the production of architectural detail. It seems likely that much of the iron fencing, iron furniture, roof cresting, and iron porch supports and decoration of mid nineteenth-century Wilmington, when the use of cast iron was at fever pitch, was produced by this works.

By February 15, 1861, the firm was advertising in the *Daily Herald,* "all kinds of iron and brass castings." One of the handsomest cast-iron fences in Wilmington, c. 1866—which appears at only four places, including the dwellings of the owners Hart and Bailey—is probably from a pattern of Bailey's. (See 219 South Third, John C. Bailey House, figs. 66, 67.)

Church records at St. James indicate that in 1847, the ironworks was responsible for "iron work for church" and in 1848 produced brass lanterns for the structure. During those two years the firm also produced lightning rods, roof flashing, and "spit pans." St. James Church records also indicate that on April, 28, 1871, Hart & Bailey bid on work at the church for "Ornamental Panels and Columns as per Architrave Drawings. . . . Cornice and Beam Mouldings not included in this estimate." This work was wood, and in 1886 the firm advertised in the February 25 *Star* "We are prepared to furnish promptly wood mouldings, brackets, newels and ornamental work of any description." The company installed iron work—including heating, stair balustrade, and newels—in the New Hanover County Courthouse in 1891–92. By this time they were also a large caster and supplier of manhole covers, water-main covers, and other items of cast-iron street furniture. Many of these can still be seen around Wilmington if one looks down as one walks.

By early in this century the company asked, in an undated advertising leaflet, "Do You Know— that we make ornamental hand rails—porch rails and other kinds of miscellaneous iron work?" Two twentieth-century examples of their work are the Oakdale Cemetery gates at the North Fifteenth Street entrance to the cemetery, erected in 1915, and the Pembroke Jones Playground gates on Market Street at North Fourteenth, erected in 1925.

The premises of the company at Orange and South Water streets evoke something of the feel of the last century; unsold gears, cogs, machines, and parts bring an immediate desire to know their use and to hear once more the hum and thump of the firm's machinery.

The remains of machines, patterns, and examples of the work of the firm are visible. The policy of the firm was to move anything not in use or not sold to a corner of the premises rather than to destroy it, so that there is an amazing amount of surviving material connected with the work of the firm. Even for the person with only limited interest in industrial archaeology but with some imagination or inquisitiveness, a walk down South Water is likely to be of interest.

Beyond what is immediately visible, the firm by its very longevity is an important survivor of the nineteenth-century city, and a present-day reminder of the interrelatedness of urban uses before the onset of modern-era zoning. The industrial Wilmington Iron Works coexists quite well with its nearby commercial and residential neighbors.

Nutt Street

Grace Street northward to Bladen

Nutt Street, probably not opened until the nineteenth century, seems always to have had mixed uses. In the 1830s the first and second blocks (the 300 and 400 street-number blocks) consisted of residences and small stores on the eastern side. On the west or water side these blocks, and the Nutt Street blocks to the north, were more heavily commercial and industrial.

Henry Nutt's Turpentine Distillery was at the northwest corner of Nutt and Red Cross streets; his office was located across the street on the northeast corner. The business was important enough and the family prominent enough to give the Nutt name to the street.

Nutt and South Water streets are the only water-oriented, basically industrial streets left in Wilmington, and the history of the surviving architecture of both streets is spectacular.

Grace Street

Nutt Street begins at Grace. Both Sprunt's and Worth's wharfs were located on the water side of the block between Grace and Walnut streets. At that time, North Water ended at Grace, so there was no street between Nutt and the river. Alex. Sprunt & Sons and Worth and Worth were connected with these wharfs and maintained buildings in the block. The Worth company was a wholesale grocer and dealer in lime and cement. Sprunt, cotton exporters and proprietors of the Champion Compress and Warehouse Company, later moved to North Front and Walnut streets. While they were in this block, Sprunt was the British consul, and the consulate was located in his office at the northeast corner of Nutt and Walnut. Wallace and Southerland, commission merchants, and Armor and Company, meat packers, were also tenants of the water, or western, side of the block at one time or another. Unfortunately, no structure remains on this side of the street—now a parking lot.

All the buildings still standing on the eastern side of the street have architectural and historical value, although the structures that anchored the ends of the block are gone. Adaptively used, the buildings that remain extend eastward to North Front Street and are part of the Cotton Exchange development (fig. 19). An area of shops, restaurants, and studios

19. Cotton Exchange, 308–16 Nutt Street. From right to left: 308–308½, 310½, 310–12 (entrance to shops), 314, and 316 Nutt Street.

on several levels, the development has maintained street facades and much finish evocative of the earlier industrial and commercial usage of the block. The 1975–76 Cotton Exchange was the first of the downtown complexes to utilize multiple existing buildings adaptively.

Building numbers within the block are confusing, and those used here are the ones used roughly from 1885 to 1915.

WHOLESALE GROCERS AND WAREHOUSES

308–308 ½ Nutt Street
c. 1900 (308 ½), and c. 1905 (308)

The only original wall surfaces that can be seen are those of the c. 1905 building, on the southern end of the structure. Both street facades were refaced in the World War II era. It was at that time that the buildings acquired their present unified Nutt Street facade with its three street openings. A two-story brick structure when built, it is now equal in height to three full stories of the older building at the northern end of the block. It is clear from the original southern end wall that the building was extended in height at the time the street facade was refaced. It is therefore possible that these c. 1900–1905 buildings were stylistic twins of 310–312 when constructed, especially since the warehouse at 310 ½, c. 1900, followed that pattern.

Former uses of these two structures are somewhat uncertain, except that they seem to have been used predominantly for wholesale grocery and related warehouse purposes. By 1915 Boney and Harper Milling Company, the dominant business in the block, was using the buildings for warehouse purposes.

WAREHOUSE

310 ½ Nutt Street
c. 1900

Labeled on the 1904 Sanborn map as a warehouse, this structure seems never to have had any other, more specific use, and its identification with specific firms is not easily accomplished. In 1893, when 310–312 was being operated as a saloon, there was an outdoor beer garden, in the best German tradition, on this site.

The structure follows the style of 310–312 (see below). When 310 ½ was built, the structures on both sides were already standing. The new construction consisted of a brick wall across the front to close the open space and wooden framing along the side walls of the existing buildings to hold the upper floor and roof of the new building. Window and door openings, bricked up when this space was enclosed, are visible on the north interior wall. It was probably the door in the center of the wall that gave access to the beer garden.

BOARDING HOUSE AND SALOON

310–12 Nutt Street
c. 1886

On the Sanborn map for 1884 a three-story mariner's saloon is shown on this site. According to the Sanborn map of 1889, that building had disappeared, and the present two-story brick building was in place. Since some of the block is shown in ruins on the 1889 map and none of the structures are the same as in 1884, it is probable that the fire of February 21, 1886, necessitated rebuilding the entire area.

The odd street numbering—with 310 ½ coming before 310—evidently reflects not only the fact that 310 existed before 310 ½ but the fact that 310 ½ was probably constructed by the owners of 310. Though it should have been numbered 308 ½, possibly 308 was then in different ownership and so 308 ½ was not used separately.

Sanborn's 1889 map shows 310–12 as a boardinghouse and saloon. By 1893 the beer garden was open to the south on the present site of 310 ½. By 1898 the boardinghouse use seems to have disappeared, but the saloon was still in operation, evidently utilizing all of the premises.

The September 30, 1900, *Star* noted the move of "Mr. W. B. Cooper from 226 North Water Street to a new store next south of Boney & Harper Milling Company here." Inasmuch as the buildings were standing, it seems likely that *new* referred to the new use for the buildings, and probably to the remodeling required for that use.

Cooper was a wholesale grocer, offering salt fish, peanuts, and other commodities. A speciality of the house was the company's own flour, "Cooper's Favorite." "Bunker Hill Flour" was another big seller.

By 1910 the structures at 310–12 are listed on the Sanborn maps as used by wholesale grocers, with peanuts on the first floor and peanut cleaning on the second. By 1915 the building was occupied by Love and Woods, wholesale grocers.

The structure is typical of better brick commercial and industrial construction of the late nineteenth century. Windows have arched brick lintels; surface planes are delineated by pilasters; and the pilasters that flank the building terminate in chimney flues.

BONEY AND HARPER MILLING COMPANY, STEAM ENGINEHOUSE

314 Nutt Street
1886

Prior to the 1886 fire that destroyed buildings in this block, Tuscarora Mills, operated by G. J. Boney, was already in operation at 316 Nutt Street, with number 314, a one-story brick structure, housing the steam engine used to power the mill. Boney suffered severe losses in the fire, and the Tuscarora name was dropped in favor of Boney and Harper, a new firm that grew out of an alliance, entered into after the fire, between Boney and Capt. J. T. Harper. Harper was a local businessman and steam-tug owner from Southport. Their new firm renewed milling operations in a mill constructed next door, to the north of the steam-engine-house.

The building at 314 would have been necessary for the operation of the mill, so it would have been either built after the fire or rebuilt within the walls of the earlier building. It continued in use as the steam-engine-house until at least 1915.

The structure has ornate brick arches and cornices. The round vent (here with brick lattice) was probably a necessity in a steam-engine-house. Here it has been made a most attractive feature of the building.

BONEY AND HARPER HOMINY AND CORN MILL

316 Nutt Street
1886

One of the best of the surviving industrial structures in Wilmington, this building was constructed for manufacturing use. In 1912 it was said to be the only mill of its kind in North Carolina, and the only one east and south of Tennessee. Its products were pearl hominy, grits, and corn meal, merchandised under the "Diamond B" trademark. In 1912 the mill was capable of producing four thousand bushels per day.

The 1889 Sanborn map notes "Power: steam; heat: coal stove in office; lights: gas; 1 hominy huller; 2 grits mills; 5 corn mills." By 1898 the listing notes: "1st flr: 10 elevators; 2nd flr: 4 run stones; 3rd flr: 2 dbl sets corn rolls, 3 run of stones, 2 hominy mills, 5 dbl purifiers, 2 fans and corn dryers; 4th flr: 12 reels." By 1915 this had changed to: "1st flr: 3 automatic scales; 2nd flr: 2 attrition mills, 2 burr mills, 2 steam dryers, 1 packer; 3rd flr: 2 stand double rolls, 1 stand single rolls, 2 germinators, 2 grist separators, 1 dust collar, 2 fans, 1 corn scourer, 1 steam dryer, 1 scale; 4th flr: 7 bolters, 1 corn scales, 1 dust collar, 1 fan, 1 scale."

In the 300-block on Nutt Street, Boney and Harper occupied numbers 316, 314, 308–308 ½, and probably 310 ½ by 1915—the major business in the block.

A four-story brick building with parapeted gable, the Boney and Harper Mill is a late nineteenth-century industrial structure and one of the least changed on the exterior of the surviving Wilmington industrial buildings. It has a corbeled cornice with patterned brick frieze. A triple-unit window in the gable consists of a round-arch unit flanked by two segmental-arch units. The four bays of the facade are delineated by monumental pilasters. Each of the bays is capped by a segmental-arch cornice cap with dropped ends. There is a diminution of bays, with each of the four bays on the ground level consisting of a double door.

Walnut Street crosses Nutt

J. W. Taylor's Saw and Planing Mill, McRae's Wharf and the Champion Compress and Warehouse Company were among the industries in this block. Flanner's building was also in the block, providing office space for commission merchants. A February 6, 1880, article on the J. W. Taylor enterprise that appeared in the *Weekly Star* is informative. It concerns the frequent devastating fires in Wilmington, the interrelatedness of Wilmington industries, and their self-sufficiency. It also concerns the source of much architectural detail on Wilmington buildings of the era.

> *Mr. J. W. Taylor commenced work at his new mill, formerly Colville & Co's yesterday. The mill is new out and out, is furnished with the latest improved machinery. He says his brother mill men have been very kind to him since his late misfortune [a fire that destroyed his mill].*
>
> *Connected with the same establishment though under different proprietorship are the Planing Mill and Sash and Blind Factory of Messrs. Altaffer, Price & Co., the former of the first and the latter on the second floor. These will be ready to commence operations on or about the 10 inst.*
>
> *The proprietors are now waiting for the boiler and engine, the former to be shipped from Richmond on Monday and the latter to be ready early in the week at the foundry of Messrs. Hart, Bailey & Co., in this city.*
>
> *The building is large and though the saw mill, planing mill and factory are all under one roof, there is an abundance of room.*
>
> *Both of these establishments have literally sprung from the ashes of the late destructive fire on the site where they have been erected.*

Red Cross Street crosses Nutt; begin 500 street numbers

Entering Nutt Street from Red Cross, one crosses into the center of Wilmington's railroad history. The nineteenth century offices and headquarters of the Atlantic Coast Line Railroad were here to the west. Both of the freight warehouses to the south are survivors of the Wilmington and Weldon Railroad. The southernmost one is Wilmington's oldest surviving railroad structure, probably mid-nineteenth century. The freight station at its eastern end, built by the Atlantic Coast Line Railroad, is a reminder of the W & W RR's successor and the importance of Wilmington as a freight terminal.

If one looks eastward along the railroad tracks where they cross Nutt Street, portions of older stone abutments are visible under the present North Front Street bridge. These are from two previous street

20. Wilmington and Weldon freight warehouses, 507 and 519 Nutt Street. The southernmost warehouse (left) is from c. 1882, with the three-story Atlantic Coast Line Freight Office (now the Wilmington Railroad Museum) at its east end c. 1900. The northernmost warehouse (right) was built before 1880.

bridges: the inner one of stone surely pre–Civil War, the middle one of stone and brick pre-1900.

Looking westward, one sees the tracks that lead past the two freight warehouses and the freight station to the waterfront and wharves that the railroads served. Freight was off-loaded in both directions, from ships to trains and from trains to ships. Abandoned machines, such as the steam crane to the rear of the southernmost freight house, are reminders of this activity.

To the north along Nutt, stretching from the tracks northward to Hanover Street, is the stone retaining wall, now stuccoed, of the Wilmington and Weldon Railroad turntable and repair shed, built about 1840.

Wilmington and Weldon tracks ran up Nutt Street to the north, joining tracks of the Central Carolina Railroad—whose depot, freight facilities, and docks were at Brunswick.

WILMINGTON AND WELDON FREIGHT WAREHOUSES AND ATLANTIC COAST LINE FREIGHT OFFICE

507 and 519 Nutt Street
507 Nutt Street (the southernmost warehouse), built before 1880; east end of southernmost warehouse and ACL Freight Office, built c. 1900; 519 Nutt Street, built c. 1882 (now the Wilmington Railroad Museum).

21. Wilmington and Weldon freight warehouse, seen from the Cape Fear River, 507 Nutt Street.

The Wilmington and Raleigh Railroad, renamed the Wilmington and Weldon Railroad, was chartered on January 3, 1834. When track was completed to Weldon and trains were put in operation between the two cities on March 19, 1840, the 161 ½ mile track made the Wilmington and Weldon the longest railroad in the world. That railroad, and others that quickly followed, were in no small way responsible for the development of Wilmington as a major port. Railroad track gave processing industries ready access to raw materials and a wide range of outlets. Wholesalers in several fields proliferated in Wilmington, serving as way stations between ship and train. Passengers were also a major item in trade. For a long period of time the Wilmington and Weldon and other early railroads earned much of their income from passengers, and until at least the mid-twentieth century the passenger train was a financially viable business.

Wilmington's 1866–67 directory lists the W & W RR; the Wilmington and Manchester Railroad; and the Wilmington, Charlotte, and Rutherford Railroad. Later, the Wilmington, Columbia, and Augusta Railroad; the Carolina Central Railroad; the Cape Fear and Yadkin Valley Railroad; and the Wilmington, Onslow, and East Carolina Railroad all operated in and out of Wilmington. By 1900, all of those mentioned had become part of either the Atlantic Coast Line Railroad, with headquarters in Wilmington, or the Seaboard Air Line Railroad.

It was the Wilmington and Weldon that made the city a major port during the Civil War. It connected with the Petersburg Railroad and that line connected with the Richmond, Fredericksburg, and Potomac. This was Lee's lifeline, which was open from the sea via blockade-runners to northern Virginia. As long as the port of Wilmington remained open and the Wilmington and Weldon operated, Lee's Confederate forces in Virginia could be supplied.

The headquarters of the Atlantic Coast Line remained in Wilmington until 1960, when they moved to Jacksonville, Florida. The ACL move left a vast area of empty buildings in this area, and took with it some thirty-five hundred people and their payroll.

22. Wilmington and Weldon freight warehouse, detail of loading bay, 507 Nutt Street.

Since then, railroad buildings in this historic transportation hub for the city have disappeared at an alarming rate. The three significant structures shown in figure 20 remain, awaiting adaptive use. Until asphalt shingle was applied to the roof of the northernmost structure in 1975, the "W & W RR" initials were still visible in the roof covering of the building.

Walls and arched bays of the freight warehouses are brick; roof trussing and framing are wood and iron. (See fig. 21.) Tracks gave access to both sides of the warehouses and directly to the wharfs on the river to their western end. Platforms abut the tracks on each side of the freight houses, and low gable roofs extend over the platforms. The two freight houses are markedly similar, and the southernmost one, already standing in 1881, could have been built at any time after about 1850. The northernmost one was constructed c. 1882.

Both freight sheds seem to have been thirteen loading bays long, with a brick arch above each. (See fig. 22.) The brick cornice is corbeled outward at the eaves. Both buildings evidence solid workmanship and attention to detail. One bay of the southern freight house was removed when the ACL freight office was built, allowing room for that structure.

The northern freight house retained its full length until recently. It is now eight bays long, the bays nearest the water having been demolished.

The three-story brick freight office at the eastern, or Nutt Street, end of the southernmost shed was constructed by the Atlantic Coast Line Railroad around 1900 to house offices for the railroad freight operations in Wilmington.

Stone paving block survives on Nutt Street in front of the southernmost structure. This extends down the south side of the building, changing to brick pavers nearer the western end of the building. The patterns and types of materials abandoned here, including machinery, are unusual transportation survivors.

As examples of industrial architecture and craftsmanship, these three buildings have few peers within the state. As the sole visible three-dimensional remnant of Wilmington's famous Wilmington and Weldon Railroad, they possess unparalleled historical importance as well.

Hanover Street enters Nutt; begin 700 street numbers

Cast-iron signs on the railroad between Nutt Street and the water read "S.A.L.R.Y. Maintenance Limit" (see fig. 13), one surviving reminder of the Seaboard Air Line Railroad. (A S.A.L.R.Y. sign is on display at the Wilmington Railroad Museum.) To many Wilmingtonians the acronym SALRY was most accurate—the railroads were the largest employers in the city. Other signs in the area refer to the Seaboard Coast Line—the merger of the Atlantic Coast Line and Seaboard Air Line railroads.

The stone retaining wall of the c. 1840 roundhouse and repair sheds of the Wilmington and Weldon Railroad is especially obvious here, as the wall forms the corner from Nutt into Hanover and runs eastward to level ground at North Front Street. The quality of the stonework is particularly good—the great engineering and construction innovators of the railroads intended their structures to last.

From about 1868 to well into the twentieth century, the Geo. L. Morton company operated in the 600 and 700 blocks of Nutt Street. A 1902 article noted that facilities included stills and other appliances and that:

23. Hall and Pearsall Warehouse, 711 Nutt Street. c. 1907.

the basis of the products manufactured is the sap of the North Carolina pine, the company buying the crude material as it comes from the trees. Spirits of turpentine, rosin and pitch are the principal products, and those of the best quality are placed at the disposal of the trade at the very lowest prices. The goods are shipped throughout the North generally, from the Atlantic to the Pacific, and as regards tar, Pennsylvania takes large quantities. The goods are sold to paint dealers, varnish manufacturers, ship chandlers and largely to steel works, who use it for blackening the steel to preserve it from rust. Rosin is principally sold locally for export. The company also deals in tar, which is supplied as required in barrels and cans. In connection, the company have a factory, making all their own cans, which is of material aid to the business.

HALL AND PEARSALL WAREHOUSE

711 Nutt Street
c. 1907: Joseph Schad, builder

Founded about 1869 as Edwards and Hall, the firm became Hall and Pearsall in 1875. A wholesale grocery firm, it specialized in rice, coffee, molasses, salt fish, and hay shipped from the west. Hall and Pearsall did much to make Wilmington a wholesale grocery center for the Carolinas.

This warehouse (fig. 23) shows attention to architectural detail that was, during its era of construction, not unusual even in such utilitarian buildings. The symmetrical treatment of the facades, the gable parapets, and the quality of the Flemish bond brickwork with colored headers are notable.

Located along the river between the tracks of the Atlantic Coast Line and Seaboard Air Line railroads, the 80 foot by 120 foot warehouse was served by private tracks to allow loading and unloading directly from the building.

THE CORBETT COMPANY OFFICE AND WAREHOUSE

704–20 Nutt Street
c. 1905: Joseph Schad, builder

A 1912 article on the Corbett Company noted that: "The company now occupy very convenient and well located premises, comprising a structure especially built for the purpose which is Mr. Corbett's property. The building is of brick of the dimensions of 60 × 200 feet. It affords the very best of receiving and shipping conveniences. It is located between the tracks of the two railroads serving the city, permitting of five carloads of merchandise being loaded or unloaded in or out of the warehouse at the same time." The building, only slightly changed, is an important part of industrial archaeology in Wilmington.

Corbett began business in 1881 as W. I. Gore and Co., wholesale grocers. About 1893 it became Corbett and Gore, finally organizing as the Corbett Co. in 1903. They distributed staple food products to jobbers throughout North and South Carolina.

Brunswick Street crosses Nutt

The Seaboard Air Line Passenger Station, Office, and Freight House, built around 1912, stood at the northeast corner of the intersection until demolished in 1976. It was the last of the Wilmington railroad passenger stations.

North Front Street

Market Street northward to Hanover Street

Consisting of some four blocks of largely turn-of-the century buildings, North Front Street evidences the best of commercial Wilmington. It is a dense mixture of structures of various heights, materials, and bulk, in an unmistakably urban setting. Buildings of relative rarity in North Carolina survive here, including two cast-iron storefronts and two early twentieth-century skyscrapers. Wilmington's native architects and architects from other parts of the country are represented, as are multiple styles. It is a superb collection historically and architecturally. Best of all, it is still used actively for the commercial purposes for which the area developed.

Market Street

The North Front mall, which includes plantings, street furniture, and controlled traffic flow, begins here and continues to Red Cross Street. Some older street lamps, posts with earlier street signs, hydrants, and other items of street furniture survive.

The brick storefont and sidewalk of the First Citizens Bank at 6 North Front Street constitute a notable remodeling of an older structure. The architect was Wes Henry of Leslie N. Boney, Architect, and the work was accomplished in 1975. The Two-Dial Post Clock at 10 North Front, manufactured by the Howard Clock Company, Boston, Massachusetts, was reerected here in the 1930s, but was old then. Such clocks are very rare today. The 1940 Bailey Theatre and two adjoining stores in stucco with simple Art Deco decoration are not only pleasing architecturally, but are on a major historic site. They replaced the Wilmington Hotel, later the Purcell House Hotel. President James Monroe was entertained by the citizens of Wilmington on the Bailey Theatre site, on April 12, 1819. The Raleigh *Minerva* reported on April 23, 1819, that while here, "he partook of a dinner with the citizens at the Wilmington Hotel." John C. Calhoun was in attendance as a member of the president's party.

ATLANTIC TRUST & BANKING COMPANY BUILDING

2–4 North Front Street
1910–12: J. F. Leitner, architect; Joseph Schad, builder.

One of Wilmington's skyscrapers, this nine-story building, flavored with Neoclassical Revival detail, treats the viewer to three facades. Because of the location, there is one facade on each of the streets and, diagonal to these, a one-bay facade at the corner. (See fig. 24.)

Wilmington's first building to exceed five stories, the new Atlantic Trust and Banking Company Building drew considerable interest and comment in its era. The 1912 Chamber of Commerce publication, *City of Wilmington,* noted:

> *Mr. Leitner is now supervising the erection of the very fine eight-story* [sic], *fireproof, new bank and office building being put up for the Atlantic Trust Banking Co., at the corner of Front and Market streets, and he is also now completing the plans for*

24. Atlantic Trust & Banking Company Building, detail, 2–4 North Front Street. J. L. Leitner, architect, 1910–12.

and will soon commence the erection of the new Union Station and Office Building of the Atlantic Coast Line, in this city. Mr. Leitner is the official architect for the Atlantic Coast Line and he has erected the largest number of their important buildings and stations in various places during the past four years.

MASONIC TEMPLE

17–21 North Front Street
1899: Charles McMillen of Duluth, Minnesota, architect; D. Gaetz & Company, Knoxville, Tennessee, builders

On the evening of November 9, 1909, President William Howard Taft, then on a visit in Wilmington, was feted at a banquet in the Masonic Temple here. The president gave a short address.

Charles McMillen, who came to Wilmington for the construction of this building and remained to open his office here, was evidently a well-known Masonic architect. Wilmington's James F. Post submitted a similar design for this structure, but McMillen's design was accepted. The *Messenger* noted on November 12, 1899, that McMillen had already designed and built fourteen Masonic temples, so perhaps that is what gave him the edge over Post.

Cornerstone for the building was laid on May 18, 1899, and it opened on November 20 with a "Great Masonic Fair," which ran through December 3. The November 12, 1899, *Messenger* described the building and its use:

The Temple will stand as a monument to the order to which it is dedicated. It is a handsome building of brown stone and press brick front. The first floor has three handsome stores. These will be occupied by Mr. H. L. Fennell as a harness store; by the Fishblate Clothing Company as a clothing store; and by Mr. James C. Munds, as a drug store. The second story is devoted to offices completed in modern style and many of these are already occupied. Among these who will occupy the office floor are Messrs Bridgers & McKetchan, Dr. W. C. Galloway, Messrs. Rountree & Carr (attorneys), The Colonial Dames Society, George H. Howell, Esq., George Harriss, Jr., Irdell Meares, Esq., E. S. Martin, Esq., Mr. Robert Ruark, Esq., Drs. Davis & Hawes, Dr. R. E. Zachary and Mr. W. H. McIlwee. The third floor will be occupied by the Masonic lodges. There will be two handsome halls, one for the Blue Lodge and one for Commandery and Chapter, with a banquet hall. The fourth floor is devoted to a beautiful ball room with an arch ceiling and parlors, reception rooms and cafe.

Mr. B. F. Miles was the stone carver for the facade ornaments; Johnson Manufacturing Company of Greensboro fabricated the metal trim; John Meaney laid the tile. The entrance to the building is Richardsonian Romanesque. The first two levels are covered by rock-faced ashlar and the upper two are pressed brick. Single and paired windows are contained in arched surrounds and the bays are separated by pilasters of increasing order. A handsome bracketed cornice caps the building, interrupted in its center for Masonic symbols. Other symbols ornament the entrance and the window heads, appearing in both stone and glass.

MACRAE BUILDING–OTTERBOURG'S IRON FRONT MEN'S WEAR DEPOT

25 North Front Street
1878

In its September 13, 1878, editions, the *Star* reported:

> *A Severe Storm of Wind and Hail—The Wall of New Building Tumbles Down, &c. . . . Several trees were uprooted and fences prostrated in various sections of the city, but the only damage of special importance so far as we were able to discover, was the falling of the wall of the new brick building on the west side of Front, between Market and Princess streets which was being erected by Mr. Donald MacRae. The accident is supposed to have been caused mainly by the frequent heavy rains that have prevailed recently, preventing the mortar from drying, together with the lack of the proper support, which would have been given it by the iron front but for the delay in receiving it and getting it into position.*

Damage was said to be slight and only to the south wall. Evidently the cast-iron storefront arrived soon, for by January of 1879 a local festival of Scots, complete with the serving of haggis, was held in MacRae's building.

By 1881 Louis Otterbourg, a tailor and clothier, occupied the building. It was Otterbourg who advertised as "Otterbourg's Iron Front Men's Wear Depot" and who called his store the "Handsomest Building in the South."

The Knights of Pythias occupied the third floor. By 1899 clothier S. H. Fishblate had succeeded Otterbourg. When Fishblate moved next door to the new Masonic building, MacRae moved in with the sales and business departments of the Wilmington Gas Light Company. He was responsible for the trolley line from Wilmington to Wrightsville Beach and had a number of other interests in Wilmington and other parts of the state.

In 1913 the building became the Grand Building, home of the Grand Theatre, a use that continued until 1923. In 1924 the theater was remodeled for McLellan Stores, their ninetieth store in the United States. The company employed sixty clerks, and nothing in the store sold for more than a dollar. Local contractors R. H. Brady and William A. Simon were responsible for the 1924 work. Surviving from their work are some of the handsome pressed-tin ceilings manufactured by the Hanover Iron Works of Wilmington. McLellan continued at this site until 1968, when it closed.

25. MacRae Building–Otterbourg's Iron Front Men's Wear Depot, 25 North Front Street, 1878.

The Renaissance Classical iron front of the MacRae Building facade (fig. 25) is uncommon in North Carolina. At least one other look-alike existed in the next block, adjacent to the old Orton Hotel, but it has been destroyed. Otterbourg's has a decidely horizontal feel and is extremely well cast and handsome. Its survival must be counted a rarity.

CHESTNUTT & BARRENTINE BUILDING

30 North Front Street
before 1884; remodeled 1895 and 1925

The 1879 Wilmington directory shows Aaron & Rheinstein in business at this address, with a wholesale dry-goods establishment. The firm later moved to their own store at 222–224 North Front.

Chestnutt & Barrentine was founded c. 1889 and remained in business until about 1913, when the firm became Chestnutt & Freeman. Their business was shoes, both retail and wholesale. The 1912 *City of Wilmington* booklet noted:

Probably no city in the South of similar population possesses a larger wholesale business than does Wilmington. Some of the important concerns here combine a wholesale and retail business and among these must be noted that of Messrs. Chestnutt & Freeman which about a year ago succeeded to the business formerly carried on as Chestnutt & Barrentine and which dates back its origin about 25 years. The firm occupy a building of four floors which covers an area of 100 × 25 feet. The store is utilized for the retail business, the upper part for the wholesale operations. The house handles full lines of boots, shoes and rubbers manufactured especially for it to fill the demands of the trade of this and neighboring sections. [p. 105]

The three-story building is of stucco over brick. Perhaps the reference above to four stories included a basement or an attic area that cannot be seen from the street. The heavily molded cornice features a modillion and dentil course and heavily scrolled brackets with paneled frieze. The Italianate building retains traces of its cast-iron street-level storefront.

Princess Street crosses North Front; begin 100 street numbers

Midway through the block on the west stood The Orton Hotel, built c. 1886–one of Wilmington's most famous hostelries until it burned in 1949. The hotel featured a multilevel porch with gingerbread decoration. The structure became one of the best known of the southern hotels, attracting conventions, smaller groups, and many well-known travelers.

Since Wilmington was a railroad town, it attracted a good amount of business from people associated with the railroads. In 1899 that business included the eighteenth annual convention of the Association of Railway Telegraph Superintendents.

The *Messenger* of May 17, 1899, enthused:

The South has never had assembled within her borders such a body of distinguished electricians and scientific experts as Wilmington has the honor of having within her precincts today. Of course the man who heads the list is the famous Mr. Thomas A. Edison, "the wizard." Of all electricians he has the most world wide fame and his discoveries and inventions have probably benefitted the world to a greater extent than those of any scientist or inventor dead or living.

Edison remained several days at the Orton. He visited Wrightsville Beach, took a boat trip down the Cape Fear, visited public schools in the city, and even listened, with a large group of Wilmington citizens and conventioneers, to one of his new phonographs.

MORRIS BEAR & BRO. BUILDING

112 North Front Street
c. 1880

In 1895, Braddy & Gaylord opened "Wilmington's Big Racket Store" at 112 North Front Street. Morris Bear & Bro. were occupying this building by 1902. The firm, founded about 1870 by Morris Bear, was continued after his death in 1889 by Isaac Bear and Samuel Bear, Jr., dealing in wholesale dry goods, notions, etc. In 1915, Morris Bear & Bro. leased 110–12 North Front Street to F. W. Woolworth Company, of New York, for twelve years.

The two-story structure is stucco over brick, with a heavily molded cornice. Windows have ornate molded cornices as well, in a leaf motif. Quoins delineate the building sides. The builder seems to have picked up features of the cast-iron structure at 116 North Front Street (see below), including window form and quoins, and adapted them to use here in brick and stucco.

GEORGE R. FRENCH & SONS BUILDING

116 North Front Street
1873

The 1884 publication of *Wilmington—Past, Present, and Future* gives George R. French the credit for developing North Front Street into a commercial avenue and has this to say about his firm:

In 1822 Mr. George R. French, Sr., came to this city from Massachusetts and established himself in his present line of business. He pursued his affairs industriously, and with the earnest purpose of building up an establishment that would eventually stand in the front rank of commercial enterprises. Of his success it is not necessary for us to enter into extended comment. In 1866 the existing firm was formed by the admission into partnership of the sons of the proprietor, and a movement was made from the old quarters on Market Street, where the business had been so long conducted, to North Front street, between Market and Princess, where, having purchased the vacant property, the firm proceeded to construct a large three-story brick building, with iron front and glass on the first floor—it being the first building of its kind constructed in the city, and was at its completion the handsomest store in the city.

At that time North Front street was either used as a place for dwellings or small stores, and being out of the usual haunts of trade, many predicted failure on their part to carry trade so far up street, but with energy and foresight the firm succeeded, and soon by building other stores and alterations of old buildings, they surrounded themselves with other lines, and the success of the movement was assured, and Front street took its place as a business street and has continued to increase in estimation of the people each year.

Business continuing to increase in a few years, the present four-story iron front building was erected by the firm and handsomely fitted up, being the first full iron front erected in the city, and the business was moved into it in September 1873. . . .

The business premises of the firm are centrally located on one of the principal business thoroughfares of the city, the buildings being 25 × 131 feet in dimensions and having four floors.

In 1912 the Wilmington Chamber of Commerce believed the firm to be the oldest established business not only in Wilmington but in North Carolina. During its almost one-hundred years, it had been in the hands of but two generations of the family—George R. French, Sr., and his four sons.

Though the street-level cast-iron front has been altered, the three levels above remain unchanged, except that window sash have been covered. The detail of the front is most visible. Each of the three levels of iron consists of four windows with flat-arched openings and a molded cornice. Windows are flanked by banded Corinthian columns. End pilasters, simulating quoining, carry up the outer edges of the front to the heavily molded cornice that tops the structure.

Evidently the French firm paid as much attention to the interior of the store as to the exterior and was not averse to expending sizable funds on beauty. The *Messenger* for February 5, 1899, noted:

Those who drop into the handsome store of Messrs. George R. French & Sons, will be struck with the metamorphosis which has been brought about by the dexterious and skilled hand of Mr. George Miller, the expert decorator. The ceiling for the entire length of the store, consisting of five panels has been decorated in the most beautiful and artistic manner. The two front and the two rear panels have been painted in solid color, a pearl gray, and the background of the middle panel is sky blue. On the background of each panel there are decorations of exquisite workmanship. There are festoons of vines, and there is a harmonious blending of green, pink, and gold tracings. Beautiful flowers complete the picture, and the eye never tires of the lovely scene. The middle panel is, however, the prettiest of all. The background represents the sky and it is studded with stars while green boughs stand out in relief against the sky. Numbers of beautiful birds sit amid the boughs while others are on the wing, making a picture of rare attractiveness. Around the chandeliers throughout the length of the room there are decorations in circles and the whole ceiling makes up a scene that is rarely met with.

The ceiling has been completed and this week Mr. Miller will finish up the walls, shelving and drawers. The shelving is to be enameled in white with decorations of gold leaf, and the drawers underneath are to be finished in oak colors. We are glad to note it when our business men show their enterprise and pride in fitting their places of business in such metropolitan fashion. Mr. Miller is an artist and in his work he has shown that he is a most skillful painter. His work by the way, is done by hand. Some of the notable work done by him was the decoration of the winter home of Mrs. Kornegie [Carnegie] on Cumberland Island, Ga., and Mr. Thos. A. Mcintyre's lodge at Verona, Onslow County, N.C.

Whatever may have happened to the French store interiors, three floors of the facade remain, not only one of the handsomest reminders of nineteenth-century Wilmington but probably the oldest unchanged storefront in the commercial area.

U.S. POST OFFICE AND FEDERAL BUILDING

152 North Front Street
1936–37: R. Stanley Brown, architect; Algernon Blair, Montgomery, Alabama, builder; R. A. Wood, construction superintendent.

A massive stone post office with tower and fine Romanesque detailing had been constructed on this site in 1889–91 under W. A. Freret, supervising architect, U.S. Treasury. Some forty-five years later, plans were announced to construct a new post office and federal building to provide additional space. Wilmington seems to have had no quarrel with the plan to construct a new building but objected to the demolition of the old building and the style of the new one.

Congressman J. Bayard Clark, who had sponsored the building, was warned by Mayor Walter H. Blair, according to the *Star* of February 20, 1936, "If Mr. Clark has been led to believe the people of Wilmington want the brick building that is being planned, then somebody has led him up a blind alley." He noted that the building as planned was "just nothing." A plan was finally advanced that would save the old building and turn it over to the city for a library, city hall annex, or community center. The new building would then be built behind the existing structure.

There were those who said that the 1889–91 building was one of the worst deteriorated in the federal system. A rather spirited preservation fight ensued, with the newspaper, trade unions, and some public officials, opposing preservation. The Wilmington Central Labor Union went on record, according to the *Star* of February 26, 1936, as opposing preservation—noting that if the building were saved, it would decrease the labor force gainfully employed by the number of men required to demolish the old building, thus adding unemployment and preventing gainful employment. The resolution read in part: "We cannot conceive of anyone wanting an old garment placed in front of a new garment as it would obstruct the beauty of the new one."

Demolition of the stone structure began on May 12, 1936. The *Star* noted on May 9 that the Ohio firm that had gotten the demolition contract had hired "a small force of Wilmington workmen." By June 12, when the paper reported that demolition was nearing a finish, it seems to have changed sides; it may have been safe by then to be pro-preservation. "One of Wilmington's ancient landmarks [it was then 48 years old, including the four years it took to build] the Old Post Office Building, will be but a memory within the week. . . . Workmen . . . could be seen yesterday, precariously perched high above the piles of debris, beating away the brick and stone which once was a part of Wilmington's most beautiful and beloved building."

On June 16 the paper carried verse by Walter Storm who:

between times as an engineer woos the muses of Parnassus, smites his lyre and bids farewell to the old Post Office building, the ragged skeleton of which for the moment obscures the eastern skyline from Front Street. It is a matter of intense interest in Wilmington for the old building was a landmark. Generations have learned to deciper time by consulting its clock, countless others have whiled away pleasant afternoons ensconced on its steps and therefore the theme of Mr. Storm is quite appropriate and worthy of more than ordinary attention. He sings:

"Farewell, old friend! Dame Progress bids you go
It is life; for nothing stands still you know.
So with regrets we may as well resolve:
That all man-made works must, in time disolve.
You have stood your ground:
you have served us well.
And in memorium, the years will tell,
Of plaudits won and checked against your score,
To live forever, and forever more.
The show is out; the curtain tumbles down,
Soon another will take your place in town.
It is life; for nothing stands still you know.
Farewell, old friend! Dame Progress bids you go."

The new building was in a Neoclassical Revival style with a recessed entrance and a Greek lantern at the roof peak above the entrance. The architect said that he had studied John Norris's Wilmington Custom House of the 1840s (now demolished) and used it as his inspiration. He also claimed to have localized the capitals of the entry columns. Since the building was in North Carolina, it was said that tobacco would be used to replace the acanthus—tobacco was,

26. U.S. Post Office and Federal Building, 152 North Front Street, lobby mural, Wilmington in the 1840's, *by William F. Pfohl, August 1940.*

after all, more appropriate for North Carolina; and the capitals are unmistakably tobacco leaf and flower.

The cornerstone for the new building was laid on September 27, 1936. It was dedicated on May 29, 1937, by Josephus Daniels—North Carolina native, member of Woodrow Wilson's cabinet, and at the time of dedication, U.S. ambassador to Mexico.

The *Star* reported on May 30 that "The building is of southern colonial style, built of brick with limestone trimming, 114 by 182 feet. The face brick was obtained from the Pine Hall Brick and Pipe Company of Winston-Salem, the limestone from Indiana, the granite for steps and water table from Mt. Airy, N. C. and the common brick from N. C. Isenhour in Sanford, N.C." The lantern features an octagonal base, fluted Doric columns surrounding a circular core, a dentil course with bell-cast roof above, and a weathervane.

Inside the lobby is a mural, *Wilmington in the 1840s* (fig. 26). Completed by William F. Pfohl of Winston-Salem in August of 1940, it is typical of the superb work done by U.S. Treasury and WPA artists. The eight plaster bas-relief groupings in the coved ceiling of the northern stair hall are also handsome. They are, unfortunately, unsigned. The mural and bas-relief are part of the national collection of depression-era federal art that is now recognized as important. The artwork here was commissioned by the Treasury Department.

Chestnut Street crosses North Front; begin 200 street numbers

The parking deck to the west interrupts the street pattern and views of the river. It is the only corner in the area where the relation of Front Street to the river has been destroyed and where the waterway is no longer an obvious part of the streetscape.

As in other blocks within the area, all the storefronts here should probably be included in an architectural survey. Certainly the mixture of facade heights and the intensive use of the area are important amenities. It is inevitable, however, that some buildings are overlooked because new facades obliterate evidence of an earlier building.

MURCHISON NATIONAL BANK BUILDING–ACME BUILDING

200 North Front and 101–7 Chestnut Streets
1902: Charles McMillen, architect; John H. Brunjes, builder

In an article on the Murchison National Bank (named for Col. K. M. Murchison of New York), the 1902 *Wilmington Up-to-Date* booklet states: "Very shortly after the publication of this volume the bank will be domiciled it its new headquarters, now in course of erection. This will consist of a handsome three story building, constructed of brick and stone, located at the corner of Front and Chestnut streets. The bank will occupy the street floor, which will be fitted up in accordance with modern requirements in keeping with the character of the institution. The upper part will be let out for office purposes, and will, no doubt, yield a lucrative return."

Organized in March of 1899, the bank had experienced a meteoric rise in business that necessitated a new building (fig. 27). A fine Neo–Renaissance

27. The Murchison National Bank Building–Acme Building, 200 North Front Street and 101–7 Chestnut Street. Charles McMillen, architect, 1902.

Classical structure, the walls are of blond brick with stone quoining, stone base, and stone watertable. H. A. Tucker & Bros. supplied the stone. The cornice is molded metal, modillioned with a brick frieze below. The cornerstone indicates the construction of the building by Acme Investment and Realty Co., which lasted from 1898 to 1904. The building passed from Murchison to Home Building Corporation and Home Saving Bank (1925), to Morris Plan Bank (1934), and to multiple other renters.

MURCHISON BUILDING–FIRST UNION BUILDING

201–3 North Front Street
1913–14: Kenneth M. Murchison of New York, architect

One of Wilmington's two skyscrapers, the Murchison Building (fig. 28) is, at eleven stories, still the tallest building in town. It is generously adorned with handsome Neoclassical Revival detail. As in most buildings of its type, the decoration seems to suggest the base, shaft, and entablature of a classical column. The two-story stone entablature consists of the ornate molded cornice of the building with copper palmette crown, Ionic pilasters, and decorative panels, and a frieze of Greek key relief that ends in wreathed rondelles with swags and draped brackets. The shaft is made up of seven stories of brick and colored stone panels with decorative crest divisions. The gray, stone, two-story base has a belt course and features the massive Doric columns that flank the round-arched entrance. In 1972 the First Union Bank took over the first floor, and other business offices are above.

In 1918 William Gibbs McAdoo—secretary of the treasury in the cabinet of President Woodrow Wilson, the husband of one of Wilson's daughters, and a presidential aspirant—visited Wilmington. The *Dispatch* of April 9, 1918, bragged:

28. Murchison Building–First Union Building. 201–3 North Front Street. Kenneth M. Murchison, Jr., architect, 1913–14.

The stage is completely and elaborately set for the coming and short stay of the city's distinguished visitor—the second biggest man in the country today—one who has honored every confidence reposed in him and one who stands second only to President Woodrow Wilson . . . will speak at the Academy of Music tonight in the interest of the third issue Liberty Loan Bond campaign.

Although Secretary McAdoo's stay here is limited he will be given an ovation and made to understand that Wilmington is delighted beyond expression to have him as her guest. In going from his train . . . the Secretary will be given the opportunity of seeing the principal downtown section. He will be given a splendid view of the harbor from the roof of the Murchison Building and will see why the city has urged that the river be utilized by the government in every possible way.

It is not known how many others, famous in their own way, have been given the opportunity to see the same view as McAdoo.

RHEINSTEIN DRY GOOD COMPANY BUILDING

222–26 North Front Street
1891–92: A. S. Eichberg, Savannah, architect

It probably can be uncontestably stated that Wilmington had no equal to this structure in commercial architecture. The 1902 *Wilmington Up-to-Date* publication called it "the most imposing mercantile structure in the city," and there can be no doubt of that fact. Four floors with brick and stone facade, the building had a proliferation of Richardsonian Romanesque detail.

The Rheinstein company was formed in 1865 as Aaron & Rheinstein and became F. Rheinstein & Co. in 1887 and the Rheinstein Dry Goods Company in 1895. It was this firm that brought architect A. S. Eichberg to Wilmington. His success with the Rheinstein Building probably had much to do with his selection to design the new county courthouse building at North Third and Princess streets. (See fig. 50.)

Except in the alley to the north, the building is not recognizable today. It has been refaced, its cornice and topping is gone, and nothing on the facade indicates its former glory, though the new facade may be a valid statement of its construction era.

BIJOU THEATRE SITE

211–25 North Front Street
1912: R. H. Brady, architect

Said to have been the first movie theater in North Carolina and one of the first in the South, the Bijou opened in a tent at this site. By the time of the construction of the 1912 theater (see fig. 29), the use of the site was well established, and the Bijou became the Wild West theater of Wilmington, presenting Tom Mix, Hoot Gibson, Buck Jones, and Tim McCoy movies and occasionally actual western heroes and antiheroes. One such was the 1918 appearance of Emmett Dalton, last surviving member of the Dalton gang. On March 13 and 14 he showed pictures depicting the "World Famous Double Bank Robbery at Coffeyville, Kansas, Oct. 5, 1892, As It Actually Happened." Emmett narrated the film and told the crowds that they had taken matters into their own hands but that he now saw their mistake.

29. North Front Street from Chestnut Street, looking north, with Bijou Theatre in left foreground, c. 1905. (Wm. Edmund Barrett collection.)

Though the theater has been demolished, its presence is noted by a surviving section of tile lobby floor with the name *Bijou*. The tile has been preserved as part of a landscaped pocket park on the site of the former theater. The park gives access to a parking deck, to the west of North Front Street.

ELKS BUILDING

255–59 North Front Street
c. 1902; interior remodeled 1906: Leitner & Wilkins, architects, Jos. Schad, contractor; front remodeled 1911: J. F. Leitner, architect, Jos. Schad, contractor

An imposing structure with arched and arcaded street-level entrances, a center pavilion with side balconies at the second level, a center-arch window, and projecting oriel with elks head and a parapeted roof, the structure was a distinctive one for downtown Wilmington.

Why the facade was so changed is not known, but the changes seems to have occurred after the Elks moved, about 1945, taking the Elks head with them. Enough of the facade remains, however, to envision the former eccentric building. Bases for the arcaded entrances remain, but the entire center pavilion seems to have been removed. Some of the roofline and cornice remain. The building now seems strangely incomplete—an unsolvable puzzle until a photograph of the Elks Building is superimposed over the current facade.

The building is of interest to architectural historians because the North Carolina Association of Architects, the predecessor of the North Carolina Chapter, American Institute of Architects, held its organizational meeting here in 1906. The *Dispatch* for July 9 headlined "The Architects in Session—First Meeting Held Saturday Afternoon at Elks' Temple." The article continued:

> *Organization Effected—Many Prominent Architects Present at Formation of Association. . . . Election of Officers. . . . The first meeting of the new organi-*

zation was held at the Elks' Temple. . . . The election of officers of the association was entered upon. The result of the election was as follows: President—Charles C. Hook, of Charlotte, Vice President—Charles W. Barrett, of Raleigh. Secretary and Treasurer—F. Gordon, of Charlotte.

The constitution and by-laws, which were adopted at this meeting, cover fully the various purposes and requirements of an association of this nature and they are based upon the rules governing the American Association of Architects.

Subsequent meetings of the new organization were held at the Seashore Hotel in Wrightsville Beach on the following Monday.

COMMERCIAL BUILDING

261 North Front Street
c. 1900

As have most of the Wilmington commercial structures, this building has lost its street-level storefront. The passerby who looks up, however, may still view a fine building. A three-bay projection is flanked by slightly recessed sections—the one to the left is quite narrow, but the one to the right, a flat-topped window, is set slightly above the level of the round arched windows of the pavilion. These are united by a single stone lintel and separated and flanked by staged pilasters. Above the windows, the keystones of the arches continue as pilasters into the entablature and break through the cornice.

I. M. BEAR & CO., BUILDING

272 North Front Street
1906–7: Hartwood & Moss, of Newport News, Virginia, contractors.

Five stories of buff brick, the building consists of a storefront with molded stone cornice, a single second-story level—probably treated in much the same manner as the original storefront, except that bay openings there were larger—and a third-story level of windows in round-arched bays, six of which march across the facade. The cornice of the building is missing, but it was likely pressed metal and elaborately molded.

I. M. Bear & Co. seem to have been the first tenants—moving from their earlier home across the street into this building, which was evidently built to their specifications. The *Star* noted on October 4, 1906: "Contractors yesterday began tearing away the present buildings at SE corner of Front and Grace streets to make way for the handsome 5-story structure which Mr. J. H. Brunjes will erect for Messrs. I. M. Bear & Co. The building will be completed as soon as possible and will be occupied by Messrs. Bear & Co., by the next Fall season." The building was later occupied by Einstein Bros. from 1909 until 1921, when Efird's Department Store began operating at this site.

I. M. BEAR & CO.

275–77 North Front Street
c. 1898

A corner store with entrance on North Front Street and a long side on Grace Street, the Bear store was three stories tall with another full story to the west on the alley off Grace. The building was brick, with fine trim, and a particularly well-detailed corbeled cornice, topped by a patterned metal cornice and by metal cresting that was especially ornate on the corner.

As of 1982, only two floors of the building remain; they are relatively unchanged on Grace Street. The top floor and the high cornice have been removed. Why this was done is not known, but the remaining detail, especially in stringcourse and brickwork, is an indication of the building's former glory.

Bear was a wholesale dry-goods and notions company, an agent for Glenham Mills. The firm, organized in 1895, maintained offices in New York at 93 Franklin Street and in a number of other cities in North and South Carolina. In 1907 they moved from this store to new and larger quarters across the street. In 1906, the building was sold to the J. Hicks Bunting Drug Company by Isaac M. Bear.

Grace Street crosses North Front; begin 300 street numbers

The block to the west is part of the Cotton Exchange, a commercial development of restaurants and shops. (See fig. 19.)

COMMERCIAL STRUCTURE

313 North Front Street
c. 1913

This structure is a three-story brick building with capped cornice of pressed metal and massive modillions. Panels of pressed metal separate the second- and third-level window banks, which contain four sets of triple windows in each level.

ALEXANDER SPRUNT & SON BUILDING

321 North Front Street
1919–20: H. E. Bonitz, architect; H. L. Vollers, builder

"Sprunt Firm to Have New Quarters" headlined the *Dispatch* of September 17, 1919, continuing:

Alex. Sprunt & Sons, Inc., cotton exporters, will erect an office building on the southwest corner of Front and Walnut streets, it is announced. Plans for the building will be drawn by H. E. Bonitz, and actual construction will start in the early future.

The building will be one story in height and of classic structure, with a frontage of 66 feet on Front Street and a depth of 80 feet on Walnut. The building will be built of material similar to that used in construction of the custom house and will cost in the neighborhood of $100,000.

The property is owned by H. L. Vollers and the building will be erected by him and taken over by the Sprunt firm on a long time lease. The company is obliged to vacate its present quarters because of inadequate floor space.

A Neoclassical Revival structure of brick and stone, the building (fig. 30) is two stories high and a wide five bays long. Bays are separated by pilasters with stylized Corinthian capitals. Windows—six-over-six at the second level and nine-over-nine at the first—with a broad panel separating them, hang beneath a single lintel and keystone at the second level. Entrance is through a stone surround topped by a broken pediment.

The 1912 publication *City of Wilmington* noted that the Sprunt firm was founded in 1866, and that it engaged in cotton exporting and operated the Champion Compresses and Warehouses. The account continued:

The number of hands employed during the season averages 800, and this greatly benefits the city in giving employment to so large a force of men. The firm ships the cotton to ports in Great Britain and the Continent. They have branch houses in Liverpool, England and Bremen, Germany, conducted under the management of resident partners. They have also offices at Havre, France and at Boston and Houston. . . . This firm also are the pioneers of the foreign steamship trade of this city, having chartered the first steamer—the Barnsmore*—in 1881. Now during the season an average of two steamships are dispatched weekly, the majority of these sailing under the British flag. Messrs. Alexander Sprunt & Sons are Lloyd's agents for this port and they are also agents of the London Salvage Association. Mr. Jas. Sprunt is British Vice-Consul here, an appointment he has held for many years.*

From just after World War II until 1968, the Wilmington USO was housed in this building.

Walnut Street crosses North Front; railroad tracks cross beneath North Front

At a site that was once the transportation hub of a major regional commercial, agrarian, and industrial center, there is now only an occasional sound of railroad activity; yet it was railroads that brought Wilmington to prominence as a port. Railroad buildings do exist to the west, and from this point there are good views of the Wilmington and Weldon/Atlantic Coast Line Railroad buildings and of the Cape Fear waterfront where land transportation meets water carriers. (See figures 20–22.)

From this site the Wilmington and Weldon Railroad—organized in 1834 as the Wilmington and Raleigh and operating 161½ miles of track by 1840—stretched both to the east and to the west. Its passenger station, freight terminals, and repair facilities crossed North Front, occupying at least the block between Red Cross and Hanover streets and Nutt and North Second streeets. Because the railroad connected with land transportation to Washington, D.C., and with steamships to the south, it was a major transfer terminal, especially for passengers traveling in either direction.

Woodrow Wilson used trains from this location on more than one occasion. It was from here in September 1875 that he took the Wilmington and Wel-

30. Alexander Sprunt & Son Building, 321 North Front Street, H. E. Bonitz, architect, 1919–20.

don when leaving Wilmington to begin studies at Princeton.

On November 9, 1909, President William Howard Taft arrived here by private railroad car. After a full day of activities in the city, he departed from this point after a banquet in his honor.

Probably the most remarkable event to occur here happened at about 2:00 P.M. on April 24, 1850, when the funeral train carrying the body of John C. Calhoun arrived in the Wilmington and Raleigh station on its way to South Carolina for burial. James Sprunt in his *Chronicles of the Cape Fear River* quotes the following newpaper accounts. From the *Chronicle* of April 24, 1850:

It is expected that the remains of Mr. Calhoun will reach Wilmington today at about 12 o'clock. The Committee of Arrangements publish the following:

Order of Procession for escorting the remains of the Hon. J. C. Calhoun.

The procession will be formed in the following order, the right resting on the railroad depot, in open order, for the reception of the corps of attendants on the arrival of the cars.

Order of Procession.
Clergy of the various denominations.
Sergeant at Arms and assistants.
Pallbearers.
Coffin.
Pallbearers.
Relations of the deceased.
Committee of the U.S. Senate.
Committee of South Carolina.
Committee of Arrangements.
Citizens of South Carolina.
Judges of the Supreme and Superior Courts.
Members of the bar.
Members of the Medical profession.
Magistrate of police and commissioners of the town, collector of customs and officers of the United States service, president and directors of the Wilmington and Raleigh R.R., members of the various societies of the town, in citizen dress, teachers of the schools and academies, captains of vessels and seamen, citizens and strangers.

. . . The citizens generally are requested to close their stores, to suspend all operations of business, and to meet at the depot at 12 o'clock. There the procession will be formed, under the direction of William C. Howard, as chief marshal, to receive the remains in open order and escort them to the foot of Market Street, where the boat for Charleston, the Nina, *will be waiting to receive them.*

A gun from the wharf of the Wilmington and Raleigh R.R. Co. will give the earliest notice of the arrival of the cars. Immediately upon the firing of this gun, the flags of the public buildings and the ships in port will be struck at half-mast; the bells of the town will commence tolling and minute guns will be fired.

The clergy and the pallbearers are requested to call at Messrs. Dawson's store for gloves and crape. The citizens will find a supply of crape at the same place.

The steamer will leave for Charleston; it is expected about five o'clock p.m.

From the *Chronicle* of May 1, 1850:

On Wednesday last, near 2 o'clock, the cars arrived from Weldon, bringing the mortal remains of John C. Calhoun, in the special charge of Mr. Beale, the sergeant at arms of the United States Senate, and senators Mason, of Virginia, Clarke of Rhode Island, Dickinson, of New York, Davis, of Missouri, and Dodge, of Iowa, and Mr. Berrien, of Georgia. . . . Mr. Venable of North Carolina, Mr. Holmes, of South Carolina, members of the House of Representatives, accompanied the committee by invitation. . . . The arrangements as to the procession, etc., were carried into effect in accordance with the program published in our last issue.

From the *Journal*:

On the arrival of the cars, the stores and places of business were closed, the shipping in port struck their colors to half-mast, the bells of the various churches were tolled, and minute guns fired while the procession moved from the depot down Front Street to the steamer Nina, *lying at Market Dock, where she was waiting to receive the remains of the lamented deceased and convey them to the city of Charleston.*

Notwithstanding the inclemency of the day, the procession was, we think the largest we have ever seen in this place. Everybody seemed anxious to pay the last respect to the statesman and orator who has so long and so faithfully filled some of the most responsible posts of his country.

The steamer Governor Dudley, *handsomely decorated for the occasion, accompanied the* Nina, *taking over a portion of the committees and guests to the city of Charleston. Both steamers left the wharf about half past three o'clock p.m.*

Across the tracks on the east side of North Front Street, the new Union Station is the last sad reminder of the former glory of this part of town and of the famous who used this site as a transportation hub in their trips to and from Wilmington.

WILMINGTON AND WELDON RAILROAD STATION BELL

North Front Street, east side, near Hanover Street
1855

Located in front of the Wilmington Railroad Museum, 507 Nutt Street, is the Wilmington and Weldon Railroad Station bell, atop a brick and concrete slab. The bell is marked, "Cast by J. Bernhard & Co., No. 78 N. 6th St. Philadelphia, 1855."

Beneath the bell on a plaque is the following: "Presented to the City of Wilmington, October 16, 1964. In commemoration of the more than 100 years that Wilmington served as the General Headquarters of the Atlantic Coast Line Railroad and its predecessor companies. This historic bell announced the departure of all passenger trains from the time it was erected in 1856 until the new station was built in 1963."

When the bell was first hung, it announced the arrival and departure of Wilmington and Weldon Railroad trains. Later, the trains were Atlantic Coast Line, Seaboard Air Line, and finally Seaboard Coast Line. The station adjacent reflects the lack of faith in the railroad's future that was evident everywhere in 1963 and the failing interest of the public in this means of efficient transportation, an interest just now being revived.

South Front Street

Market Street southward to Castle

South Front Street, which begins as commercial in the first block, adds one residence in the second and more residences plus a civic structure in the third, becomes exclusively residential in the fourth block—and what a residential street it is! The 300, 400, and 500 blocks contain no buildings that do not possess architectural value, and the 100 block contains no commercial structure without architectural value. The streetscape of these blocks is visually and historically important and exciting.

Market Street

On May 12, 1854, ex-President Millard Fillmore visited with his party. He stopped for a short period of time at "Mr. Holmes' Hotel" on the southeast corner of Market and Front streets.

VENTED COMMERCIAL BUILDING

22–24 South Front Street
Before 1884; front remodeled in 1902: H. E. Bonitz, architect, P. C. Lemoyne, builder

When Jacob W. Duls purchased the southernmost of these two properties, 24 South Front Street, in March 1886, it was described as being the southernmost store on the lot. The building is shown on the 1884 Sanborn insurance map, so it must have been built by that time.

Both buildings, or rather both street numbers, seem to have been occupied by C. Tienken as a grocery and liquor store prior to May 15, 1896, when he offered the entire stock for sale in the *Star*. Antonio Rush was operating a grocery at 22 South Front by October 22, 1878, and advertised in the *Star*, while Wescott & Taylor, a paint shop, advertised in the paper on November 17, 1878, as "In rear of Mr. Antonio Rush's store."

The Salvation Army Emergency Home for Girls was at 22½ South Front Street about 1920. Joseph Berbary's Dry Goods Store was at 24 South Front during the first quarter of the century, while George C. Simmons, locksmith and gunsmith, was at number 22 in the first decade of the century—later moving across the street. Holmes & Atkinson, grocers, was at 22 South Front by 1913, operating later as Wm. Atkinson, grocer. Starkey and Goldberg were at number 22 in 1920.

The building seems to have had a metal cornice, now removed. It is still handsome, and the stepped parapet roof is clearly visible without the cornice. Fine cast-iron vent covers survive above the windows with their ornate brick lintels. The storefront is cast iron—signed but illegible. The signature seems to read "Made by Hatta [?] a Steel Co-operative Pennsylvania." The front is decorated with molding and dentil courses and elaborate fluted modillions. Gable-topped pilasters and embossed rosettes also appear.

PECK BUILDING

29 South Front Street
before 1884

George A. Peck operated a hardware business here in 1888, in the building that he had built earlier. Hardware businesses operated by B. F. Alderman and Charles D. Foard (1897) occupied the building in later years.

This is a brick, vented, commercial structure with brick corbel cornice and plain brick binding pilasters at the corners of the building. Within the frieze are segmental arch vents with louvered covers. Windows also have segmental arches. The first floor has been obscured by remodeling, but the structure remains a handsome one. Inasmuch as the building appears on the 1884 Sanborn map, it must have been built prior to that date, with street-level changes having been made in the twentieth century.

31. B.H.J. Ahrens Building, 31 South Front Street, 1881. Addition on Dock Street (right), 1888.

B. H. J. AHRENS BUILDING

31 South Front Street
1881; addition on Dock Street, 1888

"Workmen," reported the *Star* on May 17, 1881, "under the superintendence of Mr. John Ottaway, have commenced excavating for the foundation of a large-three story brick building for Mr. B. H. J. Ahrens on the northeast corner of Front and Dock streets. It is to be of pressed brick, 44 by 32 feet in dimensions and about forty feet high, with a store on the first floor and two halls above." By May 22, the same paper reported the building above ground. On October 18, 1888, it reported "Improvements are being made on the Ahrens building . . . which when completed will add much to its appearance." Those improvements probably brought the building to its present appearance and finish.

A vented commercial structure, the building (fig. 31) and its addition at a slightly lower height remain very much unchanged. They feature fine brickwork, frieze vents with cast-iron grills, and well-detailed window surrounds. Some of the windows along Dock Street still retain cast-iron balcony-support brackets, handsome even without the balcony above. The cast-iron storefront at street level, with projecting cornice, also is still retained.

The Ahrens Building is one of the finest of the Wilmington commercial survivals.

Dock Street crosses South Front; begin 100 street numbers

Henry Clay's lodgings during his visit to Wilmington on April 9 and 10, 1844, were, according to the *Chronicle* for April 10, 1844, in the residence of Mrs. Joseph A. Hill, on the southeast corner of Front and Dock Streets.

When ex-President James Knox Polk was in Wilmington with his family on March 7, 1849, immediately after the end of his term as president, the *Commercial* reported in its March 8 edition that the presidential party was escorted to: "Mrs. Swann's boarding-house, on the balcony of which, in view and hearing of the assembled crowd, Mr. Wm. Hill welcomed the ex-president and suite in a cordial, chaste and eloquent address; during which he alluded to the birth and education of the ex-President in North Carolina, and to many of the leading measures of his administration. Mr. Polk's response was feeling and patriotic. He fondly acknowledged his attachment to North Carolina." Mrs. Swann's Boarding House is believed to have been located on South Front, between Dock and Orange streets.

A. D. WESSELL HOUSE

115 South Front Street
c. 1855

Though its South Front Street facade is obscured by additions and enclosures, the south side with vented frieze can still be seen if the Wessell House is viewed from the south or from Muter's Alley, directly across the street. What one sees is a remnant of a particularly fine Italianate structure with palmette-and-vine cast-iron vent covers and horizontal and vertical cross banding of the stucco wall surfaces, the bands serving to delineate bay openings. Among other houses of this general type in Wilmington, the Conoley-Hanby-Sidbury House at 15 North Fifth Avenue and the adjacent Von Glahn House at 19 North Fifth (see figs. 84 and 85) are similar, except that both of these houses have wide roof overhangs, rather than the projecting molded wooden cornice with modillions used here. Their plan and treatment of wall surfaces are, however, markedly alike. Both the North Fifth Avenue houses were built in the 1850s, probably the decade during which the Wessell House was also constructed.

The dwelling was occupied as early as 1885 by A. D. Wessell, a grocer at 3–5 South Second Street. Wessell, who acquired the property in 1883, maintained residence at least through 1889 and ownership into the twentieth century. He advertised in the *Messenger* on August 1, 1908, "For rent or Sale—Residence 115 South Front Street, with 13 rooms, in best condition. Water works, cisterns and necessary out houses. Terms easy." His September 10, 1892, *Messenger* advertisement was virtually the same: "Brick dwelling. No. 115 South Front Street, near the new Market, contains 13 rooms, water works, cistern and well water and all necessary outhouses. Very suitable for boarding house. Terms very reasonable. Apply to A. D. Wessell, No. 3 South 2nd Street." On January 18, 1898, he advertised in the *Dispatch*, "For rent—seven rooms over 115 South Front street. Suitable for boarding or private family." Evidently by that time the ground floor was being rented separately. On September 23, 1899, Wessell offered in the *Dispatch*: "the large commodious store, 115 South Front street, now occupied by Mrs. Canady as a millinery store."

By 1900, the store was Isham Thompson's Eating House; by 1905, Bloodworth & Dawson Saloon. Crumpler & Scott, soft drinks and restaurant, were in business here in 1915, a use that continued at least through 1938. Other uses included a boardinghouse, a thrift store, a swap shop,and in the present era, a bar and cabaret.

An extremely important survival, this residence alone exists from the many important early residences that dotted Wilmington's downtown business area.

FRONT STREET MARKET–CITY AUDITORIUM

120–122–124 South Front Street
1879; 1900, F. A. Applegate, contractor; 1912, James F. Gause, Jr., architect; 1920; 1930, Leslie N. Boney, architect; 1945

City markets are unusual survivors in most cities. Now refaced, Wilmington's 1879–80 market is little noticed; though its one-story height and bulk are relatively unchanged, its alleys still give access, and the iron gate that gave entrance to its stalls allows glimpses into the interior. It is one of three markets that survive in Wilmington, along with the North Fourth Street Market, and the Giblem Lodge on Princess Street, where the city operated a market on the first level for a number of years.

Older than the Fourth Street Market, this building was constructed for market use, while the Giblem Lodge Market was for rented space. The market was built in 1879–80 by the Wilmington Market Company and was acquired by the city in 1882. When the building opened on March 19, 1880, a Wilmington newspaper reported:

The New Market was thrown open for inspection of the public, and its spacious interior was thronged with visitors who came to view the gas-lit structure in all its perfection and completeness. A few of the stalls only were occupied, many of the proprietors being unable to make the transfer to their new quarters on the short notice given; but the suspended quarters of fat beef and sundry carcasses of plump porkers hanging on the hooks, betokened business on the morrow.

After acquisition by the city in October 1882, the market was cleaned and repaired, and a local newspaper visited in May 1883: "We looked at the new Market House and found everything as neat and trim as the stock in a millinery store. Each stall is enclosed by neat counters or shelving, which appear at a distance like the whitest of marble, and the name of the proprietor and the number of the stall appear on a neat banner-like signboard that surmounts it. The floor was also nicely sanded, and the entire arrangement was calculated to impress one favorably. It is probably one of the handsomest markets in the South, and possibly boasts of as good looking a set of butchers."

Repairs were made several times over the years. Valentine, Brown & Co. replaced the brick floors with concrete in 1892, and the moniter skylights were replaced in 1893. In July of 1895 the gaslights gave way to incandescent electric lamps, an arrangement that most stall holders seem to have found inadequate. In 1900 Contractor F. A. Applegate cleaned and repaired sash; repaired, painted, and sanded the exterior gray stucco; and whitewashed the interior. In 1912 Architect James F. Gause, Jr., prepared plans that called for screening the building and improving sanitation. A local newspaper described the work:

In the center of the market will be located flower, fruit and vegetable stalls, and on each side around the walls will be the meat stalls. The old meat counters will be removed and in their place will be sanitary refrigerator counters. The fish stalls will be moved from the alley on the north side of the market house to the rear, on the wharf. Granolithic floors will be laid in the market and in the fish stalls also, with drains, so that the whole floor space can be washed off with running water as often as is deemed necessary. Upstairs over the rear separate toilets will be provided.

In 1919, at the expiration of market leases, the market was converted to an auditorium. By January 1920 the New Hanover County Poultry Show and the Wilmington Kennel Club had already used the space for shows. The auditorium, which was capable of seating three thousand, opened officially in 1920 with the Wilmington Automobile Show and Industrial Exhibit on April 6. The Royal Highlander Band appeared and, according to a local newspaper, "An electric sign labeled 'City Auditorium' has been placed over the main entrance, and will be ablaze for the first time on the night of the opening." The Reverend Baxter F. McLendon, an evangelist known as "Cyclone Mack," preached in the auditorium in 1921, and other events were as diverse as an Old Fiddler's Convention of the same year and the Military Indoor Circus in 1926.

In 1923 a producers market for farm products, limited to women salespersons, had opened between auditorium uses. Evidently various plans for remodeling the structure were discussed, and by 1930 Leslie N. Boney had been awarded the contract for renovation of the structure for full market use. In 1944–45 the market was renovated once more. In 1948 the City Market bell was moved from this building to the market at North Fourth and Campbell streets. In 1960 the building was sold by the city council.

VON KAMPEN BLOCK: HARDIN'S PALACE PHARMACY

128 South Front Street
1894

A *Messenger* notice on Dr. John H. Hardin on February 16, 1896, calls this building the "new store," and says that "arrangement of the new store was designed by Mr. H. E. Bonitz, the young architect." This most likely refers to a new interior and location, since Hardin had been located next door in the city market before moving here.

The building does not appear on the 1893 Sanborn map, but is on the 1898 Sanborn. An 1894 construction date is confirmed by the *Messenger* of April 24: "Mr. C. F. Von Kampen has begun work on the foundation of a large brick building, which he will erect on Front street, just south of the Front Street Market." The structure seems initially to have been referred to as either the Von Kampen Block or the Van Kampen Building.

George L. Harman, tenant, advertised in August 1895: "George L. Harman is serving his delicious soda water. He has also curative cures, from corn removers to life renovators. Also a fine prescription department." Harman sold his business in October 1895 to H. L. Fentress, who in turn sold to Hardin.

32. Stemmerman's Grocery Store, 136 South Front Street. Built before 1866; repaired after fire, 1878–79. The front corner of the Von Kampen Block–Hardin's Palace Pharmacy, 128 South Front Street, 1894, can be seen at the right.

In the frieze below the stuccoed parapet, terracotta panels take the place of the vents normally found in Wilmington friezes—the cast-iron vents do appear to the rear of this building. The second floor features top, intermediate, and base stringcourses of stone through the bays, while the first floor is cast iron with shop windows remaining. (The south front corner of this building can be seen at the right in fig. 32.)

STEMMERMAN'S GROCERY STORE (NOW STEMMERMAN'S RESTAURANT)

136 South Front Street
Before 1866; 1878–79

A vented Wilmington commercial structure of brick, the low overhanging roof, cast-iron frieze vent covers, and fine brickwork typify the mid nineteenth-century arrangement of business at street level and residence above in a building that is a fine example of commercial architecture (fig. 32).

Charles Stemmerman (see color plate 8) and family, who moved from Fourth and Castle streets to this location in 1866, operated a grocery store at street level and resided above until at least 1889.

The building was evidently badly damaged by fire in late 1878. The December 25 *Star* for that year noted:

> *The brick building on the corner of Front and Orange streets, the property of Mr. C. Stemmerman, was insured for $4,000. . . . Mr. Stemmerman's stock of furniture was also badly damaged, upon which there was no insurance. . . .*
>
> *By the almost superhuman efforts of the firemen and hook and laddermen, after the flames had communicated from Lippitt's Block to Mr. C. Stemmer-*

33. Wells-Brown-Lord House, 300 South Front Street, c. 1773; remodeled c. 1857. Cape Fear River in background.

man's store on the corner of Front and Orange streets, which was partially destroyed, the fire was finally gotten under control."

J. W. H. Fuchs (name later changed to Futchs), who was granted a liquor license on December 28, 1906, was a later tenant of the building.

Orange Street crosses South Front; begin 200 street numbers

Assembly Hall, where President George Washington was entertained on Monday, April 25, 1791, was on the east side of South Front, between Orange and Ann streets. General Washington wrote in his diary: "Monday 25th. Dined with the Citizens of the place at a dinner given by them. Went to a ball in the evening at which there were 62 ladies—illuminations, bonfires, & ca." (p. 120).

A notice in the *Star* on January 4, 1874, noted: "Bids will be received at this office until the 15th inst. at 12 noon, for the construction of a Stone Wall to support the embankment on the West side of Front Street, between Orange and Ann Sts., the work to be done according to specifications, a copy of which can be seen upon application at the Mayor's office." Work was also accomplished on the wall and on sidewalks within the block in 1928, according to the *Star* of July 21.

SALVATION ARMY BUILDING

215 South Front Street
1923; J. L. Lynch, architect

The lot was purchased by the Salvation Army in October 1919, and construction of the present building was begun in July of 1923. The *Star* reported on July 19, 1923, that the two-story-with-basement building would cost about thirty thousand dollars. The basement was to be equipped with a laundry and showers, and the second floor with living quarters for Capt. and Mrs. E. W. Price, both with the Salvation Army. Stylistically, the building is a curious cross between Wilmington Italianate and Dutch Colonial—a sort of Dutch-Colonial Italian villa.

Ann Street crosses South Front; begin 300 street numbers

WELLS-BROWN-LORD HOUSE

300 South Front Street
c. 1773; c. 1857

Robert Wells, who purchased the property from John Burgwin in 1773, seems to have built this house (fig. 33). He was a ship's carpenter, and the property was described as "the lot being the upper side of the said Robert Well's wharf." Wells died prior to May 1792, when his administrator, John Brown, presented his estate inventory. Brown, who had married Wells's daughter, seems to have inherited the property. It was his in any case by May 1816, when another deed to an adjacent lot refers to a boundary as lot number ninety-one, "inherited by John Brown and now in occupation by Robert W. Brown." According to her obituary, Mrs. Brown died on December 27, 1839, on "the same lot on which she was born." In 1857 the house and lot were signed over to Columbia A. Lord, who had married a Brown. It was probably about this time that the house acquired its present exterior appearance. The property remained in the Lord family until 1941.

From South Front Street, the house is viewable only against the sky—it sits far too high above the street for any other background. Though elements of the older house survive within the present structure, what one sees here is basically mid nineteenth century. The fine quality of the sawn work and the combination of house, retaining walls, and setting is spectacular.

BAPTIST HILL

305 South Front Street
c. 1825; c. 1866

A building on this site was in use by Wilmington Baptists as a meetinghouse at least as early as 1825. The church maintained ownership and use until 1866, when they disposed of the meetinghouse and lot in hopes of getting into their new and larger building on Market Street, begun in 1859. This long and continued use and identification with the Baptists, coupled with the height of the structure above the street on its terraced site, made the name Baptist Hill a natural.

The earlier Baptist Meeting House seems to have been incorporated into the present structure (fig. 34) after 1866, possibly by John F. Stolter and John M. Bremer, who purchased the property in that year from the trustees of the First Baptist Church. In a September 7, 1890, rental advertisement in the *Messenger*, the house is described as a "large and commodious dwelling . . . with cistern, water works, gas fixtures, thirteen rooms, carriage house, & c."

A two-story frame house, it has an overhanging hip roof supported by brackets that are in line with the bay openings. A molded cornice and a plain frieze are used. The nine-over-six sash in the second level and nine-over-nine in the first level may be from the earlier meetinghouse. The four-light transom and six-light sidelights are probably from the 1866 era, along with the present interior plan.

SCHONWALD-HARPER HOUSE

309 South Front Street
c. 1847; 1903: Porter & Goodwin, Goldsboro, builders

James T. Schonwald, a doctor from Hungary, arrived in Wilmington in 1840. He is said to have spoken fluent English, French, German, Italian, and Hungarian, which made him a natural for port doctor in a city where ships of multiple registries came to call.

Schonwald bought the lot here, which runs through the block from South Front Street to South Second Street, in 1847, and began almost immediately to build his house. He located the structure in the center of the block, allowing almost a full lot in the front, which he terraced and developed with garden plants and statuary.

It was while living here in 1851, that Dr. Schonwald published his work on the diagnosis and treatment of diseases in children. Published in Philadelphia, the work was entitled *The Child: A Treatise on the Diagnosis and Treatment of the Diseases of Children, According to the Simple Law of Nature, without Medicaments.*

Schonwald sold the property in 1862 to William L. Beery of the Eagle's Island "Confederate Ship-

34. Baptist Hill, 305 South Front Street, c. 1825; c. 1866.

yard," which was then engaged in constructing vessels for the Confederate government.

In 1899 John W. Harper, captain and owner of the steamer *Wilmington,* which made daily runs from Wilmington to Southport and back with river landings in between, acquired the house for his residence. It was he who remodeled the structure to give it its present Queen Anne configuration. The *Messenger* of March 1, 1903, recorded: "The contract for the erection of Captain John W. Harper's fine residence on the east side of South Front street between Ann and Nun, has been let to Porter & Goodwin, of Goldsboro, and the work of construction will begin this week." Though the article sounds very much as if the 1903 work was for a totally new building, the work incorporated the earlier house.

The original lot survives, as does much of the landscaping and surround. Through a fine iron fence set on a wall above street level, one looks up the hill to the multiplaned house with complex roof and fine wood decoration at eaves and porch.

FISHBLATE HOUSE

318 South Front Street
1878; John H. Hanby, builder

Laura Fishblate, wife of Solomon Fishblate, bought the property here on June 28, 1875. The site was part of "Sunset Hill," a popular nineteenth-century picnicking ground. The *Star* reported on June 16, 1878, "Material is being hauled to Sunset Hill preparatory to the erection of a fine residence on the beautiful spot for Mayor Fishblate. The building contract, we learn, has been awarded to John H. Hanby."

The July 11 *Messenger* reported the residence "nearing completion." On November 10 the *Star* noted that "Mayor Fishblate has removed into his new and handsome residence on 'Sunset Hill' " and on November 19: "Mayor S. H. Fishblate was serenaded in his elegant new home on Front street, last evening, by the Cornet Concert Club. After the band

35. Fishblate House, 318 South Front Street. 1878.

had played several delightful pieces they were invited in by Mr. Fishblate and hospitably entertained for a pleasant hour, during which time many toasts were drank [*sic*] and speeches made. The occasion was an exceedingly pleasant one, and will long be memorable in the minds of those present for the splendid hospitality of the host and the good humor and pleasant intercourse which prevailed." It was later the residence of Henry C. McQueen and William P. Emerson.

Another of the vented-and-bracketed Italianate houses with center peak in both eaves and porch, the three-bay house (fig. 35) has a four-bay porch that turns at the south side of the dwelling and continues to an ell in the rear.

Sculptor Carl Paul Jennewein, whose son and daughter-in-law own the house, was a visitor here. The work of Jennewein (now deceased) is well known and includes sculpture for the Justice Department Building, Federal District Court Building, Rayburn House Office Building, Arlington Memorial Bridge, Woodrow Wilson Memorial Bridge, and other buildings and sites in Washington, D.C., as well as a number of other American cities. His local work includes carving of the Henry Bacon marker in Oakdale cemetery. (See Figure 181.)

PURNELL-EMPIE HOUSE

319 South Front Street
c. 1835; c. 1851; c. 1857; c. 1942

A one-story house said to have been built around 1835 stood on the lot in 1851 when Eliza Ann Purnell built her house, incorporating the earlier structure into it. About 1857, Adam Empie, Jr., an attorney, built a new house to the south and projecting slightly to the front of these. This is the house to the right as one faces the structure, while the Purnell, or earlier, house is to the left. The two structures were separate, with a breezeway between them, until World War II, when both houses were made into

36. Honnet House, 322 South Front Street, 1881; 1915.

apartments for government-worker housing. In the conversion they were pulled together and joined.

The house is a bracketed Italianate structure with two facade planes, each three bays wide. Detail, especially in window surrounds and moldings, is markedly different on each facade, though they were built but a few years apart. The sawn woodwork of the canopy porch is particularly fine. The dwelling is above the street, with a brick wall and openwork brick fence atop surrounding the yard.

The house was described in an August 13, 1909, for-rent advertisement: "on street car line; a commodious and convenient home, with large lot and all modern improvements and comfortable rooms for servants. In a lovely part of the city and in a first class neighborhood."

HONNET HOUSE

322 South Front Street
1881; 1915

This lot was also a part of Sunset Hill, a popular picnic and concert grounds. The *Star* of June 27, 1875, reported that: " 'Sunset Hill,' so widely known in our city for its green mounds, quiet solitude and beautiful view, this week will have another attraction added to it. The Cornet Concert Club, ever alive to musical entertainment of our citizens, have concluded to open their Sunset series at this place." It seems likely that this continued for the next three years at least. Certainly the Cornet Concert Club was still in existence in 1881, when on November 19 they serenaded Mayor Fishblate in his new house next door at 318 South Front Street (see above).

George Honnet, a jeweler who operated Honnet's Jewelry Store, bought the lot here in 1875. By 1881 he was building the house. The *Star* on October 17, 1881, stated that: "Mr. George Honnet's new residence, 'Sunset Hill,' is well underway again and will be a fine building. It will be remembered that the frame had been razed by the terrific hurricane that visited the City on the 9th of September."

Honnet had made application to erect "a wooden building" in September, as reported in the *Star* of September 6, 1881. On September 24, 1882, the same newspaper carried a "Partial list of buildings erected and improvements made during the past twelve months." Included in the list was "Geo. Honnet, a handsome and costly residence on Sunset Hill, Front Street." Evidently the building was finished within a short period after October 17, 1881.

George Honnet, Jr., succeeded his father in business in 1913, and in residence here. It was he who, in 1913–15, added the columns and the present porches. The house remained in Honnet ownership until after World War II.

A plain Italianate house with undecorated frieze, this dwelling (fig. 36) seems to have lent itself well to the 1915 Neoclassical Revival remodeling that introduced the paired Ionic columns and the porches. When Governor Dudley's Mansion at 400 South Front (see fig. 37), directly across Nun Street, retained its Neoclassical Revival porticos, the two houses were striking, vying with each other for attention.

DUDLEY-CHADBOURN HOUSE

323 South Front Street
c. 1843; after 1862

On December 30, 1842, Christopher H. Dudley, son of Governor Edward B. Dudley, purchased the lot here for $500. The house was completed by December 23, 1850, when he applied to the North Carolina Mutual Insurance Company, describing the house as, "located at the northeast corner of Front and Nun . . . made of wood, in good repair. Roof flat with scuttle and steps, 32 × 38, 2 chimneys and 8 fireplaces. East and 30 feet is the kitchen." Certainly, if the property had been new, Dudley would have said so, instead of "in good repair." For that and other reasons, the c. 1843 date seems reasonable and stylistically possible.

The house that Dudley insured seems to have been two stories high. Dudley died on January 23, 1862, at home. Finally, after a long court case over his estate, the property was acquired by George Chadbourn. According to family tradition, he added the third floor. There seems to be no reason to doubt this. It is likely that the cornice, frieze, and roof were raised, and the extra floor was built in.

Chadbourn was in business under the firm name of James H. Chadbourn & Co., commission merchants and proprietors of a steam sawmill, as listed in the 1866–67 city directory. Chadbourn resided here until his death in 1891. Mrs. James Chadbourn was still in residence here in 1898. When the property was advertised for sale on January 24, 1913, it was described as: "That desirable Chadbourn property situated on the northeast corner of Front and Nun streets. The lot is 66 by 150 feet and contains one of the best-built houses in the city. The house has twelve rooms, two baths, electric lights, gas, and furnace; also an addition of four rooms directly to the rear. For a home, the location is unsurpassed; as an investment it is certain to prove profitable."

The house is a bracketed, frame, Italianate structure, three-stories high, with a single-story porch. Its bulk and height are unusual for a Wilmington Italianate house, especially since the structure is but three bays wide. (See fig. 11.)

Nun Street crosses South Front; begin 400 street numbers

GOVERNOR DUDLEY'S MANSION

400 South Front Street
c. 1825; c. 1843; c. 1885; 1895; c. 1930

It is probable that Governor Edward Dudley's Mansion (fig. 37) holds first place among Wilmington residences visited by famous people. Daniel Webster was a guest here in May of 1847. The *Commercial* reported his May 5 arrival the next day: "On arrival at the depot they proceeded to the residence of Governor Dudley on the southwest corner of Front and Nun streets." James Sprunt reported in his *Chronicles* that in January 1890, "Cardinal Gibbons, with an Archbishop and twelve bishops were entertained here by Mr. Kerchner." According to the *Star* for January 18 and 22, 1901, Woodrow Wilson, then a professor at Princeton, visited his father, then ill in Wilmington, between January 17 and 21. The paper stated that Professor Wilson was the guest of James Sprunt during his visit. The *Dispatch* for February 7, 1918, chronicled the arrival of the Honorable William Jennings Bryan in Wilmington. According to the paper: "The great commoner . . . was met at the station this afternoon . . . and was carried to the home of Dr. James Sprunt, where he will be entertained during his visit in the city." Byran was in Wilmington to lecture at Thalian Hall. Later that year Secretary of the Treasury William Gibbs McAdoo arrived in Wilmington for the same purpose. He too, according to the *Dispatch* of April 9, 1918, was a guest at Dr. Sprunt's home.

Earlier in this century, Sprunt had also been host to President William Howard Taft at breakfast in

37. Governor Dudley's Mansion, 400 South Front Street, c. 1825; c. 1843; c. 1885; 1895; c. 1930.

this house after Taft's morning arrival in the city on November 9, 1909.

One of the desirable early sites in Wilmington, the land here was described in the title records as having a well-known spring in operation when Dr. Roger Rolf sold the lot in 1739. It was described for purchaser John Porter as "Water Lott . . . containing one-half acre in the Town of Newton and commonly known as Rolf's Rock Spring lot." As late as 1769 the site was still referred to as Rolf's Rock Spring lot. The property passed through several owners before Christopher Dudley acquired it in 1805. On October 29, 1815, according to the deed, he gave to his son Edward B. Dudley the lot on the "Brow of the Hill: including the brick warehouses, wharf, etc." From at least 1837, deeds begin to refer to the wall along the brow of the hill, so the bluff evidently was being walled to allow houses to be built on the level and fronting on South Front.

Dudley is said to have constructed the present house about 1825. It certainly was standing and was Dudley's home by November of 1843. The *Chronicle* for November 29 of that year noted: "At three o' clock yesterday a fire broke out from the roof of the dwelling of Governor Dudley, at the south end of town, and before it could be put out destroyed the roof, besides seriously injuring the body of the house. The furniture was also greatly damaged in the removal. . . . " By August 22, 1848, Dudley was offering the property for rent or sale by advertising in the *Commercial*.

Dr. S. B. Everett was in residence in 1853, when he applied for insurance. It was advertised for sale by Mrs. Everett in the *Daily Journal* of February 3,

1869, and described as: " . . . the large and elegant residence situated upon the corner of Nun and Front streets, at present occupied by Mrs. Everett, together with two vacant lots, upon which vegetables can be grown to advantage."

Francis W. and Lydia C. Kerchner were residents from c. 1871 to c. 1890; and Pembroke and Sarah W. Jones from c. 1890 to 1895. The *Star* reported during the Kerchner occupancy in October 29, 1885, that the house was undergoing repairs. In 1895, after another fire, the Joneses decided to move to Airlie as their permanent home, and James Sprunt acquired the property.

It was Sprunt who, in October 1895, added the second story to the wings, made some changes to the frieze and roof of the main block, and added a monumental Corinthian portico. At the time he acquired the house, it was a two-story dwelling, with vented frieze, low hip roof with cupola, a full porch across the front, and one-story wings. It was a handsome and nicely proportioned house. It seems likely that the vented frieze was added to the original brick house at some time after the 1843 fire, possibly when Dudley replaced the burned roof. The house appeared with the above configuration on the 1889 Sanborn map. By the time the 1898 Sanborn was published, the wings were two-story, the portico had been added, and the roof was changed. When one now looks at the house, the first level of the wings and the first two stories of the center block are from the early house, the vented frieze from the 1840s remodeling, and the rest after 1895.

The palm trees before the house seem to have been planted in 1896. The *Star* for December 19, 1896, reported that: "Thirty-two palmetto trees came by freight yesterday, consigned to Mr. James Sprunt, who will use them in adorning the yard at his residence, corner of Front & Nun streets."

Sprunt accomplished work on the house in 1899, retaining J. E. Hatch as one of the artisans to do the work. Hatch advertised in the *Messenger* for April 13, 1899, as a "Hardwood and Enamel Finisher." That same issue of the paper noted that Hatch was an "enamel finisher and decorator and painter. Mr. Hatch came here especially to do the finishing work in Mr. James Sprunt's residence."

After the property passed to J. Laurence Sprunt in 1924, he removed the portico and porches added by James Sprunt in 1895, bringing the dwelling to its present appearance.

For a period of time during World War II the house contained a restaurant. A June 10, 1944, advertisement in the *Star* suggests: "Enjoy Good Food at Governor Dudley's—Beautiful Southern Mansion—Front & Nun Sts. (Built in 1839)—Serving Hours Luncheon . . . 12:30 to 2:30 Dinner . . . 6:30 to 8:30 Sunday Hours . . . 12:30 to 5:00 Closed Mondays."

After 1945 the house was Wilmington Lodge No. 532 of the Elks. The metal Elks head from the older Elks building at 255–59 North Front was moved here and adorned the facade of this building. Most recently, Governor Dudley's Mansion has served as headquarters for the Historic Wilmington Foundation.

Edward B. Dudley was a businessman and the first president of the Wilmington and Raleigh Railroad Company, which constructed the Wilmington and Weldon Railroad. In 1836 he was elected governor of North Carolina—the first governor elected by popular vote. It was Dudley who established the reputation of the house as a North Carolina political and social center, a reputation maintained by later occupants.

Francis W. Kerchner was a well-known local businessman, first with the firm of Keith & Kerchner, wholesale grocers and agents for the Baltimore line of packet boats, and later of F. W. Kerchner, dealer in wines and liquors. Kerchner & Calder Bros., wholesale grocers, and the hardware house of O. F. Love & Co., were also Kerchner enterprises.

Pembroke Jones was a wealthy rice planter and financier who spent his last years in New York, in Newport, or at his home Airlie, just outside Wilmington. His daughter married John Russell Pope at Airlie, and Pope later designed structures at Airlie, since demolished. The Jones Mausoleum at Oakdale Cemetery is also attributed to Pope. Pope and Henry Bacon, a Wilmingtonian, are the two architects most responsible for the present containment of the Washington, D.C., Mall. Bacon worked on the overall mall design and designed the Lincoln Memorial. Pope designed the Jefferson Memorial, the National Archives Building, and the National Gallery of Art building.

James Sprunt was a rice planter, a cotton merchant, and, with his wife, Luola Murchison Sprunt, the owner of Orton Plantation. An early Wilmington historian, he wrote several works, including *Chronicles of the Cape Fear River 1666–1914*, which was published in 1914 with a second edition in 1916.

38. Parker-Saunders House, 401 South Front Street, c. 1844; c. 1871.

PARKER-SAUNDERS HOUSE

401 South Front Street
c. 1844; c. 1871

John A. Parker acquired the lot in January 1844 and deeded the property to trustees in 1859 to insure payment of debts. Parker had paid $640 for the lot; the debt for which it served as a major security in 1859 was $10,000, so there seems little doubt that the house was standing by then.

In 1871 the residence was acquired by Charles H. and Elizabeth W. Robinson. They were active members of the First Presbyterian Church, and inasmuch as the manse (on Orange Street at South Fourth, demolished) was not ready for occupancy in 1874, when the Reverend J. R. Wilson arrived to begin his pastorate, the Wilsons boarded wtih the Robinsons here. During the period, young Thomas Woodrow Wilson, later president of the United States, returned from Davidson College and joined his family. Afterwards, even when the Wilsons were in the manse on Orange Street, Woodrow Wilson is said to have been a frequent visitor to this house when in Wilmington.

The house (fig. 38) is a bracketed Italianate structure thought to have originally been stuccoed brick and to have been covered with the present frame envelope during the Robinson ownership, about 1871.

In 1868 the February 23 *Star* reported that Messrs. Russell, Fisk & Co of New York had purchased real estate in Wilmington. Among the sites mentioned as included was "the dwelling on the corner of Nunn and Front streets, known as the Parker house, for $4,200."

Charles Robinson, who later acquired the house, was a member of the commission merchant firm of Robinson & King, which had a building on South Water Street at Orange. By 1879 C. H. Robinson was listed in the city directory as in residence here. In 1904 C. H. Robinson sold the property to M. G. Saunders for $6,500.

MEARES-BRIDGERS-KERCHNER HOUSE

416 South Front Street
c. 1821: R. B. Wood, builder; c. 1887: moved and rebuilt / enlarged; 1899, annex, James F. Post, architect / builder

This house began its life at 152 North Front Street on the corner of Chestnut, the present site of the post-office building. The property there was acquired by William Belvedere Meares in 1821, and the house was constructed soon thereafter, certainly before 1841, when Meares, a lawyer who had also been a member of the House and State Senate, died. When the property was insured by Catherine G. Meares in February 1849, it was described as "made of brick covered with tin," forty-six by thirty-eight feet, two-story, basement and attic, with four chimneys, and twelve fireplaces. The Greek Revival detail of the first two floors of the house would suggest that the structure was built before 1841, so that there is little doubt about its being the Meares house.

After Wilmington was occupied by Federal forces at the end of the Civil War, this brick house, on a commanding position downtown, was used as a hospital for federal troops. From April 2 to May 30, 1865, it was a hospital for the 7th Connecticut Volunteers, and later it was used as an office for Lt. B. Williams of the 3rd Ohio Volunteers, then commanding an ordinance depot.

In 1887 the property was owned by Edward R. and Margaret E. Bridgers, who on July 8 sold it to the United States government for the construction of a post office. In this sale, Margaret Bridgers "reserved the right to remove for her own use all buildings upon the granted premises, the removal to be made 60 days after notice is given by the agent." The house had been occupied by R. R. Bridgers before passing to Edward and Margaret and was, according to the *Star* of March 21, 1890, built by contractor and builder R. B. Wood.

Notice was evidently given quickly, for the house seems to have been moved in 1887 to its present location on South Front Street—then owned by F. W. Kerchner, a prominent local merchant, wholesale grocer, and wine dealer. The original house site was at 152 North Front, and there would have been no barriers to moving it down Front to its present location. The *Messenger* reported on April 7, 1888, that "Col. F. W. Kerchner's new residence on South Front street, rebuilt out of the Bridger's building, will be quite an addition to that part of the city." On April 24 the same paper reported that "The Kerchner mansion on Front Street is being pushed to an early completion."

On the new site the house was shown on the Sanborn map for 1889 as three-story; the third level above the second-floor window lintels was added at the time of the move. Though the newspaper account uses the term "rebuilt," the house seems to have been moved relatively intact, as will be observed by examining the building and noting the differences between the first two levels and the third.

In addition to Kerchner's reputation as a successful businessman, he evidently had something of a military reputation as well, and was called Colonel. The October 17, 1899, *Dispatch* noted: "Col. F. W. Kerchner will leave here tonight for Baltimore to attend a reunion of the survivors of the Harper's Ferry raid in 1859. The reunion will be held tomorrow which is the anniversary of John Brown's surrender. Col. Kerchner was in command of the company that effected Brown's capture." Robert E. Lee commanded the party that took Brown and J. E. B. Stuart was another member, so Kerchner would have been in good company.

T. H. SMITH HOUSE

420 South Front Street
before 1881; c. 1890

On Gray's 1881 map, this house (fig. 39), which is prominently marked "Thos. Smith" and Governor Dudley's Mansion, then occupied by F. W. Kerchner, were the only houses on the west side of South Front Street between Nun and Church. The configuration of the Smith House on Gray's map leaves no doubt that the house now standing was there in 1881. Indeed, the 1879 city directory lists T. H. Smith, grocer, as residing at "Front corner Church."

The house is a vented-and-bracketed Italianate dwelling with canopy porches. The bay window at the right and the two-part dovecote that tops the roof peak and is crested with iron are probably later additions, c. 1890, but may well be within the period of Smith ownership, for the Smiths did not dispose of the property until 1892. The additions give the house a jaunty Steamboat Gothic character that is most memorable.

Albert Gore was a later resident. The *Star* reported

39. T. H. Smith House, 420 South Front Street, before 1881; c. 1890.

his death here in its January 11, 1895, edition: "After a long and brave battle for life, Albert Gore died at his residence in this city yesterday afternoon in his 37th year. He was the son of William Irdell and Rachel Ann Gore, was born in Little River, S.C. and came to Wilmington with his parents in 1869. In 1881 he married Miss Bessie Ledford, who with five children, survives him. He was a partner in the firm of W. I. Gore & Co., and for some time in that of Corbett and Gore." On January 14, 1901, Bessie Elma Gore married Cuthbert Martin. The *Star*, which noted the event in its January 15 edition, reported that "The entire lower floor of the residence was handsomely decorated and the parlor, in which the ceremony was performed, was beautifully decorated with palms, ferns, bamboo and other ever greens." The Martin couple returned from their honeymoon to live here, a residence they maintained for some years.

McCLAMMY HOUSE

423 South Front Street
1914: Revelle and Page, builders

On June 23, 1914, the *Dispatch* reported: "A building permit was issued yesterday to Mr. R. P. McClammy for the erection of a handsome residence on the northeast corner of Front and Church Streets on the site of the dwelling he has occupied for several years. This building will contain 10 rooms and the estimated cost is $5,000. Revelle and Page were awarded the contract." McClammy was the publisher of the *Wilmington Dispatch*, the paper that reported construction of his house. McClammy resided here for some thirty-four years.

A two-and-a-half-story brick Neoclassical Revival house with some Italian villa features, the dwelling has especially fine leaded glass in the upper part of

40. Wessell-Harper House, 508 South Front Street, c. 1846.

the one-over-one first-floor sash and in the transom and sidelights of the entrance. Lilies in lead, repeated, carry across the windows and into the entrance glass. The chimneys are also handsome and well detailed with their iron tie bars. They are markedly similar to those used in the MacRae House at 108 South Third, which was designed by Henry Bacon. (See fig. 55.)

Church Street crosses South Front; begin 500 street numbers

WESSELL-HARPER HOUSE

508 South Front Street
c. 1846

Seemingly built c. 1846 by Jacob Wessell, the house was long associated with the Wessell and Harper families.

The dwelling (fig. 40) is without a doubt the highlight of the Greek Revival era in Wilmington. The form, basically the same as other Wilmington plain houses, encompasses the Federal era, sometimes transitional to Greek Revival, which has the massing, arrangement, symmetry, and look of the Federal era but is essentially plain, without the decorative elements of the style used elsewhere. Its low hip roof and strictly contained corners with Ionic pilasters lift this structure above most of the other transitional houses with Greek detail, however. When this house was built, the Italianate was already beginning its ascendancy in Wilmington. This final statement of the Greek Revival style is therefore all the more important.

Since 1971 the structure has served as offices for the Wilmington Housing Authority.

North Second Street

Market Street northward to the railroad tracks

As were most of the streets in the downtown area, North Second Street was developed at an early date and, as was typical of early urban areas, was a street of mixed uses. Residences, stores, factories, theaters, saloons, churches, and governmental buildings were often in adjacent structures or even in the same structure. It was only with the onset of modern zoning that we began to limit uses—residential, commercial, mixed residential, etc. As of 1976 the process of separation is almost complete on North Second Street—only one residence remains, at 303 North Second. There is, however, still a fine mix of structures.

William Hooper, one of the North Carolina signers of the Declaration of Independence, lived in a small shingle-covered house at 24 North Second. The *Star* reported its demolition on October 25, 1882.

41. City Laundry, 22–28 North Second Street. Grossman-Mahler, architects, 1910–12.

CITY LAUNDRY

22–28 North Second Street
1910–12: Grossman-Mahler, architects, builders

Joseph H. Hinton, Wilmington area hotelier, was president and a 1907 founder of the City Laundry Company. Hinton, who owned The Orton Hotel, may have been fulfilling a business need, since the new laundry specialized in hotel, theatrical, and ship work. As this structure indicates, the enterprise was a financial success.

The two-story brick building retains portions of its stone cornice but is minus its original pilaster caps and projecting three-part parapet. The street-level shop windows survive, and the building facade is essentially unchanged. Stylized stone leaf decoration and walls composed of combinations of pressed and rough-faced brick in recessed panels demonstrate greater attention to detail in commercial structures of this era than is thought necessary today (fig. 41). This building has been restored and is now a part of the Cooperative Savings and Loan Complex, a good example of adaptive use.

Princess Street crosses North Second Street; begin 100 street numbers

NEW HANOVER COUNTY, OLD JAIL (LATER GARRELL BUILDING)

104 North Second Street
c. 1840; 1906: H. E. Bonitz, architect

The county jail was located in this area from at least 1799, when the New Hanover Court Minutes for December 19 describe an exercise area for prisoners at roughly this location. That courthouse and jail burned on January 17, 1840, and the new jail was built.

Early in this century, W. B. McKoy reminisced

42. Cape Fear Club, 124 North Second Street. C.H.P. Gilbert, architect, 1912–13.

in Sprunt's *Chronicles of the Cape Fear River*, (pub. 1914), "I recall as a small child its massive doors, its cells and the heavy gratings at the openings and at the steps on each floor, the heavy trap-doors on a level with the floor, the timbers and boards thick and heavy. In my mind I pictured it as resembling the keep of some ancient castle or fortress. . . ."

The structure was advertised for sale in the *Commercial* on June 13, 1854, and called "The jail." A sale advertisement in the November 20, 1866, *Daily Journal* called the structure "that valuable three-story brick building, situated upon the northeast corner of Second and Princess street, known as the 'Old Jail.' "

The *Star* for October 3, 1906, reported "Since the exterior walls have been stuccoed and the scaffolding has been removed, it is the remark of the town that the old jail building at northeast corner of Second and Princess streets, now owned by Mr. Jno. F. Garrell, is one of the prettiest structures downtown." It is not known what portions of the original building exist, though the rear walls, foundations, and portion of the outer walls and roof certainly do, within the 1906 overlay.

CAPE FEAR CLUB

124 North Second Street
1912–13: C. H. P. Gilbert of New York, architect; J. F. Leitner, supervising architect; Kenneth M. Murchison, New York, consulting architect; Wallace and Osterman, builders

Said to be one of the oldest social clubs in the south, the Cape Fear Club traces its origin to 1852, when thirteen Wilmington men organized to provide a common downtown meeting place. In operation until 1861, the club was inactive during the Civil War. Reorganized in March 1866, largely by Confederate veterans, it was incorporated as the Cape Fear Club by an act of the legislature in 1872. The group met at several locations before constructing this building. One early visitor to the club was Henry Walters, of New York, Baltimore, and Airlie in Wilmington. Walters founded Walters Art Gallery in Baltimore to house his art collection; he also gave paintings to the club.

A Neoclassical Revival structure, the Cape Fear Club building (fig. 42) is notable both for its residential scale and setting and for the boldness of its decoration, including coffered ceilings on both entrance portico levels.

Confusion exists over the architect of the building. The *Dispatch* for July 23, 1912, reported that J. F. Leitner had prepared plans for the building, and Leitner's name was still being mentioned as architect after the structure was completed. The *Dispatch* noted on September 3, 1912, that "Mr. C. H. P. Gilbert of New York City, was selected by the building committee as the architect to design the new building." In 1913, while the building was under construction, the *Star* reported on September 18, "Architect Robinson of New York, who was here on one of his regular trips inspecting the Cape Fear Club's handsome new home, states that work on the structure is progressing satisfactorily." Robinson was either from Gilbert's office or that of New York architect Kenneth M. Murchison, who was a member of the club and has been credited with the design. In the absence of contrary information, it seems likely that Gilbert was the architect and Leitner the local supervising architect, with Robinson as liaison and Murchison as consultant.

The *Dispatch* reported on January 10, 1913, that ground had been broken for the new building the previous day. It was occupied in December of 1913.

Chestnut Street crosses North Second; begin 200 street numbers

The Hotel Cape Fear, which fronts on Chestnut, occupies most of the western side of the block and is the dominant structure in the area. (See fig. 108.)

During his visit to Wilmington on April 12, 1819, President James Monroe was entertained in the home of Robert Cochran, whose house stood on the east side of North Second Street, near the corner with Chestnut. The Cochran house was destroyed about 1885.

Red Cross Street crosses North Second

Along North Second Street between Red Cross and the railroad tracks, color variations in the paving block, from beige through red to almost black, give indication of the long use of the street. Original paving block was laid, and the street was later patched in whatever brand was available at the time. "Catskill Block" predominates, but "Reynolds Block," "Southern Clay Mfg. Co." block, and the products of other pavers also appear. Granite curbing survives.

The street slopes steeply to the railroad tracks. Across these to the north are the nineteenth-century brick and stone retaining walls of the railroad cut and some of the foundation and baggage section of the late nineteenth-century Union Station.

These tracks and the remnants of buildings represent one of the lifelines of Wilmington. The railbed here has been in use since at least the mid-nineteenth century. Travelers arriving in Wilmington by train came to this area, and freight shipped from the waterfront used the track as consolidation began and a union terminal was established.

PORT CITY COLD STORAGE (NOW KNOWN AS NEW HANOVER COLD STORAGE COMPANY)

518 North Second Street
1912; 1923

Transporting perishables by either train or ship required cooling, and ice plants were a fixture of most ports and railroad towns. Because of the development of newer means of refrigeration, few survive.

W. E. Worth and Co., "Ice Manufacturing," was in operation on this site by c. 1885. The company was the Wilmington Ice Factory by 1893, Worth Ice and Fuel Company by 1898, and the Independent Ice Company by 1910. In 1912 the Independent Ice Company Cold Storage Plant, the main structure seen here, was in operation. Some of the structures in the complex survive from earlier eras, and a part of the remaining complex is evidently also from about 1923. The *Star* reported on April 1, 1923, that The Southern Packing Company was being offered for sale. "The sale will include nine tracts of land, on one of which at Second and Campbell streets, is located the cold storage plant of the company, which is modern, and which was recently built at an expense of about $350,000."

South Second Street

Market Street southward to Castle Street

Both fine residential and commercial structures survive in the first block of South Second Street. The Van Amringe Building, at 7–11 South Second, was built in 1904, after plans of L. A. H. Koeth, architect. The small brick office at 21 South Second appears on the Sanborn maps first in 1910. It was built around 1906 on the DeRosset House property, probably by C. P. B. Mahler of the architectural firm of Grossman-Mahler. Mahler acquired the DeRosset House in October, 1905, and his family maintained ownership until 1946.

The street within this block is still surfaced with brick pavers, predominantly "Augusta" block.

DESTRAC-RANKIN HOUSE

19 South Second Street
c. 1842

William Destrac, listed in the city directory of 1866-67 as a baker, acquired this property in April 1841 and sold it in June of 1845. The 1845 sale price, when compared with the purchase price, indicates that the structure (fig. 43) was standing, a conclusion enforced by the Greek Revival detail of the house.

43. Destrac-Rankin House, 19 South Second Street, c. 1842.

Robert George Rankin was a resident here from about 1845 to 1865. During the Civil War he served as captain, Company A, First Batallion, North Carolina Artillery. He was killed at the Battle of Bentonville in 1865.

It is likely that, even if the house did not from the very beginning combine first- or street-level commercial uses with dwelling uses above, it was used in that manner from a very early date. The topography of the street—the land rises sharply to the east, or from front to rear of the dwelling—makes such a use a natural, offering ground-level entrances on both the commercial, or street, level and the dwelling, or second, level.

DEROSSET HOUSE

23 South Second Street
1841: C. H. Dahl, carpenter; c. 1854: northeast addition; 1874: Italianate detail, cupola, conservatory added; 1914: southeast addition, Grossman-Mahler, architects.

The grandest of Wilmington's pre–Civil War dwellings, this five-bay, two-story frame house (fig. 44) features a low hip roof capped by a tall cupola. The wide vented-and-bracketed frieze is accented by a low center pediment. Both the cornice and the cupola are part of 1874 Italianate changes to the Greek Revival house. The academic Greek Revival portico with fluted Doric columns and a classical frieze remains.

An ell to the rear and the glass-enclosed side porch on Dock Street were already in place by the time Sanborn drew his 1884 map. They are part of the 1874 changes; H. Vollers, a builder who acquired

44. DeRosset House, 23 South Second Street. 1841; c. 1854; Grossman-Mahler, architects, 1914.

the house in 1882, probably made no changes.

The last enlargement / addition to the house (c. 1914), enclosed the ell and extended the house on Dock Street. The structure had been converted to apartments, and this addition increased space noticeably. It blends well with the earlier structure, echoing such elements as brackets, low roof, and siding. Slightly offset to the south and east, the addition adds greatly to the bulk of the structure.

This massiveness is enhanced by the dwelling's imperial position, on a high terraced hill overlooking the Cape Fear River. The deep terraces of the garden remain, constructed of brick, as is the high foundation of the house.

Dr. Armand DeRosset III, (born 1807; died 1897) acquired the property on which this house stands from Anne Younger of Arkansas in 1841. He evidently began building this house soon thereafter. In 1849 DeRosset insured it for $5,000 and the furniture within the house for $1,000. The structure is described as "his dwelling house . . . corner Second & Dock streets, part of Lots No. 18 & 23 . . . wood covered, south tin has 2 scuttles & stair in good repair 40 by 48 feet 2 stories high with brick [foundation] four chimneys & 12 fireplaces, ashes are not deposited about the dwelling."

Member of a confusing line of DeRossets—all named Armand—Armand III was sometimes called Armand Jr. He attended medical school in Philadelphia and returned to practice in Wilmington. He married Eliza Lane Lord, and they had eleven children. One of them, their daughter Annie, was the first person buried in Oakdale Cemetery. He is said to have given up the practice of medicine after a child he was treating died. Mrs. DeRosset died at the Philadelphia Exposition in 1876, and the doctor later remarried.

DeRosset headed DeRosset & Company, general

shipping and commission merchants, who were agents for the Underwriters Agency of New York and for wines and mineral oils as well. Failing fortunes forced the sale of the house in 1882. Dr. DeRosset and his second wife, Catherine, moved to the DeRosset House at Third and Market streets, where the doctor had been born. His wife died there in 1894; he died there in 1897.

H. Vollers acquired the property in 1882. In 1893, it was willed to Luhr Vollers. The family maintained ownership until 1905. Although both the Vollers were builders, they seem to have made no changes in the house.

In 1905 the property passed to Carl P. B. Mahler and his wife. Mahler was also a builder and a member of the architect / contractors firm of Grossman-Mahler. They made the last and largest addition to the house.

Acquired by the Historic Wilmington Foundation in 1975, the structure is being restored. The foundation was organized in August 1966 by four Wilmingtonians: Thomas H. Wright, Jr., Kelly W. Jewell, Jr., R. V. Asbury, Jr., and Wallace C. Murchison. The historic-district zoning ordinance in Wilmington allowed ninety days as a waiting period in which alternatives could be sought for demolition to historically and architecturally significant buildings within the established historic district. The nonprofit Historic Wilmington Foundation, financed entirely by membership contributions, established a revolving fund to be used in rescuing architecturally significant buildings from demolition. The foundation intended to demonstrate by rehabilitation that deteriorated older dwellings can become sturdy, attractive residences and businesses. It has a full educational program and has affixed plaques to a number of Wilmington structures. It is one of several organizations whose aim is preservation of historic Wilmington, its revolving fund providing the monies so frequently lacking to preservation organizations faced with an emergency. The intent of the fund is to rescue, occasionally to rehabilitate, and then to sell—so that the funds are recouped to be used again for a similar purpose.

Dock Street crosses South Second; begin 100 street numbers

The USO Building at 120 South Second Street was constructed during World War II for entertainment and housing of white military personnel; a matching structure for black military personnel was on North Eighth Street at Nixon. This building is typical of such structures throughout the country—militarily planned, quickly constructed, and, during their era, intensely used and successful. All too seldom they are saved as a reminder of that era. An August 14, 1943, article in the *News* suggested that the building might be enlarged:

> *Arrangements are nearing completion for an application for funds to double the size of the USO building at Second and Orange streets, in the name of the City of Wilmington, to be filed with the Federal Works Agency in Richmond.*
>
> *Leslie N. Boney, architect, who is now preparing plans, said the application will "probably go to Richmond Wednesday night." He declined to comment about the cost of the additional construction, or its size.*
>
> *In describing the present USO clubhouse, Mr. Wellott, field recreation representative, said it was a Type A building, or one of the larger types of buildings being built by the government for occupancy by the United Service Organizations.*

BALLARD-POTTER-BELLAMY HOUSE

121 South Second Street
c. 1846

Jethro Ballard—who is shown in the 1850 census as a merchant with real estate valued at $18,000, unusually high for this area in that era—built this house. He acquired the land in 1844, paying $1,000, and sold it in 1851 to Samuel R. Potter for $8,000. When Potter applied for insurance from the North Carolina Mutual Insurance Company on April 2, 1851, he described the house (fig. 45) as: "made of wood, tin roof, nearly new . . . has a scuttle, two-stories high, 54 × 45. Four chimneys and eight fireplaces . . . no stoves."

Potter died in 1856, but his wife remained at the property for some years. On April 11, 1880, she advertised in the *Star*: "For Sale or Rent—One of the most desirable corner Lots in Wilmington for sale, with handsome Dwelling House, Stables, and Flower Garden. Lot fronts on Second Street 99 feet and on Orange 165 feet. The stable lot would make a good building lot. Terms very easy. Apply on premises."

Evidently by 1883 Mrs. Potter had died without

45. Ballard-Potter-Bellamy House, 121 South Second Street, c. 1846.

a sale, for J. H. Boatwright, guardian for Eliza A. and Sallie F. Potter, offered the property for sale in September 1883. He was unsuccessful, and on November 20, 1884, the house was sold at public auction at the courthouse door. Mary W. Bellamy was the highest bidder, and the lot was deeded to her.

Mary Bellamy was Mary Williams Russell, who had married John D. Bellamy's son William James Harriss Bellamy. The younger Bellamy was a surgeon, who had left the University of North Carolina in 1864, when just twenty years old, to serve in the Confederate army as a private. Bellamy returned to school after the war, received his degree, and practiced medicine in Wilmington for many years. His office was to the rear of the house, on Orange Street. A clipping from an unidentified paper, dated November 14, 1885, calls the structure a "new office," which Dr. Bellamy had recently built. Dr. Bellamy died in 1911, his wife in 1921.

A two-story bracketed-and-vented Italianate structure, the house features a full porch with academic fluted Doric columns and paired Italianate brackets above each, a curious use of Greek form and columns in an Italianate setting. Traces of the terraced gardens remain.

Orange Street crosses South Second; begin 200 street numbers

South Second Street within this block is relatively narrow, with good trees and pleasantly undefined boundaries; for part of its eastern side there is no sidewalk. The street descends toward the south, reaching a low point near the Ann Street end of the block before beginning to climb again. The Tan Yard Branch ran through the block, just south of Northrop's Alley. The Tan Yard House, built as early as about 1830, may still survive at 225 South Second.

46. Wright-Murphy House, 212 South Second Street, c. 1830.

Probably the oldest house within the block—now stuccoed and much modified, though its fine lines are still discernible—is the Burch-Cowan House at 208 South Second. A free school was conducted there as early as 1832 by the ladies of Wilmington.

The fine Victorian-era structure at 216 South Second is the E. D. Sloan House, built in 1899 by builder J. C. Stout.

WRIGHT-MURPHY HOUSE

212 South Second Street
c. 1830

William A. Wright was deeded a vacant lot here in the division of his father's estate in March of 1829. He must have built by 1833, when a notice locating the Wilmington Free School appeared in the *Peoples Press & Wilmington Advertiser* for December 4, noting that a Mr. Shuter lived just south of the free school. Since this lot is south and no Mr. Shuter owned property in the area, this seems to have been the house, and he seems to have been a renter.

This agrees quite well with the stylistic evidence. The house (fig. 46) is a handsome Wilmington Plain house, frame and two-stories high with gable roof and full porch. The entrance has a molded architrave with three-light transom and three-light sidelights, typical of the Greek Revival era of its construction.

William A. Wright sold the house to Mary Ann Murphy in 1846. On her insurance application in 1849 she noted that the house was not new. Miss Murphy resided here until her death in 1889.

NORTHROP-CARR HOUSE

213 South Second Street
c. 1829

Another of the Wilmington Plain houses, this structure seems to be typical of the Federal era. A two-story frame structure with gable roof, the house has starkly different front and rear facades. On South Second Street, it has an almost full porch at the first level, three bays wide, with a low hip roof, four-part open wooden posts, and a spoke balustrade. To

47. Walker-Cowan House, 302 South Second Street, 1869.

the rear is a full double porch under a shed extension of the gable roof, quite different in treatment of bays and finish.

By 1829 Isaac Northrop, a merchant and tanner, owned the house. A sheriff's writ of that year mentions the house as "now in the occupancy of Isaac Northrop." In 1851 when he insured the property, he noted in the application that the house had been "lately repaired throughout."

When the dwelling was sold to Dr. Thomas B. Carr, a dentist, in 1856, it did not pass out of the Northrop family; Carr had married Isaac Northrop's daughter.

Later occupants of the house, as indicated by the 1889 city directory, were A. D. Cazaux, a ship broker, and his three sons: J. M. Cazaux, assistant fire chief, and E. D. Cazaux and O. P. Cazaux, clerks.

Ann Street crosses South Second; begin 300 street numbers

South Second Street climbs southward from Ann Street to Nun Street, where it reaches its high point and begins to descend once more. Street trees remain within the block, which is residential in character.

WALKER-COWAN HOUSE

302 South Second Street
1869; James Walker, builder

"Mr. James Walker was granted the privilege of erecting a two-story building on the corner of Ann and Second streets, provided it be covered with tin or otherwise made fire-proof," the *Star* reported on April 20, 1869.

A portion of the house (fig. 47) is said to have been constructed by William A. Gwynn shortly before he sold the property to James Walker in 1869. Walker, an architect and builder, evidently acquired the property as an investment. He never lived here, but maintained ownership until his death in 1901, using the house as a rental unit. Certainly the dwelling would have been of his design and construction.

Among the nineteenth-century residents of the house were the Reichman brothers, who operated a dry-goods business at 26 Market Street, and later in the century, Isaac Shrier, a clothier whose business was also at 26 Market.

From about 1905 to 1922 James Hill Cowan was in residence here. By 1905, Cowan, a reporter for the *Messenger*, had (according to city directories) become editor of the *Dispatch*, an important Wilmington newspaper. He was elected mayor of Wilmington for a term of office from 1922 to 1926. After his death on September 11, 1924, his wife, Katherine Mayo Cowan, finished out his term, thereby becoming the first woman mayor in North Carolina. Louis F. Harper, a contractor and carpenter, purchased the house around 1922.

The dwelling has the height, low roof, canopy porch, and arrangement of the Wilmington Italianate house. Its has a distinctive molded cornice, with dentil course, and plain frieze. One would assume that Walker, the architect and builder, chose this entablature rather than the more usual vented and bracketed one.

McRAE-BEERY HOUSE

303 South Second Street
c. 1850

In 1904 this house was moved southward from its corner location and was renumbered 303. The H. P. Munson House, 301 South Second Street, was subsequently built on the original McRae-Beery House site.

John McRae acquired the southeast corner lot on South Second at Ann Street in 1831. The $500 he paid included this lot and the present lots of 301 and 305 South Second. In 1851, when McRae sold to Samuel J. Beery, the purchase price was $2,000, indicating improvement on the property, probably the construction of this house.

When Beery applied for insurance with the North Carolina Mutual Insurance Company on the house in March of 1851 he described it as "Made of Wood, Old, lately repaired. House 2 stories, 40 × 18 feet; 2 chimneys and 4 fireplaces." Why the house is described as old is not known. Perhaps McRae incorporated an older house into the 1851 structure and labeled that "repaired." The house in its present configuration and finish conforms quite nicely to the stylistic era of c. 1850.

The house is a vented-and-bracketed Italianate side-hall structure of frame—two-stories high and with an entrance featuring transom and sidelights.

THE CHAIR HOUSE

305 South Second Street
c.1822; remodeled c. 1905

An 1822 deed of William C. Lord and John Wooster to Uz. Wood mentions this lot, fronting on Second Street and including "the Chair House and Stable." In Samuel J. Beery's above-mentioned application for insurance in March of 1851 on the house at 303 South Second Street (it was then numbered 301), he mentions "on south of house and kitchen distant about 50 feet a 2-story house made of wood," the right location for the Chair House and probably this house, since no other structure is known that could fit the location.

Evidently the Chair House was a manufactory, possibly for cabinetmaking. Gray's 1881 map of Wilmington clearly shows the house and lists it as Kerchner & Calder, evidently then a business rather than a dwelling. The house is remembered by some as a relatively open barn or factory, remodeled by T. D. Love about 1905 to its present early twentieth-century appearance.

The structure is perched atop a hill and sits well back from the street. Even if the structure had no interesting history, the site alone would give the house great charm.

LOUIS J. POISSON HOUSE

308 South Second Street
1886–87; extended westward c. 1890

In reporting permits for construction, the June 9, 1886, *Star* recorded a permit to: "L. J. Poisson, to erect a two-story frame tin roof dwelling on west side of Second street between Ann and Nun, and also a one-story shingle roof stable. Petition for erection of these buildings was granted, provided the stable be covered with tin."

Poisson is said to have come to Wilmington from San Francisco and to have patterned his house here after a San Francisco town house that he admired. This may well be true. The house (fig. 48) is a vented-and-bracketed Italianate structure, but its massing and finish are different from most Wilmington houses of its style, and it does have counterparts in San Francisco.

The gable roof with its fine pediment, the bay window, and the porches—certainly individualize

48. Louis J. Poisson House, 308 South Second Street, 1886–87; c. 1890.

the house. The dwelling is said to have featured a bathroom with a built-in copper bathtub encased in cypress. This was a first in Wilmington and was especially intriguing to neighborhood children.

A conservatory on the southern side of the house was locally famous, mainly because of the gardening success of Mrs. Poisson, later Mrs. Brooke G. Empie; she was renowned for her care of plants and her stocking of the conservatory.

Poisson died in the summer of 1888 of typhoid fever. The enlarging of the house c. 1890 is said to have been necessitated by relatives who then came to live with Mrs. Poisson.

Nun Street crosses South Second; begin 400 street numbers

WORTH HOUSE

410 South Second Street
c. 1880

A fine Queen Anne–style cottage, one-story with attic, full porch, and corner tower, the house has a complex roof with many gables on which shingle is lavishly used as wall covering and decoration. The house appears on Gray's 1881 map of Wilmington in the same position and relation to the street as the present structure. Inasmuch as the Worth family, David G. and his wife Julia A., owned the lot from 1872 to 1904, there is little doubt that they built the dwelling.

During most of the first quarter of this century, the house was occupied by George T. Hewlett, to whom Mrs. Worth sold the property in 1904. Hewlett was a salesman for S. & B. Solomon.

McGOWAN-QUELCH HOUSE

418 South Second Street
1897; Preston Cumming, builder

Preston Cumming bought the lot here at a private sale in 1896, acquiring clear title on January 15, 1897. On May 16 he sold the property to W. A. and Maud McGowan at almost four times the purchase price. This is an indication that a house had been built, a fact confirmed by the *Star* for August 22, 1897. In an article titled "Wilmington Progressing," the paper lists dwellings built during that year. Under "one story houses, tin & shingle roof," it lists "Second, between Nun & Church, for Mr. Preston Cumming." Obviously Cumming constructed the house as an investment, and it must have been a good one from the quickness of the sale.

Cumming was a woodworker who later founded a general woodworking company on South Water Street at the foot of Dock Street. In addition to general woodwork, the company produced mantles, cornices, and moldings.

The McGowans maintained ownership until 1902. Between then and 1910, there were three owners. In that year John P. Quelch acquired the property, probably through marriage to Mary Allen. She was the daughter of James and Marion Allen, who had owned the house since 1904. The Quelch couple maintained ownership until at least 1949.

A one-and-a-half-story Queen Anne–style cottage with complex roof, the structure features a hexagonal bay beneath a gable roof projection on the south front, and a projecting square tower on the north front. Patterned shingle, sawn gable ornaments, brackets, and applied panels are used as decoration. The tower finial and the roof cresting survive.

Church Street crosses South Second; begin 500 street numbers

REAVES-STONEBANKS HOUSE

508 South Second Street
c. 1900

The property here was acquired by William J. Reaves in 1894 and was not sold until his son Rob-

49. Reaves-Stonebanks House, 508 South Second Street, c. 1900.

ert MacDonald Reaves transferred it to Nellie C. Stonebanks after the death of the elder Reaves in 1917. The house was constructed c. 1900, during the period of Reaves ownership. The Reaves family was heavily involved in real estate dealings and in building. The W. J. Reaves Manufacturing Company, a general woodworking company, was formed in 1905. W. J. Reaves was also a vice-president and manager of the Wilmington Iron Works. The house here is one of a row of at least four—at 508, 510, 512, and 514 South Second Street—constructed by the Reaves family. At various times a member of the family may have lived in each of the four dwellings.

A superb Queen Anne–style house, the structure (fig. 49) has detail and decoration that set it apart from other houses of its style in Wilmington. A frame, two-story dwelling with hip roof, the house has a front cross gable with molded cornice and returns. Windows are variously treated, from the three-unit gable decoration of window flanked by vents, through the double second-level unit with its pedimented overwindow in the cross gable, to the paneled hexagonal bay with pedimented cornice caps. The centrally located door also has a pedimented cornice cap, and there is spindle decoration on the screen. A round-arch window with stained glass is to the right of the entry.

Its porches are the highlight of the house. At the second level there is a one-bay recessed porch in the L formed by the cross gable. It has turned posts, sawn brackets, and a turned balustrade. The first-level porch with its hip roof projects in front of the second-story porch and runs the width of the facade. It has turned posts, turned balustrade, and turned and sawn brackets. The right bay on the first-floor porch is outlined by a bentwood curve—it is as if Teddy Roosevelt had returned from an African game hunt and braced a pair of elephant tusks in an appropriate porch opening. A turned newel is used here instead of a straight post to flank the steps on the right and to emphasize the curved framing of the bay.

WILLIAM J. REAVES HOUSE

514 South Second Street
1900

Though somewhat modified, this Queen Anne–style house is a fine example of the genre. Of particular interest are the elaborately sawn and carved gable ornaments spanning the peak of the cross gable of the east, or front, facade and that of the north facade. The eastern gable ornament has the letter R worked into it—symbolizing construction and occupancy by the Reaves family. The equally ornate and well-planned gable ornament to the north contains an even greater surprise, for worked into its center is the date 1900. Though such markings may have been quite common, this is the only such monogramming and dating of construction known to exist in Wilmington.

W. J. Reaves and his son Robert McDonald Reaves seem to have occupied, at various times, 510, 512, and 514 South Second Street, three of the four or more houses they built in this block. The Reaves family is also known to have built the house at 508 South Second. The house at 514 seems to have been constructed as the home of the elder Reaves and was occupied by him from the time of its construction until about 1911, when the family moved to the Winter Park area of Wilmington.

At the time these houses were constructed, the area was a prime residential one, and many fine houses of the turn-of-the-century still survive.

North Third Street

Market Street northward to Chestnut

Along with Market Street and Fifth Avenue, Third Street is one of the three Wilmington boulevards, which are ninety-nine feet wide rather than the sixty-six foot standard for other streets. Though North Third should be a major thoroughfare—after all both the New Hanover County Courthouse and the Wilmington City Hall (102 North Third Street) have North Third addresses—it is little more than a broad street channeling traffic through the area. There are no street trees nor is there any curbside landscaping here, and the center plaza, landscaped and planted on the other main boulevards, has been eliminated on North Third Street.

Market Street

NEW HANOVER COUNTY COURTHOUSE

North Third Street at Princess, southeast corner
1891–92: A. S. Eichberg, Savannah, Georgia, architect; James F. Post, supervising architect; Valentine-Brown & Co., Brunswick, Georgia, builders.

Eichberg's building (fig. 50) is an unusually symmetrical High Victorian Gothic structure, the sole area representative of a strong national style, although seldom used in the South. It is a remarkably well-preserved example of the style, one of immense architectural importance.

Rock-faced ashlar is used in stringcourses, in the foundation, and in the first level of the central entrance pavilion that breaks through the roof above to form a bell and clock tower. The clock still works, its chimes adding a delightful sound to downtown Wilmington. The final stage of the tower contains open balconies on each of the four faces. Its exaggerated pyramidal roof is broken by dormers containing the clock faces.

End bays are treated as nascent towers through the use of low pyramidal roofs. Window openings are archtopped and outlined with molded brick. Engaged columns—some in a quasi-Corinthian form, others in a curious unacademic Ionic order with short twisted shafts—occur between the windows.

Other ornament consists of complex bracketed cornices, spherical and crocketed finials, brick molded into panels, and foliated and plain columns.

High Victorian Gothic structures derive their individuality in part from Gothic forms, in part from color and the use of two or more kinds of material. Here several types of brick are used with contrasting stone, creating the desired polychroming. The overall effect is showy, but solid—the High Victorian Gothic is not characterized by the fragility of the earlier Gothic Revival.

The versatility of Wilmington's nineteenth-century architectural giant James F. Post is amply demonstrated by comparing the courthouse with the city hall, 102 North Third Street, (fig. 51), across Princess Street to the north. Construction of the two structures was nearly a half century apart, but Post was supervising architect for both. Though neither of the plans was his, he was responsible for changes and for the quality of the finished structures, as well as for on-site interpretation of the architectural design.

Land for the new courthouse was acquired in May of 1891. Designs for the new building had already been invited, and on June 11 the *Messenger* reported, "After carefully examining designs and plans submitted by four architects, the Board of Commissioners accepted those submitted by Mr. A. S. Eichberg, the well-known architect of Savannah, Georgia." On August 18 the same newspaper noted that a "very handsome picture" of the building had been shown a reporter and on August 29 that "A. S. Eichberg, the architect of the county court house, presented the plans and specifications for the structure, thus relieving himself of the forfeit of $100 for every day after the 28th of August they were not submitted." On September 1, the substitution of granite for brown stone was reported; on November 17, the acceptance of the bid of Valentine and

50. New Hanover County Courthouse, North Third Street at Princess, southeast corner. A. S. Eichberg, architect, James F. Post, supervising architect, 1891–92.

Brown, of Brunswick, Georgia, as the builders. On that same day the article on the builders also described the building.

The new court house will be of stone and brick and will front 101 feet on Princess street and 72 feet on Third street. It will be two stories high exclusive of basement. The first story will be intersected by two wide corridors running at right angles through the building from north to south and east to west, a feature that will not only add to the convenience of the building but will enhance its comfort in securing all the draught necessary at all seasons of the year.

The main entrance will be on Third street side and will be through the base of a graceful tower 110 feet in height above the side walk. There will also be an entrance on Princess street through the base of a tower 60 feet in height, surmounted by a flag staff 25 feet in height. There will be smaller towers with dormer windows on the two front corners of the building. The main tower will front on Third street and will be to the south of the corner which will run up at Princess and Third streets. Provision has been made in this tower for a clock, the dials of which will be 90 feet above the pavement. The clock will have four dials, north, south, east and west. We understand that the clock is to be a striker, and will be lighted at night by electricity. The top story of the tower will contain open balconies on all four sides, 68 feet above the sidewalk.

The building is to contain no wood, with the exception of the floors, and will approach nearer to a fire proof building than structures of this class usually are. The substructure is to be all stone, which will run to a height of six feet above the pavement. The front will be of pressed brick and stone and the building will also be ornamented from top to bottom with stone. The cornices will be of galvanized iron and the roof will be of slate. A roomy verandah will run along the south side of the building and will front on what is to be made a beautiful park.

The roof will be steep and will be hipped on all four sides, while the front will be ornamented in the most elaborate style, that with the handsome entrances and towers will make the structure one of the handsomest county buildings in the Southern states.

Mr. Eichberg, the architect, who by the way, is also the architect of Mr. F. Rheinstein's fine building, is one of the leading architects of the United States. He is not only known in the South, but has a national reputation in his business, and has designed many of the most modern buildings in the Southern and Western states.

The *Star* reported the selection of James F. Post as supervising architect on December 1, and by December 20 it reported that "the old shanties on the lot for the new court house" were being pulled down. By January 3 the *Messenger* noted that the foundation had already been dug and piles were being driven. On April 21 the *Star* could state that the cornerstone had been laid the previous day. Rain dampened the enthusiasm of the crowd, and after the "Impressive ceremonies of 'laying the cornerstone,' " the "doors of the Opera House were . . . thrown open" and the rest of the ceremonies were held there.

Burr & Bailey, successor to Hart & Bailey and the predecessor to the Wilmington Iron Works, was awarded the heating contract, as noted by the *Star* of June 7, 1892. Evidently the firm did other ironwork for the building as well, including iron railings and newels. On November 6 the *Star* recorded:

Mr. William J. Furlong, a machinist employed at Messrs. Burr & Bailey's shops, was painfully hurt yesterday morning. He was seated on the floor, working on an iron newel-post for the new Court House, when a fellow workman wheeling a truck accidentally knocked over another iron newel-post leaning against the wall of the building. The iron column weighing about 400 pounds fell on Mr. Furlong's head, cutting a deep gash and severely mashing and breaking a blood vessel in his right foot. . . . Last night he was resting easily.

By July 17, according to the *Messenger*,

The brick work on the new court house is now completed with the exception of the middle tower, fronting on Third street, which is to be run up 50 feet above the top of the building. This will give it a height of 130 feet from the level of the pavement below. Two towers, each 85 feet high, on either corner of the Third Street front, have been completed and the roofs are being put on. The work of slating the roof of the entire building is now being pushed vigorously and Mr. H. J. Lavey, foreman of the carpenter force has laid the floors in some of the rooms.

Evidentally all the floors had been laid by November 6, when Burr & Bailey were putting the finishing touches on the stairways.

The two-thousand-pound bell for the clock was on hand before October 16, when the *Star* notified its readers of its safe arrival. By October 23 that paper could report that the Southern Electric Company, Baltimore, Maryland, was almost finished with the electric lighting. "There will be about 250 incandescent lights in the building, starting with 24 in the tower—six behind each clock dial and others distributed throughout the building. The fixtures will be of brass and of the combination pattern for gas and electricity—and will be very handsome."

On January 18, 1893, the contract for vaults was reported by the *Star* as awarded to the Fenton Metallic Manufacturing Company of Jamestown, New York. Contract for furnishings was given to Thos. C. Craft on March 7, according to the paper of that day. On April 9 they reported:

The new Court House, erected by the county of New Hanover, corner of Third and Princess streets, will be thrown open for the inspection of the public to-morrow and Tuesday, between the hours of 10 A.M. *and 6* P.M. *It is well worth a visit. The exterior of the handsome building has been universally admired, alike by citizens of Wilmington and visitors from other places, and an inspection of the interior will no doubt add to the satisfaction that the good people of New Hanover feel in possessing not only the most handsome, but the best arranged and most complete building of the kind in all its details and appointments, in the State of North Carolina.*

. . . The building throughout will be lighted by gas and electricity, and in cold weather warmed by hot water pipes. The ventilation throughout is perfect. A large brick cistern, built on the latest improved plans, will furnish an ample supply of water for all the rooms and offices.

The court room, on the second floor, covers the whole front of the building. It is furnished with benches for spectators. The floor is covered with matting. The bar is enclosed with railing and furnished with chairs and tables for members; the jury box, the stand for witnesses, the clerk's desks are conveniently placed and furnished. On this floor are two petit jury rooms, furnished with chairs and tables; the Judge's private room, a room for lady witnesses, the Solicitor's room, and a room for the Clerk of the Criminal Court.

On the first floor is the Sheriff's Office—two rooms; Clerk of Superior Court—one room and vault; Register of Deeds—one room and vault; ground jury room; room for the Superintendent of Public Instruction, and the County Commissioner's Office.

First actual use of the building for its intended purpose began with the spring term of the superior court in April. The *Star* noted that the first case heard "was a suit for divorce, which the Judge remarked was a 'bad beginning.' "

Two final bits of work remained to be done. The clock was installed, and it was first illuminated on the evening of August 22, according to the *Star* of the next day. On September 5 the paper noted that J. T. Riley had been awarded the contract for furnishing the brick sidewalk around the building.

Today many find it difficult to appreciate the building as its contemporaries did. To them it was a marvel. A *Star* writer suggested on October 28, 1892, "The new county Court House is the handsomest building in the city, is what nearly everyone says, and what everybody says must be so—don't you know?" Beneath today's dirt and grime, the New Hanover County Courthouse is, without a doubt, one of the South's finest examples of the High Victorian Gothic.

Princess Street crosses North Third; begin 100 street numbers

The corner of North Third and Princess streets is one of the architectural delights of the city. The simple two-story structure on the southwest corner is a functional commercial building. Across the street on the southeast corner the New Hanover County Courthouse is a tour de force of the High Victorian Gothic, while on the northeast corner City Hall is equally impressive with its Classical Revival portico and Italianate walls. On the northwest corner the contemporary building of the Waccamaw Bank is a striking Brutalistic addition to the city scene. It is a corner on which to stand, to walk around, and to savor architecture.

WACCAMAW BANK

101–3 North Third Street
1969–71: Ballard, McKim and Sawyer, architects; W. E. Carter, Whiteville, builder

The use of tinted glass, brick, and stone banding reflect similar uses of material and color in the New Hanover County Courthouse diagonally across the street. There the similarities end, however. The bank building is starkly and startlingly Brutalistic in its style. Its multiple massing of blocks and moatlike sunken garden add to the fortresslike feel of the building. The recessed entrance between walls that splay outward reinforces the effect.

The building is cut away at the street corner, where the overhanging block shelters a window. On Princess the structure presents asymmetrical masses that descend, step fashion, to the street. Along North Third Street the brick masses cut vertical slashes through the horizontal marble band. A white paved sidewalk and patio area outside the entrance, planted with pampas grass, echoes the white marble bands.

The building is a striking example of the premise that good, innovative architecture is not dead, nor is the day of its practice past. It does not imitate, though it does blend. Given slight chance of overwhelming either the city hall or courthouse, it makes a straightforward and bold architectural statement of its era and time of construction. In doing so, it buttresses the existing architectural collection in a most exciting manner.

WILMINGTON CITY HALL

102 North Third Street
(See 305 Princess Street [figs. 114, 115], for the Thalian Hall part of the building.)
1854: design John M. Trimble, New York, architect; 1855–58: construction, James F. Post, supervising architect; Robert B. Wood, John Wood and George Rose, builders

On the afternoon of November 9, 1909, President William Howard Taft reviewed a parade in his honor from a platform erected on the steps of this building. Governor Thurmond Kitchen introduced the president to the crowd of some twenty thousand people.

Wilmington's mammoth Italianate/Classical-Revival City Hall–Thalian Hall must be understood in the context of the city of its day, a port with a population of some five thousand. The size and finish of the building for a town of that size is most certainly unusual, as is the fact that the city hall and theater-cultural center are combined in one building.

The Thalian Association, for which the theater was built on Princess adjoining City Hall, was an early institution, important to the town, and established in use of the site, so that a new building that did not include a stage and theater hall was rejected. One half of the funds from the sale of the property to the city went to the theater group and was promptly offered to the city to be used in constructing a new theater building in connection with the city hall. The city agreed, and the state legislature authorized the issue of bonds for a combined building. Though there were some difficulties between the Thalians and the city, they ultimately agreed that the city would construct the building, finish the exterior, and begin the interior, which would be finished by the city in the city-hall portion and by the Thalians in the theater portion.

The city hall building (fig. 51) is highlighted by a colossal Classical Revival portico carried on fluted Corinthian columns. A molded water table marks the division of the basement and first levels, and a belt course occurs between the first and second levels. At the second and third levels the bays are marked by Doric pilasters between which occur pairs of round-arched, two-story windows united beneath molded semicircular relieving arches supported on corbels. A cornice of acanthus modillions carries around the two street elevations. The portico pediment is closed and undecorated. The entablature is wide and carries around the building on the North Third and Princess facades.

Architecturally and stylistically, the genesis of the building is something of a puzzle. On Tuesday evening, October 12, 1858, the *Daily Journal* carried an extensive article on the "Town Hall and Theatre."

In the fall of 1855, the "Old Academy" was pulled down, and the erection of the present building commenced. The original plans were drawn, we believe, by Mr. Trimble of New York, but subsequently modified in some of their details. The pediment and portico on the Western or Town Hall front, for instance. The Corner Stone, inserted in the North East Corner of the Town Hall was laid with Masonic Ceremonies on Saint John's Day, being the 27th Dec. 1855. The building is in the form of an L, being 170 feet on Princess street and 100 feet on Third street. The Town Hall is 100 feet in length by 60 feet in width—the Theatre is 110 feet long by 60 feet wide. The building is of uniform height—54 feet, and is of the Corinthian order, as far as applicable.

The western or Town Hall portion of the building has a basement fitted up for Guard rooms, a principal story having rooms for the various municipal offices, while upstairs is the large hall intended for public meetings, etc., occupying the whole length and breadth of the building, and making a most noble and lofty apartment. . . .

As we stated at the beginning of this sketch, the plans for the whole pile of building were made in 1855 [actually 1854] by Mr. Trimble, of New York, and adopted by the Commissioners, the chief external variation made subsequently has been in substituting the pediment end and pillars forming the front of the Town Hall, for a small portico like that at the Theatre, which was the original design. The change adds elevation and dignity to the principal front.

The contracts were taken by Messrs. J. C. & R. B. Wood for the masonry, and by Mr. G. W. Rose for the carpenter-work etc., Mr. James F. Post being appointed superintendent. Now that the building approaches completion we can begin to appreciate its size

51. Wilmington City Hall, 102 North Third Street. Plans, John M. Trimble, architect, 1854; construction, James F. Post, supervising architect, 1855–58.

and beauty, and we feel confident that, when finished, it will compare favorable with any municipal building in the South.

The general arrangement of the theatre, is after the plan of Mr. Trimble, but the details and their adaptation to the circumstances, have been all executed under the supervision of Mr. Post and the officers of the Thalian Association.

There seems no doubt that Trimble, Post, the Wood brothers, and Rose were the principals responsible. The problem is what they did. Trimble's plans were in hand by the end of 1854, when they were reported in the *Commercial* on December 30. By that date the plans had been studied, and modifications were being discussed. Trimble was a well-known theater designer from New York, and it is likely that he had been asked to submit a design because of the inclusion in the building of the theater. Possibly his designs only sketched in the City Hall and were more specific for the theater. Trimble's design seems to have been in the Italianate style, as indicated by the newspaper and the present building. The style was then flourishing nationwide, and he designed other era buildings in that mode. Wilmington, then beginning its Italianate love affair, may have requested a building in that style.

Certainly it could not have selected masons, carpenter, and superintending architect from any group more qualified to work in that style. George W. Rose had either already completed or was just completing his own Italianate residence in wood at 519 Grace Street, the Grace-Rose-Covington House, when, on November 1, 1855, he was chosen by the commissioners as one of the builders. J. C. and R. B. Wood and James F. Post had several years of experience in the style, beginning as early as 1851 with the construction of the masonry Edward and Henry Savage House at 120 South Third (see fig. 59). The 1851–52 MacRae-Dix House, at 108 South Third Street (see fig. 58) and the 1852 Zebulon Latimer House at 126 South Third Street (see fig. 62) were also the handiwork of these three men. So they all knew the style and had worked with it before.

On December 8, 1855, the Commissioners' Minutes (now located in the city clerk's office, Wilmington, City Hall) note that "forty dollars be allowed Mr. R. B. Wood for drawing plans and specifications for the city hall." Post's contract with the city as supervising architect—all the choices for builder and supervising architect were made at the November 1 commission meeting—stated "that he will furnish all the working plans nceecessary for the due execution of the work."

It seems likely that Post actually was responsible for the design modifications of the city-hall portion of the building, also, as he was for the theater (as reported in the *Daily Journal,* October 12, 1858.) Post had been hired for the job of supervising architect, charged specifically with furnishing working plans, and he seems to have emerged as the architect of the group. Post's grandson suggested in the *Star* on January 25, 1939, that Post designed the North Third Street portico, along with another for the Princess Street entrance to the theater that was not used. He also suggested that Post journeyed to New York to arrange for construction of the columns. Post certainly erected similar columns at the Bellamy Mansion (see figs. 130–32) on Market at North Fifth Street in the 1850s, and regardless of the commission note about payment to Wood for plans and specifications for city hall, Post still seems the best bet for the local design modification. Whoever was responsible, the result was to give individuality and identity to each of the two sections of the building.

Land for the building was purchased by the town in July of 1854. The Post ledgers indicate that work had begun by November 5, 1855. The cornerstone was laid December 27, 1855 and the first performance in the theater was in April of 1858. City Hall had been occupied before October 1858, and the theater had its grand opening on October 12, 1858.

One of the most pleasant views of the city is from the sidewalk slightly to the north of City Hall (see fig.10). As one looks to the south, the Classical Revival portico of City Hall dominates the foreground, with the towers of the New Hanover County Courthouse slightly to the south. In the distance the crenelated tower of St. James rises, and one sees, atop the hill, the massive attenuated stone spire of the First Presbyterian Church. It is a vista that gives the viewer the feel and character of the city.

South Third Street

Market Street southward to Queen

The architecture and history of South Third Street are consistent for these seven blocks—exceptional. Third Street is one of the three main thoroughfares ninety-nine feet wide rather than the normal sixty-six feet, and South Third was developed in the 1880s with broad center plazas, intensive programs of street plantings and improvements, and with street furniture of iron and marble. Fountains for watering animals, fountains to be used by residents, and fountains to look at—all were in the center plaza of South Third, which later acquired marble statuary as well.

One of the fine vantage points for viewing the town and pondering its past and future is the intersection of Third and Market streets. The contrast between the northern and southern parts of Third Street is great here, as is the difference between lower and upper Market Street. Both denuded streets and greenery are visible. Both major public buildings and lesser structures can be seen.

Within the first block, St. James Episcopal Church, which should be viewed from all sides, is the dominant building on the east, along with the MacRae House at 19 South Third Street, now a part

1. Wilmington—looking northeast from the Cape Fear River Lift Bridge.

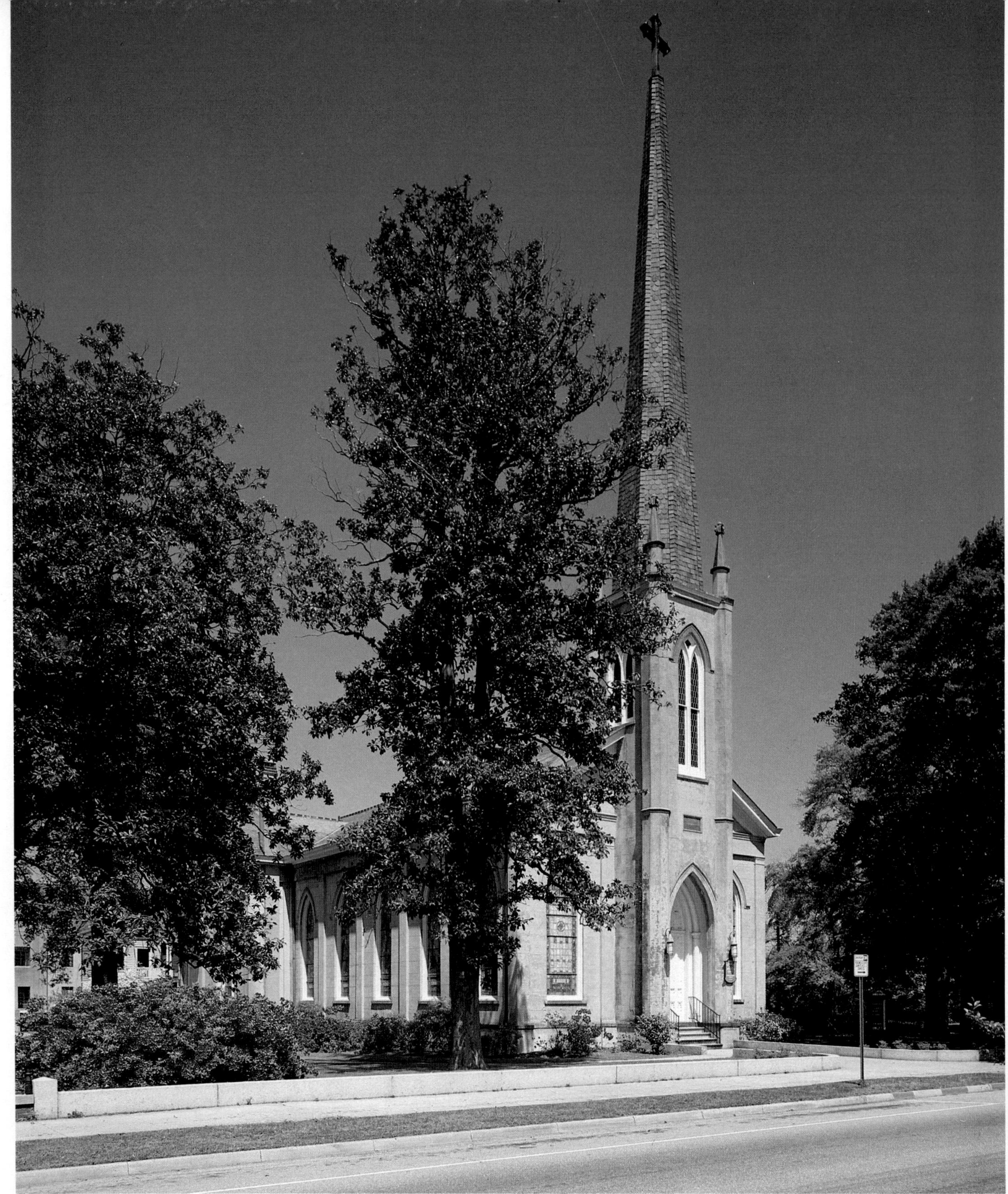

2. St. Paul's Evangelical Lutheran Church, 603 Market Street. H. Vollers, architect, James F. Post, supervising architect, 1858–69.

of the St. James complex. To the west, the side of the Burgwin-Wright House presents itself to the viewer, as does the garden entrance to that complex. To its rear and above it is the DuBois-Boatwright House. These buildings and their surroundings provide a fine frame for introducing the viewer to South Third Street.

Within the next several blocks, at least to Church Street, there is not a building without architectural interest on South Third Street.

Market Street

ST. JAMES EPISCOPAL CHURCH

1 South Third Street
1839–40: Thomas U. Walter, Philadelphia, architect; John Norris, New York, supervising architect; J. C. Wood, principal mason; C. H. Dahl, principal carpenter; Robert B. Wood, builder
1871, church roof and ceiling: Henry Dudley, New York, architect
1885, chancel, organ chambers, choir room, and south transept: Henry Dudley, New York, architect
1888, work on church foundation and floors: J. H. Hanby, builder/architect
1889, side galleries removed: architect unknown
1892, Bridgers Memorial Building: architect unknown, Valentine Brown & Co., builders
1912, cloisters between church and Bridgers Memorial Building: architect and builder unknown
1923–24, The great hall: Hobart Upjohn, New York, architect
1955–56, Milton Hall: Leslie N. Boney, Architect, architect
1956, cloisters from Milton Hall to MacRae House: Leslie N. Boney, Architect, architect

Public buildings, such as St. James in Wilmington, are frequently the work of nonnative professional architects and therefore are stylistically in step with national trends and vogues—in sharp contrast to the domestic architectural fabric of the city. Thomas U. Walter, best known for his 1865 cast-iron dome to the United States Capitol, designed St. James Episcopal Church (figs. 52–53) in a simple, academic Gothic Revival style.

A square entrance tower, accented with octagonal pinnacles at the corners and containing a clock and

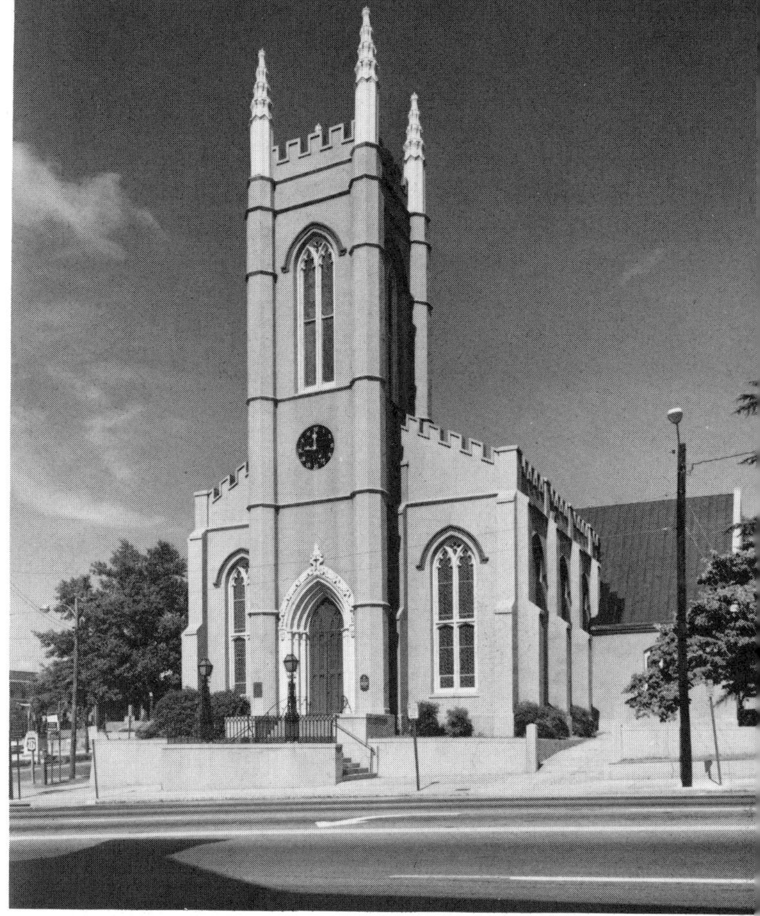

52. St. James Episcopal Church, 1 South Third Street. Thomas U. Walter, architect; John Norris, supervising architect; 1839–40.

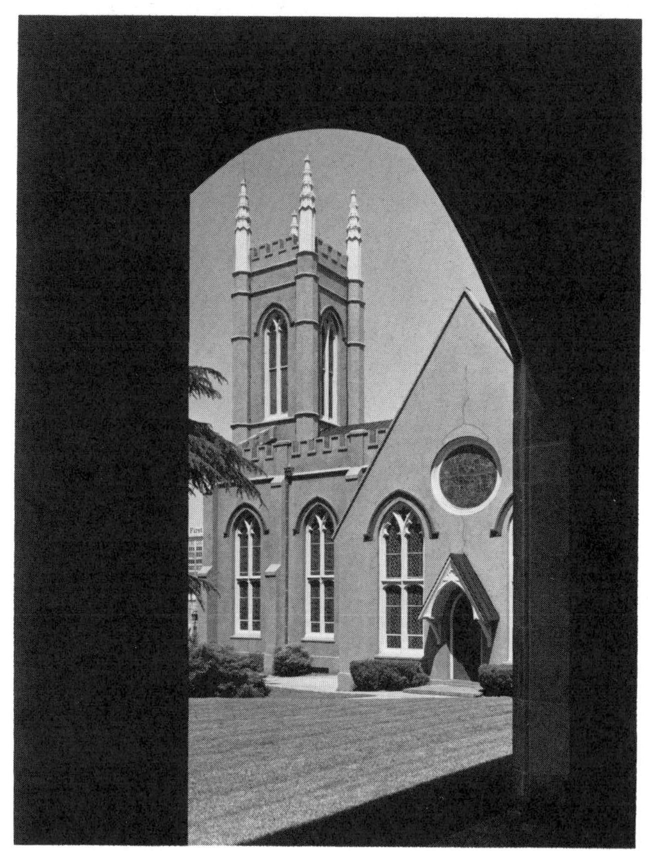

53. St. James Episopal Church, from the 1912 cloisters between the church and the Bridgers Building.

a bell, rises through the body of the building and is its chief focal point. Ornament on the stucco edifice is minimal, consisting mainly of crenellated battlements, molded stringcourses, and molded labels over the lancet windows. The recessed entrance is beautifully framed by engaged triple colonnettes that carry pointed arches outlined by crockets. The masterful work of J. C. Wood, principal mason, and C. H. Dahl, principal carpenter, executed under the direction of John S. Norris of New York and Robert B. Wood of Wilmington, is in a remarkable state of preservation.

When the North Carolina General Assembly passed an act establishing New Hanover Precinct in 1729, it did not mention St. James by name, but it was common practice at that time to lay out the parish concurrently with the precinct/county. St. James was mentioned as early as 1734, when St. Martin's Parish was created and ordered to pay its arrears to St. James Parish, indicating that St. James was already in existence.

Erection of the first church building was authorized in 1751 on land already set aside for the church and acquired over a period of time after 1747. Though the block between Third and Fourth streets on Market—which runs southward some one hundred twenty feet on each of the numbered streets—was designated as "ye Church yard or burying ground" and is mentioned in other deeds, it was not immediately used or built upon and had to be resecured at later dates from those who held it either in their own right or on behalf of the church. A clear deed was acquired from James Smallwood in July 1749, and the early church location, nearer South Fourth in the present cemetery area, was acquired. The building was begun in 1751 but was not completed before 1770, when the assembly authorized funds for its completion. The building was used until March 25, 1839, when it was demolished prior to construction of the present church building.

At least one unusual item of furnishing from the earlier church survives, the painting *Ecce Homo.* It was taken from one of three Spanish ships that attacked Brunswick Town in 1748. In 1759 the assembly authorized the division of proceeds from the sale of booty from those pirate ships between St. Philip's and St. James. The *Ecce Homo* was assigned to St. James.

The congregation acquired the site of the present church in 1841 from Armand J. DeRosset, though at the time the church building had already been standing on the property for almost a year. The rest of the land occupied by the church complex was acquired over the years, culminating with the acquisition of the MacRae House, 15 South Third Street (fig. 55) in 1956.

An account of the cornerstone laying for the present church of St. James carried in the *Wilmington Advertiser* for April 5, 1839, has been reprinted in several church publications. It notes the ceremony on April 3 at which the Reverend Robert Brent Drane gave an address and read a paper to be deposited in the cornerstone. The paper read in part:

> *This cornerstone of St. James' Church is laid this 3rd day of April, in the year of our Lord one thousand eight hundred and thirty nine (1839). The Rt. Rev. Levi Silliman Ives, D. D., LL. D., being Bishop of the Diocese of North Carolina. The Rev. Robert Brent Drane, A. M., being the Rector of the parish and officiating on the occasion.*
>
> *Dr. A. J. DeRosset, W. C. Lord, Church Wardens, Dr. Thomas H. Wright, Dr. A. J. DeRosset, Jr., W. B. Giles, W. A. Williams, James T. Miller, Vestrymen.*
>
> *The plan of this building was designed by T. U. Walter of Philadelphia, and executed under the direction of John S. Norris of New York by J. C. Wood as principal mason, and C. H. Dahl as principal carpenter. May the gates of Hell never prevail against it.*

Brick from the older church was used in the construction of the new building. Work was completed and the present building consecrated on March 29, 1840.

Though none of Thomas U. Walter's drawings of the church are known to exist, his written description presented to the vestry is in the Vestry Minutes, dated February 7, 1839.

The tower clock seems to have been manufactured by George H. Hollbrook of East Medway, Massachusetts, and was installed here in October 1840, with George J. Read of the Hollbrook firm superintending the installation. Hollbrook's guarantee noted: "The clock is hereby warranted to be a good time keeper and the Bell warranted not to break for one year from the date hereof or one year after the same shall be put up." Perhaps the bell was not installed initially, or perhaps the first bell did crack, for the present bell was "Cast by George H. Hollbrook, East Medway, Mass., 1843. Presented to St.

James Church, Wilmington, N.C. by P. K. Dickinson."

Hart & Bailey, a local firm that would evolve into the Wilmington Iron Works, accomplished a good deal of work in the church. In 1847, when the firm was Hart & Polley, they installed the electric rods/lightning rods and provided "spit pans." They also billed the vestry for unspecified "iron work" for the church and in 1848 provided "brass lanterns" and nails and billed for soldering the roof. When the 1871 work was being accomplished, the firm bid for the decorative woodwork: "Below we respectfully submit for your inspection an Estimate for Ornamental Panels and Columns as per Architrave Drawings for St. James Episcopal Church of this City. Material to be Yellow Pine work to be put together to fit Templets—the same to be furnished us by the Carpenter in charge of the work And we to deliver the work when finished to the church door. Price for each Architrave as above specified One Hundred 100.00 00/100 Dollars. Cornice and Beam Moulding not included in this statement."

The bronze chandeliers and some of the pulpit furniture were purchased during the Reverend Dr. Drane's ministry, or before 1862, and presented by the ladies of the church. The marble baptismal font was acquired during the same era, and has been in its present location since 1888.

The Reverend Dr. Drane served St. James from 1836 to 1843, resigned, and after a year was reinstalled in 1844. He was still serving as rector in 1862, during the great Wilmington yellow fever epidemic. Drane remained at his post, though much of the population fled the town. The minister at the First Baptist Church and the priest at St. Thomas the Apostle Church also remained. All three died of yellow fever, with Drane succumbing on October 14, 1862.

In February of 1865, after Union forces entered Wilmington near the end of the Civil War, church services were disrupted at St. James. The Reverend Alfred Augustine Watson, the rector who had been installed on January 1, 1865, when ordered to include prayers for the president of the United States, argued that he had no authority to pray for the president, but could only pray for "those in authority." The church was seized by the 104th Ohio Volunteers, and church services were halted on February 26. The pews were removed from the church, and it was used as a hospital. It was returned to the congregation during the summer, and enough repairs were effected to allow resumption of services on December 8, 1865. Watson was consecrated in St. James in 1884 as the first bishop of the Episcopal Diocese of East Carolina.

In August 1871 Henry Dudley of New York provided plans for a new roof and ceiling and evidently accomplished the work. In 1875 the brass lectern was installed on Easter Sunday. The *Star* recorded the fact in its March 31 edition and noted that at the Easter celebration "the most prominent feature was a new and handsome lectern, composed of solid brass, ordered direct from Europe."

In 1885, when the church was enlarged through the addition of the chancel, organ chambers, choir room, and south transept, Henry Dudley was again charged with accomplishing the work.

It is interesting to note that both Dudley and Walter were among the thirteen architects who founded the American Institute of Architects in 1857. Hobart Upjohn, who designed a later addition to this church, was the grandson and successor of Richard Upjohn, another of the thirteen.

By 1888 work was needed on the foundations and floors, and it was accomplished by J. H. Hanby, a local builder/architect.

The interior was still not finished to the satisfaction of the congregation, and in 1889 the side galleries were removed and the interior painted, additional stained glass installed, etc. The "Report of the Committee on Church Interiors," dated April 23, 1889, indicates the attitude of the committee making these changes in the church. After alternatives had been discussed, the report continued:

Our opinion is that the only proper and desirable style of decoration is fresco painting put on in accordance with designs by a competent artist who has made ecclesiastical decoration a study, and by skilled workmen under his direction.

Such work, while more expensive at first, would be more desirable, more churchly and more permanently satisfactory and pleasing, and therefore, better worth the outlay, if not more economical in the end.

Our only estimate for such work is that of Mr. E. J. Neville Stent, Decorative Architect, previously submitted to you, for $600. We are not prepared to say whether this included scaffolding and preparations of the walls, but think it most probably does, the latter, at least.

If the Vestry does not now feel at liberty to undertake such a work, we recommend that the walls be made uniform where defaced by alterations, and the work be postponed until it can be well done.

We have obtained from Mr. E. V. Richards a proposal to fill in the round window in the transept with stained glass of pleasing colors and design for the sum of ten dollars, which he says is barely the cost of his materials.

We think the price very low and recommend that this be done at once.

The congregation, vestry, and ministry at St. James seem always to have been aware of the architectural, historical, and cultural importance of the building and to have authorized change cautiously, and then only after careful study by experts.

The 1892 reredos and altar, designed by Silas McBee was carved by him. He came to Wilmington especially to accomplish this work. The central bronze panel and the east window were also designed by McBee, and the work was done by Charles Lamb and Company artisans in New York.

In 1966 the Cassavant Frères organ was installed, and the old organ, purchased from George Jardine of New York and installed in 1848, was given to a church in Newport News, Virginia.

The Right Reverend Robert Strange (1857–1914) and the Right Reverend Thomas Atkinson (1807–81), and Mrs. Atkinson, are buried under the chancel. Strange and Atkinson were both bishops of the Episcopal Eastern North Carolina Diocese.

There may be remnants of an older structure than the present church in the St. James complex. Society Hall was built by the Women's Working Association in 1834. After the new church was constructed, Society Hall served as the parish house until 1892, when a new parish house, now the Bridgers Memorial Building, was built. This was connected to the 1834 building and incorporated part of it. The 1892 parish house was supplanted in 1922 when Hobart Upjohn signed a contract to design a new parish house. Work began on the building, now known as the Great Hall, on May 3, 1923, and it was completed by March 6, 1924. Milton Hall, or the church house, was started in the fall of 1955 and was completed by October 29, 1956 after designs by the firm of Leslie N. Boney, Architect. The cloisters that connect the Church and the Great Hall were built in 1912; those between Milton Hall and the parish house (MacRae House) were erected in 1956. The firm of Leslie N. Boney, Architect, designed the 1956 cloisters after the earlier one.

DUBOIS-BOATWRIGHT HOUSE

14 South Third Street
c. 1765 and later

John DuBois, merchant and alderman of the town of Wilmington, wrote his will in September of 1767, bequeathing to his wife "the house wherein I live and adjoining lots, during her widowhood or life, then to daughter Anna Jean." The evidence indicates that the house now standing is the one in which DuBois lived before his death in 1768. The house has since been somewhat modified, mainly in changes to the porches, the erection of foundation walls to the street, and changes to the facade bays. The basic form and finish of the dwelling, one of the Wilmington Plain houses, remains stable. One of some five Georgian-style buildings in the city, this house (fig. 54) is also the oldest of the Wilmington Plain houses. Architectural historian Janet Seapker described it for the National Register of Historic Places:

The DuBois–Boatwright House is reportedly the oldest of a type of domestic structure which in the city was built throughout the century 1770–1870. This type of dwelling is a very plain rectilinear frame structure covered by a gable roof finished by a molded rake board. In all but two cases the chimneys are interior. Generally the characteristic Wilmington plain dwelling is two bays deep but ranges from a substantial house five bays wide to a tiny cottage. This type of house has a one-or-two level porch that usually runs the full length of the building. Most of the surviving Federal and Greek Revival–style structures in Wilmington have the characteristics of this plain house type.

Anna Jean DuBois married Thomas Younger, who died in 1798. She inherited the house when her mother died in 1803 and offered it for rent on February 3, 1807. The advertisement in the *Wilmington Gazette* offered immediate possession to the "house on the hill."

The property passed in the 1840s to John and Lucy Wooster, who built a newer and larger house on Dock Street, next door to the south. Through marriage the Wooster ownership passed to the Boatwrights, who in the 1930s sold the Dock and South Third Street house and moved back into the earlier Wooster home. Boatwright heirs continue in occupancy and ownership.

54. DuBois-Boatwright House, 14 South Third Street, c. 1765 and later. The Burgwin-Wright House (224 Market Street) outbuildings and gardens are on the right.

DONALD MACRAE HOUSE

15 South Third Street
1901: Henry Bacon, architect

Henry Bacon, who lived in Wilmington and graduated from Tileston School, was not primarily a residential architect. He is known more for his work at Wesleyan University in Middletown, Connecticut, for which he was campus planner and designer of a number of buildings, and for his work with various sculptors—culminating in his design of the Lincoln Memorial in Washington, D.C., for which Daniel Chester French was the sculptor.

In the Wilmington area Bacon designed "Live Oaks," the 1915 Walter Parsley residence on Masonboro Sound; remodeled the Hugh MacRae residence on Market Street (now demolished); and designed this house (fig. 55) for Donald MacRae. These and "Chesterwood," in Stockbridge, Massachusetts, designed in 1900 for Bacon's friend and fellow worker Daniel Chester French, make up the bulk of the architect's residential work. The MacRae House indicates just how good Bacon was when he chose to devote his time to residential design.

This is Wilmington's Shingle-style house par excellence. Beautifully detailed, it is brick throughout the first level and shingled above. Basically the house is an L with a polygonal tower. Simple eaves brackets support the hip roof, while the porch, which projects beyond the end of the dwelling, is composed of plain posts joined with pegs—a sort of stylized Oriental Stick-style motif. One-over-one sash is used throughout, with the upper sash divided into diamond patterns. The entry glass is beveled and leaded.

55. Donald MacRae House, 15 South Third Street. Henry Bacon, architect, 1901.

The heavy slab-brick chimneys with their iron ties are a prominent feature of the design, as are the dormers and the red tile roof.

Both on the exterior and the interior, the dwelling remains very much as built. Bacon himself did much of the superintending, giving special attention to detail. The Beautelle Manufacturing Company was responsible for executing the interiors, and H. M. Beautelle, president of the company, supervised on site. The February 7, 1901, *Messenger* noted, "the floors and furnishings will be of hard wood, mahogany, granite, quarter-sawed oak, cherry, etc." Many of the light fixtures combined gas and electricity and remain in the house, as does most of the hardware.

Donald MacRae, for whom the house was constructed, purchased the land here in 1898. Construction was begun on the house in 1901, and it seems to have been finished the same year. The family is known to have been in residence in April of 1902, when their daughter Monimia MacRae was born. In 1956 the house and lot were acquired from her by the vestry of St. James Episcopal Church. The dwelling is now used for church offices and various meeting functions.

WOOSTER HOUSE

20 South Third Street
c. 1845; c. 1913

John Wooster, an attorney, acquired the property in 1844 and built the house soon thereafter. By the time of the publication of the city directory in 1866–67, he was in residence. The structure is one of the Wilmington Plain houses and a fine one, with Greek Revival detail: a construction date of about 1845 is certainly probable.

Wooster did not build his dwelling to face Third Street, but to front on Dock. It was a large house, two-stories with low hip roof, seven bays long on Dock Street and five bays wide on South Third. The single-story porch over the full basement that jutted into Dock Street—the dwelling was built before the street was paved and the sidewalk laid—became a landmark in the Dock Street block between South Second and South Third. Since the porch was high above the street, it was an obvious impediment to traffic, and by 1913, when S. M. Boatwright owned the house, it was ordered to be taken down. The *Star* reported on September 13: "Council decided to pay to Mr. S. M. Boatwright $150 as damages for the removal of the piazza of his house at corner of Third and Dock streets, the same having projected over the sidewalk on Dock Street, and was built there before the street was opened. The payment of the amount was recommended by the former Council."

Boatwright removed the porch, reoriented the house from Dock Street to South Third, and built a new porch there with Neoclassical Revival elements. The entrance door was removed from the center bay of the Dock Street side to the center bay of the South Third Street side. Where the door had been, an exterior brick chimney was built. The earlier door and surround survives on South Third, where window architraves from the Dock Street facade were copied.

Dock Street Crosses South Third; begin 100 street numbers

The center plaza of South Third Street begins here with a prime piece of street furniture, the Confederate Memorial. Street trees, which also start here and continue for the next several blocks, are frequently sizable, though most are recently planted replacement trees. The plaza and grassy street sides are thriving, however, and the trees and other plantings are beginning to reassert themselves.

On the east side of the street, early houses have been demolished, and the First Presbyterian Church property occupies most of the block. The church parking lot took the place of two houses, but was planned to leave street trees and some yard trees along with the street side walls and iron fences. Cottage Lane, which begins in the center of the block, is given delineation by the fine walls and cast-iron fences, which mask the parking lot behind them to the east, flanking Cottage Lane. (See Hart Carriage House, 309 Cottage Lane, fig. 141).

The northernmost of the cast-iron fences was erected around the residence of Levi Hart, a partner in the iron firm of Hart & Bailey. Bailey's home survives at 219 South Third (see fig. 66) and has an identical fence. They are both believed to have been produced in the Hart & Bailey foundry, later Wilmington Iron Works.

CONFEDERATE MEMORIAL

Center Plaza of South Third Street at Dock Street
1924: F. H. Packer of New York, sculptor; Henry Bacon, architect

One of the prime items of Wilmington street furniture and of civic art, this monument (fig. 56) with its two bronze figures—one representing courage, the other self-sacrifice—is also a fine piece of sculpture and work of civic art.

56. Confederate Memorial, center plaza of South Third Street at Dock Street. Henry Bacon, architect, F. H. Packer, sculptor, 1924.

57. Bridgers House, 100 South Third Street. Charles McMillen, architect, 1905.

Designed and erected with a bequest from Gabriel James Boney, the monument was dedicated to "the Soldiers of the Confederacy." Packer's bronze figures stand atop a pedestal and against a granite shaft that rises behind them. In such cases the architect is normally responsible for the setting and the sculptor for the figures, so that the granite monument and the relation of the bronze figures to it evidence Henry Bacon's work, accomplished in collaboration with Packer.

It was this type of work that Bacon liked to do best, and his best-known works are those executed with sculptors. His Lincoln Memorial in Washington houses the seated Lincoln sculpted by Daniel Chester French. Packer worked with French on the seated Lincoln, so he must have worked with Bacon as well. It is uncertain if Bacon came to be involved in work on this sculpture first because he was a local boy and Packer then won the commission through Bacon, or whether Packer secured the commission and then asked for Bacon's assistance.

Bacon died before this monument was unveiled. It is one of only two major monuments in North Carolina known to have been designed by him—*The Women of the Confederacy Monument* on Capitol Square in Raleigh, sculpted by Augustus Lukeman and erected in 1913, is the other. Bacon's work also appears here in grave markers in the Bacon plot in Oakdale Cemetery. (See fig. 181.) Packer accomplished other Wilmington work as well (see George Davis Statue, Market Street at Third Street [fig. 121], and T. E. Sprunt Monument at Oakdale Cemetery).

BRIDGERS HOUSE

100 South Third Street
1905: Charles McMillen, architect; Joseph Schad, builder

Mrs. Elizabeth Eagle Haywood Bridgers built this house (fig. 57) to serve as her residence. She was a granddaughter of John Haywood, well known treasurer of North Carolina; a descendant of Richard Eagles, for whom Eagles' Island on the opposite bank of the Cape Fear River was named; and widow of Preston L. Bridgers, the son of Rufus Bridgers, who was a nationally known railroader with the Wilmington & Weldon, and later with the Atlantic Coast Line Railroad.

If Mrs. Bridgers intended to build a house as grand and as noticeable for its day as the Bellamy Mansion and the DeRosset houses were for their eras, then there is little doubt that she succeeded. She chose her architect, site, and material well. It is at the top of South Third Street as it climbs from Market and at the top of Dock Street as it climbs from the river, or at least as it stops its most precipitate climb. The Right Reverend Leo Haid, O. S. B., Vicar Apostolic of North Carolina, sold the land to Mrs. Bridgers. In chronicling the sale, the February 8, 1905, *Star* stated "It is learned that Mrs. Bridgers will have erected on the lot a very handsome residence and that work upon the same will begin in a few weeks." To design the structure, Mrs. Bridgers chose Charles McMillen, who had come to Wilmington from Duluth to build the North Front Street Masonic Temple and remained here to establish a practice.

They decided on a house of stone. Joseph Schad was chosen as builder. The stone was shipped from an Indiana quarry to South Carolina, where it was shaped and cut and then sent to Wilmington for placement. J. H. Niggel, then foreman of the Columbia Stone Co., which cut and shaped the stone, came to Wilmington to work with Schad in the construction of the house. After the Bridgers House was completed, Niggel remained in Wilmington to found the Carolina Cut Stone Company.

A massive Neoclassical Revival structure, the house is two and one-half stories of rock-faced ashlar with rock quoin bindings at the corners. The most notable feature of the striking house is the grand semicircular portico supported on colossal freestanding Ionic columns. The interiors are easily as impressive as the exteriors. The 1912 chamber of commerce publication *City of Wilmington* called the structure "one of the handsomest houses in the state." Recently renovated for an adaptive commercial use, it must still be regarded as handsome.

58. MacRae-Dix House, 108 South Third Street, 1851–52.

MACRAE-DIX HOUSE

108 South Third Street
1851–52: J. C. and R. B. Wood, James F. Post

It seems likely that the Wood brothers were the masons and builders for this house (fig. 58) and that Post was involved both in design and in production of the wooden detail. Entries in Post's ledgers indicate his work on specific items for the house. In 1852 he billed for "Entry on Mr. McRaes [sic] house," evidently meaning the door and probably indicating that the dwelling was not finished until the year following its start.

Upon its completion, Donald MacRae seems to have sold the house to John W. K. Dix. Dix married Sarah E. Martin on July 30, 1851, and bought the property here on September 13, 1852. The city directories for 1881–82 show Sarah Dix, widow of John, living here, the same residency shown on Gray's 1881 map. She was still in residence in 1885.

This is one of the Wilmington dwellings that closely follows the plan, elevations, and ornamentation for a "Cubical Cottage in the Tuscan Style" recommended by A. J. Downing in his *The Architecture of Country Houses,* published in 1850. Both this house and its neighbor, the Edward and Henry Savage House at 120 South Third (fig. 59), built during the same period and by the same craftsmen, follow the Downing recommendations. A bracketed Italianate structure of stucco over brick, this house has exposed rafters supporting the wide overhang of the low hip roof, with brackets beneath the rafters—the house at 120 South Third has no brackets. A plaster band runs along the cornice, the corners of the house, and the water table of this dwelling, outlining and delineating wall surfaces.

The three-bay iron porch is cast in a lyre pattern that is draped across the top and hung as a balustrade below.

SAVAGE-BACON HOUSE

114 South Third Street
c. 1850; c. 1909

Built by Henry R. Savage, c. 1850, the house seems to have been a bracketed-and-vented Italianate dwelling, though the brackets are now missing. They were probably removed as a part of the Neoclassical Revival remodeling of c. 1909. The cleaned-up frieze, center pavilion, present porch, and entry are from that era and were probably accomplished by D. C. Boyce. The *Morning Star* for June 19, 1909, carried the following: "For a consideration, said to be $15,000, Mr. Percy R. Albright, assistant to the general manager of the Atlantic Coast Line, has purchased from Mr. D. C. Boyce, the handsome residence at 114 South Third Street, recently improved by the owner. The residence is one of the prettiest and most eligibly located in the city." The improvement mentioned is probably the present house configuration. If not then, it was brought to its present state soon after 1909, possibly by Albright.

Henry Bacon, Sr., and his family were probably the most important occupants of this house, though the Bacons never owned it. Bacon, who moved here from Southport c. 1881, lived in this house until his death in 1891. Bacon was an engineer, responsible for the dam between the Cape Fear River and the Atlantic Ocean that closed New Inlet.

Constructed between 1875 and 1881, with additional work as late as 1886, and known locally as The Rocks, the dam contains some one hundred eighty-one thousand and six hundred cubic yards of stone; sixteen thousand, seven hundred fifty six gross tons of heavy granite; and an untold amount of logs and brush that provided the mattresses on which the stone rests. New Inlet, cut by a storm in 1761, had formed a second mouth to the Cape Fear that by the 1870s was threatening to close the channel into Wilmington, thus ending its usefulness as a port.

Bacon's dam—he not only designed and built it, but evolved much of the machinery with which it was constructed—averages thirty-six feet in height and is from ninety to one hundred twenty feet wide. It had the desired effect of reestablishing flow in the river, thus cleansing the channel so that commerce by ocean going steamers was once more possible into Wilmington. "The Rocks" is a prominent American engineering landmark, chosen in 1975 during the celebration of the United States Corps of Engineers as one of only twelve "Best Ever" projects completed during the two hundred year history of the corps.

Two of Bacon's children who lived here grew to international renown and success. Henry Bacon, called "Harry" in Wilmington to distinguish father from son, graduated from Tileston School on May 30, 1884. Later, as an architect he designed much civic and some domestic architecture, and with such sculptors as Karl Bitter, James Earle Fraser, Augustus Saint-Gaudens, and Daniel Chester French, he designed some of the best-known monuments and memorials of the twentieth century. Some of young Henry's work is visible from this house, since he was architect of the Confederate Memorial in the center plaza at South Third and Dock streets, and of the Shingle-style MacRae-Dix House at 108 South Third Street (fig. 58), now a part of the St. James church complex.

Francis Bacon, an older brother and an archaeologist, worked as draughtsman for the American Archaeological Society/Harvard University excavations at Assos, Turkey, near Troy, from 1881 to 1883 and subsequently. Francis later edited and wrote the explanatory notes on the expedition, while drafting most of the plans and details of the major report on the dig, published first in 1902 and then in 1911. One of the report drawings by Henry Bacon, who visited Francis at Assos, was for the Tomb of Publius Varius. From stelae shown in that drawing came Bacon's first design for the tombstone that marks his grave at Oakdale, as well as his design for the family marker there. Francis Bacon later turned to furniture designing and manufacture, earning na-

59. Edward and Henry Savage House, 120 South Third Street, 1851.

tional and international fame and working with some of the best-known architects of the day, including his brother Henry.

EDWARD AND HENRY SAVAGE HOUSE

120 South Third Street
1851; J. C. and R. B. Wood; James F. Post

Edward Savage built the house (fig. 59) but sold it to his younger brother Henry in 1863. The house remained in Henry's family until 1953, so that the name Henry Savage House has long been in use.

Henry Savage, who had married a daughter of O. G. Parsley, worked for O. G. Parsley & Co., commission merchants and importers. His obituary appeared in the August 2, 1904, *Star*.

Captain Henry Savage was born in Wilmington in 1834 and was, therefore, in the 70th year of his age . . . and before the war was engaged in the commission business on the wharf.

In 1853 he was one of the organizers of the Wilmington Light Infantry. Served as a captain in the 18th N.C. Regiment during the war. In 1863 he was appointed by Pres. Jefferson Davis collector of customs at the port of Wilmington, and depository for the Confederate States treasury, and the duties of this position occupied him until the close of the war.

After the fall of Fort Fisher, he retired to Raleigh, and later establishing his office in a railroad car, moved west as necessity demanded until the fall of the government.

He held the office of City Clerk and Treasurer from 1877 to 1883.

The contract with the Wood brothers and with Post was entered into October 1851, and construction began soon thereafter. This is one of the purer of the Italianate houses, similar in elevation, plan, and ornamentation to the work of A. J. Downing. (See the MacRae-Dix House, 108 South Third Street, fig, 58.) Edward Savage may well have liked the Downing design and asked for a house like it. The house is one of at least three—two of them within this block at 108 and 120 South Third Street and the other at 520 Orange Street—that are markedly similar. Two houses in the first block of North Fifth Avenue—the Conoley-Hanby-Sidbury House, 15 North Fifth Avenue (see fig. 84), and the Von Glahn House, 19 North Fifth Avenue (see fig. 85)—and the Wessell House at 115 South Front Street also have elements in common with these three houses.

In this house the roof overhang is wide, but the projection is supported by rafter extensions instead of the more common brackets. The roof itself is a low pyramidal hip. The frieze, just under the eaves, is unadorned. There is no wall decoration to the water table, which is also plain. Bay openings are set in flat surrounds that project beyond the wall surface and sit on simulated blocks.

The single-story canopy-roofed porch is of steamed and fitted wood, except for its posts, canopy, and balustrade, which are of cast iron in foliated curvilinear and geometric patterns. Cresting in iron also appears on the canopy porch roof. The cast-iron fence that runs along the front of the narrow lot has an arrow shaft with central modillion pattern hung from tapered posts with flaming urn finials.

The house faces the east, and one of the great joys of the building watcher is observing the shadow-detail cast on the stucco facade of the house by the delicate cast-iron porch. That detail is such that the house presents ever different and changing faces to the visitor and viewer.

FIRST PRESBYTERIAN CHURCH

121 South Third Street
1859–61: Samuel Sloan, architect; James Walker, builder; 1926–28: Hobart Upjohn, architect; J. L. Crouse, Greensboro, builder; 1925–28; Education Building: H. L. Cain, architect; K. M. Murchison, consulting architect; U. A. Underwood, builder; Hobart Upjohn, architect for modifications to Cain/Murchison plan

There seem to have been Presbyterians in Wilmington as early as 1760, when the Reverend James Tate, a minister of that denomination, arrived in Wilmington from his native Ireland. Tate worked in Wilmington as a teacher. By 1785 there was an organized Presbyterian church, but the congregation was not constant until 1817, when the First Presbyterian Church was organized and accepted into the Fayetteville Presbytery. From that year until the present, except for a short period during the Civil War when the church was without a full-time minister, the church has been an active one.

The cornerstone for the first church building erected by the group was laid on May 12, 1818. A round broadside commemorating the occasion survives in the church records. It shows James Marshall and Benjamin Jacobs as builders. That first structure was said to have been on Front Street, between Dock and Orange. Within a short period of time, on November 3, 1819, the building was destroyed in an area fire, one of the many that swept downtown Wilmington in the eighteenth and nineteenth centuries.

A new structure was begun almost immediately on the northeast corner of Front and Orange streets. The 1818 cornerstone of this building was discovered in 1926, when the walls of the 1859 church building were being razed. It was, reported the *News-Dispatch* of December 13, 1926:

> *. . . imbedded in the walls . . . in a position to which it did not show, a flat, rectangular brown stone about 2 × 5 feet in size, with the following inscription upon it:*
>
> *"The Corner Stone of this Church was laid May 19th, 1818. The Church was dedicated to the service of Almighty God May 10th, 1819. It was destroyed by Fire in the dreadful conflagration of the Town November 1819 and rebuilt 1820."*
>
> *The stone was broken in removal and one or two words were hard to read, but the above is very nearly the exact writing.*

The handsome structure was completed in 1821. On April 13, 1859, this building was destroyed by fire. It is said that the Presbyterians, who had no insurance on the building, began subscription for a new building on the spot, even as the building was burning. They decided to move eastward into a more residential area and purchased land on South Third at Orange, the present site.

The 1859 burning of the Presbyterian Church came in the aftermath of a great spiritual awakening in Wilmington, part of a nationwide revival in mid-1858. The revival had been strongly felt in Wilmington, when the Presbyterians constructed Chestnut Street United Presbyterian Church, 710½ Chestnut Street (see fig. 109), as a thank offering for their own awakening; the Lutherans formed and began construction of St. Paul's Evangelical Lutheran Church, 603 Market Street (see color photo

60. First Presbyterian Church, 121 South Third Street, Hobart Upjohn, architect, 1926–28.

2), and the Baptists began construction of their major new First Baptist Church building, 421 Market Street (see fig. 126).

Samuel Sloan of Philadelphia, architect of the building being erected by the Baptists, was also chosen by the Presbyterians to design their new building. James Walker was the builder. As did Sloan's Baptist building, the Sloan design for the Presbyterians featured an attenuated spire that was long a Wilmington landmark. The building was finished before the Civil War—the Baptists and the Lutherans had to wait until after the war to dedicate their buildings—and was dedicated on April 28, 1861. During the Civil War era the Presbyterians were able to give their completed church building less than full use. The Reverend M. B. Grier, who had been minister while the church was being built and had spearheaded its construction, held ideas about the Union that were not the same as those held by a majority of the congregation. Consequently he resigned at the beginning of the war to go North. It was not until May 6, 1866, that another full-time minister was installed, though the congregation had maintained a relatively regular schedule of services.

One of the best-known ministers of the congregation, the Reverend Joseph R. Wilson, was installed on November 1, 1874. He served until April 1, 1885, and later preached often in the First Church. Wilson, a well-known theologian in his own right, was the father of Woodrow Wilson, president of the United States during World War I. Though young Wilson was already in college when his father was installed, he spent much time in Wilmington: in the manse that stood on Orange Street to the rear of the present church, in the church building that preceded this one, and in other homes and buildings still standing in the area. A fine plaque, erected in 1928, commemorates Wilson, one of a large number of memorials within the narthex of the present church structure. The Wilson plaque carries a bas-relief of the president, the state seals of Virginia and North Carolina, and the following text: "Sacred to the Memory of Woodrow Wilson, 1856–1924, World War President of the United States, 1913–1921, Son of Rev. Joseph R. Wilson, D.C., Pastor of this Church, 1874–1885. The Father of the League of Nations. A scholar, Statesman, and Christian, a Lover of Righteousness. Once a citizen of Wilmington, and member of this Church. A ruling Elder in the Presbyterian Church."

When the First Church celebrated its seventy-fifth anniversary in December 1892, the Reverend Mr. Grier and the Reverend Mr. Wilson returned to assist others in the service.

In 1893 a large addition to the church was built. Dedicated on February 11, 1894, it was used for Sunday school and other educational purposes. By late 1925, the facilities were inadequate, and a contract was signed to complete a new building. The *News-Dispatch* for November 14, 1925, headlined "Contract Awarded for Big Annex to 1st Presbyterian:"

Contract for the annex to the first Presbyterian church has been awarded to U. A. Underwood, and construction will be started at once. This work is expected to be completed within nine months.

Cost of the annex will be between $75,000 and $100,000, and it will afford as modern and beautiful sunday school accommodations as can be found in the south, it is stated. The annex will be used for the elementary and primary grades, the present Sunday school then being turned over for the sole use of the young people.

This annex will be built in two ells, one of these being located on the present playgrounds. The ells will be two stories high, and the portion facing on Orange street will have an English chapel effect.

Within the building will be class rooms, cloak rooms, cabinets, store room space and all modern conveniences and facilities. One feature will be a large and complete gymnasium.

The structure will be known as the James Sprunt Memorial building, in memory of those who have contributed toward the funds for its erection. H. L. Cain, of Richmond and Philadelphia, an expert in church and Sunday school work, is the architect, with Kenneth Murchison, well known here, and now living in New York, as the consulting architect.

Even as work on the annex was beginning, fire struck the church once more. In a conflagration discovered about midnight on December 31, 1925, the church buildings burned—the third time the church had lost its home through fire. This time the buildings were insured, and to this money and the funds already on hand for the annex, new contributions were added. The *News-Dispatch* for March 9, 1926, noted that Col. Walker Taylor had been selected chairman of the building committee, and that:

61. *First Presbyterian Church, north side with chapel.*

Hobart Upjohn, noted church architect, has been selected as the architect for the new First Presbyterian church edifice to replace the one destroyed by fire several months ago. Announcement of the selection of Mr. Upjohn was made yesterday, at which time the personnel of the church building committee was also announced.

In the selection of Mr. Upjohn, the building committee and the congregation, are very much pleased. He is said to be one of the nation's greatest church architects having designed buildings in many sections of the country.

In the April 26, 1926, edition of the same paper, it was reported that Upjohn was in the city and that plans had been placed before the building committee and the congregation. Of the some $360,000 necessary for construction, it was reported that $300,000 was already on hand.

It was announced that about one half of the entire amount required for the edifice will be expended on the Sunday school plant, a building which is expected to be one of the finest in the entire south.

The plans were drawn by Hobart Upjohn, well known church architect, who has drawn plans for many religious edifices in the south, including some in Wilmington. Mr. Upjohn was in the city last week in conference with the building committee, and at that time presented the plans which were opened for inspection yesterday.

Upjohn used the south foundation wall of the Sloan church "as well as part of the west wall," under the nave of his building, labeling those areas clearly in his drawings. Brick from the Sloan-designed building was cleaned and reused in the Upjohn building. New foundations for the Cain-Murchison gymnasium annex were already in when the old church burned, and windows and other trim had already been ordered. Upjohn's drawings indicate that the "new concrete foundation will be used as it stands," and that window frames already ordered and stored at the site were to be used.

Church construction was fully underway by late December 1926. The cornerstone was laid in the spring of 1927, and enough work had been completed by October 13, 1927, to allow a meeting in the session room of the new building (fig. 60), the first use of the new structure.

The firm of Roach and Rowe of Greensboro contracted for the stonework of the sanctuary and chapel. On July 13, 1927, William Roach, in Wilmington to inspect the work of his firm, was killed in a fall from the tower, which at that time seems to have been at the thirty-foot level. The *News-Dispatch* noted that he slipped after stepping on new construction that had not yet set.

J. L. Crouse, also of Greensboro, was the general contractor for construction of the new Upjohn buildings. Presumably U. A. Underwood continued construction of the Cain-Murchison-Upjohn educational portion of the complex.

The complex was completed and dedicated on November 18, 1928. The organ was completed and first used in 1928 as well. Built by the E. M. Skinner Organ Co., it was designd by C. H. Atkins, and the casework in front of the pipes at the front of the sanctuary is by Angelo Laualki, of Cambridge, Massachusetts. Since work on the organ casework was going on simultaneously with the construction of the sanctuary, it is likely that these men worked with Upjohn, as did the designers of the lighting-system fixtures installed in 1928, and of the rose window and chapel windows, also installed in 1928. These windows are by G. Owing Bonawit, Inc., of New York and are the only original stained-glass windows that remain, except for those in the narthex.

In a systematic program, begun in 1950, other windows have been replaced by glass from the Willet Stained Glass Studios of Philadelphia. Willett described the discipleship window—number five of the south clerestory windows (starting from the right nearest the chancel)—as a "four lanced clerestory windows . . . our finest craftsmanship and materials, a thoroughly staunch and watertight job, strongly barred and leaded. All painted portions to be fused in the kiln a sufficient number of times to render them absolutely fadeless as the work of the medieval glass artists which has stood the test of centuries. The choicest mouth blown pot-metal glassed and Norman slabs to be used throughout. No enamels to be introduced." The discipleship window was completed and dedicated in 1968. The side-aisle stained-glass windows and the nave and chancel door lights are also by Willet. The church has issued excellent publications on the symbolism of the various windows.

The chancel carvings were done in or near Chicago by a group of German woodcarvers, originally from Oberammergau. The carvings, received in 1927, were installed before the church was dedicated in 1928.

The pulpit Bible is of more than passing interest. It was printed and bound in London in 1855 and was used in the church until the end of the Civil War, when it was taken from the church, presumably by a Union soldier. In Annapolis, Maryland, in late 1865, Lt. Sidney G. Cooke purchased the Bible from another soldier for sixteen dollars. It was preservd by the Cooke family until 1928, when Thurston Cooke, of Kansas City, Missouri, returned it to this congregation. It may well be that the removal of the Bible from the church and its preservation by the Cooke family saved the volume from being burned in the midnight fire of December 31, 1925.

Among the well-known ministers who have appeared in this building was the Reverend Peter Marshall. He was in Wilmington in the fall of 1939 and again in 1940. The *News* announced in its September 20, 1940, edition that from November 11 to 15, Marshall would preach "at the First Presbyterian Church at 8 o'clock" each evening.

Built of rough-cut random stone, the sanctuary is in the late Gothic Revival style, consisting of a gable roof basilica beside a square four-stage tower crowned by a stone needle spire. The spire is capped by a rooster weathervane cast by the Wilmington Iron Works. An enormous tracery pointed-arch window fills almost the entire facade; reduced versions of the arched window mark the seven bays that are supported by pinnacled buttresses.

The small stone chapel to the north (fig. 61) is designed in a Norman Gothic mode, while the educational and other buildings in the church complex to the rear of the sanctuary and chapel and on Orange Street are Tudor, with brick half-timbering and stucco.

Noticeable design differences between the three parts of the grouping and the harmonious relationship of the parts to their setting, give the complex its great architectural importance.

ZEBULON LATIMER HOUSE

126 South Third Street
1852: J. C. and Robert B. Wood; James F. Post

Zebulon Latimer purchased the lot here on July 23, 1845, and constructed the present dwelling (fig. 62) in 1852. He was a native of Connecticut, who came first to Edenton and then to Wilmington, arriving here in the 1830s. For a number of years he was a partner in the W. & Z. Latimer dry goods firm with his brother, and for a time he was a member of the firm of Latimer & Anderson. He was a director of both the Commercial Bank of Wilmington and the Bank of the Cape Fear.

The elder Latimer died in November 1881 while in New York; his wife Elizabeth died in Wilmington in November 1904. The oldest son, William, bought this house from his father's estate in 1889 and lived there with his mother until her death. He married Margaret Iredell Meares on October 3, 1905. They maintained ownership until 1956, when the property passed to heirs who in turn, in 1963 and in 1967, sold the house and the grounds to the Lower Cape Fear Historical Society.

Now utilized as headquarters for the society and for their extensive archive of local history, the house is also maintained as a historic house museum open to the public on a regular basis. (The interior is shown in color plate 5.)

A bracketed-and-vented Italianate structure, its design differs subtlely from other houses of the genre in Wilmington, mainly because of its richness—it almost seems overdone. The house is stuccoed masonry with corner quoins. Frieze brackets are heavy, of cast metal, while vents are round and delineated

62. Zebulon Latimer House, 126 South Third Street, 1852.

by graceful wreaths. There are curious low-gable roofed dormers, and windows are capped with heavy, ornate cast-metal cornices. The classic porch with its Corinthian columns of wood on South Third Street contrasts sharply with the Orange Street piazza with its canopy roof and delicate cast-iron supports, balustrade, canopy, and cresting. The Sanborn maps indicate that at least by 1884 the porches were as they are today; at least the Orange Street porch was then cast-iron, even if the South Third Street porch was not. The South Third porch seems to crowd the window lintels and to obscure some of the entrance with its fine overdoor, transom, sidelights, and heavily molded door. It is likely that it is a later change from an earlier cast-iron trimmed porch.

The cast-iron fence (said to have been moved here from Oakdale Cemetery), the servants quarters to the west rear, and the landscaped surround complete a significant complex that is vitally important in depicting life in Wilmington during the opulent pre–Civil War era. The complex is listed in the National Register of Historic Places.

In the yard to the north, the three-tiered fountain of cast iron is part of the Wilmington street furniture, moved here from the reduced center plaza of South Third. It is probably from the 1880s street development.

Orange Street crosses South Third; begin 200 street numbers

The center plaza of the street continues through this block and the first of the series of utilitarian pieces of street furniture is in the center of the block, within the center plaza. This is a combination water fountain and horse-watering trough. A fine architectural diversity of style exists, along with mixed public and private uses.

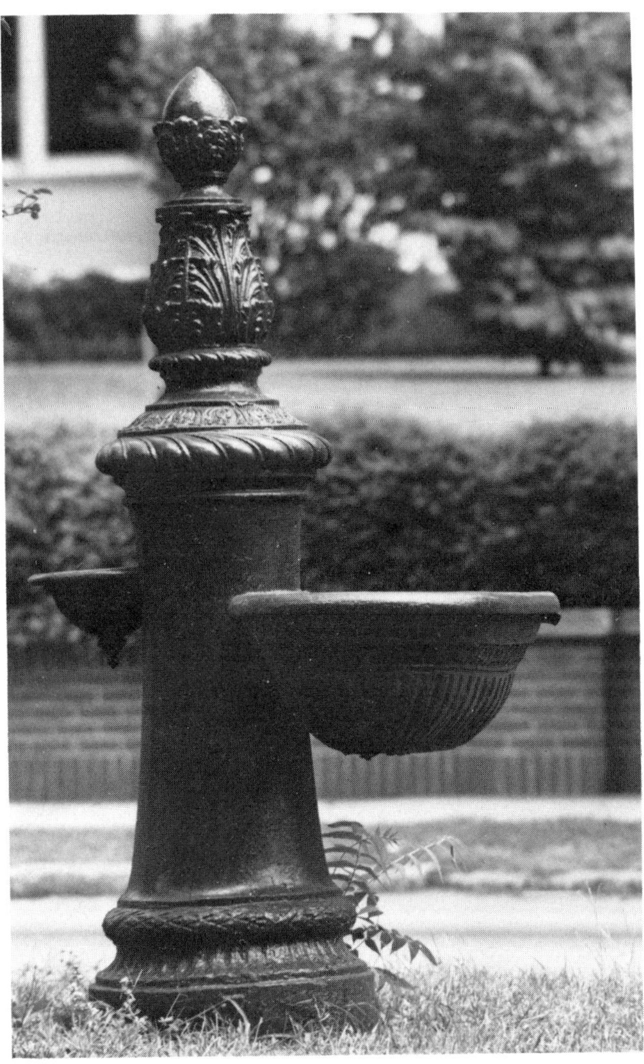

63. Fountain and horse watering trough, center plaza of South Third Street between Orange and Ann streets. J. L. Mott Iron Works, c. 1880.

FOUNTAIN AND HORSE WATERING TROUGH

Center plaza of South Third Street, between Orange and Ann, and between Ann and Nun
c. 1880: J. L. Mott Iron Works, caster and builder.

Pieces of street furniture such as the fountain and watering trough here (fig. 63) were more commonplace in Wilmington than in some cities. They were part of the boulevard development of Market and Third streets and Fifth Avenue. Begun in the 1880s under the administration of Mayor J. Fowler, the street development and enhancement has largely disappeared, though an attempt is being made to reestablish the plantings.

During the 1880s development, the streets were planted with curbside trees, and the grassy center plazas were delineated and landscaped. Fountains and watering troughs were a vital part of the effort, both for horses and other animals and for the human population. The three-tiered fountain that once graced the plaza between Dock and Orange streets is now in the garden of the Zebulon Latimer House at 126 South Third; a fine ornate dual-purpose fountain with basin and urn finial is between Orange and Ann streets; and a simpler elongated tub-like basin (fig. 64) is between Ann and Nun. They are, along with the Confederate Memorial, the only Third Street survivors of the many such items of street furniture, civic sculpture, and citizen convenience that once were part of Wilmington's street landscaping.

Items of street furniture such as these are rare, and their survival here is all the more astounding since South Third Street is a major traffic artery. These items are being cared for, and replacement plantings have recently begun to restore trees cut from the center plazas when they were reduced in size and from the curbsides. In time, the utility poles that supplanted the earlier trees will, it is hoped, be replaced by trees.

64. Horse watering trough, center plaza of South Third Street between Ann and Nun streets. J.L. Mott Iron Works, c. 1880.

HENRY LATIMER HOUSE

202 South Third Street
1882–83: James F. Post; J. C. and R. B. Wood

65. Henry Latimer House, 202 South Third Street, 1882–83.

On Gray's 1881 map there are four houses at the corner of Orange and South Third streets on the sites that are now occupied by this house and the Edward Latimer House (208 South Third Street; see below). On June 11, 1882, the *Star* reported: "the Messers Latimer are pulling down the houses at the southwest corner of Third and Orange streets, and making necessary preparations for the erection of such buildings as will be an ornament and improvement to that locality." On November 22 the same newspaper reported "a fine new residence is going up on 3rd Street. . . . Mr. Henry G. Latimer will occupy the corner residence when completed." On February 27, 1883, the paper once more noted the Latimer houses: "The large and handsome brick residences in course of construction at and adjoining the southeast [*sic*] corner of Third and Orange streets, the property of the Messrs. Latimer, are nearing completion. They will be a great improvement to the neighborhood."

James F. Post's ledgers provide the authority for Post and the Wood brothers as the artisans responsible for this and the Edward Latimer House next door. Both houses have the same plan, though reversed, and the windows, entrances, and wall surfaces are almost exactly alike. It is only in the roof—this building has a mansard roof, thus another story—that the two dwellings differ noticeably. The Henry Latimer House (fig. 65) has a bracketed frieze, without vents—though there is evidence that the vents were there originally and were closed when the later Mansard roof was added to the structure. It is likely that the roof was added within a few years of the construction of the house, though that is by no means certain, and the date could be as late as the early twentieth century, when the house passed from Latimer to Kenan ownership.

This house began as a mirror image of 208 South Third, a bracketed-and-vented, two-story, brick late Italianate dwelling. It is now a bracketed late Italianate structure with a fine Mansard roof and well-executed brick chimneys.

The carriage houses and servants quarters for both this house and the Edward Latimer House survive, facing on Orange Street and Hoskin's Alley to the rear of the house. They were constructed concurrently with the houses, 1882—83, and are unusual and particularly important survivors.

Henry Latimer was a student of art and the oldest of the three sons of Zebulon Latimer. He worked with his brothers in the family firm of W. & Z. Latimer, dry goods merchants, and participated with them in the founding of Acme Manufacturing Company. Latimer lived here until 1898, when he moved to Auburn, New York, his wife's home. Latimer later returned to Wilmington and died in this city on January 27, 1929.

Later the house was the residence of several members of the Kenan family. One of these was Mary Lily Kenan Flagler Bingham whose funeral was held here in July of 1917. She had married the multimillionaire Henry M. Flagler in 1912 and, after his death, the Kentuckian Robert Worth Bingham. Flagler's death had left her one of the nation's richest women. Her sister Sarah Kenan, who had married her kinsman Graham Kenan, was another resident here, along with her husband. His obituary in the February 7, 1920, *Star* noted that he was an attorney who had practiced in Wilmington until 1918, when he removed to New York, where he

died on Thursday night in his apartments in the Gotham Hotel. . . . Funeral services will be held from the late residence, 202 South Third St., tomorrow. Interment will be made in Oakdale Cemetery.

Mr. Kenan was licensed to practice law in 1905 and came to Wilmington to practice his profession. He was associated with the law firms of Kenan and Herring, Kenan & Stacy and Kenan & Wright.

ELLIOTT HOUSE

207 South Third Street
c. 1913

Certainly one of the finest of the Wilmington Georgian Revival houses, the Elliott House seems to have been constructed about 1913. The property was acquired by Mrs. Mabel Elliott, wife of George B. Elliot, in late 1909. The house is not on the Sanborn map of 1910, but does appear on the 1915 map, so that the approximate date of 1913 for construction is obvious. Elliott was president of the Atlantic Coast Line Railroad.

The house retains its essential exterior features: windows with splayed arches and keystones, finely detailed dormers and sash, classical portico with closed pediment and Tuscan columns. The style of the dwelling is typical of buildings constructed during its era; all drew their detail and plans primarily from American buildings of the Georgian and Federal periods. The house seems so architectonic that it most certainly had an architect. The financial capability of the Elliot's also argues for an architect, though no architect's name has yet been discovered.

In 1948 the house was acquired by the Ladies Benevolent Society of Wilmington to serve as the new Catherine Kennedy Home, which had been moved here from an earlier home at 903 Princess Street. The association was started in 1845, incorporated in 1852, and reorganized in 1868. In 1889 the home operated by the Ladies Benevolent Society was renamed Catherine Kennedy Home, in honor of Catherine DeRosset Kennedy, first president of the organization. Once restricted to women residents, the home is now open to members of both sexes.

The brick wings to the home were designed by William J. Boney of Leslie N. Boney, Architect, and were completed in 1950 and 1958.

EDWARD LATIMER HOUSE

208 South Third Street
1882–83: James F. Post, J. C. and R. B. Wood

This house, begun on or about November 22, 1882, was occupied by Edward Latimer, one of three sons of Zebulon Latimer. The Edward Latimer House and the house at 202 South Third, originally its mirror twin, were built after Zebulon Latimer's death in 1881, so that each of the three sons could have equal houses—one of them remained in the original house. The *Star* reported on November 22, 1882, that " a fine new residence is going up on 3rd Street. . . . Mr. Edward S. Latimer will take the one just commenced." The paper reported on February 27, 1883, that the houses "are nearing completion."

The house is almost identical to the Henry Latimer House at 202 South Third (see fig. 65), except that their plans are reversed. If one looks carefully, the windows, the entrances, and even the bay windows match. While the house at number 202 has had a Mansard roof added, the original vented frieze remains here, with the vents providing light, circulation, and decoration for the attic story beneath the low hip roof. Its bracketed and vented frieze and roof were once echoed next door, as were its chimneys.

Edward Latimer was a member of the dry goods firm of W. & Z. Latimer and a founder of the Acme Manufacturing Company.

ELLEN SAVAGE WADDELL HOUSE

218 South Third Street
1885

William Latimer bought the property here in 1882 for $1,250 and in 1886 deeded it to Elizabeth Latimer for $5,000, the rise in price probably indicating the construction of the house. This is reinforced by a report in the *Star* on December 6, 1885, that: "The Fire Department turned out in a hurry yesterday at one p.m. in answer to an alarm for a fire on Third between Orange and Ann streets. It was in a new building in process of construction for Mr. Wm. Latimer, in a pile of shavings in one of the rooms. The fire was put out without much difficulty, and the services of the department were not required." The house is a simple, brick, two-story, pedimented and bracketed, plain Italianate house with full porch at the first level.

On May 4, 1886, Elizabeth Latimer deeded the property to her sister, Ellen Savage Waddell, who was the second wife of Alfred Moore Waddell. The Waddells moved into the new house in 1886, and it was their residence until about 1900, when it was sold by A. M. Waddell, Jr., to Sophy G. Campbell.

Waddell was a United States congressman, a well-known orator—he seems to have spoken at almost every cornerstone laying and dedication in the city in the last half of the nineteenth century—and a writer. He was a lawyer who edited the pro-Union newspaper *Wilmington Herald* in 1860–61, but he later served in the Confederate army. Waddell was elected mayor of Wilmington in 1898, and in 1909 he published his history of New Hanover, Brunswick, and Duplin counties.

JOHN C. BAILEY HOUSE

219 South Third Street
c. 1864.

John C. Bailey, born in Sweden, came to Wilmington about 1852 from Nashville, New Hampshire, and began working as a patternmaker in the Clarendon Iron Works. Evidently he had experience in that type of work, and in 1859 he entered into partnership with L. A. Hart in the iron foundry business.The firm of Hart & Bailey remained the domain of these two until Bailey died in 1880 and Hart in 1882. Ultimately, under Bailey's heirs, the firm evolved into the Wilmington Iron Works, which is still in operation

In 1863, Bailey bought the property here—which already contained a house at the corner where the church now stands—paying $10,000 in "lawful money of the Confederate States of America." He must have begun almost immediately to build a new house and was probably soon in residence. The house (fig. 66) is similar to several others nearby, irregularly massed, with coupled windows, a bay window, simple porch with canopy roof and fine Inalianate entry door. It retains the low hip roof and bracketed-and-vented frieze of the Wilmington Italianate, with paired vents over paired windows. The house remains virtually unchanged—the two-over-two sash from the later nineteenth century being the only noticeable exterior change.

The superbly cast and designed iron fence and gate (fig. 67) is one of the handsome features of the house and setting. Only three other fences of this design are known in Wilmington. One of these is around the Bellamy Mansion site at 503 Market Street (see fig. 130); a second was at the Cape Fear Club in the Dawson House at North Front and Chestnut streets; and a third is around the parking lot of the First Presbyterian Church, 111 South Third Street,

66. John C. Bailey House, 219 South Third Street, c. 1864.

which was the site of L. A. Hart's now-demolished house. Since two of the four known fences of this design are in front of the houses of the partners in the iron foundry of Hart & Bailey, it is reasonable to believe that they were cast in the Hart and Bailey foundry and used as advertising displays. The fences were probably manufactured sometime shortly after the Civil War, and inasmuch as Bailey began as a patternmaker, it is not too much to suppose that the design was his.

Polley & Hart, the predecessor firm to Hart & Bailey had done iron work for St. James Episcopal Church in 1847 and 1848, and in 1871 the firm contracted to do all the work for "ornamental panels and columns as per architrave drawings for St. James Episcopal Church." This work was wood. Given the certain knowledge that the Hart & Bailey firm produced wooden architectural detail it seems likely that the wooden detail used here was sawn and was also produced by the firm. They would not have used any product but their own.

The combination of Mr. Bailey's almost unchanged house and Hart & Bailey's cast-iron fence and ornamental wooden house detail shows the capability of the man and the firm—a rare combination and an extremely important dual survival.

The house was later the residence of Ida Brooks Kellam, author, genealogist, archivist, and major compiler of data about Wilmington and her people.

GAFFORD-PARSLEY HOUSE

224 South Third Street
c. 1854

John Gafford bought this property from John Gillett in 1850 for $350, a price that indicates there was no house on the lot. Stylistically, however, the

67. John C. Bailey House, fence and gate. Hart & Bailey, c. 1864.

house would seem to fit into the 1850s era, and when Gafford sold to Oscar G. Parsley in May of 1854, the price was $1,500—the rise in price probably indicating construction of this house.

From 1854 until well into the twentieth century, the house was in Parsley family ownership. Oscar G. Parsley lived elsewhere initially and died elsewhere, but some member of the family may always have been in residence here. In 1877 George D. Parsley, a son, was in residence. The 1881 resident was Oscar G. Parsley, Jr., who served as Brazilian consul.

In February of 1889 the property passed to Anna M. Wiggins, wife of Octavius A. Wiggins and daughter of Anna and Oscar G. Parsley. The February 4, 1889, will of Anna Parsley, by which Anna Wiggins inherited, identified the house as the one "in which I am now living." By 1926 P. W. Davis, who had married Mary Wiggins, was in residence. Davis was treasurer of Davis-Moore Paint Co., and acting treasurer of Atlantic Paint and Varnish Works, Inc.

Parsley family businesses included O. G. Parsley and Co., commission merchants and importers; Parsley & Wiggins, saw mills; and Hilton Steam Saw and Planing Mills.

A vented-and-bracketed Italianate house, the structure features two canopy porches, one on each street facade. Since the house is above the street on the Ann Street side, there are particularly good views here of the porch framing and of the frieze detail. The house seems relatively unchanged on the exterior from its c. 1893 appearance on the Sanborn maps.

Ann Street crosses South Third; begin 300 street numbers

At the beginning of the block there are fine walls and fences along Ann Street, which maintains some of its earlier paving material to the west.

HASELL-PARSLEY-FRENCH HOUSE

302 South Third Street
c. 1810; c. 1860: James F. Post, architect; c. 1910

William S. Hasell, who built his brick house here c. 1810, published the *Wilmington Gazette* from October 11, 1808, until his death in 1815. Hasell also owned the press that printed the *Gazette,* did other printing, and established both a reading room and a circulating library—both Wilmington firsts. Hasell mortgaged his property to provide capital, a usual way of raising operating funds, and in 1812 he mortgaged, by deed of trust, among other things, "his house and lot on South Third Street," so that the house was standing by that time.

When the Hasell lots passed to William Smith in 1822 the conveyance specifically mentions "the three story brick building formerly the residence of William S. Hasell, Esq." James Sprunt noted in his *Chronicles of the Lower Cape Fear* that the house was standing in the 1840s "on the south west corner of Third and Ann streets, set back from either street, and fronting on Ann Street, a house, showing decided marks of the ravages of time, but still a building of massive proportions, pink stuccoed and bearing indications . . . of having been the residence of people of wealth."

It evidently was standing in 1852, when Oscar G. Parsley purchased the lot and house from John McRae. The Hasell House may have been in bad condition, and Parsley seems to have wanted to change the orientation so that his dwelling would front on South Third rather than Ann Street. To do this, he had to change the topography of the site considerably, a task that he accomplished c. 1860 by building the retaining wall that one sees now on the Ann Street side and the west, or rear, of the lot. This created a flat lot on the western side of South Third and in the process buried at least the first story of the Hasell House.

Parsley had retained James F. Post to plan a house for him, and Post's ledgers (now located in the archives of the Lower Cape Fear Historical Society) include bills "to plans and cost for house at 3rd and Ann streets" and "to superintending the erection of a house on 3rd street." It is likely that Post's work included planning and erecting the retaining walls. Once this was done, the first floor and foundation of the former brick house was used as the foundation of the new house built facing South Third. The hip-roofed building atop the wall on Ann Street was evidently also constructed at this time.

Parsley maintained ownership of this house only until 1871, and in 1877 it passed to George R. French, Jr., a member of the firm of George R. French & Sons, wholesale and retail dealers in boots and shoes. His will on October 19, 1912, left the house and lot "where I now reside" to his wife, and she maintained ownership until 1931. It seems to have been the French family that brought the house to its present appearance, with work on the porches c. 1910.

Examination of the basement of the present house leaves no doubt of the existence of the Hasell House, and certainly the above-ground Italianate house, bracketed and vented, is a fine one, well planned for its site. The staggered facades and fine porch add measurably to the value of the house, as do the surviving wall and outbuildings.

MURCHISON HOUSE–DIOCESAN HOUSE

305 South Third Street
c. 1876: James Walker, architect; c. 1910; c. 1915

The brick stable, carriage house and quarters, which can be seen through the cast-iron gates at the south end of the lot, is older than the house and seems to have been the first structure built on the lot by its Murchison owners. Lucy W. Murchison acquired the property in 1872, and on October 29, 1873, she obtained an easement from George A. Peck, who lived next door to the south, which stated that "party of the first part [Murchison] has had built a brick building for a carriage house at s/e corner of her lot on the dividing line between the two lots." Evidently the carriage house was slightly over the line, and this had to be cleared with Peck, who owned the property onto which the carriage house encroached.

James Walker is said to have been the architect of the house, (fig. 68) built about 1876. Very little of the early house seems to remain except for its form and possibly the rear wing, which can be seen from Ann. The two-story porches there with radiating canopy ornaments and Chinese Chippendale balusters are quite handsome and may be from the earlier house.

The c. 1876 house seems to have had a mansard roof and a tower. The Sanborn maps (1884–1904) list the house as two stories with "french roof," and at the entrance a tower of three and one-half or four stories. The house had changed by the time the 1910 map was published, with the addition of the wing to the north (left) and the bay window in the ell. It had changed again by the publication of the 1915 map. By that time the mansard roof had been removed and the tower topped and the structure had received its present roof balustrade and possibly some of its finish. It is likely that framing of all the window openings is from the c. 1915 era—that in fact what one sees is basically the house as modified in the 1915 era. It is an extremely handsome and important Neoclassical Revival–style structure, in a good setting, with its surround of cast-iron fence, brick walls, gates, carriage house, and other buildings still retained on a sizeable lot. This, together with the quality of the trees and other plants at the site, add up to an especially fine complex.

Lucy W. Murchison, who owned the property, was the wife of David R. Murchison, and the couple resided here. Murchison, a Confederate veteran, was educated at the University of Virginia and accumulated wealth as a merchant. He became a director of the Bank of New Hanover and was president of the Wilmington Produce Exchange, of the Wilmington Compress and Warehouse Company, and of the Express Steamboat Company. He later also gained control of the Carolina Central Railroad.

Murchison died in 1882. His widow, who later married Clayton Giles, died in 1913. Her daughter, Lucille, who married Walter Marvin, conveyed the property some fifteen years before her death in 1968 to the Episcopal Diocese of East Carolina with an

68. Murchison House–Diocesan House, 305 South Third Street. James Walker, architect, c. 1876; c. 1910; c. 1915.

endowment for maintenance. It is now used as an office and diocesan house.

Wilmington architect James F. Post did at least some work on this house. His ledgers indicate that he was retained in 1897 for an "addition to butler's pantry & bath room wing."

HEIDE-BRIDGERS HOUSE

308 South Third Street
c. 1835; c. 1869; 1891: James F. Post, architect

A house was on the site as early as 1835 and is believed to have been incorporated into the present structure, a vented-and-bracketed Italianate house of c. 1869. R. E. Heide, of the firm of Heide and Company, was then resident, and it was probably he who enlarged and remodeled the early house, converting it to the Italian idiom of the era. The projecting gable, vented frieze and paired windows are features of several other houses of the immediate area from the 1860s era.

Heide's firm was located on South Water. They were ship brokers and chandlers who engaged in a regular ship agent's business. A 1902 chamber of commerce publication noted that Heide & Co. owned the 9 South Water Street premises, had been on the site for some thirty years, and while supplying vessels "does not transact a city grocery business." Heide was from Denmark, and at various times he

69. 300 block of South Third Street. Showing (left to right) are: 320 (not discussed); 318 (before 1880; c. 1885; c. 1912); 316 (1886); and 312 (c. 1840; c. 1890) South Third Street.

and his brother, A. S. Heide, were vice-consuls for Norway, Sweden, and Denmark. R. E. Heide died in 1895.

Mrs. M. E. Bridgers purchased the house from Heide in May of 1890. The widow of Robert R. Bridgers, president of the Wilmington and Weldon Railroad, she was connnected with several area houses. In September of 1891 she retained James F. Post to remodel this structure. On the exterior, Post added the bay window to the north and made some changes in the porch and sash but retained the basic Italianate exteriors. Mrs. Bridgers continued in residence until 1904.

PECK HOUSE

311 South Third Street
c. 1868

A bracketed-and-vented Italianate house, the dwelling seems to have been built c. 1868 as the family residence of George A. Peck. The house appears little changed on the exterior, except for sash, porch ornament, and porch ceiling. The property remained in the Peck family until recently.

Listed in the 1866–67 city directory as being in the hardware business, Peck was then residing at the home of Treat F. Peck on Second Street between Market and Dock. The 1875–76 directory lists George A. Peck as in business at 15 South Front Street and as residing on Third Street between Ann and Nun—already in this house. In the same directory T. F. Peck is shown with a business at Front and Dock and a home on Third between Ann and Nun—evidently the two were still sharing a business and a residence. By the time the 1883 directory was published, the two had established separate business and residence addresses. George A. Peck is listed as residing at 309 South Third, an address that does not exist. The 1885 and subsequent directories list him as residing at 311 South Third, the correct street address for this house.

In one bad pun, oft quoted locally, the *Star* reported on December 7, 1874, that "The fowl house of Mr. George Peck, who resides on Third Street between Ann and Nun streets, was broken open Friday night and robbed of two fine turkeys which were being fattened for Christmas. Of course, the thief is in a 'Peck' of trouble."

McKAY-GREEN HOUSE

312 South Third Street
c. 1840; c. 1890

Murdock McKay, long the New Hanover County Register of Deeds, purchased land here in 1817. He died in 1843. It was likely his son Kenneth Murchison McKay who built the house, though he too soon died and the property passed to McKay heirs.

The house seems to have been updated and given an Italianate look about 1870. On March 27, 1873, it was advertised in the *Star:* "For Sale, on the 27th instant, we shall sell at the exchange corner that valuable house and lot situated on the west side of Third Street, between Ann and Nun streets, at present occupied by Dr. D. M. Buie. The lot has a front of 66 feet on Third Street, running back west 165 feet. The improvements consist of a dwelling containing six rooms, kitchen, water and all necessary outhouses on the premises."

Gray's 1881 map shows the southern part of the house as it is today, with Dr. William Henry Green in residence. Dr. Green, a druggist, added the northern wing c. 1890 and that brought the house to its present size and decoration.

The dwelling is interesting for the manner in which each of the styles is frankly expressed (see fig. 69). Little effort was made to integrate them or make them compatible. The southern house is unabashedly Italianate; the northern house is as obviously Queen Anne in style. Even elements such as window surrounds and sash differ, though the bracketed-and-vented frieze does carry around both houses. The combination of the two design eras in distinct parts of the dwelling and the use of the unifying frieze is unique within the area.

J. WILLIAMS MURCHISON HOUSE

316 South Third Street
1886

Henry Bacon, Sr.—writing to his wife, then in the north, on September 1, 1886—described the effect of the earthquake of the previous night on Wilmington. After general observations and noting that some chimneys had been damaged he continued: "So was one [chimney] of Mr. Murchison's (new house) and a small piece of the wall at the bay-window just under the cornice was shaken out. It is only one thickness of brick you know." Bacon's reference to the dwelling as "new house" works out well with the directory and map evidence, and there seems no doubt that the Murchison residence was being finished in late 1886, so that the construction date can be fixed on that year.

The Sanborn maps indicate that there were porches on the front and south sides of the house, removed in the twentieth century when the present entry was added. Otherwise the basic Wilmington Plain house character remains, lifted to Chateauesque style by the roof, with its sharp pitch and patterned slate-shingle design and by the finish of the street facade (see fig. 69). The roof maintains an overhang, with brackets and a paneled frieze. There is also a molded wood cornice above the corbeled brick atop the second level windows.

Basically this house and the Burruss House next door to the south at 318 South Third have the same plan. It is the material from which they are constructed and the design of the finish and ornament used that give them such individuality.

BURRUSS HOUSE

318 South Third Street
before 1880; c. 1885; c. 1912

Edwin E. Burruss, founder and president of the First National Bank of Wilmington and one of the organizers of the Clarendon Water Works Co., bought the property here in 1880. There was a house standing at the time, and some of it to the north rear seems to have been incorporated into the present structure built by Burruss around 1885 (see fig. 69).

The family has a tragic history. A six-year-old daughter, Katie, died on September 2, 1886, on Greenville Sound. Mr. Burruss died in March of 1887, and his wife, Elizabeth Northrop, survived him by only four months. Another daughter, Elizabeth, died here of typhoid fever in 1910. After the death of the parents in 1887, Mrs. William A. Cumming, whose husband had died in 1886 and who was Mrs. Burruss's sister, moved into this house to care for the small children left by the Burruss couple. The two sisters were members of the family of Northrop and Cumming, one of the prime mercantile and industrial families of the late nineteenth century in Wilmington.

The dwelling is a cross between the Italianate Wilmington house and the Wilmington Plain house in its massing and form, but is lifted from those styles by its finish and decoration. Some of the detail has Eastlake characteristics, and some of it Stick-style characteristics, though the entire dwelling might be called Carpenter Queen Anne.

Whatever the style, the finish of the house is superb, and essentially unchanged since construction—the porch extended only across the front until c. 1912, when it was extended around the north side of the house within the L—and one of the outstanding Wilmington houses of its era. The eaves' decoration of bargeboard, the rafter brackets and gable ornament, the vertical framing, and the carved frieze course are matched in complexity and beauty by the porch of clustered open posts, sawn balustrade, carved frieze, and entry ornament.

70. Stick-style Queen Anne–style house (Lucy M. Giles House), 321 South Third Street, c. 1895.

STICK-STYLE/QUEEN ANNE–STYLE HOUSE (Lucy M. Giles House)

321 South Third Street
c. 1895

The Sanborn maps for 1893 show the Nathan Green House (see fig. 83) on this site. In 1898 the Nathan Green House is shown as having been moved diagonally across the block eastward and turned to front on South Fourth, its present location. On the South Third Street site, two new houses had been built by Charles and Lucy M. Giles. The structures at 317–319 and 321 South Third were almost identical to each other.

Of the two, number 321 (fig. 70) remains almost unchanged on the exterior. It features a gable roof with false gablet and tower above the true gable. The roof overhang is supported by cut brackets, and stick ornament appears in gable and porch decoration. The second level of the facade, above the porch, is shingled. The porch features chamfered posts with brackets forming arcades. A cut circle frieze appears above the bracketed arcade. A double-tiered, symmetrical balustrade is used along with tent-topped newels at the entrance.

The house is a fine example of the eclecticism of the 1890s—essentially a vertical Italianate form with Queen Anne massing and roof forms to the street and Stick-style ornamentation.

KING HOUSE

326 South Third Street
c. 1872

A bracketed-and-vented Italianate house, the structure features a facade on two planes with canopy porch in the L. The facade projects to the south front, where there are paired windows and a peak in the roof above. The exterior appears to be relatively unchanged from its early appearance.

The property was purchased by Charles and Mary J. King in 1872. Presumably they began construction almost immediately. By the time Gray published his 1881 map, the house is shown with its present configuration and labeled "Chas. King." The King couple maintained ownership until 1895, when the house was sold to Ann and Oliver P. Meares.

71. Stemmerman-Whitehead House, 401 South Third Street, c. 1885.

Nun Street crosses South Third; begin 400 street numbers

Within the 400 block of South Third the fine architectural character of the previous four blocks is continued. The houses are of consistent scale and materials with landscaped surrounds. The fine iron fence of the former R. W. Hicks residence at 418 South Third (now demolished) remains. At the southern end of the block stands the Cape Fear Apartment building. When it was nearing completion in 1911, the October 9 *Dispatch* called it "One of the Handsomest Buildings of its Kind to be Found in This Section" and continued:

After months of steady work on the part of carpenters, brick masons, electricians, plumbers and other artisans, the Cape Fear Apartment at the northwest corner of Third and Church is now practically completed. It is one of the handsomest and most convenient apartment houses in the state and will undoubtedly prove most popular with renters. The real estate firm of M. C. Darby & Co. has the agency for the building and many of the apartments have already been rented. However, there are others left, well situated, and persons who are seeking a desirable home in one of the most select sections of the city would do well to interview the real estate agency without delay. The structure is four stories in height. It is modernly constructed and splendidly equipped. There are sixteen apartments, as well as a large cafe. The apartments range from three to six rooms in size. All are equipped with modern conveniences.

STEMMERMAN-WHITEHEAD HOUSE

401 South Third Street
c. 1885

A two-story, frame, Queen Anne–style house (fig. 71), the dwelling has a noticeable roof overhang with brackets, geometrically sawn bargeboards, and iron cresting. A radiating gable ornament shingle siding, and a band frieze are used. Separating the levels on the north is a shingled pent. The porch is high and hip-roofed with chamfered posts and a

72. McKoy House, 402 South Third Street. James F. Post, architect, 1887.

double-tiered spoke balustrade. The handsome house seems little changed on the exterior.

Evidently the dwelling was constructed for Charles H. Stemmerman, who first operated a grocery on Castle Street before moving to his grocery on South Front. The house passed from Stemmerman ownership shortly after it was built, and by 1895 was occupied by William A. and Cornelia Whitehead. The house remained in Whitehead family ownership until 1972.

McKOY HOUSE

402 South Third Street
1887: James F. Post, architect; Alfred Howe, builder

Post's authorship of this house (fig. 72), Wilmington's best representative of the Stick style and a first-rate example for any area, is based on the partial survival of his drawings. Plans labeled "Map of Plan," "Foundation Plan," and "Roof Plan," and signed "James F. Post, architect, 210 Princess Street, Wilmington, N.C., March 1887," survive.

Stick-style buildings like this one feature tall proportions, steep roofs, complex plans, and irregular massing. To this is added the use of stick framing and decoration. In the McKoy House this is especially noticeable in the gables, which are articulated with grids, fans, brackets and bosses. As with others of its style, the verandas are extensive. The McKoy House may well have been painted two or more colors when built, the colors emphasizing the style and directing the eye to the varied design elements.

William Berry McKoy, local attorney, built the house and lived there with his family until his death in 1928. It is still occupied by his descendants. McKoy graduated from Princeton in 1876, read law with George J. Strong in Raleigh, and was admitted to the bar in 1879. In 1876 he organized the Historic and Scientific Society of Wilmington, a public manifestation of his lifelong interest in local history. A title lawyer, McKoy made extensive abstracts of New Hanover titles, which he later used in his historical writing.

On December 15, 1886, McKoy married Katherine Bacon, daughter of Henry and Elizabeth Bacon and sister of the architect Henry Bacon, and of Francis Bacon, an archaeologist, furniture designer, and builder. All were frequent visitors in this house.

The authors Henry Bacon McKoy and Elizabeth F. McKoy, who have written extensively on Wilmington history, were both born and raised here.

KENLY HOUSE

405 South Third Street
c. 1891

This Queen Anne–style house seems to have remained unchanged on the exterior since its construction c. 1891. The single-plane porch seems somewhat unusual for the multiplaned house, but its stick balustrade and spindle course are typical of the style in this area.

John R. Kenly was first general manager and later president of the Atlantic Coast Line Railroad. It was he who built the house as a family dwelling. One of the Kenly children, Eleanor, married Carl Kelton Bacon, another of the sons of Henry Bacon, Sr., at a wedding here in October 1902. Mrs. Kenly, who died here in June of 1917, was, according to the *Dispatch* of June 25 "the first president of the local Young Women's Christian Association (YWCA) and was one of the most ardent workers for its foundation."

ALLEN-GREEN HOUSE

406 South Third Street
c. 1886: J. S. Allen builder; c. 1929: Lynch & Foard, architects

With the 1929 remodeling, this Stick-style structure added Neoclassical Revival elements. A balcony above the entrance and balconies beneath each of the full-length windows of the first level replaced the earlier porch. The effect of the changes is to emphasize the verticality of the dwelling.

J. S. Allen, who built the house, was a local contractor and builder who constructed this house as his own dwelling. He is said to have been working on the house in 1886, when the Charleston earthquake hit Wilmington. Allen studied damage in Wilmington then traveled to Charleston to study damage there. Based on his examination of the 1886 damage, he incorporated changes into his own house that were intended to allow it to withstand sizable earth tremors or quakes. The house is said to move noticeably during a high wind.

Allen sold the house to Hector and Ida D. Green in 1891. A frequent visitor during the time the Green couple lived here was Paul Green, a nephew of Mr. Green. Paul Green, author of *The Lost Colony* and *The Common Glory,* was the originator of the outdoor symphonic drama, usually based on historical themes and particularly popular in the south.

The Green couple occupied the house until they sold it to Mrs. William Joseph Woodward in 1927. Mrs. W. D. McMillan, who remodeled the house in 1929, was her daughter.

HOGE-WOOD HOUSE

407 South Third Street
1891: From Dr. Hoge's drawings; A. B. Cook, builder

A fine Queen Anne–style house, this is a two-story structure with complex roof and a cross-gable plan. The house remains remarkably unchanged since 1891, except that c. 1895 the porch was continued around the north end of the house to the hexagonal-bay tower. The dwelling exhibits the multiplaned and multiple-roof hallmarks of the style.

The Reverend Peyton H. Hoge, minister of the First Presbyterian Church from January 4, 1886, to July of 1899, built the house during his ministry and lived there until 1899. It was the Reverend Mr. Hoge who gained fame as the minister who performed the marriage ceremony for Mary Lily Kenan and Henry H. Flagler during their wedding at Liberty Hall in Kenansville.

After the Reverend Mr. Hoge moved in 1899, George Rountree purchased the house and made it his residence. Rountree, an attorney, was a member of the firm of Rountree and Carr, and served as a state legislator, judge of the Superior Court, and president of the North Carolina Bar Association.

Judge Rountree sold the property to Dr. Edward Jenner Wood in 1910, and Dr. Wood lived in the house until his death in 1928. His obituary in the

Star called him "an authority on Pellagra-Sprue," and noted that he had studied at the University of North Carolina and practiced and studied medicine at the University of Pennsylvania and in Germany at the University of Munich.

Dr. Wood was one of the first to recognize the national danger of pellagra and to publicize its existence here. He wrote *A Treatise on Pellagra* published in 1912, and a large number of articles on the disease. His interests led him to study abroad, where he found his speciality recognized. One article in the *Star*, on May 16, 1920, noted one such period abroad:

> *Dr. Edward Jenner Wood, of this city, has just received the degree of doctor of tropical medicine in the Royal College of Physicians and Surgeons. This is a degree held by very few American physicians, owning to the fact that English colleges are the only ones which now offer the course.*
>
> *He was also graduated in the distinction group of the London School of Tropical Medicine. This is a subject in which Dr. Wood has long been interested, and his friends hope that he may contribute some valuable discoveries in this branch to the profession.*
>
> *Having finished this work, Dr. Wood expects to go back to Guy's Hospital in London, and spend a month or two there. June and July he will be in Edinburgh studying with Dr. Thomas Lewis, the greatest living authority on the functions of the heart; and in September with Sir James McKenzie at St. Andrews.*
>
> *After a short visit to Lady Osler, the widow of the distinguished court physician, at Oxford, Dr. Wood expects to sail for home, arriving in Wilmington the latter part of September.*

Dr. Wood was the son of Dr. Thomas Fanning Wood, an equally famous Wilmington physician. The elder Wood was the first secretary of the state board of health, edited the *North Carolina Medical Journal*, and earned national reputations as both a physician and a botanist.

C. W. WORTH HOUSE

412 South Third Street
1895: D. Getaz of Knoxville, Tennessee, contractor; c. 1910

C. W. Worth, who acquired land here in 1889 and was listed in the city directory as in residence by 1894–95, was a merchant engaged in the wholesale grocery trade. He also dealt as a commission merchant in cotton and naval stores. The main buildings of the Worth Company, established c. 1859 and operating under various other names before C. W. Worth came into partnership, were at Nutt and Grace streets. By 1905 Worth was also president of the Cape Fear Machine Works. This company and the Worth Company remained his major commercial interests, though he was connected with several other firms. The family maintained occupancy of the house until 1930.

Worth built his Queen Anne–style house in 1895. It featured a great center projection, curving gently outward from the southern facade and sweeping back to the recessed north end of the facade. A porch ran across in front of the towerlike projection. Within a relatively short time after its construction, c. 1910, the house was severely remodeled to give it a more Neoclassical Revival character. The northern side of the front facade was brought out, the center bay was greatly enlarged and made more oval, a tower was added at the southeastern corner of the front facade, and several changes were made in the south facade. The porch was contained on either side of the center tower, as now, but it jutted outward as an uncovered patio before the tower.

ATKINSON-BATES-STEVENSON HOUSE

419 South Third Street
c. 1873; 1895: remodelling by Stout, contractor; c. 1904

Built either by Edward Kidder or by John Wilder Atkinson, the structure seems to have been a relatively straightforward Italianate house with a flat facade. Kidder sold the property to Atkinson in 1873 for $3,000. He had purchased it in 1846 for $650, and the sale price to Atkinson would seem to indicate that a house was standing in 1873. Atkinson maintained ownership until 1882, when the property passed to Isaac Bates. James C. Stevenson and Elizabeth Jocelyn Stevenson purchased it at sale in 1895. It was the Stevenson family that made the c. 1895 and c. 1904 changes in the dwelling.

The 1895 remodeling added the bay window and some of the trim. It is likely that the major Neoclassical Revival remodeling came about 1904. The center pavilion, the present porch, and the sunburst and floral swag frieze are probably from this era. With these changes, the new entranceway (the older entrance remains on the original wall plane, while

3. Thalian Hall, interior, 305 Princess Street. John M. Trimble, architect, James F. Post, supervising architect, 1854–58; 1871; 1881; 1895; 1904; H. E. Bonitz, architect, 1909.

4. St. John's Masonic Lodge, overmantel, 114 Orange Street, J. J. Bellanger, artist, c. 1809.

the pavilion forms a recessed entry for it), and indeed the entire facade, received almost a totally new outlook.

For those who study the facade, the old house can still be seen peeking through, especially in the vented-and-bracketed Italianate frieze and the earlier entrance.

L. N. BONEY HOUSE

425 South Third Street
1925; L. N. Boney, architect

"A handsome dwelling is being erected at the northeast corner of Third and Church streets by L. N. Boney, well known architect" (*News Dispatch*, June 8, 1925).

Designed and built by the architect as his own residence, this Georgian Revival house is two story, brick, and with a gable roof. Dormers are pedimented with finely detailed sash and pilasters. The Paladian windows in the gable ends, the dentil cornice, and the fluted pilasters with Corinthian capitals of the portico continue the classical detail. The entrance is beneath an elliptical fanlight and is flanked by sidelights. Though the columns of the portico have been changed, they were originally Tower of the Winds and paired at the corners, as are the replacements.

Boney was probably the most important of the Wilmington architects of the 1920s, succeeding the architects who had dominated the Wilmington scene at the turn of the century. He first worked in Wilmington with W. J. Wilkins & Co., and in 1922 he established his own firm, which is still in operation. Boney lived here until c. 1940.

Buildings designed by Boney include the New Hanover County High School on Market Street; Trinity Methodist Church on Market Street; the New Hanover County Courthouse Annex on Princess, the annexes to Tileston School, 400 Ann Street, 1936 and subsequently; and a large number of residences and other religious, civic, and commercial buildings. His three sons, Charles H. Boney, Leslie N. Boney, Jr., and William J. Boney, all architects, continue the architectural firm established by their father, Leslie N. Boney, Architect.

Church Street crosses South Third; begin 500 street numbers

Castle Street, at the far end of the block, was a major late nineteenth- and early twentieth-century commercial artery. Both Castle and Church streets led to major passenger and freight wharfs and terminals on the waterfront.

WILMINGTON PLAIN HOUSE

508 South Third Street
Mid-nineteenth century

One of the Wilmington Plain houses, this is a two-story frame structure with a low gable roof, flush raking cornice, and molded box cornice. The present double porch is probably a later addition, though it may have replaced a similar porch and goes quite well with the house.

The six-over-six sash and the entrance with six-light transom and four-light sidelights are indicative of a mid-nineteenth century era of construction, as are other design elements. This stylistic evidence fits well with the assigned tax date of c. 1850.

From 1912 to 1922 the house was the residence of the Reverend and Mrs. J. S. Crowley; the Reverend Mr. Crowley was a popular Presbyterian minister and pastor of the Immanuel Presbyterian Church. During his occupancy here, he performed the marriage ceremony for many Wilmingtonians in this residence. Mrs. Crowley died here in July 1917.

Castle Street crosses South Third; begin 600 street numbers

Though Castle and Queen streets are not included in this volume and it covers less than it should on South Third Street, that should not be taken to mean that these areas are not worth architectural and historical notice.

THE PATENT STONE HOUSE

610 South Third Street
1905: R. H. Brady, builder

Robert Henderson Brady, a local contractor and builder, received a building permit in February 1905 for construction of this house to be built of artificial stone and brick and to be used as a family residence. Evidently Brady intended to move from his home at 408 Church Street to the newer house on South Third, but if he did so, he also maintained the property on Church Street, and by 1907 he was living there once again. In subsequent years the house was occupied by the Peterson and Pollock families.

By advertisement in the May 26, 1907, *Star*, the house was offered "For Sale—On South Third Street, brand new stone dwelling, nine rooms, electric lights, porcelain tub, sewerage, etc. Good deep lot, alley on site." The asking price was $3,500, and according to the *Star* of June 2, 1907, H. L. Henderson purchased the dwelling.

The Sanborn insurance maps show this site as vacant in 1904 and as having a "patent stone" house there in 1910. A *Dispatch* article on May 28, 1903, identifies patent stone as, "hollow concrete stone, which was recently introduced into Wilmington. The new stone has created a most favorable impression here and before long it is expected that many buildings will be constructed with the material, which is cheaper than brick and as durable as stone." The Wilmington Stone & Construction Company seems to have been the early manufacturer.

A large number of residences and other buildings were indeed constructed of this stone. The 1904 Boys Brigade Armory at Second and Church Streets, constructed through funds from Mary Lily Kenan Flagler and from plans by architect Charles McMillen, as well as several houses in Carolina Place and businesses in all parts of the city, also used the material.

This is one of the few large houses so constructed that still survives in very much its original condition. It is a handsome structure in a simple Queen Anne mode, with full porch featuring Tuscan columns and turned balustrade. It is the house itself—with walls of large rough-hewn block, cast to resemble granite such as that used in the Bridgers House at South Third and Dock streets—that proves the capability of patent stone. Water table and window lintels are cast, as is the frieze just below the eaves; it features a running band of ivy vine and leaves. If Brady intended to use the house as an advertisement for the capability of the stone, it must have been successful. The house is also important as an example of his craftsmanship, for he was one of the preeminent builders in turn-of-the-century Wilmington.

Queen Street crosses South Third

ALFRED HOWE HOUSE

301 Queen Street; northeast corner of Queen and South Third
c. 1870: Alfred Howe, builder

Alfred Howe, a black contractor and builder, is listed in the 1866–67 city directory as living on Queen Street at South Third. This house may either be an enlargement of the house he then occupied, or a new house of c. 1870. It is shown on Gray's 1881 map and must have been constructed by Howe himself, since he was then in the business of house contracting and construction.

The dwelling is one of the few mansard, or French Second-Empire, houses in Wilmington and the only one-story dwelling of this size and bulk. Others are two-stories plus the roof story and seem quite tall and vertical. This house is one story high plus the mansard-roof story and seems quite wide and horizontal. Somewhat modified with new siding, roof covering, and porch, its fine lines and basic awareness of the style are still obvious.

Howe, his brothers Anthony and Pompey, his sons John and Valentine, and his grandson Valentine, Jr., were all carpenters, builders and contractors, and all important in construction in Wilmington. Alfred was a member of St. Marks Episcopal Church, 220 North Sixth Street (fig. 99) and held various political and civic positions. He built the Mary Jane Langdon House, 408 Market Street (fig. 122) and was a builder of St. Marks. No full list of buildings by Alfred or any of his kinsmen has yet been compiled, but this house and other buildings that he is known to have worked with certainly show him to have been a major builder.

In noting his death, the October 7, 1892, *Messenger* carried the following: "Alfred Howe, a well known colored citizen of Wilmington, who has amassed a fortune of some $25,000 or $30,000, died yesterday. He was aged 75 years and leaves two sons and two daughters. He was senior warden of St. Marks Episcopal church. He and his two brothers, Anthony and Pompey, were carpenters, but purchased their liberty when young men. He and his brothers all accrued property and gave their children good educations." Another note in the same edition of the same newspaper carried the death announcement: "Died. In this city, Thursday, October 6th, 1892, at 12:15 p.m., at his late residence, corner Third and Queen streets, Alfred Howe, aged 74 years 9 months and 7 days. The funeral services will be held at St. Marks P.E. Church this Friday afternoon October 7th at 4 o'clock."

North Fourth Street

Market Street northward to Campbell Street and the railroad tracks

Chestnut Street crosses North Fourth; begin 200 house numbers

SCHULKEN HOUSE

222 North Fourth Street
c. 1880; c. 1895

The lot on which the house stands was acquired by Margarethe Bailey in 1878 and sold in 1888 by James B. Bailey and wife to Margarethe Schulken. This was probably a transfer within the family, with Margarethe Schulken and Margarethe Bailey being the same person. It is likely that the house was built during the ten year period from 1878 to 1888.

It was evidently the Schulken couple who made the late nineteenth-century changes to the house, adding the bay window, changing the roof to a gable form, and adding paneled and corbeled brick chimneys, possibly atop the older flues. Englehardt Schulken is listed in the directories as a grocer, as a salesman, and as secretary-treasurer of Adrian Co., wholesale grocers. The dwelling remained with heirs until 1971.

A vented-and-bracketed Italianate house, the structure is given great individuality by later changes. A brick wall with corbeled top encloses the yard of the house, which sits slightly above street level.

Grace Street crosses North Fourth; begin 300 street numbers

PEARSALL HOUSE

309 North Fourth Street
c. 1875

Gray's 1881 map lists the house as the residence of O. Pearsall. Pearsall maintained ownership at least through 1890, residing at this address. The dwelling is typical of the vented-and-bracketed Italianate genre, except for the porch, which may be later. The porch has a turned balustrade and chamfered posts with paired brackets above the molded neck.

Oscar Pearsall seems to have worked with the firm of Edwards & Hall, wholesale grocers, until 1875, when he became a partner in the firm, and its name was changed to Hall & Pearsall. Pearsall remained a member of the firm, acting as its manager until 1907, when he withdrew to form the firm of Pearsall & Co., wholesale grocers and fertilizer manufacturers. Their fertilizer factory was located at Fernside, employed from twenty-five to forty hands, and made several types of high-grade fertilizer. The wholesale grocery part of the business dealt mainly in staples such as flour, rice, coffee, meal, grain, hay, and sugar. A 1912 description in a chamber of commerce publication noted that "In flour they make specialities of 'Uzit,' 'North Star,' and 'Lotus' in full patents, and 'Pillsbury's Best,' a spring wheat bakers' flour."

Red Cross Street crosses North Fourth; begin 500 street numbers

ST. ANDREWS PRESBYTERIAN CHURCH–HOLY TRINITY CHURCH

520 North Fourth Street
1888–89: A. G. Bauer, architect and builder;
1910–11: Sprunt Memorial Hall Annex, Rhodes & Underwood, builders

The Second Presbyterian Church was an outgrowth of the religious revival that swept Wilmington in 1858, leading the First Presbyterian Church to construct a chapel on Chestnut as a thank offering. Soon the Second Presbyterian Church was organized and began worshiping in the Chestnut Street building. The congregation remained there until after April 11, 1862, when, because of chaotic conditions created by the Civil War and the yellow-fever epidemic then raging in Wilmington, the church be-

73. St. Andrews Presbyterian Church–Holy Trinity Church, 520 North Fourth Street. A. G. Bauer, architect, 1888–89.

came inoperative. The remaining members of the congregation returned to the First Presbyterian Church to worship. In 1866 a committee was authorized to sell the Chestnut Street building, and it was sold to a black congregation, the Chestnut Street United Presbyterian Church, in 1867. (See 710½ Chestnut Street at MacRae Street, fig. 109.)

At a January 2, 1872, meeting, the Second Presbyterian Church was reactivated, and on February 12, 1872, land was purchased on the southeast corner of North Fourth and Campbell. A church building was erected on Campbell and dedicated on May 4, 1873.

By a September 19, 1888, vote of the congregation, a change in the name of the church was authorized. St. Andrews was suggested, and the name was adopted on the first ballot.

In June of 1888, amid discussions of changes in the 1873 building, a resolution was adopted to build a new church. Plans and specifications were furnished by Adolphus Gustavus Bauer. Bauer, who had worked with Samuel Sloan in the construction and design of the governor's mansion in Raleigh, was at the time considering locating for business in Wilmington. The 1889 city directory lists him as both architect and contractor and builder. Though this building (fig. 73) stands alone as an identifiable result of his Wilmington practice, Bauer was an important architect, and this building is valuable as an area example of his work.

On October 1, 1888, the groundbreaking for the new church occurred. The cornerstone was laid on October 16, 1888, and the building dedicated on June 9, 1889. St. Andrews then had some two hundred twenty-six members.

An account of the dedication in the *North Carolina Presbyterian* for June 12, 1889, noted that seats were furnished for eight hundred people during the dedication services, and "no one was crowded . . . as the church is furnished with opera chairs. These chairs are of very fine quality, finished in cherry and crimson plush, and go far in contributing to the great beauty of the building as well as its comfort. The congregation thinks there is no handsomer church in the state. . . . One point was watched with anxiety, the acoustic properties of the building, but all anxiety was dispelled, for the hearing was perfect."

These seats may have been supplied by a local firm. The *Weekly Star* noted on June 14, 1889, that "most of the inside and outside finishes were made at Parsley & Wiggins' mill." The June 8 *Messenger* had noted:

> *The pulpit is quite a handsome piece of furniture and was made by Messrs. Parsley & Wiggins. It is made of curly pine and trimmed in walnut.*
>
> *The communion table is also made of pine, trimmed with walnut, and has in walnut letters in relief the inscription "In Rememberance." The piece of furniture is the handiwork of Mr. George Ziegler.*

At least one other part of the church furnishings was of local manufacture, the fiber matting used to carpet the gallery. The June 8 *Messenger* said it was "presented by the Acme Manufacturing Company."

By 1900 the church was ready for redecorating, and the *Star* announced on July 7: "The interior of St. Andrews Presbyterian Church will be thoroughly remodeled by Duryea and Potter, the well known New York designers. Contractor Thad F. Tyler will begin putting in the scaffolding today." A new organ, made by Henry Pilchir's Sons, Louisville, Kentucky, was installed in early 1906. The *Dispatch* reported on February 23 a recital to inaugurate it and called it "a very handsome instrument." The organ remained in the building until late 1976, when it was removed for renovation and subsequent use by another church.

A permit was issued for the construction of Memorial Hall in late 1910. The *Star* noted on December 15, under "Building Permit": "St. Andrews Presbyterian Church; two-story, slate roof, brick structure, extension of the church on Campbell, near Fourth street, building to be known as Memorial Hall, given by Mr. W. H. Sprunt; estimated cost, $14,000; Rhodes & Underwood, contractors." On October 9, 1911, the *Dispatch* reported the structure completed and noted that J. C. Stewart was superintendent of construction.

Though the source of glass and other furnishings is not known, at least some of the later windows were German. The *Star*, on January 16, 1912, reported on the dedication of "two handsome windows . . . to the memory of Mrs. Jane Dalziel Sprunt and Mrs. Julia Fillyaw," and noted that both windows were "made in Munich, Germany."

A new manse was constructed at 516 North Fourth Street, just south of the church, in 1908.

St. Andrews ceased to exist on June 1, 1944, when the congregation merged with the Church of the Covenant on Market Street at South Fourteenth. The new churches adopted the name St. Andrews–Covenant Presbyterian Church, utilizing the Market Street property and selling the St. Andrews property. The cornerstone of St. Andrews, some of its stained glass, and some of the furnishings are now in the St. Andrews–Covenant building.

Holy Trinity Church assumed ownership of the North Fourth Street property, where ministers such as J. W. Primrose and Alexander Doak McClure preached.

Campbell Street crosses North Fourth; begin 600 street numbers

CONSOLIDATED MARKET AND FIRE ENGINE HOUSE NO. 3

602–6 North Fourth Street
1907–8: H. L. Bonitz, architect; R. H. Brady, builder

As early as 1745, regulations were adopted by the city to lessen the danger of fires and to regulate operation of the town market. As the town grew, more markets were necessary, and several were built on the borders of the city or at convenient locations. As fire-fighting equipment became available, the city also assumed the expense of maintaining and equipping a fire department—not surprising in a city that had had so many devastating fires. It is also not surprising to see fire and market houses combined.

Fire Engine House no. 3 was located here at least as early as 1905. A picture made that year shows the fire engine and the horses that pulled it in front of the station. That building was torn down in 1907 for construction of the present dual-use structures, which was designed for horse-drawn equipment and included a stable.

74. Consolidated Market and Fire Engine House no. 3, 602–6 North Fourth Street. H. E. Bonitz, architect, 1907–8.

The two-story building (fig. 74) at the corner of Campbell, 602 North Fourth Street, was the fire engine house. Of fine decorative brick, the first story of this and the adjacent market is in horizontal brick bands. Though the firehouse has been painted, it is likely that this building, which also has Flemish-Bond brickwork, was decorated with darkened headers as are the market-house first floor and its center section. Both buildings are marked by corbel-based capped turrets that pierce the cornice and rise above the corbeled edge.

While the fire station has a relatively flat stepped parapet at the roof line, the market, at 606 North Fourth Street, has a stepped gable, a center oculus with corbel key on the cornice above, and paneled sides.

A center entrance to the market, of herringbone-batten double doors, has a gauged-stone arch surround. Storefronts to each side consist of double doors with two flat panels beneath an elongated glass panel. This is topped by a transom. Transoms are also atop the store windows that flank these doors. The side units are sixteen-light sash.

Several alterations have occurred in the fire station, but all of the bays, with the exception of the center fire-engine entrance, are topped with flat stone arches and keystones, so that they are easy to spot even if they have been sealed. A brick stringcourse separates the first and second levels of both buildings. On the street corner of the firehouse a stone arched base interrupts the stringcourse on each facade to support the slightly projecting corner tower. Beneath each of the stone arches is a panel in a stone surround. The panel on the North Fourth Street side bears the following legend: "Consolidated Market and Fire Engine House, A.D.—W. E. Springer, Mayor—1908, Market Committee, H. Rathjen, Chairman, W. E. King, J. A. Kerr, Chas. Schnibbin—Chief of F. Dept., H. L. Bonitz, architect, R. R. Brady contractor." The other panel is blank.

At the corner a single turret terminates the tower, with an arched corbeled course supporting the entablature. Adjacent to the tower on each side and at the end of the Campbell facade of the building, the turrets are in threes. The corner set of turrets is shorter and has a panel beneath each side. The panel on the North Fourth facade contains the date 1907; those on the Campbell facade contain rosettes.

The buildings are handsome, evoking more of the nineteenth century in appearance than the twentieth. This is not surprising because, though they were built in the twentieth century, they were intended for fire equipment that was horse drawn. The market was constructed for farmers and merchants who also still depended largely on horses for transportation and drayage; the automotive age would not fully arrive until the post–World War I era.

North Fourth Street crosses the railroad tracks by bridge over the cut

In its editions of February 19, 1891, the *Star* suggested "Quite an interesting panorama is presented nightly to loungers standing on Fourth street bridge and watching the moving of trains with their many lights and the long row of lights at the station in the distance." Though the trains are gone and the station has been replaced, the bridge is still a fine place to view the influence of the railroad on the city. To the east the vista to the North Sixth Street Truss Bridge is particularly fine (see fig. 100).

The area across the tracks to the north is Brooklyn—Manhattan and the Bronx were farther out along Wrightsville Avenue. It was the Brooklyn area and its nineteenth-century development that led to the location of the fire station and market at North Fourth and Campbell. The trolley line, which ran from North Front up Red Cross Street, branched northward along North Fourth. The traffic and accessibility that the trolley generated accounted for much of the development along the street during the later part of the nineteenth century.

The Brooklyn Baptist Church was at the corner of North Fourth and Brunswick, and Gray's 1881 map shows the area already well developed. Evidently the name was applied to an earlier development. The *Star* for April 29, 1874, reported: "forty-one stores in successful operation in that part of the city north of the Wilmington and Weldon railroad, as reported by a gentleman who went to the trouble of counting them a few days since. Another one is in process of erection and arrangements are being made for the establishment of an auction house in that locality. The improvements in that part of the city have been very rapid in the last few years."

South Fourth Street

Market Street southward to Castle

South Fourth Street is narrow and tree lined and has a pleasant mix of residential, civic, and other uses. Street paving remains brick through much of the area. Sidewalks of brick survive at several places, as do brick carriage ways, granite curbing, and Belgian paving block.

Market Street

TEMPLE OF ISRAEL

1 South Fourth Street
1875–76: Alex. Strausz, architect; James Walker, supervising architect; Abbott's Building Company, builders; Captain R. S. Radcliff, construction superintendent

A fantastical structure in the Moorish style, the temple (fig. 75) is unique to the city. A gable-roofed structure, its gable end facing the street is flanked with square three-stage towers topped with diminutive onion domes. Window openings in the facade and towers are paired and have a variety of arched heads, including several trefoil variants and a pointed arch. The entrance, centered beneath the gable peak and massive double windows of the pediment, has

75. Temple of Israel, 1 South Fourth Street. Alex. Strausz, architect, 1875–76. From City Cemetery/St. James Cemetery—the First Baptist Church is in the near center.

a round-arched head and is approached by stairs from the sides. The iron balustrade and upright lanterns emphasize the approach.

The Temple of Israel is the oldest synagogue in North Carolina, though it was not organized until 1872. An earlier Wilmington group was founded in 1867 and met for awhile, acquiring a building on Marcus (now Church) Alley, between Dock and Orange streets. That movement was soon dormant, and it was not until December 8, 1872, under the influence of the Reform movement, that the Temple of Israel was organized, insuring the local collective a place of worship.

Wilmington has a long Jewish history, generally conceded to have begun with the arrival of settler David David in 1738. By the time Aaron Lazarus arrived late in the century, he was part of a steady stream of Jewish immigrants to and through Wilmington, and many of the present members of the temple can trace their origin to these late eighteenth- or early nineteenth-century settlers. Judah P. Benjamin, later senator from Louisiana and member of the Confederate States cabinet, spent some of his youth in Wilmington. By 1852 the community was large enough and stable enough to form a Jewish burial society; by 1855 the Hebrew Cemetery (see fig. 178) within Oakdale was open; by 1875 this temple was under construction.

The construction firm that built the temple is referred to in Temple publications as Abbott's Building Company, probably a group headed by Joseph C. Abbott. The architect, Alex. Strausz, was once a member of the same firm as Abbott, which traded under the name Cape Fear Building Company. They advertised in the *Star* on December 17, 1869, noting "estimates and plans given and contracts made for the erection and completion of Dwelling Houses, Public Buildings, Warehouses, Offices, Bridges, & c."

By the time the Temple of Israel was constructed, Strausz seems to have been with the firm of Strausz and Rice, in partnership with L. E. Rice—also once with the Cape Fear Building Company firm. Evidently the division of the Cape Fear firm was amiable, since Strausz and Abbott both worked on this building. The design attribution is somewhat clouded, with both Strausz and James Walker mentioned as architects. It is likely that Strausz was responsible for the Moorish design and that for some reason, now unknown, Walker was retained as supervising architect.

Ground was broken on May 20, 1875. On July 15 the cornerstone was laid with full Masonic ceremony and an address by Alfred Moore Waddell. The building was dedicated on May 12, 1876, with Rabbi Samuel Mendelsohn participating. Mendelsohn remained in Wilmington as rabbi of the congregation, a job he retained until 1921.

Biblog, a 1976 publication of the temple, quotes a local newspaper description of the new building at its opening in 1876:

On entering, the eye is dazzled with the colors of blended light that stream through the richly stained glass windows. The carpet is brilliant with flowers of the warmest hues, scattered in garlands and bouquets on the emerald surface. The altar is covered with imperial purple velvet, and on each side of it stand the seven typical lights supported by two bronze columns, in front of which are two marble basins filled with flowers upheld by marble cryatides. Vases of flowers are stationed in graceful profusion and crowns of roses and evergreens hang from the chandeliers around the room. The Ark is of white marble and grey stone, excepting the two black tablets of stone which are of black marble, bearing on their surface the Ten Commandments traced in Hebrew with glittering gilt letters. The "sanctum sanctorum," which was exposed to view in one part of the interesting and impressive ceremonial, seems to be draped with the same rich Tyrian dye as the altar, combined with folds of lace. In the Holy of Holies were deposited the "Scrolls of the Law" enclosed in silken coverings, on which were inscribed two Hebrew characters, abbreviations for "The Crown of the Law."

Dr. Isaac Mayer Wise, around whose prayer book the Reform movement began, noted in his *American Israelite* (1876) that "for simple elegance this temple is unsurpassed in the United States."

ST. JAMES GRAVEYARD

South Fourth Street at Market, southwest corner
c. 1745–1855

The public burying ground in this block was already in use by June 28, 1745, when Michael Higgins deeded a corner at Market and Third streets to James Smallwood, noting that it contained the lot "commonly called churchyard or burying ground." This was reinforced on January 1, 1747, when James Smallwood deeded to William Farris two lots on the east side of Third Street bounded on the north by Market Street and on the east by "ye burying ground." Property was deeded to the church wardens of St. James parish in 1747 on South Fourth running down Market 165 feet for a church graveyard and for "no other use."

In 1751, when construction of St. James at 1 South Third (see figs. 52, 53) was authorized and a cornerstone laid, it was toward the western end of this (present) cemetery. With the construction of St. James, the cemetery developed a closer association with the church, though adjacent areas near Dock Street on South Fourth continued to be used as a city cemetery. Evidently the boundaries of both graveyards were somewhat fluid and were not defined until after Fourth Street became a fixed thoroughfare in the nineteenth century. As late as 1909 both markers and tombstones were found on the eastern side of South Fourth Street. In that year the Duncan Cameron stone of 1790 (see fig. 180), now at Oakdale along with Cameron's remains, was found at number 7 South Fourth while excavating for construction of the Frank L. Huggins House.

The cemetery remained in use until at least 1855, when interments began at Oakdale and local ordinances prohibited additional burials within the city limits. Some graves were moved from the St. James Cemetery and the adjacent city cemetery to Oakdale at that time, as well as later, when space was needed for expansion of the St. James Church complex and construction of the Wilmington Fire Station and headquarters, 20 South Fourth Street.

The cemetery is an integral and important part of the St. James Church complex and possesses great historical importance both as a burial ground and for those interred here. Massive trees and other plant material of significance within the cemetery are oak, cedar, dogwood, and English boxwood. The area is cool, and shaded and is enclosed partly by segments of the St. James Church and Wilmington Fire Station complexes and partly by low walls of stuccoed brick topped with brownstone. Even though the cemetery is adjacent to heavily traveled Market Street, there is a feeling here of peace and quietude.

Some one hundred twenty-five marked graves survive, featuring many types of markers from tabletop to finely carved upright stones. There are but two slate stones in the cemetery, and it is likely that both are imports. One dated 1808 with a magnificent design incorporating a capped urn and a bent tree (the weeping willow was not yet in wide use) is the stone of Capt. Ephraim Symonds of Salem, Massachusetts. The other is the stone of Capt. Daniel Durfey, who died in 1793. Its epitaph evidences the inability of the stonecarver to fit his letters and words into the allotted space, but his ability to make do in a charming manner with this uncertain verse:

Great God is this our certain doo[m.]
And are we still secure
Tombs
Still walking downwards to our
And yet prepared no more.

The stone of Joseph Kellog, 1826 is from the weeping-willow era and features a fine tree over a draped urn. Three 1788 markers appear to be by the same stonecarver, quite possibly local. They all feature a quaint angel with unrelieved wings, upright curls in its hair, and enormous round eyes of a small circle within a large circle, as if the angel were wearing glasses. The 1788 marker of Sarah Stone also has a fine top and floral surround. The gravestone of Frances Wilkinson and son William Wilkinson is also from 1788 and with the angel, except that this one is in a flat-topped stone with the angel as a deep bas-relief in a panel near the top. The angel also appears on the 1788 stone of William Millor.

The carving on the stone of Letitia Kitty Robeson, 1849, is particularly fine, providing legend and decoration. It is also one of the few signed stones in the cemetery, marked "Lauber of Fayetteville." Lauber was evidently a superb calligrapher. Mary Ann Robertson Kirkpatrick of Baltimore, Maryland, is memorialized by a plump obelisk atop a large pedestal. At the base of the obelisk are Masonic eyes in pediments. The 1887 monument is signed "Gaddess & Benton, Balt., Md."

Best of the signed markers is that of William Hunt, nineteen-year-old son of John and Sarah Hunt of "Elizabeth Town in N. Jersey," who died in 1757. The stone is topped by a well designed and executed angel. At the sides is a surround of tulips. Dogwoods are within the border of the legend, and at the base are two daisies with an arcaded course carving arched between them. Within the arcaded arch, one letter or period per, is "PRICE. ENGRAVOR." Anyone who doubts that gravestone carving is sculpture and can be fine art needs only to view this stone. The epitaph is also particularly poignant and a fine adaptation of a common eighteenth-century theme.

How lov'd how Valu'd once; avails thee not.
To whom related or by whom begot.
A lump of Dust alone, remains of thee.
It's all thou art & all the proud shall be.

The 1801 stone of Joseph Milne contains a more common version of the theme.

Stop here my friend and cast an eye
As you are nou [sic] so once was i[sic]
As i am now so you most [sic] be.
Prepare for death and follou [sic] me.

Among other stones is that of Joseph R. Gautier, 1816, which features a deeply carved and draped urn with fine medallions in the corners of the stone. There are also a few brick, domed and walled tombs. One is marked "Henry Toomer & Charles Jewkes Family Vault 1786."

There are also many historically important persons in the cemetery, including a number of Revolutionary soldiers, but at least three such persons should be pointed out. First is Thomas Godfrey, born in Philadelphia in 1736, died in Wilmington in 1765. The marker notes that he was: "Author of the Prince of Parthia, the first Drama written by an American and produced upon the Professional Stage in the Colonies." Second is Cornelius Harnett, a Revolutionary hero, whose grave marker is a replica of the original stone, which was broken. Harnett died a British captive in 1781. His epitaph reads:

Slave to no sect
He took no private road
But looked through nature
up to nature's God.

(See Market Street at South Fourth text on the Harnett Obelisk for more on Cornelius Harnett.) Third, and one of the most interesting historically, is George Washington Glover. His marker bears the following text: "The body of Major George Washington Glover of Charleston, South Carolina, who passed on at Wilmington, N.C., June 27, 1844, was buried in this cemetery. Erected by trustees of funds of his wife Mary Baker Eddy." Mrs. Eddy, the founder of Christian Science, was in Wilmington at the time of Glover's death and attended his funeral here.

This well-cared-for cemetery is an interesting open area and one of the fine museums and sculpture gardens in the city. The vista from its northeast corner is one of the best in Wilmington. There is a European feel about the scene. Looking east-northeast, the Temple of Israel, 1 South Fourth Street (fig. 75), is in the right foreground, with the Carolina Apartments, 420 Market Street (fig. 125), just visible behind it. Market Steet and the Harnett Obelisk and Kenan Memorial Fountain (fig. 127) are in the left center. Trees in the foreground are small and young, increasingly larger and older in the distance. To the left center is the John A. Taylor House, 409–11 Market Street (fig. 123), behind that the First Baptist Church, 421 Market Street (fig. 126), the Bellamy Mansion, 503 Market Street (figs. 130, 131), and jutting above the trees, the attenuated steeple of St. Paul's Evangelical Lutheran Church, 603 Market Street (fig. 134). A better mixture of styles, textures, and sheer beauty is difficult to picture.

A. M. BALDWIN HOUSE

3 South Fourth Street
1895

A multiplaned house with complex roof and porch, this dwelling epitomizes the Queen Anne house (see fig. 76). A hexagonal bay on the right side of the house has a high peaked gable with patterned shingle and spindle canopies at the junction of the bay and gable eaves. At the opposite side of the house, the porch terminates in an octagon, with octagon-shaped peaked roof topped by a finial.

The porch has turned posts and balustrade and a

76. A. M. Baldwin House, 3 South Fourth Street, 1895.

spindle course. Sash is predominantly one-over-one within lightly molded architraves, and the entrance door has a one-light transom in the same architrave. A small stained-glass oculus in a kaleidoscopic pattern is on the diagonally cut wall behind the octagonal porch bay.

The Morning Star for June 6, 1895, carried the following: "Workmen were engaged yesterday in tearing down the building on the lot next south to the Jewish Synagogue, on 4th Street, preparatory to the erection of a handsome residence for Dr. A. M. Baldwin, the owner of the property." Evidently construction of this dwelling was begun almost immediately and was completed within the year.

WILMINGTON FIRE BELL, FIRE STATION, AND FIRE DEPARTMENT HEADQUARTERS

20 South Fourth Street at Dock Street, northwest corner
1886, bell; 1955, station: Leslie N. Boney, Architect

Wilmington has been plagued with several disastrous fires, yet it was not until 1856 that a full

77. George R. French House, 103 South Fourth Street, c. 1850.

volunteer fire department was organized. On December 1, 1897, the department became professional, with the city assuming the expense of hiring fire fighters and undertaking maintenance of equipment and buildings. The original headquarters fire company moved from North Fourth and Princess streets to this site in 1886. A wooden building already on the site was used. The pumper company entrance was on South Fourth, the hook-and-ladder entrance on Dock Street.

The Wilmington Fire Bell, cast in 1886, was hung in a standing wooden tower. In 1915 the bell was moved to the new station at Fifth Avenue and Castle Street—where it sounded alarms until 1918, when the last of the city's horse-drawn equipment gave way to mechanization. The bell continued to hang in the Fifth and Castle tower until 1955, when it was brought here and installed on its pedestal—a prime and important piece of street furniture. The bell, on a round concrete base, carried the legend "strike on this line." It was evidently rung by hand in a numerical pattern, with the number that was rung indicating the location of the fire. It also carries the following: "Meeneely & Co., West Troy, N.Y., 1886; City of Wilmington, North Carolina; E. D. Hall, Mayor, C. D. Meyers, Chief of Fire Department; Board of Aldermen, S. Bear, Jr., D. G. Worth, V. Howe; Committee of Fire Department, E. H. Darby, H. L. Dudley, C. Giley, G. J. Boney, G. Rouard, W. Doescher."

The new fire station and headquarters, third on the site, is a building of the International style. Horizontal bands of concrete aggregate alternate with bands of glass. The foundation is of green-colored aggregate, which carries around the entrance. On the first level of the South Fourth Street facade there are five equipment bays and four office bays. Though the emphasis is horizontal, vertical aluminum framing members are exposed.

Dock Street crosses South Fourth; begin 100 street numbers

Paving brick, predominantly "Southern Clay Mfg. Co." (see fig. 155), is used throughout the entire 100 block of South Fourth Street. Cottage Lane enters the street from the west. This block of South Fourth is one of Wilmington's super blocks, both in streetscape and in architecture.

VOLLERS-HARDIN HOUSE

102 South Fourth Street
1896: L. H. Vollers, builder

Luhr H. and Susan A. Vollers purchased land here from George W. and Florence Kidder in June 1896. A building permit was issued in August. Vollers was a builder and contractor, and it must be surmised that he built his own house. In June of 1900 the Vollers couple sold to John H. Hardin, a pharmacist, known locally as Dr. Hardin. The Hardin family maintained ownership until 1957, though the dwelling was converted into two apartments in 1934.

A fine Queen Anne house featuring shingle ornament in gables, a sawn and applied wooden frieze, and a porch with low, turned balustrade, it has a spindle course draped between turned posts.

GEORGE R. FRENCH HOUSE

103 South Fourth Street
c. 1850

George R. French, of George R. French & Son, operated the largest boot and shoe business in Wilmington, catering to both the retail and the wholesale trade. The company, established in 1822 as Hathaway and French, later became George R. French and then George R. French & Sons. From 1873 the firm operated from a handsome cast-iron store at 116 North Front Street that is still standing. French was a staunch member of the First Baptist Church and active in civic affairs. His interests included the Seaman's Friend Society, Chamber of Commerce, Bank of Wilmington, the Atlantic National Bank, the Wilmington Gas Light Company, and the Wilmington Seacoast Railroad—all of which he served as president or director. He was also one of the founders of Oakdale Cemetery.

The house here (fig. 77), transitional with both Greek Revival and Italianate forms, was built about 1850. French applied for insurance on it in that year and described it as on the east side of Fourth Street at Dock, of wood, "new, not finished," with tin roof, two stories tall, forty-one by fourteen feet, two chimneys, four fireplaces, no stoves to be used. The application noted that there was a wooden dwelling in the rear. It still stands, fronting on Dock Street.

One of the fine Wilmington Plain houses, the ornate porch, also an excellent example of its construction era, is from a somewhat later period.

The house was described in an August 23, 1889, "For Rent" advertisement in the *Star* as "The residence . . . formerly occupied Geo. R. French, Sr., containing nine rooms, water closet, bath rooms, and all modern conveniences. Apply at store. George R. French & Sons."

WILLIAM FRENCH HOUSE

107 South Fourth Street
1871: Alex. Strausz, architect

William French, one of the three sons in the "& Sons" part of George R. French & Sons, a wholesale and retail shoe firm, attended college at Wake Forest, then returned to Wilmington to join his father in the shoe business. William also followed his father in other business activities, becoming president of the Wilmington Cotton Exchange.

This house is on part of the George R. French lot that was acquired in 1847. There seems to have been a house here at least by 1849, and George French probably occupied it while his own house at 103 South Fourth was being built about 1850. It was then available for William, and he was living here on May 10, 1871, when the *Star* reported that a fire had destroyed his home. On June 21 the same paper reported that construction had begun on a new residence at the site. Plans for the large residence—forty-three feet in front and fifty-four feet six inches deep, with ten rooms and all modern conveniences—were, according to the paper, prepared by local architect Alex. Strausz. William continued in residence here until his death, as did William Jr., and his widow, Lillie French, who lived here until after World War II.

A bracketed-and-vented Italianate house with facade on two planes and a fine porch, it features double windows framed above by brackets and echoed

78. Italianate dwelling, 109–11 South Fourth Street, c. 1870. The 1872 brick sidewalks and carriageway of 107 South Fourth appear in the left foreground.

by paired vents in the frieze. A portion of the carriage entrance and the earlier street survives before the house to the south. Belgian paving stone is between the street and the beginning of the brick carriage way, with stone runs for the carriage wheels. This is probably the sidewalk laid around the French residences in 1872, when this house was new. The *Star* reported on January 30: "Messrs. George R. and Wm. A. French are laying a most substantial brick pavement [sidewalk] on Dock and Fourth Streets, around their dwellings." It is one of several Wilmington sidewalks and streets that can be dated.

ITALIANATE DWELLING

109–11 South Fourth Street
c. 1870

Of the bracketed-and-vented Italianate houses, this is one of the small number that has a shallow center-gable peak or pediment in the roof frieze, which is echoed in the porch frieze (fig. 78).

In a *Messenger* "For Rent" advertisement on May 26, 1892, the structure is described as: "That desirable residence, No. 111 South Fourth street, between Dock and Orange streets, containing 8 rooms, with kitchen, water works, and all modern improvements. Will be rented furnished if desired. Possession given immediately. Apply on premises."

79. Wilkinson-Belden House, 116 South Fourth Street, c. 1810; c. 1885; c. 1900.

WILKINSON-BELDEN HOUSE

116 South Fourth Street
c. 1810; c. 1885; c.1900

A confusing historical progression of ownership makes this house (fig. 79) difficult to trace, but its architectural evolution seems rather straightforward. A two-story section to the right, or north, rear is described on the 1889 Sanborn map as "built not later than 1830." An interior examination leads to the conclusion, based on architectural detail, that a c. 1810 date is supportable. The front part of the house, its major block, seems to have been built c. 1885; it does not show on Gray's map of 1881, but does show on the Sanborn map of 1889. The one-story projection to the left rear on Cottage Lane appears on the Sanborn map in 1904, so it must have been added c. 1900.

The facing of all sections is Italianate, in the bracketed and vented manner. The massiveness of the cottage is an illusion, created in part by the porch, which turns the corner on the northern end of the house, and by the wings that project on both sides at the rear. The porch has a narrow frieze with double brackets over each post. Posts are chamfered above and below a double neck molding, are linked by a turned balustrade, and have a scalloped drape at their top.

William Giles acquired the land here in 1810, and the $1,100 price he charged in 1813, when he sold the property to William Wilkinson, indicates that a house was standing. The rear section of the house is probably the structure built by Giles c. 1810. The Wilkinsons owned the property until the mid-nineteenth century, when John Williams became involved in ownership. In October 1887 Isabel Williams Belden came into possession of the house and lot. It is likely she and Louis S. Belden built the rest of the house. Isabel died in 1907 and Louis in 1914. The house passed to their daughter Isabel, who married William Love Moore. Mrs. Moore lived here until 1965.

The house still maintains a pleasant relationship to both Cottage Lane and brick-paved South Fourth Street with its granite curbs. The dwelling retains its brick sidewalk.

80. Williams-MacMillan House, 118 South Fourth Street, 1889.

WILLIAMS-MACMILLAN HOUSE

118 South Fourth Street
1889

The Sanborn insurance maps dated May 1889 show a two-story frame dwelling "being built" on this site. The configuration leaves no doubt that the house being built is this one (fig. 80). Also shown on the lot is an older house, marked "to be removed."

John Williams had acquired the land where the house stands by 1842. He died in 1855, leaving this and other adjacent property to his grandchildren. By October 1887, William Arthur Williams, who had married Jane Iredell Meares, came into full possession of the lot. It was this couple who began construction of the house. Williams is shown in the 1889 city directory as living at 118 South Fourth Street. Previously he had been listed elsewhere. He is listed in the directories variously as timber inspector, as president of the Auburn Lumber Company, and as clerk for the Board of County Commissioners.

Jane Iredell Williams was actively interested in the arts and studied woodcarving and botany. A combination of these interests led her into carving elements for the house and into painting wildflowers in watercolors and on china, which she fired in a kiln in the backyard. Mrs. Williams designed and fired the fox and grape tiles of the dining room fireplace. The stair newels and balustrade are also of her design, with the newels said to have been fashioned by her from bedposts. In July of 1923, she became first chairman of the Wilmington Art League upon its organization. Her obituary in *The Wilmington News*, September 8, 1935, called her "a talented artist . . . well known for her paintings of flowers and her collection of studies of wild flowers in North Carolina."

The property was purchased by Henry Jay MacMillan in 1919. It passed to his wife, Janie Meares Williams MacMillan, daughter of the builder, at MacMillan's death in 1920. MacMillan was a prominent businessman, and Mrs. MacMillan carried on the business after his death. She was active in supporting the arts in the city, became president of

81. Sutton-Hedrick House, 222 South Fourth Street, c. 1820.

the Wilmington Museum of Art when it was established in the mid-1930s, and in 1943 was appointed a member of the citizens' committee for a state art gallery. Janie M. Williams and Henry MacMillan were married in 1905 and had three children. One of the MacMillan children, Henry J. MacMillan, is a nationally known artist and the present occupant of the house.

Though we do not know the name of the architect, the house must have had one; the various elements and the overall manner in which they are blended are too good to have simply evolved. The architect is said to have practiced in Norfolk at a later date and to have been one of that city's best known designers. The style of the house causes decided arguments among architectural historians, who describe it variously as Bungaloid, Queen-Anne, or Shingle style. The house is a mass of planes and forms unified by a dramatic roof and seems to be of the Shingle style. It is a large frame house covered with a gable roof that begins above a simple canopy arched porch and swoops upward a full three stories. A dormer and a cross gable interrupt the roof at each end but do not disturb its line. Shingle is used freely in the upper stories. The house is a striking and beautifully designed and crafted structure. The quality of its style and finish is matched by the maintenance of the building and its surrounding landscape.

Orange Street crosses South Fourth; begin 200 street numbers

Paving brick at the intersection and throughout the 200 block of South Fourth Street survives, most of it unmarked. There are massive live oak street trees within the block, especially near its Ann Street end.

SUTTON-HEDRICK HOUSE

222 South Fourth Street
c. 1820

Probably the purest of the Wilmington Federal-era houses, this structure (fig. 81) is two stories,

82. Bell House, 306 South Fourth Street, c. 1893.

plus attic, with gable roof in the Beaufort style, covering a double-tiered porch to the front and an extension of the main block of the house to the rear. The house has wide and random beaded siding. The narrow and vertical windows, which retain much early glass, are six-over-six sash on the second level and nine-over-nine on the first. Window surrounds are flat and lightly molded. Chimneys are brick and exterior, with single weatherings. The porch has chamfered posts, a balustrade of spokes rectangular in section, and a rounded handrail. The entrance is a double door, opening in the center, with three panels in each leaf,—a six-panel door of the Federal era that has been halved. Paneled pilasters flank it, and it is topped by a rectangular transom with lights in an oval pattern. Atop the transom is a delicately carved pierced dentil course and molded cornice.

The door is not original to the house but came from the Freeman House at Second and Orange streets, no longer standing. The house also contains mahogany salvaged from Samuel Sloan's 1859 First Presbyterian Church after it burned in 1924, as well as other salvaged architectural material.

Although set almost on the street with a cast-iron hitching post at curbside, the house is nonetheless difficult to view, since it nestles among the live oaks and shrubs that shade its site. The effect is one of privacy and beauty.

Martha Sutton purchased the property here in 1822 and willed it in 1832 to Martha Ann Hedrick, her granddaughter. The will notes specifically that she is "to have my house & lot on Fourth Street." Martha Ann Hedrick married Thomas H. Howey in 1842. Either Mrs. Sutton built the house, or it was already standing when she purchased the property. When the house was insured in 1849, it was described as "two stories high, frame, with two piazzas, two chimneys and 'old.' "

Ann Street crosses South Fourth; begin 300 street numbers

Paving brick, predominantly "Southern Clay Mfg. Co." (see fig. 155), is used at the intersection and throughout the block. "Augusta Block" is used in patching. One of the fine views of the components of the Tileston School complex on Ann is from the intersection of Ann and South Fourth streets.

BELL HOUSE

306 South Fourth Street
c. 1893

Henrietta and Benjamin Bell acquired the property here in January of 1886. They had moved to the block c. 1880, but lived in number 316 rather than in this house. This dwelling (fig. 82) is on the 1893 Sanborn map, however, and the Bells are listed in residence in the 1894–95 city directory.

Benjamin Bell was partner in the printing firm of Jackson and Bell. His December 16, 1923, obituary in the *Star* included the following information:

> *In 1877, with J. W. Jackson, he established the job printing firm of Jackson and Bell, and this firm with the same partners has existed until this time. This was generally recognized as one of the longest established job printing partnerships in the United States in which there had been no change in principals during the existence of the firm. On the death of H. W. Bonitz, then publisher of the Wilmington* Messenger, *Messrs. Jackson and Bell, in 1891, bought the* Messenger, *and they continued in active direction and control of that publication until its suspension in 1908. Since that time they had concentrated all their activities on their job printing plant, and had only recently moved into new and enlarged quarters on North Second Street.*

Zack K. Bell, who succeeded his father as member of the printing firm, died in 1963. He had assumed the presidency of the firm in 1928, when Jackson died.

One of the premier Queen Anne houses in Wilmington, the structure is two and one-half stories, frame, with a complex roof and multiplaned surfaces on all facades. It features gable decoration of bargeboards decorated with bull's-eyes, radiating sun panels, and multipaned colored glass, and has panels of shingles, batten work, and vertical siding. The porch has turned posts with bracket tops, a spindle course, and a balustrade of decorative turnings and arch cutouts.

NATHAN GREEN HOUSE

312 South Fourth Street
c. 1849

Sanborn's 1893 map shows no house on this lot, but the present structure (fig. 83) was there by the time Sanborn's 1898 map was published. A handsome Wilmington Plain house in the Greek Revival mode, it obviously predates 1898, and even though it is now covered with asbestos shingle, the age is obvious from plan and detail such as the nine-over-six sash on the second level and nine-over-nine sash on the first, the molded box cornice with flush raking cornice, and the interior end chimneys.

A house that has the right dimensions and materials to be this one is shown on the 1893 Sanborn map, but it is at 319 South Third Street. The lot at 312 South Fourth is empty. There was nothing between the house on South Third and the empty lot

83. Nathan Green House, 312 South Fourth Street, c. 1849.

on South Fourth except outbuildings. The 1898 Sanborn map shows at 312 South Fourth, the structure previously at 319 South Third. Its configuration is quite distinctive, with a two-story front section and a one-story extension to the rear. The South Third Street lot had been freed for more intensive development, and this house—having no topographical and distance barriers to the move—was turned from facing west to face east and was moved one block. Two new houses had been built on the South Third site.

The house on its original site was described by Nathan Green in an 1849 application for insurance as "2-story, of wood, piazzas whole length of house, 2 chimneys and 'new.' " Evidently Green, who, along with his mother, had been freed from slavery in 1792, built the house. In 1898, it was the residence of Mrs. H. A. Donnelly.

COOK HOUSE

321 South Fourth Street
c. 1830

This one-and-a-half-story frame house presents a gable end to South Fourth Street and a facade to Nun Street—now obscured by the later house built in the front yard of this structure. The facade has a five-bay porch with chamfered posts and simple balustrade and brackets. The Greek door of two vertical panels is set in a surround of an eight-light transom and three-light sidelights. On the roof plane above are two gabled dormers with six-light sash and plain pediment. Sash at the first level is six-over-nine, though the pane size is larger than normal for that sash. An old brick building in the east yard also faces Nun Street. A picket fence along South Fourth, the orientation of the house, and trees in the yard give it great privacy and allure. It is also one of a very small number of dormered cottages in Wilmington. The date of the house has been variously estimated as from late eighteenth century to mid nineteenth century. Stylistically the house would seem to fit well into a c. 1830 construction date.

A Capt. William Cook was in residence here by 1845, when he sold the house to John Steward Richards. Capt. Silas Martin, a sea captain, was a later resident. It was he who is said to have placed his daughter Nancy in a keg of rum when she died at sea, and so preserved her until she could return to Wilmington and an Oakdale burial.

William Anderson of the firm of Brown and Anderson, jewelers, lived here in the late 1860s. He hanged himself in the backyard, and in 1886 E. H. Keathley, a watchmaker, bought the house from the Anderson estate.

SUTTON-WORTH HOUSE

323 South Fourth Street
c. 1850

This house is in the two-story Wilmington Plain house style, but evidences Greek Revival massing and detail. Its gable roof, interior end chimneys, porch with simple posts and spoke balustrade, door with transom and sidelights, and six-over-six sash in flat architraves are typical elements of other area houses of the Greek Revival era.

William Sutton purchased this lot sometime between 1849 and 1866 from the front yard of the Cook House at 321 South Fourth. When he sold it to Clark Baker in 1866, the purchase price indicated that this house, built in front of the Cook House dwelling, was already standing. The architectural evidence bears this out. Baker deeded the house to his daughter Mary, the wife of Joseph B. Russell, the same year he purchased it. The city directory of 1866–67 shows the Russell couple as residing at the corner of Fourth and Nun, or in this house. They sold it in 1870 to Barzilla G. Worth—a Quaker, but a member of the First Presbyterian Church. Gray's map of 1881 lists the house as the residence of "J. B. Worth."

Together with T. C. Worth, B. G. Worth—a wholesale grocer and cotton and naval stores merchant—founded in 1850 the Worth Company, which by the turn of the century was a dominant firm in its field in North and South Carolina and Georgia. In Wilmington the firm Wm. E. Worth & Co., begun by B. G. Worth's son, which operated the Wilmington Refrigerator and Ice Works, was formed in 1885.

ITALIANATE HOUSE

326 South Fourth Street
c. 1870

This is a fine two-story Italianate frame house with a low hip roof and the vented-and-bracketed frieze typical of Wilmington. The canopy-roof porch is one of the most visible of the city's canopy porches because the house is sited atop a retaining wall high above the street. From street level the interior framing of the porch roof is clearly visible, with its rafters steamed and joined to frame the canopy.

The house is of an architectural type that could have evolved in the 1870s. When the property was sold to Abraham and Eliza Cook in 1872, the purchase price indicates that a house was there. One is shown on Gray's map of 1881, but on another part of the lot. The Sanborn map for 1893 shows the house on this site, but without its porches or rear wing. It had its present configuration by the time the 1898 Sanborn was published. One wonders if the porches were not salvaged from another house similar to this one and reused. The house seems too fine and of too early a design to have been constructed c. 1898.

Sold at public auction in 1897 by a receiver for the Bank of New Hanover, the house was bought by Godfrey Hart, who sold it in 1900 to Ellen Kure.

Nun Street crosses South Fourth; begin 400 street numbers

MILLER HOUSE

401 South Fourth Street
c. 1882; c. 1920

"Dr." F. C. Miller bought the property here from the estate of Joseph Francis King in 1881. He may have already lived in a house on the site, for the 1879 city directory shows him as residing at Fourth and Nun. In 1884 he and his wife Annie mortgaged the property to Mary E. Russell, possibly for money with which to construct this house. The mortgage was satisfied in 1885.

The 1881–82 city directory lists "Dr." F. C. Miller, a druggist, as living on South Third Street, with a store at the corner of Fourth and Nun. Perhaps the house he formerly occupied had been torn down and the new one was being built. The 1883 directory lists Miller with a drugstore at 324 South Fourth Street and a residence at 401 South Fourth Street. Evidently this house had been completed by that time, and the Miller family was in residence. About 1893 a small drugstore called The German Drug Store was erected in the corner of the lot within the L of the house, and this was the Miller drugstore until c. 1910.

A bracketed-and-vented Italianate dwelling, the Miller House has a facade on two planes. Originally the porch was one-story across both planes of the facade. The present two-story porch, from the 1920s, is handsome and covers the same area as the earlier single-level porch.

North Fifth Avenue

Market Street, northward to Campbell Street

The name of Fifth street, extending from northern to southern city limits, is to be changed to Fifth avenue. City council practically decided to make the change, upon petition of 51 citizens considered at the meeting today.

News-Dispatch, *December 9, 1914*

One of the wide boulevards of Wilmington, landscaped in the 1880s under the administration of Mayor John J. Fowler, the street was given the added distinction of being called *Avenue* in 1914. North Fifth retains its landscaped center plaza and its street trees. The Kenan Memorial Fountain, at the intersection of Fifth Avenue and Market Street, (see Kenan Fountain, Market Street, and fig. 127) joins both North Fifth and South Fifth at their dividing line. The first block of North Fifth remains a fine residential block, its street trees meeting overhead to form a double canopy.

ALDERMAN-CARPENTER HOUSE

12 North Fifth Avenue
c. 1848

Built by Henry M. Bishop, who acquired the property in April 1846; or by William Jones, who acquired it in May of 1847; or by William L. Smith, who acquired it in October 1848, the house is a plain Greek Revival two-story frame house with a fine, later Victorian-era porch. Smith retained ownership until 1863, and if not actually the builder, he was certainly the first owner to maintain a sustained residence there.

Mary Alderman lived here from at least 1905 to 1934. She operated the Alderman Select School, a kindergarten, first at 15 South Fourth Street and later in this house. The dwelling was acquired by W. F. Carpenter, Miss Alderman's brother-in-law, in 1918. Laura Carpenter, Miss Alderman's niece, continued the school until 1942.

CONOLEY-HANBY-SIDBURY HOUSE

15 North Fifth Avenue
1852: James F. Post, architect

James F. Post's ledger does not prove his authorship of the design for this house (fig. 84), but it does indicate a good deal of work done for John J. Conoley in late 1852. Among other items are "putting up blocking course on dwelling house," "hanging gate," and "Marble work at Brown and Anderson," including stone sills and lintels. This is certainly enough to establish Post as working on a

84. Conoley-Hanby-Sidbury House, 15 North Fifth Avenue. James F. Post, architect, 1852.

house for Conoley, and this is believed to be that house. It is markedly similar to other houses of the era on which Post worked.

Conoley maintained ownership until 1860. He was a clerk who later had his own book and stationery business, Conoley & Yates, at 47 Market Street. Charles M. Whitlock seems to have been in residence in 1898, when the *Dispatch* recorded, in its May 26 edition, a burglary while the Whitlocks were eating dinner. On June 7, 1904, a *Star* advertisement offered room and board for gentlemen here.

John H. Hanby acquired the property in 1904. He was listed in the 1883 city directory as an architect and later as a contractor and builder. The January 11, 1895, *Star* announced, "Mr. John H. Hanby, who has for eleven years filled the responsible position of Supervisor of Buildings of the Atlantic Coast Line Railroad system, has retired from that service and now resumes his old work as general contractor and builder. His skill and experience in his line of business are so universally recognized here that it is not likely he will be often 'out of a job.' " By the time Hanby acquired this house, he was proprietor of the Atlantic View Hotel in Wrightsville Beach.

Verlinza Sidbury acquired the house in 1916 from Charles D. Foard, Hanby's brother-in-law. The elder Sidbury died in 1943. His son, Dr. J. B. Sidbury, also resided here. The younger Sidbury attended Trinity College, now Duke University, before receiving his M.D. degree from Columbia in 1912. He served internships at Roosevelt Hospital in New York and at New York Foundling Hospital before returning to Wilmington to open an office in the

Carolina Apartments in 1915. On June 6, 1920, Dr. Sidbury established Babies Hospital at Wrightsville Sound to provide advanced pediatric care to children of the area and to those of summer visitors.

At Dr. Sidbury's death, the house passed to the First Baptist Church, which currently uses it as church offices. It is one of several significant historical and architectural structures used and maintained by the church.

A two-and-a-half story stucco-over-brick dwelling with low hip roof, it is an academic Italianate structure with vented-and-bracketed frieze. Vents are covered with iron grills. The paneled walls, Italianate entrance and door, and well-detailed porch with Tuscan columns tie together this house and the Von Glahn House at 19 North Fifth Avenue, built during the same decade. (See below.)

KNOHL HOUSE

16 North Fifth Avenue
c. 1860

Frederick William Knohl acquired the land on which this house stands in 1856 and constructed the house soon thereafter. His will, probated in the March Court of 1866, gave the property to his widow "as long as she remains a widow." In case of a remarriage, it was to be divided equally between mother and daughter. In 1876, in the August 16 *Star*, the property was advertised "For Rent, the dwelling, known as the Knohl House, on Fifth Street between Market and Princess."

Later residents included Alfred M. Waddell, attorney and mayor of Wilmington for several years in the early twentieth century. The Waddell firm was Waddell and Peschau. W. R. Hudler, dispatcher for the Atlantic Coast Line Railroad, was a resident after 1915 for a few years.

POLLEY-MORRISON HOUSE (later Hamme House)

18 North Fifth Avenue
c. 1870

Tax assessors' records list 1870 as the construction date for this house. From its Wilmington Plain style, there seems no reason to question the date. The structure appears on Gray's 1881 map, so it was certainly standing before 1881. It was remodeled from dwelling to apartments just prior to World War II and was converted to office use after 1950. These diverse uses brought several changes in the character of the house. It is a two-story frame dwelling, with paired windows on the sides. These, along with the low gable roof, are prominent features of the structure.

The lot on which the house stands was acquired in August 1867 by Lewis M. Williams and Alexander H. Moore from Hirman and Mary Jane Polley. They may have forfeited after building the house, for the property was still in Polley ownership in 1892, when it was sold to Nora, J. D., and Lila H. Morrison. The property was still owned by Nora Morrison in 1942, when it was sold to Sophie Hamme.

VON GLAHN HOUSE

19 North Fifth Avenue
c. 1859

Henry Von Glahn, a Wilmington merchant from Germany, was already in residence here in 1859, when he acquired the house in which he was living and the lot on which it was sited from Thomas Southmayed and John H. Conoley, his former landlords. Conoley's house (see fig. 84), next door to the south at 15 North Fifth, was already built, and it seems likely that Von Glahn liked the Conoley structure well enough to use it as his design inspiration for the new house he built here. The two are almost identical except that the Von Glahn House (fig. 85) is somewhat bigger and has a wing.

The house remained in the Von Glahn family until 1965, when the property went, by will, to the city. It now houses offices of the city government, including the mayor's office—a significant governmental preservation and adaptive use.

A vented-and-bracketed Italianate structure with cast-iron vent covers, it is a two-story house, stucco over brick, with a full basement. A plaster water table runs around the structure, forming a base for the plaster pilasters that run from water table to frieze between the bays. A belt course intersects the pilasters between the first and second levels. The entrance is in the right bay of the first floor level—there is also a full basement level. The Italianate four-panel entrance door appears in a segmental arch surround with two-light segmental transom. The door is flanked by sidelights with glass etched in floral patterns.

85. Von Glahn House, 19 North Fifth Avenue, c. 1859.

Whether the August 26, 1899, *Messenger* article on the work at the house referred to rustication or marbleizing of the plaster surface is not known. That article noted "Mr. H. Von Glahn is having handsome improvements made to his beautiful house on the SW corner of Fifth and Princess streets. The house is being remarbled outside and repaired inside."

Princess Street crosses North Fifth

The Southern Bell Co. building at 107 North Fifth Avenue was completed in 1976, following plans of Holloway-Reeves, architects of Raleigh.

HOUSE

115 North Fifth Avenue
c. 1900; porch, c. 1920

Built about 1900, probably as a duplex with one dwelling unit up and one down, the house is a relatively plain two-story frame structure.

About 1920 the Bungalow-style porch was added. The hip roof, plain frieze, overhanging cornice, and material of the main block of the house was carried over, but there the similarity ends. The first porch level features paired Tuscan columns on brick piers. Second-level posts are frame, with siding and corner boards used to create square posts that have bases and pedestals. Bay openings are asymmetrical on both levels, with the right bay smaller than that to the left. On the second level, bay openings are framed with gently rounded corners, and the porch is screened.

A relatively common house and porch type in early twentieth-century America, it is a type that disappeared far more quickly than other, earlier types, so that it is becoming increasingly rare.

Chestnut Street crosses North Fifth

The fence/wall and entrance gates to the Hemenway School, designed by B. H. Stephens and built in 1914, survive the school, which burned in 1971. Massive magnolia trees on the site, which runs through the block to North Sixth Street, make it prime park and open space. There is a well-developed park here now, with gazebo and play equipment. The park was a 1979 bicentennial project.

BEAR-BEST HOUSE

307 North Fifth Avenue
c. 1880

The house—shown on Gray's 1881 map abutting Sampson's Alley to the south and facing North Fifth—is a late Gothic Revival cottage. Of a type that is relatively rare in Wilmington, this cottage epitomizes its Gothic heritage in its gable-end decoration. The gable, perpendicular to the street, has a centered, three-part elongated vent. Two lancet-topped louvered openings occur, with a diamond louvered vent above them to fill the lancet-shaped frame. Siding within the gable is flush and set vertically—except above the vent, where the siding follows the lancet shape of the vent, continuing the shape visually to the gable peak. Evocative of the Italianate are the cottage's low canopy porch roof and full-length front windows.

Solomon Bear acquired the property in 1861 and evidently built the house. He sold to R. W. Best in 1885 and Best maintained ownership until 1914. According to the Wilmington city directory of 1918, J. Albert Farley, cashier for the *Morning Star* newspaper, resided at this address.

Red Cross Street crosses North Fifth; begin 500 street numbers

Campbell Square to the east contained a cemetery in its center prior to 1855. By 1881 it contained a public school on the cemetery site and a black Methodist church on the North Fifth corner with Red Cross and a black Baptist church on the North Fifth corner with Campbell. That use continues today. (see St. Mark's Episcopal Church, North Sixth Street at Red Cross)

ST. STEPHEN A.M.E. CHURCH

502 North Fifth Avenue
1880–88: Lewis Hollingsworth, architect-builder;
1913: St. Stephen A.M.E. Annex

On November 9, 1909, President William Howard Taft greeted the black schoolchildren of the county from a stand on the steps of this church. Taft, then on a visit to Wilmington, had earlier greeted white schoolchildren at the intersection of Market and Third. Governor Thurmond Kitchen and other dignitaries accompanied the president.

Bishop Francis Asbury wrote in his journal for Tuesday, February 8, 1803, of his arrival in Wilmington and his preaching, noting: "I met the people of color, leaders and stewards; we have eight hundred and seventy-eight Africans, and a few whites in fellowship." The Front Street Methodist Church became the church home for all Methodists in Wilmington, spawning all the other downtown Methodist churches, black and white. St. Stephen was founded in May of 1865, when six hundred forty-two black members withdrew from the Front Street Methodist Church and joined the African church under the leadership of Rev. W. H. Hunter, a black chaplain with the federal forces then occupying Wilmington.

In 1866 the group constructed its first place of worship, on Red Cross, between North Fifth and North Sixth. Land at this corner—the site of the present building—was transferred to the trustees of the church on March 18, 1867, and the congregation then owned not only its own church but the land upon which it stood.

Rev. James A. Hanby became the first minister; he was succeeded in 1880 by Rev. Joseph Fry. Under the Reverend Mr. Fry, work began almost immediately on a new church building. Lewis Hollingsworth, a member of the congregation, drew the plans for the building. Bricks were furnished by Daniel Lee, another member, who had a brickyard. Six master carpenters and six master masons, all of them members of the church, began work. Little is known about any of these artisans, though they were obviously superb practitioners of their professions. It would be particularly interesting to know more about Hollingsworth, since the church building makes it evident that he was a highly skilled designer.

The *Star* reported on July 17, 1880, that the existing church, built in 1866, was being demolished and, on August 11, that the foundation of the new church was being dug. On August 18 the paper could report that laying of the foundation had "commenced yesterday," and on September 15 it recorded:

The corner stone of St. Stephen's new brick A.M.E. Church, now being erected on the northeast corner of

Fifth and Red Cross streets, will be laid on Monday, the 27th inst., with appropriate ceremonies. The building committee and the members generally of this church deserve great credit for what they have already accomplished financially towards the erection and completion of what promises to be a large, substantial and handsome church edifice; and they have desired us to express their gratitude and appreciation to the white people, who have contributed liberally to this end.

The Building Committee consists of R. F. White, Jos. E. Sampson, Thomas Rivera, J. Johnson, Josh. Meares, Jas. Green, Rev. J. W. Telfair, Wm. Holmes, G. L. Mabson, David Jones and Henry Turner.

By June 11, 1881, the paper noted the "frame of the roof has been raised, and the work of covering it will now be proceeded with." According to the *Star* of August 16, 1881, "The first services in St. Stephen's A.M.E. Church, now nearly completed, were held in the basement of the edifice on Sunday, the pastor, Rev. J. G. Frye, officiating. There were four distinct services during the day, the first at 5 A.M., the second at 10 A.M., and third at 3 P.M., and the fourth at 8 P.M., and the large building was literally packed on each occasion."

Evidently the church had reached the limits of its resources, for the building was to remain unfinished for almost four years. Work began again in 1885, according to the *Star* for January 7:

The brick work of St. Stephen's A.M.E. Church, corner of Fifth and Red Cross streets, was completed some time since, but the body of the church, inside, has remained in an incomplete state, and the congregation have worshipped in the basement. Now workmen are engaged in doing the inside work, much of which is nearly complete, including the galleries and that portion of the building above the same. The galleries will be very handsome and the beautiful scroll work that adorns the upper portion of the building will be very attractive, and will set off the interior arrangement of the edifice to a great advantage. Below the galleries the walls will be neatly wainscotted, handsome pews of modern style will be introduced into the body of the church, and a neat pulpit will occupy the niche in the eastern end of the building. When all the work is completed, including the spire, which is yet to be erected, it will be a handsome, well finished church, and a credit to the body of Christians who are to worship in it. Lewis Hollingsworth, colored, is the contractor.

It was not until April 25, 1886, that the paper could report completion of the building: "St. Stephen's A.M.E. Church is so nearly finished that the congregation expects to worship in it today." A new pipe organ, operated by a water motor, was installed in November 1895 and, according to the *Messenger* for November 24, was first used that day. The church was essentially completed for use by 1886 and was brought to its present form by 1888.

A late Gothic structure with center gable, flanking shed roofed wings, and a four-stage tower on the southwest corner, the church (fig. 86) maintains both its fine horizontal Gothic exterior and its interiors today. Indeed, the interior (fig. 87) is one of the most impressive in Wilmington. Gas light-fixtures remain on columns and behind the pulpit. The gas chandeliers are intact, their mirrored reflectors still polished and used. Early electric-light chandeliers survive as well. There is fine stained glass (fig. 88), particularly the symbolic windows in the clerestory above the balconies. Balcony screening and arches are sawn and the roof trussing is decorated. Through the screens above the balconies the impression of two tiers of gallery seating is created. The overall combination of ornate dark woods, polished brass, brilliant light fixtures, and red carpeting creates a feeling of Victorian era opulence and richness. It is a rare visual experience that cannot be enjoyed in many surviving interiors of the era.

The 1913 Annex is a noteworthy building architecturally, and its early use gives it unusual importance, for it seems to have been a combined school, clinic, hostel, and public bath, carefully planned to serve as a community center. The August 2, 1913, *Star* gave a fairly full description of the new building and its intended uses:

Members of St. Stephen's A.M.E. church, colored, corner Fifth and Red Cross streets, under the leadership of their pastor, Rev. A. J. Wilson, D.D., are building a handsome brick annex to the church which will cost in the neighborhood of $15,000, and which will be used by the Sunday School. There will also be a number of other features such as a swimming pool, public library and the teaching of domestic science. The membership of the church is 1,600 and it is one of the leading churches of the colored people in the State.

The new edifice will be four stories and will be built of brick. Work was begun this week and the foundations have been laid. For some time the church has

86. St. Stephen A.M.E. Church, 502 North Fifth Avenue. Lewis Hollingsworth, architect, 1880–88.

not been large enough to hold the large number of Sunday school pupils and it was decided to erect a building especially for its use. In view of the fact that the colored people have nothing in the way of a Y.M.C.A., the pastor and his people have planned to make the annex serve the same purpose for the colored people that the Y.M.C.A. and Y.W.C.A. does for the white people.

Dr. Wilson stated yesterday that a teacher of domestic science would be secured, and the entire fourth floor used for this department. By reason of the fact that a large proportion of the colored women cook for white people he will have the hearty cooperation of the citizens of the city who are interested in those movements which make for the public good.

In the basement there will be a swimming pool, rest rooms for old people and a doctor's office. It is expected that later a physician will be stationed at the church to minister to the physical ills of the church members and others who may need his services. There will also

87. St. Stephen A.M.E. Church, interior.

be public baths so that those who do not have these facilities at home can have them at the church.

On the second floor there will be the pastor's study and several classrooms. On the third floor there will be classrooms for the Sunday School and a public library. The classrooms are so arranged that they can all be thrown together making a large auditorium seating 800 people. There will be in all 18 classrooms for the Sunday school, so that each class can have a separate room thus insuring more thorough teaching than is possible with one large auditorium.

The foundation idea, the pastor states, is to make the church of real service to the people it serves and to minister not only to their spiritual needs but to their physical needs as well. There is a large field for this kind of work among the colored people and little has been done in the past by the church to help them.

The combination of sanctuary and annex at St. Stephen possesses tremendous historical, architectural, and social importance.

88. St. Stephen A.M.E. Church, stained-glass window.

MAHN HOUSE

515 North Fifth Avenue
before 1881

William D. Mahn, an administrator of the estate of Eli V. Kelly, who had earlier owned this lot, acquired it himself in February 1868. The property remained with the Mahn family until at least 1912, when Hattie M. Mahn sold it to Katie C. George. The house appears on the Gray 1881 map of Wilmington, and was constructed before that date. Because of the long ownership by the Mahn family, it is likely the house was constructed by them.

John C. Rowan, listed in the city directories as a "moulder" (presumably a mold maker), was living here by 1899.

The house, an Italianate cottage, features all of the distinguishing characteristics and stylistic marks of the Wilmington house of that style. The low hip roof, the frieze with vents and brackets, and the canopy porch with full-length facade windows are all displayed to good advantage here. The entrance has both transom and sidelights in the Greek manner. The sidelights are framed by a round arch that echoes the rounded Italianate arches of the door panels. The porch balustrade is simple, as are the fluted columns with their bracket capitals. This is one of several houses in the city that utilize brackets as capitals, approximating the Corinthian order.

At the southeast corner of North Fifth Avenue and Campbell Street is the contemporary building of the First Baptist Church, completed in 1977. The congregation began in 1843, when 17 blacks were accepted into membership at First Baptist. By 1861 the church had 173 black members. On November 7, 1864, the black members of the predominantly white church received permission from the congregation to withdraw and construct a new church. Initially, a building on Walnut Street between Fourth and Fifth was used, but a frame church was built on the present site in 1869. That building, altered and rebuilt in 1896, and remodeled in 1948, stood until February of 1974, when it burned. The contemporary structure, with its modern stained glass, is a fine addition to the ecclesiastical architecture of Wilmington.

South Fifth Avenue

Market Street southward to Queen

South Fifth Avenue is tree lined, and its center plaza survives. Several houses in the first block have carriage- or horse-mounting blocks at curbside, a vivid reminder of the preautomotive city.

GRAINGER HOUSE

7 South Fifth Avenue
1901

Charles S. Grainger received the land on which this house was built on October 28, 1899, from William L. and Josie Smith. Mrs. Smith, the widow of Isaac Bates Grainger, was Charles' mother, and the property was an early inheritance. Members of the Grainger family maintained ownership until 1954 of the house they had built in 1901. In 1973 the dwelling was adapted to use as law offices.

Charles S. Grainger was a cashier at Murchison National Bank and secretary-treasurer of Wilmington Underwriter's Insurance Company.

A Neoclassical Revival house, the structure retains its exterior essentially unchanged, except that the upstairs porch over the entrance has been enclosed for conversion to a bath.

WILLIAMS HOUSE

10 South Fifth Avenue
c. 1868; wing to south, c. 1886

A three-story, frame, bracketed Italianate structure, the dwelling features a one-bay center pavilion and a single-story porch on the facade and on the south side. The front porch is three bays wide with square posts and crowned with a balustrade in an oculus pattern. The cornice is held by brackets with double flutes and a stringcourse that runs over the bracket bases. The posts are paneled. The main door has a semicircular transom and an elaborately paneled and tiled vestibule beyond the missing outside entrance door. The recessed inner entrance door remains. The paneling and tile of the vestibule probably date from 1886, the same date as the hip-roof addition with patterned tile and brackets to the south. The addition also features a bay window with hexagonal pointed roof.

The structure, now used as apartments, is a perfect marriage of the Italianate and Queen Anne styles, each complementing the other but remaining separate.

In 1867 George Williams purchased the lot on which he constructed this house. He was building by 1868. There was already a house on the lot, constructed by 1843, and Williams may have incorporated it into his new dwelling. He was a partner in the firm of Williams & Murchison, commission merchants, wholesale grocers, and agents for New York steamers. The Williams family maintained ownership until well into the twentieth century.

McKAY-BERRY HOUSE

11 South Fifth Avenue
c. 1818; c. 1849; c. 1900

The *Cape Fear Recorder* noted on September 5, 1818, that the "new house on the hill lately erected by Mr. William McKay" was for rent, stating further that "Its site is one of the most pleasant and healthy in town. It has a good yard, garden and every convenient outbuilding." After Dr. William Augustus Berry acquired this building, he moved the old house slightly and altered and added to it. The 1849 "Specifications of the workmanship and materials to be used in the alteration and addition of the building on Fifth street" survive in the Lower Cape Fear Historical Society archives. The structure was once again remodeled c. 1900, this time by Daniel O'Connor. Each remodeling incorporated parts of the previous house. By 1913, the dwelling was the residence of Egbert Kedar Bryan.

What one sees here is distinctly Queen Anne, with little or no exterior clue to the older houses whose parts it contains. The cast-iron fence from the last, or c. 1900, era is in an arrow design signed "The Stewart Iron Works, 3rd and Culvert St., Cincinnati, Ohio."

QUEEN ANNE HOUSE

15 South Fifth Avenue
before 1882; c. 1889

A vented-and-bracketed Italianate house, already standing when Gray drew his 1881 map, this dwelling acquired Queen Anne detail and additions around 1889. The complex roof of the house is in sharp contrast to the tower to the right, since the Italianate frieze with vents and brackets survives on the tower. The multiplaned facade seems to undulate, its use of patterned shingles and various bay forms adding to the illusion.

Mary McIntosh bought the land here on October 17, 1846, and was in residence before 1855. In court papers (New Hanover County Court House, Register of Deed Office) ordering the sale of the property after her death, it is described as "being the lot on which Mrs. Mary McIntosh resided at the time of her death." James C. Smith bought the property at a public auction on June 12, 1855, for $1,440, indicating a structure was then on the lot. When John E. Pierce sold to John G. Bauman on January 1, 1861, the price was $2,000. It is possible that the dwelling being transferred included the nucleus of the existing house.

The house had a tragic late-nineteenth-century history. On August 22, 1898, the *Dispatch* recorded the death of Miss Bessie C. Hill at the residence of her uncle, W. Harris Northrop, 15 South Fifth: "The deceased young lady was the daughter of Mrs. Wm. E. Hill, of this city and had been ill for several weeks with typhoid fever. The particular sad part of the death is the fact of her mother, sister, Miss Julia Hill and brother, Master Willie Hill, are all seriously sick in the same house with the dread malady." Dr. Thomas S. Burbank was a later resident. The *Dispatch* recorded his move to this address in its December 27, 1902, edition.

COSTIN HOUSE

20 South Fifth Avenue
c. 1849; c. 1875

Built by Miles Costin c. 1849, the structure (see frontispiece) is said to have been remodeled by him c. 1875 in the French Second-Empire style, one of

89. Wessell-Hathaway House, 120 South Fifth Avenue, 1854.

a small number of Wilmington houses in the style. The concave mansard roof used here not only added another story, stretching the structure from two stories plus basement to three full stories, but also matched the concave, or canopy porch roof. The porch with its curved stairs at each end—"come-and-go stairs," according to one area resident—may have survived from the earlier house. The bracketed eaves may also be a carry-over.

According to the *Star* of October 24, 1885, "Col. J. W. Atkinson," then in residence at 20 South Fifth Avenue, "is making extensive improvements on his residence corner Dock and Fifth streets." A clipping of December 30, 1923, notes additional work on the house: "Dr. L. E. Farthing, of this city, has purchased the handsome colonial residence on the NW corner of 5th and Dock streets. The building is a 3-story and basement residence of the old southern type. The work of completely remodeling and improving will be started next week. Dr. Farthing's intention is to remodel so as to have his office there."

Dock Street crosses South Fifth; begin 100 street numbers

WESSELL-HATHAWAY HOUSE

120 South Fifth Avenue
1854; James F. Post, builder

James Wessell, a native of Germany, acquired the land for the house on May 23, 1853, and in 1854 contracted with James F. Post for construction. Post's ledger (located in the Lower Cape Fear Historical Society archives) for April 10, 1854, has a $1,099.66 entry "to contract building House" for J. Wessell. He billed for columns and capitals on April 20 and on May 1 for freight on columns and for hauling same, so evidently they were ordered from an architectural supply house. On May 9 he billed for a newel, balusters, and mahogany for rail and on June 10 for "hauling 24 loads" that included balusters, seven transoms, and eight pair of sash. On August 5 he billed "to putting up front door" and for putting up chamber doors; on August 7 for the work of three men "to building fence"; and on September 9, 1854, "to putting up front gates." The design of the present cast-iron fence before the house (fig. 89) indicates that this is the original 1854 fence.

If Wessell ever lived here, it was for only a short time before leaving Wilmington for Fayetteville. Next-door neighbor H. B. Eilers managed the property for Wessell, finally selling it in 1858. Eilers was an attorney and evidently Wessell's business partner as well. The *Daily Journal* for January 23, 1852, reported: "J. Wessell and H. B. Eilers having, on the 8th December, 1851, formed a co-partnership under the firm of Wessel & Eilers having taken stores No. 1 & 2, of P. K. Dickinson's Building, on North Water Street, Wilmington, formerly occupied by Miles Costin, where they intend to keep on hand a general assortment of groceries, liquors and provisions at wholesale."

The sale of the house on January 5, 1858, was to James L. Hathaway. A partner in Hathaway & French, boot and shoe store, Hathaway later operated the firm of Hathaway & Son, selling cheese, coffee, molasses, cotton, and yarn. His obituary in the June 26, 1892, *Messenger* noted that "when he resided in our city he did a large shipping business with the West Indies."

Hathaway, from Fall River, Massachusetts, left Wilmington during the Civil War and never returned, selling the property in 1866 to Avon E. Hall, also a merchant. Hall maintained ownership for only two years, selling in 1868 to Dr. W. W. Harriss. The house was described in a *Messenger* sale notice on June 4, 1899, as: "The very eligible lot and dwelling, recently damaged by fire, on Fifth Street, No. 120, next corner of Orange, lots 66 and 165. Large cistern and well on the premises, sewerage connection. Complete. Residence formerly occupied by Dr. W. W. Harriss." By 1913 the Howard McClintock family was in residence.

Since 1940 the house has served as residence for the Leslie N. Boney, Sr., family and as office for the Leslie N. Boney, Architect, architectural firm, located in the basement of the house. The Boney firm has played a major role in designing civic, commercial, and residential structures in Wilmington since the early twentieth century.

The house is basically Italianate with Greek Revival detailing, especially in the handsome Tower of Winds capitals atop the fluted columns of the full-length, five-bay porch. The floor-length first-level windows, and simple bracketed frieze with wide roof overhang, emphasize its Italianate origins. Tall "come-and-go" stairs once led to the handsome eclectic center entrance.

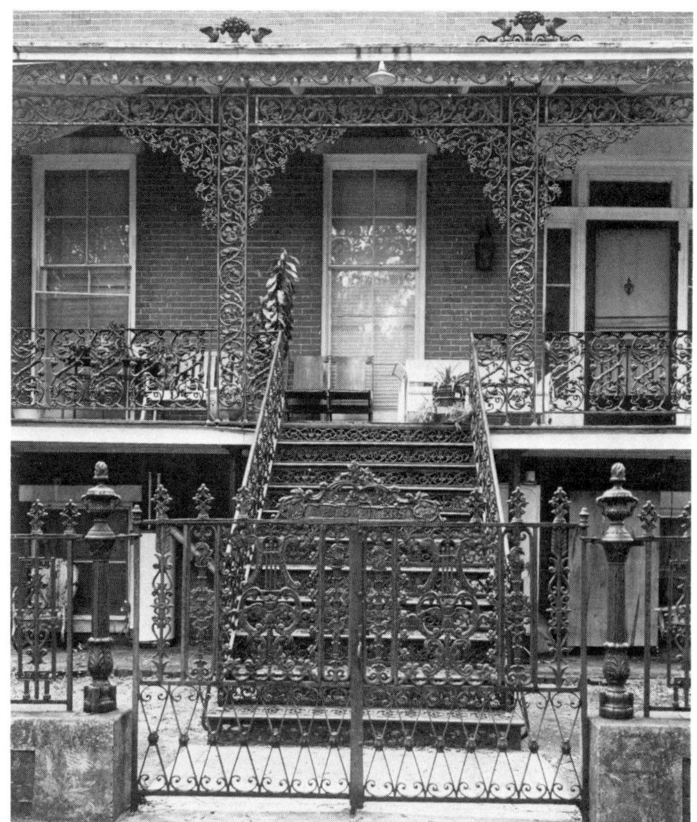

90. H. B. Eilers House, 124 South Fifth Avenue, 1852. (detail of 1852 iron).

H. B. EILERS HOUSE

124 South Fifth Avenue
1852

H. B. Eilers, an attorney and partner with J. Wessell in a wholesale grocery and liquor business, acquired this corner lot in 1850. He had completed his house and erected the fence that surrounds the yard by 1852. The property remained in the Eilers family until 1927.

The house, a vented Italianate structure of exposed pressed brick, stands alone stylistically for the purity of its execution and for the completeness of its survival. It is all here: the exterior detail, the cast-iron fence, and even its carriage house around the corner on Orange Street.

The quality of the cast-iron fence and gate (fig. 90) with its H. B. Eilers, 1852, marking and of the porch iron and iron grills in the frieze vents is unmatched by any other in the city. The porch is com-

91. Richard Price House, 125 South Fifth Avenue, 1840.

plete with cast-iron columns, canopy, steps, anthemia, and cresting, all handsome and in good repair. The entrance location at the second level, above a full basement, gives this porch more visibility than any other iron porch in Wilmington.

RICHARD PRICE HOUSE

125 South Fifth Avenue
1840

On November 1, 1840, Catherine Price, who had married her cousin Richard Watts Price, wrote a friend: "I shall soon be in my new home. Cousin Richard has bought a lot and is building." Cousin Richard had written his sister-in-law in 1839 that he was engaged in "ship carpentering business." He was later a merchant and a harbor master for the Port of Wilmington.

Following the Civil War Mrs. Price took in boarders, advertising in the *Star* for May 27, 1868, that "three gentlemen can be accommodated with pleasant board." During the same period, her daughter operated a school. In the same paper she advertised on September 29, 1868, "Miss B. K. Price will resume the exercises of her school at the residence of her mother, corner Orange and Fifth streets on Thursday, Oct. 1st." A news article in the same issue declared: "Miss Price has conducted her school successfully for several years, and is well known to our citizens." On April 23 the paper carried an advertisement for piano students. "Wanted. Mrs. Hudson wants a few more scholars to fill out her class of instruction on the piano. . . . Those desiring pupils may call at Mrs. Price's corner of 5th and Orange."

R. W. Price and G. M. Altaffer operated a sash and blind factory at the foot of Walnut Street until the factory burned on December 29, 1882. It is probable that some of the doors, sash, and shutters on the house were manufactured in the family factory.

A Wilmington Plain house built during the Greek Revival era, it has many of the hallmarks of that style (fig. 91). It is a two-story frame structure, with gable roof, box cornice and cornice returns, a center entrance with transom and sidelights, and porches to the front and the south. The fenced corner lot with its fine trees and excellent landscaping add much to the charm of the house.

Orange Street crosses South Fifth; begin 200 house numbers

92. The St. Mary Church, 220 South Fifth Avenue, 1908–11.

TOWNES-EMPIE HOUSE

209 South Fifth Avenue
1916

W. A. and Annie DeRosset Townes purchased the land in 1915. Mrs. Townes died in childbirth in 1916, while the house was being built, and it was never occupied by the Townes couple. First residents were the Herbert Bluethenthals, newlyweds who lived here while their own home at 1704 Market Street was being built. Townes sold the house in 1919 to Theodore and Evelyn Pearson Empie. After Mr. Empie's death in 1944, Mrs. Empie continued in residence until 1964. Empie was president of the Carolina Metal Products Company.

A Shingle-style structure, the house features a shingled second story with pent over a brick first story. The entrance hood with brackets, door, and other detail are Colonial Revival in style.

THE ST. MARY CHURCH

220 South Fifth Avenue
1908–11: Rafael Guastavino (father) and Rafael Guastavino (son), builders; Father Patrick Marion, construction superintendent

A Spanish Baroque church in brick and tile, St. Mary (fig. 92) is beautiful both in style and in the quality of its finish. One hardly expects to find a major Spanish Baroque cathedral among the live oaks on South Fifth Avenue in Wilmington, North Carolina!

Built without steel or wood beams or framing and without nails, the building employs brick and tile structurally as well as decoratively. Its plan is that of a Greek cross with a high dome over the crossing. (See fig. 93.) The facade features tall twin towers capped by domed cupolas. These flank a wide baroque gabled entrance. Some of the glass in the

93. The St. Mary Church, dome, exterior; from the Cape Fear River Lift Bridge.

church is signed "Mayer & Co., Munich/New York." The porcelain Stations of the Cross do not seem to be signed but are very fine. Some of the furnishings are from the earlier church of St. Thomas The Apostle Church, 208 Dock Street, moved here when St. Mary replaced St. Thomas as the Catholic Pro-Cathedral of Wilmington.

Ground was broken for the St. Mary Church on May 20, 1908, and the first brick was placed November 20 of that year. The cornerstone was laid October 21, 1909, by Bishop Abbot Leo Haid, then Vicar Apostolic of North Carolina. First services were held in the church on December 17, 1911. On April 28, 1912, St. Mary was consecrated and dedicated St. Mary Pro-Cathedral by Cardinal Gibbons. Gibbons' interest in Wilmington and the success of the church in North Carolina are in no small part responsible for the construction of such a large and impressive cathedral here. St. Mary Pro-Cathedral returned to being the St. Mary Church in 1925, when the Diocese of Raleigh was established.

The church building is the work of a father and son, both named Rafael Guastavino. Though the older Guastavino was an architect who had won competitions and accepted commissions, he is not known primarily as an architect. He arrived in the United States in 1881 with his son, a knowledge of Spanish building techniques, and enough money to begin a new life. The son studied architecture in New York and won an architectural competition, but he then practiced little architecture, preferring, with his father, to push their system of cohesive construction. George Collins noted in an article on the Guastavinos in the October 1968 *Journal of the Society of Architectural Historians* that:

This is ironic because through the employment of their several favored forms of tile vault, the two Guastavinos as contractors and builders probably exerted as much aesthetic influence on the "imperial" spaces of early twentieth-century architecture and on the neo-

94. The St. Mary Church, detail of dome, interior.

Gothic naves of the following decades as did the actual architects of the buildings.

In 1886 Guastavino failed to win the competition for the Arion Club in New York City, but did get the contract to install the floor vaults. In this case he was forced to make the vaults thicker than was necessary (or wise), but from that time he was more frequently consulted than advised by the architects with whom he worked. There was no known precedent for the Guastavino vault on this side of the Atlantic.

Guastavino vaults consist of tiles that are held by mortar so strong that the tiles will ordinarily crack before the mortar separates. (See fig. 94.) Collins noted that: "The vault with which we are dealing is very thin, consisting of little more than a surface, and derives its rigidity not from massiveness or thickness but rather from its particular geometric form, viz. its type of curvature." Their vaults and domes were so strong that, unlike ordinary construction that required scaffolding or supports to hold the structure in place while the vault or dome was being built, the Guastavino system required no artificial support, and workmen might actually support themselves and their materials on the work completed the day before.

The two Guastavinos incorporated their Guastavino Fireproof Construction Company in 1889. The father had patented his process for "Construction of Fireproof Buildings" in 1885, and by 1939 the two held some twenty-five patents. These patents went a long way toward making the Guastavino system an exclusive one and brought architects such as McKim, Mead and White; Bertram G. Goodhue; Hornblower and Marshall; Richard M. Hunt; and a host of others to the Guastavino firm for assistance in construction. The two accomplished several commissions for members of the Vanderbilt family, including work at Biltmore House near Asheville, North Carolina. They took up residence in the country at nearby Black Mountain, and there the Guastavinos began experiments, in a small kiln, with tile manufacture. Later they established a manufacturing plant near their home in Woburn, Massachusetts, for production of the structural, acoustical, and decorative tile they needed, tile such as that used in St. Mary Church.

The father and son also demonstrated their work in such buildings as the Cathedral of St. John the Divine, New York, with architects Heins and La Farge, and the Boston Public Library and the rebuilding of Jefferson's Rotunda at the University of

95. Steljes House, 324 South Fifth Avenue, 1882.

Virginia with McKim, Mead and White. In Washington they worked with Hornblower and Marshall on the Museum of Natural History Building of the Smithsonian Institution. One could scarcely imagine a better group of buildings or a better-known list of architects—all using Guastavino techniques and tile in unique vaults and distinctive domes.

The Guastavino design attribution for St. Mary has been long claimed, as it has for the St. Lawrence Church in Asheville. Whether or not the actual design was theirs, the techniques and tiles used were, and they were the builders. The elder Guastavino died in North Carolina while working on St. Mary, and his son completed the commission. Father Patrick Marion, a priest who had superintended the construction of St. Lawrence, also superintended here.

The actual design attribution of St. Mary has still to be proven. If Guastavino was the architect, then St. Mary is one of his very few American buildings and of immense importance. Whether the actual design was his or not, the inspiration must have been. After all, it was the techniques and knowledge of the father-son team, their Spanish origin, and the materials that they developed and manufactured that made the church possible. There can be little doubt that the structure is theirs.

Ann Street crosses South Fifth; begin 300 street numbers

STELJES HOUSE

324 South Fifth Avenue
1882

The city directory for 1881 lists Diedrick Steljes, a grocer, as residing at Sixth and Queen streets. The *Star* on September 24, 1882, in a partial list of buildings erected during the years 1881 and 1882, includes: "D. Steljes, fine residence, corner of 5th and Nun streets." In the city directory for 1883 he is shown residing at 324 South Fifth.

A vented-and-bracketed Italianate structure, the house (fig. 95) features the typical low hip roof and porches of the style. Because of its corner location, it is able to display two canopy-roofed porches, one on South Fifth Avenue and one on Nun Street.

96. Fifth Avenue United Methodist Church, 409 South Fifth Avenue. B. D. Price, architect, 1889–90.

Nun Street crosses South Fifth; begin 400 street numbers

FIFTH AVENUE UNITED METHODIST CHURCH

409 South Fifth Avenue
1889–90: B. D. Price of Philadelphia, architect; Porter and Goodwin of Goldsboro, builders; E. V. Richards, stained glass; 1921: Soong Memorial Building

The Fifth Street Church was organized in 1847 from the Front Street Methodist Church to serve communicants in the fast-developing southern part of the city. At first the new congregation met in members' homes, but in 1848 it acquired this land by donation from Miles Costin. A church was erected almost immediately. The first building was a simple frame structure, repaired in 1875–77 and enlarged in 1884–88. By that time it was inadequate, and the present structure (fig. 96) was undertaken. The cornerstone for the new building was laid November 13, 1889, and the church was dedicated on September 26, 1890. It is said to have had the largest seating capacity in the state, 1,150 when completed.

A handsome Gothic structure, it has double towers, recessed on either side of the roof gable. Entrance is through the smaller tower. The interior of the church, with its soaring roof and diagonal plan, exposed trussing, and combined gas and electronic chandeliers, is particularly beautiful. The stained glass is exceptional (see color plate 7), as is the quality of the furniture.

Local artist E. V. Richards, who also did some of the glass at St. James, seems to be responsible for the glass here. The *Messenger* for December 21, 1889, noted that "Mr. E. V. Richards, of this city, has been awarded the contract for making the stained glass windows for Fifth Street M. E. Church." Almost a year later, on September 6, 1890, the same paper reported "Mr. E. V. Richards, the artist, finished the last of the handsome cathedral glass windows for the new Fifth Street M. E. Church yesterday."

The altar may be the original. The *Star* for October 12, 1890, noted its installation: "Electric lights will probably be used in Fifth Street M. E. Church tonight. The new altar has arrived and has been placed in its proper position. A door has been cut on the north side of the tower and steps built on the outside, so that the chimeringer can have access to the chimes." The chimes were evidently not satisfactory. On March 5, 1891, the *Star* carried the following:

> *A new set of chimes has been ordered by Mr. Jno. C. Davis for Fifth Street M. E. Church to replace the set now in use, which have not given satisfaction. They were from the McShane Foundry at Baltimore, which agreed to receive them back and furnish others, and Prof. Van Laer was engaged by Mr. Davis to visit Baltimore and test the new set; but being unable to do so on account of sickness, Mr. Davis wrote to Mr. L. L. Curtis, formerly choirmaster of St. James Church, but who is now a resident of Baltimore, asking him to go to Baltimore & inspect the new bells.*

Mr. Curtis must have found them satisfactory, for the *Star* chronicled their arrival in its March13, 1891, edition: "The new chimes ordered by Mr. Jno. C. Davis for the Fifth Street M. E. Church have arrived, and will probably be used for the first time next Sunday. There are ten bells, said to be similar to those of Trinity Church, New York."

The education building of the church, the Soong Memorial Building, was erected in 1921 and named for Charlie Jones Soong, baptized in the earlier church on this site November 7, 1880. Soong, a young ship stowaway, was discovered aboard ship in Beaufort, North Carolina, and was saved from deportation by the Chadwick family, who later moved to Wilmington. Under the sponsorship of the church, Soong attended Trinity College (now Duke University) and Vanderbilt University before returning to his native China. He married there and is better known for two of his daughters than for his own accomplishments. One of the Soong daughters became Mme. Sun Yat-Sen, another Mme. Chiang Kai-Shek.

Castle Street crosses South Fifth Avenue; begin 600 street numbers

FIRE STATION NO. 2

600 South Fifth Avenue, corner with Castle
1915; James F. Gause, Jr., architect; L. H. Vollers, builder

Land was acquired here by the city in 1890 for a market and engine house. The *Star* noted a hitch in getting clear title in its November 14 paper, but evidently by the time of the December 24 edition the title had been secured, and the mayor was directed to "procure plans and specifications for a new truck house for the Fifth Ward Hook and Ladder Company." By January 6, 1891, according to the *Star* of that day: "Bids were opened yesterday in the Mayor's office for building a truck house for the Fifth Ward Hook and Ladder Company, at Fifth and Castle streets. Mr. Frank Swann's proposal to do the work, including painting at $685, was considered the lowest, as the other bids did not include the painting." According to the December 24, 1890, *Star*, the building was to be "forty by twenty-five feet and two stories in height."

The present station (fig. 97) replaced the earlier building in 1915. The Wilmington Fire Bell, first hung in 1886 and now part of the fire marker at 20 South Fourth Street, was in the tower here from 1915, when the station was completed, until 1956. It sounded alarms until 1918, when the last of the horse-drawn fire engines was phased out.

97. Fire Station no. 2, 600 South Fifth Avenue at Castle Street. James F. Gause, architect, 1915.

One of Wilmington's diverse and excellent collection of fire stations, this one is basically Italianate with Dutch Revival detailing. It is highly eclectic and pleasing, designed by local architect James F. Gause, Jr. Only slightly modified for its adaptive use as an insurance agency office, the structure is a fine example of its era of construction, of the importance of this area of the city, and of the taste of the city government and citizenry during the period of its construction.

North Sixth Street

Market Street northward to Harnett

Market Street

North Sixth Street is typical of fine residential streets in Wilmington and in most other cities. There are a number of interesting examples of domestic architecture that range from large, highly developed residences to small, plain cottages. Also located in this ten-block area are a commercial structure of unusual material, the only remaining railroad truss bridge in the area, a nineteenth century educational and religious site of historical importance, and a twentieth-century school.

98. Helig House, 15 North Sixth Street, c. 1885.

HELIG HOUSE

15 North Sixth Street
c. 1885

Originally constructed as an Italianate-style cottage in the bracketed-and-vented manner, the house (fig. 98) derives much of its architectural interest from a turn-of-the-century Queen Anne remodeling. The highly individual combination of the various Queen Anne elements—turned columns, spindle course, bay window, gable ornament, gable decoration—are a charming overlay to the older cottage.

Chestnut Street crosses North Sixth; begin 200 street numbers

ST. MARK'S EPISCOPAL CHURCH

220 North Sixth Street
1871: Emerson and Fehmer, Boston, architects, and Alfred Howe, probable supervising architect and builder; 1897: renovation and enlarging, Valentine Howe, Sr., probable architect and builder

Organized in 1858 as a mission of Saint Paul's Episcopal Church, 16 North Sixteenth Street, and with a mixed congregation, St. Mark's evolved into a black mission in 1866, received its first black minister in 1869, constructed this building (fig. 99) in 1871, organized as a parish in 1872, and was accepted into the diocese the same year.

The Episcopal Board of Missions' home mission magazine, *Spirit of Missions,* noted the consecration of the church in its September 1875 issue:

On Friday, June 18, was consecrated by the Bishop of North Carolina—the Rt. Rev. Thos. Atkinson, D.D.—in the city of Wilmington, North Carolina, St. Mark's (colored) Church.

This being the first Church consecrated in the Dio-

99. St. Mark's Episcopal Church, 220 North Sixth Street. Emerson and Fehmer, architects, 1871.

cese for colored people, a corresponding interest attached itself to the ceremony. . . .

The edifice is sixty-one feet by thirty-five feet outside measurement: Height to the ridge forty-one feet; to the eaves, twenty feet. It is of brick and church-like in style. The designs were furnished by Emerson and Fehmer, of Boston, Mass. The roof is sharp, the chancel recessed, the windows pointed Gothic.

Upon the north-west corner is a small tower, fifty feet in height to the base of the cross, and furnished with a bell. The plan provides for a larger tower upon the south-west corner. But that is still in the future. The chancel is toward the east, and is furnished with Altar, Credence and Bishop's chair, all of chestnut. A suitable Lectern has not yet been obtained; that in use being only a temporary piece of furniture. Possibly this communication may meet the eye of some one who will think it a privilege to supply the want.

The corner-stone was laid March 23, 1871. Since that time the work has been steadily carried on as the funds have come in; always upon the principle of not running into debt.

The whole amount received and expended thus far, inclusive of the cost of the ground, has been about $6,000. Of this a part has been raised by the congregation itself; a part has been contributed by its friends among the other Churchmen of Wilmington; and we may thankfully add, a part of other friends who do not call themselves Churchmen. But, to a considerable extent, the congregation has been indebted for its success in this undertaking to the good will and liberality of Churchmen in other parts of the country. Particular mention should be made of the very liberal contributions from New York, Boston, and Washington City, from which sources about $4,000 has been received.

The Reverend Charles O. Brady, a black minister, took charge of the Wilmington mission in December 1869. He was shortly received as a clergyman by the Episcopal Diocese of North Carolina upon presentation of a letter from the Bishop of Connecticut. By May 1870 he was reported "serving with acceptance and success as a Deacon, a colored congregation in Wilmington."

In February 1871, the Reverend Mr. Brady reported to the Board of Missions that his congregation was worshipping in Saint Paul's, but had raised "by their own exertions" nine hundred dollars. With this they had purchased a "desirable lot of ground, in a central position, on which they contemplate the erection of a chapel, according to ecclesiastical rule." Among other contributions, he reported, sixty dollars from "Messrs. Emerson & Firmer [*sic*]" *(Spirit of Missions)*. It is likely that Emerson and Fehmer also contributed their plans for the contemplated church building.

By June 1871, Brady was able to report that the cornerstone was laid on March 23, and walls were "almost up to the window tops." Evidently the construction was carried out speedily, for he wrote the Board of Missions that, "Our first service was on the Sunday after Christmas, the last Sunday of the old year [1871]. The Bishop opened with the Holy Communion at 9 A.M., and made a touching address. Regular service was held at 11 A.M., and half past 7 in the evening by myself. . . . Large congregations were present at both the morning and evening service. . . . Our new St. Mark's looks neat and churchlike, and all who see it are most pleased with its appearance. We still however need means to complete it, which I have faith to believe we shall get in due time." On Easter Monday of 1872, Brady wrote, "We organized, according to the canons of the Diocese of North Carolina as St. Mark's Parish, with wardens and vestry duly elected by the baptized members of the congregation" *(Spirit of Missions)*.

While other black Episcopal churches in North Carolina may be older than St. Mark's, their congregations worshiped in schools or other such buildings, or in churches built for white congregations. St. Mark's is believed to be the oldest black Episcopal church in North Carolina built by and for a black congregation.

St. Mark's interior was refurbished in 1880 according to the *Star* of June 30, and "the present neat appearance of the walls, pews, etc., reflects credit upon all concerned." When the ceilings were lowered and the church enlarged in 1897, it reached its present dimensions. According to the *Dispatch* for March 9, 1903, a new pipe organ was being "installed in St. Mark's Episcopal Church." The memorial pulpit was installed in 1909. A newspaper noted on May 2:

St. Mark's Episcopal Church has just completed a series of improvements that places it in the front rank of progressive ecclesiastical organizations in the city. The interior walls of the church have been thoroughly renovated, painted and decorated; a new velvet Brussels carpet has been laid in the chancel, choir and all the aisles; several electric lights have been added to further light the chancel and choir and a memorial pulpit of brass and oak has been installed and will be dedicated today. The memorial pulpit is pentagonal in shape with moulded base resting on a prepared platform two steps above the chancel floor. The five panels are formed by twisted panels of brass, the centre bay filled by an equilateral cross with Ionic finials surrounded by a circle containing a circlet pierced by elongated spearheads. In the left hand panel is the monogram I.H.S., the Greek form of the Holy Name, and in the right hand column is the complement, the Chi Rho, the second part of the sacred name, while two annulated columns complete the outline.

Below the symbolic letters run horizontal panels, filled with the tendrils and leaves of the passiflora and the upper panels containing duplications of the conventional Fleur de Lys. All the above is of highly polished brass. Above this metal work is a wide hand rail or support of oak and arranged in connection with this is an adjustable sermon desk pierced with three Fleur de Lys of brass, emblematic of the blessed Trinity.

The memorial inscription is engraved on a brass plate attached in the mouldings of the base and runs as follows: "To the Glory of God and in Memory of Rev. Charles Otis Brady. Born 1829 Died 1886 Faithful, Zealous and True Minister of this Parish for eighteen years: Beloved by All. 'He Being Dead, yet Speaketh' Hebrews II:4."

An April 25, 1915, clipping from an unidentified newspaper concerns the unveiling of a new altar. "At the 11 o'clock service of St. Mark's Episcopal Church today one of the most beautiful altars in any of the colored churches of the South will be unveiled. This altar has been installed by the congregation of St. Mark's as a memorial to the four deceased Bishops of the Diocese. It is a beautiful altar made of a fabric called 'Regalico' [*sic*] by a Chicago firm. The front is decorated with four columns in orange and gold effects, one for each of the Bishops—Atkinson, Lyman, Watson, and Strange." The altar—marked "Copyright 1906, Deprato Statuary Co., Chicago" on its north side, and on the south side, "Hardest Composition Ever Made, Rigalico Trade Mark"—is still in use. An early wooden altar with paneled front in quatrefoil design is now in the chapel.

The organ is marked "Hood and Hasting, Boston" and may have been installed in 1903, prior to the installation of the new altar. It is in the chancel addition. The painted organ pipes survive, superb in their blue and gilt. Much fine stained glass also remains, especially in the altar window and the east window on the south side. The entrance windows are the oldest.

Church furniture is relatively simple and probably from the 1897 remodeling. The lowered ceiling is in five panels—the two at each end are sheathed diagonally in tongue and grooved wood, while the center panel is horizontally sheathed but with cross framing and an intersecting boss. All wood is stained a dark color.

A *Star* writer had noted on October 19, 1871, that the new St. Mark's building was "one of the neatest edifices of the kind in the state." The church could hardly have had a finer firm of architectural designers. William Ralph Emerson and Carl Fehmer were two of the nine founding members of the Boston Society of Architects in 1870. They continued in partnership as Emerson and Fehmer from before 1870 until 1885, when they established separate offices. Both became well known in the field—especially Emerson, who was one of the early proponents of the Colonial Revival style and later a foremost practitioner of the Shingle style.

St. Mark's is a highly pleasing Gothic Revival structure of stuccoed brick. The sharply pitched roof emphasizes the verticality of the style, a verticality that is echoed in the entrance, lancet windows, and buttresses. The octagonal corner tower is scarcely larger than the church. While the eaves of the church are at twenty feet above the ground and the apex of the gable at forty-one, the tower is only fifty feet high to the base of its cross. The plans provided for a larger tower on the southwest corner, an asymmetrical plan similar to that of the First Baptist Church, 421 Market Street (fig. 126). The fact that the larger tower was never constructed serves to emphasize the vagaries of finance for a fledgling congregation rather than to diminish the architectural importance of the church.

It is likely that Alfred Howe, a black builder, was in charge of the 1871 construction. Howe was involved in the purchase of the church lot and was elected senior warden of the first vestry in 1872. Since funds and material were in short supply and the construction of the building was a self-help project, it would have been logical for Howe to build the church. His execution of the Mary Jane Langdon House, 408 Market Street (fig. 122), indicates that construction of the church was within his capability.

When the church was renovated and somewhat enlarged in 1897, it seems equally likely that Valentine Howe, Sr., accomplished the work. Valentine Howe had learned his trade from his father and was a vestryman of St. Mark's from 1885 until his death in 1905. Howe also engaged in major construction projects and at the time of his death in 1905 was building the James Walker Hospital Annex.

Jackson Hall, the St. Mark's Parish House, 601 Grace Street, adjacent to the church, was completed in 1953–54 and dedicated April 25, 1954.

Red Cross Street crosses North Sixth; begin 500 street numbers

CAMPBELL SQUARE

West side of North Sixth Street to North Fifth Avenue; Red Cross Street on the south, Campbell Street on the north
1845

William S. Campbell deeded this square, block 236, to the city of Wilmington on June 30, 1845.

Traditionally, there was a Quaker cemetery within the square, possibly dating from the eighteenth century. It was evidently used later as a black burying ground, as reported in the *Star* of March 8, 1893. Whatever its use, there was a cemetery in the square at the time of the 1845 deed.

In 1866, the board of aldermen passed an ordinance dedicating the block to the use of the black population of Wilmington. This was supplemented by ordinances of June 7, 1886, and March 7, 1893. On March 18, 1867, the black Methodist Episcopal church was deeded the southwest corner of the block, where St. Stephen A.M.E. Church now stands. At the same time, the center of the block—with fifty-foot-wide entrances reserved on each of the four streets on the block perimeter—was deeded to "The Wilmington Colored Educational Institute." On September 16, 1876, the northwest corner of the block was deeded to the First Baptist Church; on June 24, 1886, the southeast corner was deeded to the First Colored Presbyterian Church. On September 13, 1883, the northeast corner of the block was deeded to St. Mark's Episcopal Church. In 1919, according to the *Star* for August 24, the Presbyterian and Episcopal lots along North Sixth were deeded to the city for school use.

The schoolhouse in the block was noted by the *Star* of November 20, 1868, as being "finished, but not in use." This was likely the first Peabody School, which replaced a wooden structure built about 1866. In 1867, George Peabody, a wealthy Boston merchant, established a fund, endowing it with one million dollars. He added an additional million in 1869. The funds were to be used without regard to race to "encourage and assist educational effort in those portions of our beloved and common country which have suffered from the destructive ravages of war." Exactly when the school here came to be known as Peabody School is not certain, but it was so known by May 1, 1884, when the *Star* announced an opera house entertainment by students of the "Peabody colored school."

The *Star* for February 7, 1885, reported that the building has "just been finished with new blinds and nicely painted and it now presents a neat and genteel appearance." The building partially burned in February of 1893. On February 23 the *Messenger* noted: "The fire department responded promptly but in the meantime the fire burned through the floor and up the walls to the roof. The result was that most of the roof was burned off and the building otherwise considerably damaged. The desks and furniture were also more or less damaged, as well as the school building." By October 10, 1894, the paper reported, "The Peabody school house (for colored children) has been thoroughly equipped and furnished with the latest school paraphernalia, and has two new rooms added, making it the finest colored school in the state."

Evidently the present building was constructed in 1919, after the deeding of the corners of the lot to the city. The *Star* for August 24, 1919, reported "an additional school building is to be constructed at an approximate cost of $30,000." Additions to the school were constructed in 1942 by Robinson Bros., Inc., of Asheville, according to the *News* of April 9.

Campbell Street crosses North Sixth;
begin 600 street numbers

SIXTH STREET TRUSS BRIDGE

North Sixth Street over the railroad tracks
1910–11: Des Moines Bridge & Iron Company

This truss bridge (fig. 100) is not only an excellent example of its type, but is the only such bridge that survives in Wilmington. Constructed in 1910–11, the bridge was jointly built by the Atlantic Coast Line Railroad and the city of Wilmington. A thru-bridge on two concrete abutments, it is 145 feet long and 45 feet wide.

Bill Reaves's column in the *Star-News* of August 22, 1976, gives the best history of the bridge.

The Sixth Street Bridge was originally constructed to join a city divided.

For many years the northern section of the city remained undeveloped, largely due to the Wilmington & Weldon Railroad tracks which divided the city, north from south.

The first bridge was of wood, built about 1873. The Wilmington Board of Aldermen ordered the railroad company to construct bridges across the 'cut' at Second, Third, Fifth, Sixth, Seventh, and McRae streets. At this time only one bridge existed and it was located on Fourth Street and was called the Boney Bridge, but it was considered too narrow for heavy traffic.

The bridge on Sixth Street was to be 25 feet wide.

In 1866, the Sixth Street Bridge was condemned and a new bridge was built, again of wood. This

100. Sixth Street Truss Bridge, North Sixth Street over the railroad tracks. DesMoines Bridge & Iron Company, 1910–11.

bridge was rebuilt again in 1891 and 1895. In 1902, the Wilmington Dispatch newspaper reported that "the old wooden bridge over the Coast Line tracks at Sixth street is to be repaired and a contract will be let in about ten days. The bridges will be kept in good repair and when the Fifth Street bridge is finished there will be three 'first-class' bridges connecting Brooklyn [the section of the city north of the tracks]."

In December, 1909, the wooden bridge was condemned and removed.

The same month, negotiations began for a new bridge constructed of steel with wood floor. In July 1910, an advertisement for bids for a steel bridge at Sixth Street appeared in newspapers. The bids were opened in August 1910, and a contract was let in September. The bid accepted was made by the Southern Construction Company of Burlington, N.C. Its proposal was $7,500.

The contract made with this company proved to be a disaster. From the beginning they had trouble making the required bond and in May 1911, the contractor left town, leaving many of his laborers with wages unpaid. The construction firm also left unpaid bills, among which was a large one with the Des Moines Bridge & Iron Company who supplied the steel for the bridge. The sheriff attached the unfinished bridge and all the materials yet to be used. The press referred to this situation as the "Sixth Street Muddle."

On June 17, 1911, it was announced that A. D. O'Brien, a Wilmington Civil Engineer, had been awarded the contract to complete the bridge on Sixth Street. His bid was $1,400. The bridge was completed in the fall of that year and dedicated.

Included in the national Historic American Engineering Record, the bridge has been photographed and recorded for permanent record. Its inclusion attests to its value as an example of the style and to its relative rareness as an area survivor. At one time, all Wilmington streets crossed the railroad tracks on truss bridges of one type or another. This bridge alone survives.

The narrowness of the bridge and ramp approaches, which highway engineers are fond of listing as two of its major drawbacks, may also be viewed as part of the value and charm of such bridges. They force us to slow down, and they remind us of the role the railroad played in the development of the area. Vistas from this bridge not only show the deep cuts that the tracks made through Wilmington, but the many commercial and industrial structures along the right-of-way, all railway-oriented. To the northwest, dwelling along the tracks are also visible.

Bladen Street crosses North Sixth Street; begin 900 street numbers

SHOTGUN HOUSES

909, 911, 913, 915, and 917 North Sixth Street; western side of the block
Late nineteenth century

These houses are all adaptations of the shotgun house, so named because of the manner of stringing rooms one behind the other in a long, deep structure, one room wide, rather than the traditional cluster arrangement of rooms and halls. If one fired a shotgun in the front door, the shot would pass through all rooms and go out the back door.

Development here was probably concentrated in the last quarter of the nineteenth century. Among real estate transactions in the area was the one below advertised in the *Star* by John D. Love on May 27, 1874: "Buy real estate in the new and thriving part of a city. I offer for sale because I need the money, four unimproved lots, each 150 × 66 feet, fronting on Sixth between Bladen and Harnett Streets, nearly equidistant from three railroad depots, and convenient to the street cars." Houses such as these were an integral part of the city, offering low cost housing to a great many citizens.

CORNELIUS HARNETT SCHOOL (LATER JAMES B. DUDLEY SCHOOL)

920 North Sixth Street
1914: Burett H. Stephens, architect; Rhodes and Underwood, builders

Begun as the Northside School, the structure was named the Cornelius Harnett School upon completion. From 1948 to 1952 it was known as the Peabody Annex. In 1952 it was renamed the James B. Dudley School.

Constructed as a school for white children, the building was opened to blacks in 1948. It was renamed to honor the prominent black educator and Wilmington native James B. Dudley, teacher and president of A & T College, Greensboro. From 1971 to June 1978, the building was used as a junior high school for exceptional children without regard to race. Since 1978 it has been a fifth and sixth grade center.

A Neo-classical Revival structure with monumental Ionic portico, the building is part of a superb collection of civic architecture in Wilmington. The facade decoration features bas-reliefs of children. These sculptures are themselves significant as civic outdoor art and are part of the large collection maintained by the Wilmington school system.

South Sixth Street

Market Street southward to Nun; then to intersection of South 6th and Queen Streets

Market Street

A pleasant residential street, South Sixth is bordered with massive live oak and other street trees that meet above the thoroughfare in many places.

WEIL HOUSE

21 South Sixth Street
1895–96: H. E. Bonitz, architect, L. H. Vollers, builder

Julius and Rachel Weil, local merchants who operated a dry goods store, acquired this property in 1895 and retained Bonitz as their architect and builder. Bonitz evolved a Queen Anne–style scheme somewhat more ornate than his clients desired, requiring changes. The original plans, which have remained with the house, show stained glass and a porch surrounding the house. The glass and some of the porch were omitted in construction.

Typical of Queen Anne–style houses of its era in Wilmington, the Weil House (fig. 101) is interesting because of its design by Bonitz and the survival of the plans, which can be compared with the standing dwelling. Since the builder is also known, the house evidences the capability and taste of Wilmington ar-

101. Weil House, 21 South Sixth Street. H. E. Bonitz, architect, 1895–96.

chitects, builders, and their clients during the last decade of the nineteenth century.

To intersection of South Sixth and Queen streets

Though there may have been empty spaces, undeveloped streets, and countryside between Market Street and this area in the early nineteenth century, there was considerable pre–Civil War development in the area of South Fourth, South Sixth, Queen, Castle, and Church streets.

With structures at all four corners, this intersection is a good example of that development. The paving block at the intersection is late nineteenth century, as are the two Victorian-era structures at the northeast and southwest corners of the intersection. At the other corners are an early twentieth-century church and a mid nineteenth-century house.

CHURCH OF THE GOOD SHEPHERD

515 Queen Street; northwest corner of South Sixth and Queen streets
1911–12: Upjohn & Conable of New York, architects

On November 8, 1892, the *Messenger* noted that:

The northwest corner of Sixth and Queen streets has been much improved in the past few months. The Parish of St. James' has bought this corner lot, turned around the small dwelling which occupied one side of the lots and has erected a church, seating 200 persons, and a hall some twenty five feet square, both facing Queen street.

The opening services at the church Sunday night were attended by a large and interested congregation. Hereafter, divine service will be conducted in this church, named the Chapel of the Good Shepherd, every Sunday. . . .

The work is chiefly the same that has been carried on at St. James' home for many years. They have added some important features and trust it will be more useful and practically helpful than ever. The location has been changed simply to get closer to the people and nearer to the centre of the field work.

By March 26, 1907, the *Star* could note the creation of a new parish, with the chapel becoming the Church of the Good Shepherd. "The organization of the parish," wrote the reporter, "marks a new epoch in the history of the great work that has been maintained under the jurisdiction of the parish of St. James."

The present building replaced the earlier structure in 1911–12. On October 31, 1911, the *Dispatch* carried an architectural rendering of the new church building and an article on its construction. The drawing was signed Upjohn and Conable, a young New York firm. Both architects, Hobart Upjohn and George W. Conable were later to become famous, and after establishing his own firm, Upjohn returned to Wilmington to design at least two other buildings, the St. James Parish House, or Great Hall, 1 South Third Street, in 1923–24 and the First Presbyterian Church, 121 South Third Street (fig. 61), in 1926–28. The Church of the Good Shepherd is an adaptation of the English Gothic country church and features a stuccoed corner tower and brick parapeted walls. The cornerstone was laid with Masonic ceremony on All Saints Day, November 1, 1911, and the building was occupied the following year.

MALPASS HOUSE

701 South Sixth Street
c. 1850

Known as the Malpass House after its owners since 1923, the dwelling seems to have been built c. 1850, possibly for a combined dwelling/office or dwelling/commercial use. It is a Wilmington Plain house from the Greek Revival era. There is an entrance from the street in the gable end on South Sixth, though the house faces southward toward the interior of the block along the eastern side of South Sixth. A four-bay, two-story porch covers this facade. Posts are square, and the balustrade remains only at the second level. On the first level, the porch floor is missing from its normal position, and the ground-level floor is indeed even with the ground.

A city cemetery was established in the block early in the nineteenth century. It was evidently closed about 1855. The *Messenger* for September 2, 1892, noted:

A citizen requests us to call the health authorities of the city to the bad condition of an old burying ground in the middle of the square surrounded by Queen and Wooster streets on the north and south and Sixth and Seventh streets on the east and west. It is overgrown with rank weeds and bushes, and the residents in the community are apprehensive that it will cause sickness. They would like for it to be cleaned out, and if possible, to have the remains of those buried there removed to one of the cemeteries or to some spot outside the city limits. The burying ground has not been used for thirty years and is now surrounded by residences.

Perhaps the Malpass House had some connection with the cemetery. Could it have been a keeper's residence? Could it have been moved to this spot from some other spot? Legal records indicate a jump in the value of the property between 1903 and 1904, possibly indicating when the house was moved to the site—if it was moved. The increase in value clearly does not indicate original construction, for the house had already been standing for at least a half century in 1903.

Inasmuch as the style of the house is unusual in survivals in Wilmington and the structure is located in an area of early development, the Malpass House warrants more careful investigation.

North Seventh Street

Market Street northward to Red Cross

A pleasant tree-lined street, North Seventh is almost entirely residential. Though several dwellings have been destroyed, many residences remain. Their construction spans a period of at least a century and a half.

The street retains early paving material, curbing, and sidewalk and is a good study of late nineteenth-century brick pavers. "Ragland Block" appears in the first block, along with granite curbing. These pavers continue into the second block (100 street numbers), where there are also "Augusta" and "Peebles Block, Portsmouth, Ohio" pavers. The third and fourth blocks (200 and 300 street numbers) are predominantly "Peebles" pavers, while "Reynolds" pavers appear at the intersection with Walnut Street, where they are set into patterns that wash across the intersection.

Princess Street crosses North Seventh; begin 100 street numbers

This block seems to have been a favorite for the residences of Wilmington architects and craftsmen. James F. Post, Wilmington's master carpenter and architect, resided at 110 North Seventh Street from at least 1885 to 1896. He died in 1899 at the home of James F. Post, Jr., at 112 North Seventh. Both houses have been demolished. Gerald M. Altaffer, builder and craftsman, lived at 105 North Seventh from at least 1900 until his death in 1907. That house too has been demolished. Osborne G. Foard, architect, also lived in this block. (See Bowden-Foard House, 114 North Seventh Street.)

CAPT. JOSEPH PRICE HOUSE

101 North Seventh Street
1882

The *Star* reported on September 24, 1882, that Capt. Joseph Price's "new residence at the corner of Seventh and Princess Streets [is] a very handsome building and just about completed." Price is listed in the 1883 city directory as being in residence at 101 North Seventh. A Confederate naval hero, Price commanded the ironclads *Georgia* and *Neuse*. He was later harbor master for the port of Wilmington.

One of the Wilmington Plain houses, the structure is somewhat boxy, without ornament, and reminiscent of an earlier Greek Revival style. Stylistically, it contrasts sharply with other houses in the block and with Wilmington's romance with the Italianate style.

H. T. DULS HOUSE

109 North Seventh Street
1897

According to the *Messenger* for July 31, 1897, "Mr. H. T. Duls' handsome new residence on Seventh street, between Princess and Chestnut streets, is receiving the finishing touches." Those finishing touches were indicative of the Victorian era. As reported in the *Dispatch*, September 30, 1897: "Mr. H. T. Duls's residence on Seventh between Princess and Chestnut streets has just been completed and dressed off in a beautiful cream color trimmed in dark olive and terra cotta. The house is decidedly one of the prettiest dwellings in the city. The painting, which was executed in a skillful manner, was done by Alford Hall, colored."

The house is a flamboyant Victorian structure that must have been most noticeable in its 1897 colors.

BOWDEN-FOARD HOUSE

114 North Seventh Street
1882–83

Mary C. and Joseph J. Bowden bought the property in 1882, built the house, and were in residence in 1883. Bowden, first a clerk and later a conductor with the Carolina Central Railroad, lived here for

102. Burns-Huggins House, 224 North Seventh Street, c. 1855.

more than twenty years. Several members of the De Vane family, who later occupied the house, worked with the Atlantic Coast Line Railroad.

From 1924 (when he purchased this small house) until after 1946, this was the residence of Osborne G. Foard, of the architectural firm of Lynch and Foard, and his wife Elsie, teacher and later principal of Cornelius Harnett School. Foard's architectural firm was responsible for the design of Saint Paul's Episcopal Church at Sixteenth and Market streets, Fire Station no. 5 at Seventeenth Street and Wrightsville Avenue, and many other significant Wilmington structures.

Another bracketed Italianate cottage with vented frieze, the house is one-story high beneath a low hip roof. The porch is almost full length, with pierced columns, a turned balustrade, and a hip rather than a canopy roof.

Chestnut Street crosses North Seventh; begin 200 street numbers

CURRIE-BOONE HOUSE

212 North Seventh Street
c. 1870

Stephen A. Currie bought the lot here in 1867 for $880. By the time he sold it to his sister Mary J. Gibbs in 1876, the price had risen to $4,317, indicating that the house had already been constructed. Though there are variations in the price of the property during other nineteenth century transfers, the house was definitely there in 1881, when Gray's map was published, and had reached its present configuration by 1893, when Leighton L. Boone was the owner. Boone, a blockade-runner during the Civil War and then a foreman at the Navassa Works, later became president of the Wilmington Lumber Company. He died at this address in June 1921.

A bracketed Italianate house, it is sited on a well-landscaped lot. The porch, with its turned balustrade and spindle course, is probably from the late nineteenth-century era of Boone family ownership.

BURNS-HUGGINS HOUSE

224 North Seventh Street
c. 1855

A country house later surrounded by the city, this frame structure (fig. 102) predates its neighbors. One outbuilding, possibly a kitchen, survives.

A Wilmington Plain dwelling, the building is listed in the tax records as having been built in 1832. Owen Burns acquired the lot from Jacob Wessel in 1853 for $600. Burns mortgaged the property to Oscar G. Parsley in 1857, and Parsley sold it to Richard H. Grant in 1858 for $2,100. This would seem to indicate that there was not a house on the property in 1853, but that Burns had built before he lost the property to Parsley. From an exterior examination of the house, there is no reason to doubt a c. 1855 date. The low hip roof with slight overhang and molded cornice, the side entrance with transom and sidelights, and the shutters of two panels of movable louvers are evocative of the Greek Revival era. The porch that surrounds the house on the two street facades is less Greek, with its clustered posts and simple balustrade, but is one of the factors that gives the house great memorability.

When Burns acquired the lot in 1853, the neighborhood would have been only sparsely developed, but one where streets were already marked out and there was a good deal of real estate activity. After the opening of Oakdale Cemetery, the house was on a major thoroughfare to the cemetery.

The property passed to the Huggins family in 1860. From that time until well into the twentieth century, it was in either Huggins or Whitney family ownership. W. A. Whitney, turn-of-the-century resident, was clerk and later watchmaker with the G. W. Huggins firm.

Walnut Street crosses North Seventh; begin 400 street numbers

WHITEMAN HOUSE

404 North Seventh Street
1899: W. H. Willis, builder

The 1871 city directory lists John H. Whiteman, timber inspector, as living on "N. 7th, near Church." There was already a house on the lot by the time Gray accomplished his 1881 map. The Sanborn map of 1893, which includes North Seventh Street, also shows a dwelling here. The Whiteman family believes that John H. Whiteman, Sr., tore down the earlier structure in 1899 and built the present house. That contention is borne out by the *Messenger* of November 8, 1899, which noted: "W. H. Willis, the contractor, has succeeded in getting the frame work for the residence of H. H. Whiteman, colored, well up again and about ready for the weatherboarding. It will be remembered that he had the frame about up before when the storm swept over this section last week and blew it down. The building when completed is to cost about $3,000."

Distinctive because of the unusual facade it presents to the viewer, the house is basically a bracketed-and-vented Italianate house, though it is reminiscent of Steamboat Gothic dwellings. This resemblance derives partly from dual paint colors and the fact that the frieze vents are directly above the windows and seem to be vented transoms for the second-level windows. It also derives partly from the use of Stick-style elements on the facade to outline openings and from the balustrade and spindle course of the full porch. It is the bay, however, that is the most unusual feature. While one would expect three, or at the most four, planes in a bay window such as this one, it has seven planes, so that rather than being demioctagonal, it seems almost round. The overhanging cornice emphasizes this, as do brackets that delineate each of the planes. Another factor is the narrow siding on the facade, which contrasts with siding of a more normal width on the sides of the structure. On the second level of the facade, the siding is horizontal; on the first level beneath the porch, it is placed diagonally between the bay openings and is used decoratively.

Both John Sr. and John Jr. Whiteman were listed in city directories as wood dealers. John Sr. was later listed as secretary of United Charities.

The family produced several well-known teachers and educators in the early twentieth century. Annita Whiteman taught at Peabody School; Gladys taught at Williston Primary School; and John Jr. was superintendent of black schools in Columbia, South Carolina, and after the system was integrated, was the first black supervisor of education for the system. Addie Whiteman Dickerson became a lawyer in Philadelphia, achieving distinction in a field traditionally difficult for a woman, much less a black woman.

South Seventh Street

Dock Street southward to Church Street

South Seventh Street is pleasantly residential, maintaining street trees and a consistent scale to its residences, especially in the first two blocks.

After the establishment of Oakdale and Pine Forest cemeteries, Seventh seems to have become a thoroughfare for funeral processions. A May 24, 1874, *Star* article noted that prior to the building of the street railway "Seventh Street was considerably used for funerals to both cemeteries from the southern portion of the city." By 1874 the street was in deplorable condition, and the newspaper "suggested to the city authorities to sawdust the same." On May 13, 1894, a Wilmington newspaper reported "The city authorities have constructed a good shell road on Seventh Street from Market to Castle."

Dock Street crosses South Seventh; begin 100 street numbers

PENNY HOUSE

109 South Seventh Street
c. 1888

B. F. Penny purchased the lot on which this house stands in January 1888 and probably began building soon thereafter. The block was still largely undeveloped in 1881, with only one house facing on South Seventh within the block. Penny built in the prevailing vented-and-bracketed Italianate style. Even with changes to balustrade, porch, and trim, the house is striking. The five-bay facade is on two planes, with three bays projecting and covered by an almost full, two-tiered, three-bay porch. All bay openings have molded architraves and heavily molded cornice caps and projecting sills. The double entrance door is beneath an arched transom.

Penny is listed in the 1895 city directory as a clothier. The 1909–10 directory lists the firm as B. F. Penny and Co.

Orange Street crosses South Seventh; begin 200 street numbers

Though no building-by-building survey has been accomplished on South Seventh Street beyond Orange, several historical and architectural sites to do with black history should be mentioned.

At 209 South Seventh Street is the Ebenezer Baptist Church. Already in existence in 1880, the church building was listed on the Gray map of 1881 as "Col. Baptist Church." A new building begun in 1896 was evidently a fine structure, for the *Dispatch* reported that year on March 21 that "Mr. James F. Post, the architect, completed plans for Ebenezer Baptist Church." Though the present late-Gothic building dates from 1927, the basement of the Post-designed building survives, with one level of brick arched windows.

At 419 South Seventh, Gray's 1881 map lists St. Luke's Methodist Episcopal Church. The congregation, now St. Luke's African Methodist Episcopal Church, was organized in 1861, and they built at this site at least as early as January 21, 1878. The church bell, cast by "McShane Bell Foundry, Henry McShane Co., Baltimore, Md., 1886." was used from the time it was installed in 1886 to the destruction of the 1878 church by fire in January 1944. The bell is now displayed atop a pedestal to the north of the rebuilt church. The 1944 building was designed by Leslie N. Boney, Architect, and was built by U. A. Underwood Co.

As with other black churches of Wilmington (and indeed a majority of all churches), there is no published history of either of these congregations. Certainly a good share of the black history of Wilmington is embodied in these two churches, and if that history is as good as the architectural heritage of the two, it is well worth recording.

On South Seventh Street between Nun and Church is Evergreen Tabernacle no. 9, built in 1899.

The April 4, 1899, *Messenger* recorded issuance of the building permit to the Tabernacle "of the N.V.G.O., of the Brothers and Sisters of Love and Charity, to rebuild their hall on Seventh Street. . . . This was the office of the Negro newspaper, The Daily Record, destroyed by fire on the memorable 19th of November 1898, when some citizens of Wilmington wrecked the office of the newspaper." The incident, part of the Wilmington riot of 1898, formed the basis for Thomas Dixon's book and play *The Leopard's Spots.*

North Ninth Street

The block between Chestnut and Grace streets

Chestnut Street crosses North Ninth; begin 200 street numbers

GRAFFLIN HOUSE

206 North Ninth Street
before 1881; remodeled c. 1898

A story-and-a-half frame house set well back from the street on a large lot, the dwelling was built before 1881, when it appears on the Gray map. Its original style and finish are unknown; some evidence indicates Gothic Revival, however.

The present character of the Grafflin House likely comes from remodeling during the era of the M. E. Grafflin family's ownership from 1898 through the first quarter of the twentieth century.

The starkly symmetrical structure is a highly individual Queen Anne cottage. The cross gable roof, with front projecting bay, is echoed in the pedimented porch that terminates in flanking conical roofed gazebos. A square cupola crowns the roof at the intersection of the cross gables. The effect is one of spaciousness and height, evoking images of turn-of-the-century life-styles such as porch swings and rocking chairs, Victorian gardens and croquet on the lawn.

Red Cross Street

Cape Fear River eastward to North Seventh Street

Red Cross was one of the major streets of old Wilmington, with access to the largest rail terminal in Wilmington, that of the Wilmington and Weldon Railroad, and to important waterfront docks on the river. Champion Compress and Warehouse Company was located on Red Cross at the river for a number of years in the nineteenth and early twentieth centuries, along with Alexander Sprunt and Sons warehouses.

Freight facilities of the Wilmington and Weldon were located at Red Cross and the water from the mid-nineteenth century. Later, the general offices of the Atlantic Coast Line Railroad were also located on Red Cross between Nutt and North Front streets

103. Marshall-Chasten House (later Schubert Hall), 210 Red Cross Street, c. 1840.

and North Front and North Second streets. Built in the early twentieth century from the plan of architect J. F. Leitner, the Atlantic Coast Line General Office Building at the northeast corner of Front and Red Cross was intentionally demolished on July 12, 1970, in an early-morning dynamite blast. The Union Station—combining facilities of all railroads into Wilmington at Red Cross and North Front streets and to the north of the railroad tracks—has also been demolished.

The trolley that ran northward up North Front Street turned eastward on Red Cross, running out to James Walker Hospital (now demolished) on Rankin Street (Red Cross Street extended) at Dickinson. St. John's Episcopal Church (now demolished) was on Red Cross Street at North Third, and the street was also a street of prime residences.

In 1976 the Cape Fear Technical Institute was located on Red Cross west of North Front Street. The street still begins at the river, where the Alton F. Lennon Oceanographic Laboratory, located in a converted ferryboat, is moored.

North Second Street crosses Red Cross; begin 200 street numbers

Once a thriving residential block, only two residences remain. They retain their street trees, which have been destroyed in the rest of the block.

MARSHALL-CHASTEN HOUSE (later Schubert Hall)

210 Red Cross Street
c. 1840

Thomas Marshall acquired the land here in August of 1838 and probably began construction of this house (fig. 103) soon thereafter. Marshall maintained ownership until 1851—when the property passed to Zeno H. Green, who kept it until 1871. Acquired by the Chasten family in 1885, it remained their home until well into the twentieth century.

R. H. Chasten, who is listed as residing here in the 1889 city directory, was identified as "Inspector." It was his daughter, Cannie Chasten—a musician and music teacher who opened a music studio here in October 1892 and gave lessons for at least a quarter of a century—who christened the dwelling "Schubert Hall."

This is a two-story frame house with the Beaufort-type gable roof that is commonly found in the town of Beaufort, North Carolina. The double-tiered front porch is an integral part of the structure, beneath a gable roof that has more than one pitch to each of its planes. A Wilmington Plain dwelling, the house has similarities in plan to the Burgwin-Wright House, 224 Market Street. (See fig. 120 and color plate 6.)

North Third Street crosses Red Cross; begin 300 street numbers

GREEK REVIVAL RESIDENTIAL-COMMERCIAL STRUCTURE

320–22 Red Cross Street
c. 1850

A Greek Revival–style building in a city where that style is relatively rare, this two-story frame structure with low hip roof features a molded cornice, a plain frieze, and intermediate and corner pilasters. Dwelling spaces are above the corner and to the south along North Fourth Street, while the store (which is now a restaurant) is along Red Cross with a diagonally cut entrance at the corner of Red Cross and North Fourth streets.

The dwelling entrance on Red Cross, with its transom and sidelights within a molded architrave, is typical of the Greek Revival era. The structure is a handsome one and a surviving example of many other such Wilmington structures that combined dwelling use with neighborhood businesses. Its continuance in active use is as important as its style.

The 1885 city directory lists this as the residence of Seth W. Davis, auctioneer. In 1890, N. Hullen operated a saloon here. By 1904 it was the residence of H. H. King. The *Star* reported the death of Mrs. King at 320 Red Cross Street on June 3 of that year. The building was owned by C. P. B. Mahler and family from 1898 to 1923.

North Fourth Street crosses Red Cross; begin 400 street numbers

LATE ITALIANATE DWELLING

407 Red Cross Street
c. 1870

Evidently the house was moved to this site after 1915, and its origin is unknown. It does not show on the 1881 Gray map, or on the Sanborn maps through 1915. From the design, however, there can be no doubt that it is an earlier house, and on the basis of style alone it could have been built c. 1870.

A late Italianate structure, the house is different both because of its bulk and because of the equal-size cross gables of the roof. The molded cornice is supported by sawn brackets with drop pendants. The three-bay double-tiered, pedimented porch on a five-bay facade has an oculus vent in the closed pediment simple posts and turned balustrade. Window architraves are molded, and cornice caps project. Entrances are central on both levels, with doors beneath transoms—the lower one arched.

ITALIANATE DWELLING

409 Red Cross Street
before 1881

A vented-and-bracketed Italianate dwelling, the house features a canopy-roofed porch with molded cornice and plain frieze. Double brackets crown openwork posts with side brackets sawn in a floral pattern.

The 1885 city directory lists E. Van Laer, "professor of music," at this address. In 1890, W. B. Hartsfield, coppersmith for the Wilmington and Weldon Railroad, died here.

QUEEN ANNE–STYLE SHOTGUN HOUSE

413 Red Cross Street
c. 1895

Probably the best finished and most ornate of the narrow Wilmington shotgun houses, this Queen Anne cottage (fig. 104) is a fine example of its type. One story, frame, with gable roof perpendicular to the street, it presents a most ornate facade to the viewer. Decorated with carved rafter ends, molded bargeboards, patterned shingle, a louvered gable

104. Queen Anne–style shotgun house, 413 Red Cross Street, c. 1895.

vent, and sawn-and-shingle gable ornament, the roof gable is echoed by a projecting gable-roofed central bay. This is decorated with a radiating gable ornament, patterned shingle, and a tin panel decorated with swags that surround the bay and serve as a frieze atop the windows. Windows are elongated and sit atop a shingled wainscot.

The house features recessed interior porches on each side of the central bay, so that there are actually nine planes to the very narrow house facade. The porches have spindle courses, plain posts, sawn brackets, and turned balustrade. Doors are topped with transoms.

It is significant that three dwellings as varied as those at 407, 409, and 413 Red Cross Street appear adjacent to each other within a single block. The differences in their bulk and finish are great, making them a good study of nineteenth-century Wilmington tastes and styles.

North Fifth Avenue crosses Red Cross; begin 500 street numbers

St. Stephen A.M.E. Church Annex dominates the north side of the block. It is in Campbell Square in the Peabody School block.

Walnut Street

North Water Street eastward to North Seventh

There are good views of the Cape Fear River and of occasional water traffic from Walnut and North Water streets, though the waterfront now has little relation to its former importance.

During the late nineteenth century Sprunt's Wharf and the Alexander Sprunt and Sons Company were located on the south side of Walnut at Nutt. Water Street did not cut through this far until recently. The Cape Fear Flour Mills were also at Nutt and Walnut streets on the south side. On the north side between Nutt and the river were the buildings of the J. W. Taylor Saw and Planing Mill and McRae's Wharf, one of the major Wilmington wharves. A short time later Sprunt moved across the street in this area, constructing warehouses and operating the Champion Compress Company.

At Walnut and North Front streets, the Wilmington Hotel operated from the late nineteenth century until well into the twentieth, one of the city's best known and handsomest hotels. Its 1914 building, a major downtown landmark, was demolished in 1974.

Though this could scarcely be recognized from the present state of Walnut Street, it was once a major commercial and industrial waterfront area.

North Third Street crosses Walnut; begin 300 street numbers

WACHOVIA BANK AND TRUST COMPANY

301 Walnut Street
1952

A modernistic structure of horizontal brick and stone bands, the bank is a stylistic maverick in Wilmington. It is a curious structure that seems, like the Waccamaw Bank two blocks away at 101–3 North Third, to have borrowed material and color from the New Hanover County Courthouse. In addition to brick and stone, there are green stone bands, giving an odd polychroming to the structure.

A large, central, stone panel, with stepped false-gable front trimmed with green stone and containing a seven-bay window band at the second level, dominates the Walnut Street facade. The windows have multipaned glass, with stone lintels, and molded stone sills. Within the band the windows alternate with green log-shaped rolls. Below the windows the name of the bank appears in a panel, flanked by oc-

105. Wachovia Bank and Trust Company, detail, 301 Walnut Street, 1952.

tagonal plaques with stylized Art-Deco eagles (fig. 105). The entrance is centrally located and has a green surround and an aluminum slab hood.

On the North Third Street facade, there is a smaller stone panel in the northwestern corner of the building.

North Sixth Street crosses Walnut; begin 600 street numbers

JOHNSON HOUSE

602 Walnut Street
c. 1850

Fannie A. Johnson, wife of Alexander Johnson, purchased the lot on which this house stands in October of 1872. The purchase price seems to indicate that there was a house already standing, and tax records give a construction date of 1850. These two facts, coupled with the style of the dwelling, seem to indicate that the tax date is probably correct.

A large frame structure, the house features a centered Greek Revival entrance with sidelight and transoms, a low hip roof, and wide unadorned frieze. The house is five bays long on Walnut and three wide bays deep on North Sixth. The western bay on the ground floor is also an entrance with a three-light transom above, possibly indicating an early combined residential and professional or commercial use of the structure. A four-bay porch with chamfered posts and turned balustrade almost covers the Walnut Street facade. The house is revetted somewhat below street level, indicating a building up of the level of Walnut Street in front of the house.

The structure is prominently displayed and labeled "A. Johnson" on the 1881 Gray map of Wilmington, indicating a building and owner of consequence.

Grace Street

(formerly Mulberry Street)

From North Water Street eastward to North Ninth

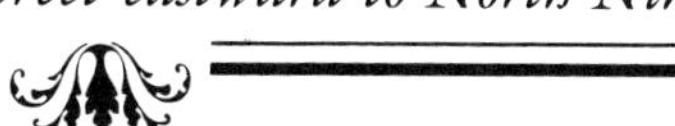

On Gray's 1881 map of Wilmington, Mulberry Street stretches to the Cape Fear River. Worth's Wharf is at its foot to the north. To the south, nearer Chestnut Street, is London's Wharf. The Mulberry waterfront was intensely commercial and industrial, with North Water Street beginning to the south near the waterfront and Nutt Street somewhat farther east and to the north. Nutt Street gave access to the freight and passenger terminals of the major Wilmington railroads and to their docks, while North Water Street led to additional wharfs and the main commercial area. Since both ended at Mulberry Street, it became a major traffic artery for people and goods leaving or approaching the waterfront.

When Front Street Methodist Church relocated from North Front Street to Mulberry at North Fourth Street in 1887, the congregation changed its name to Grace Methodist Church. This was a large and important Wilmington congregation, and Mulberry began gradually to be known as Grace Street, after the church. By 1895 the name was so well fixed that the street became Grace Street. Though *Mulberry* was dropped from official designations, the name died hard, and until well into the twentieth

106. Lazarus House, 314 Grace Street, c. 1816: c. 1854; c. 1895.

century, the street was identified on maps and in documents as "Grace or Mulberry."

North Third Street crosses Grace; begin 300 street numbers

LAZARUS HOUSE

314 Grace Street
c. 1816; enlarged and remodeled c. 1854; iron porch and fence on Grace, c. 1895

The Lazarus House (fig. 106) exhibits a continuum of architectural styles rarely found in Wilmington or elsewhere. Throughout its lifetime of remodeling and enlarging, the owners added to rather than changed so that much design evidence from each era remains. The house displays Adamesque, or Federal, detail in the three bays to the east, or left side of the house, from the early era; Greek Revival detail to the west, or right, side, from the c. 1854 era.

In its early configuration, the house was the only dwelling within the block between Grace and Chestnut, North Third and North Fourth, streets. Facing Chestnut, it had a well-developed lawn, gardens, and orchards between the house and the street.

It was during the phase of the house that evolved around 1854 that it became a full-blown Italianate building and changed its entrance to Grace Street. A center pavilion, three bays wide and one bay deep, seems to have been added at that time to serve as the new entrance.

Cast iron remains on both facades of the house. The double porch and steps on the Chestnut Street facade are early. Quite Gothic in character, they are probably from the mid-nineteenth century phase of the house. Iron on the Grace Street facade, including the porch and the lawn fence, is late, probably not installed until c. 1895.

This house is one of the few in the city that maintains any of its Federal-era character—not surprising considering the devastating nature of the frequent fires that swept the city and the Wilmington love affair with the Italianate, which tended to push all other styles aside. Its isolation within its own block gave it protection from fire; the taste of its owners protected it from stylistic stripping. In the Lazarus House there is a reconciliation of the stylistic eras of construction in a superb exhibit of taste and character. The house is not only a visually dominant Wilmington landmark, but stylistically, one of its most valuable.

Aaron Lazarus came to Wilmington from Charleston early in the nineteenth century. He established a mercantile empire here, with warehouse and commercial properties on the waterfront. His interests extended to shipping and to the Wilmington and Weldon Railroad, which he helped found and served as director.

Lazarus died in 1841, while on business in Petersburg, Virginia. He was buried in Richmond, there being no Jewish cemetery in Wilmington. There was also no synagogue, and Lazarus worshipped in St. James, where he is said to have once remarked that he could worship Jehovah in any temple. Lazarus left a large family, among whom his holdings, including this house and block, were divided.

Dr. F. J. Hill, who was also associated with the Wilmington and Weldon Railroad and had sizable mercantile interests, acquired the house from the Lazarus heirs. It was he who changed the orientation of the dwelling to Grace, thus adjusting for the diminished property and bringing the structure into the mainstream of Italianate Wilmington through his additions and changes.

On February 24, 1874, when a Wilmington newspaper reported the auction of the property, it must still have been an impressive complex: "The valuable property known as the old Lazarus Place, belonging to the estate of Dr. F. J. Hill, deceased, was sold yesterday at private sale. This property fronts 26 feet on Third street, 222 feet on Fourth street and 210 feet on Mulberry street. On it there is a large dwelling, offices, kitchen and stable, all of brick."

North Fourth Street crosses Grace; begin 400 street numbers

GRACE UNITED METHODIST CHURCH

401 Grace Street
1914–16: old education building; 1949–50: sanctuary, Harold E. Wagoner of Philadelphia, architect, W. A. Simon, builder; 1956–60: new education building, Harold E. Wagoner, architect

William Meredith, a Wesleyan missionary who came to Wilmington from the West Indies in the late 1700s, established Methodism in this area. The first church building, erected by 1797 at North Second and Walnut streets, burned. By 1815 another church had been built. Bishop Francis Asbury preached in both these buildings.

The second church building was on the northeast corner of North Front and Walnut streets and took its name from the location—Front Street Methodist Church. A burial ground had been established adjacent to the church by 1831. The church was enlarged in 1843 before it burned on April 30. The third church, a fine Greek Revival structure, was built in 1844. On February 21, 1886, that structure was also destroyed by fire.

Since land at the Front Street site was restricted and the city was developing to the east, the decision was made to seek a new location, and property was purchased on Mulberry at North Fourth. The cornerstone for the new church to be erected there, the congregation's fourth, was laid on November 24, 1886. When the church acquired a lot in Oakdale Cemetery and, in 1887, moved remains from the Front Street Methodist Church Cemetery to Oakdale, there no longer remained any ties to Front Street. On May 2, 1887, the congregation chose the name Grace for the new church. Occupied in 1887, the new debt-free building on Mulberry was dedicated on December 7, 1890. In 1895 the name of the street officially changed from Mulberry to Grace.

Between 1914 and 1916 an educational building was added; in 1945 the church repaired and remodeled the 1886–87 building. On March 21, 1947, the 1880s church burned—the fourth time the church buildings had been destroyed by fire. The education building survived, as did the walls and tower of the sanctuary building, but the decision was made to take them down and start anew, retaining only the education building. Harold E. Wagoner of Philadelphia, a nationally known church architect, was chosen to design the new building. The building committee presented him with a mo-

107. Grace United Methodist Church, 401 Grace Street. Harold E. Wagoner, architect, 1949–50; 1956–60.

tion stating that the church "not be colonial type but simple modified Gothic in style."

Ground was broken for the new stone church May 11, 1949, and the building opened for worship on December 24, 1950. On May 16, 1951, the bodies of former ministers George Daughtry and William Meredith were placed in a vault beneath the pulpit. Altar windows were dedicated February 18, 1951; the debt-free church building was dedicated on May 15, 1955, and the new Moller pipe organ and new stained-glass windows were dedicated on March 27, 1966.

The bell in the present building, with the marble font in the baptistry, and the brass cross on the altar are from the 1880s church, salvaged from the fire. The stained glass is new, much of it from Willett Stained Glass Studios of Philadelphia, installed at various times from 1954 to 1966. Willett, one of the best known glass-makers in the country, has supplied glass for the National Cathedral in Washington, D.C., and for many other fine churches. In Wilmington, Willett glass also appears in the First Presbyterian Church at 121 South Third.

Between 1959 and 1960, the remaining part of the Wagoner plan for the church was completed. The new education building is in front of the 1914–

16 building, though the older building is visible between the sanctuary and the newer structure. (See fig. 107.)

In 1960 Grace Church faced a fifth crisis, one almost as devastating as the fires that had plagued it. With the announcement that the Atlantic Coast Line Railroad would move its headquarters from Wilmington to Jacksonville, Florida, came the realization that Grace would lose some two hundred members—railroad employees who would move. This, coupled with the changing character of the area, and the deterioration of the adjacent neighborhood as urban renewal and clearance created a wasteland, left the church with the decision of abandoning downtown or recognizing changed circumstances and congregation—the classic dilemma of downtown churches in the twentieth century. Recognizing the assets of the existing church, especially its heritage and ability to serve a wider and more diverse area than any new church could, Grace decided to remain downtown, where it had just finished constructing major new facilities. In a Statement of Mission adopted April 9, 1972, the congregation vowed to be "involved in the struggle of the stuff of life; that we must be concerned about the welfare of those not only in our fellowship, but also in the Wilmington community and of all men everywhere; and this concern shall be expressed by an active program of community involvement, to the end that all men shall come to share the fulfillment of love and joy and peace that God intends."

CUTTS HOUSE

416 Grace Street
c. 1886

Not shown on the Gray's 1881 map, the house does appear on the 1889 Sanborn map. In the 1889 city directory the Cutts family is listed as in residence at 416 Mulberry. A. H. Cutts, who had been a conductor on the Wilmington and Weldon Railroad, is listed as Capt. A. H. Cutts, gatekeeper, Atlantic Coast Line Railroad. John A. Cutts, conductor, and Jimmie Cutts, clerk, both for the Atlantic Coast Line, also resided at number 416. The property had been purchased by Annie L. Cutts in 1885, and construction on the house must have begun immediately. The Cutts family remained in residence until 1905.

Though property had not been selected by the Methodists for their new building when the Cutts acquired their lot, the church site, directly across the street, was chosen soon thereafter. Almost overnight the block became significant and highly visible. This house is the only survivor of the vented-and-bracketed Italianate structures built on the south side of the block. It is probably indicative of the quality of the others.

North Fifth Street crosses Grace; begin 500 street numbers

Fine vistas along North Fifth show the street much as it appeared in the late nineteenth century. Trees and shrubs remain at the sides and in the center plaza, giving the broad street the true feel of an avenue.

ROSE-COVINGTON HOUSE

519 Grace Street
c. 1855; George W. Rose, builder

George W. Rose acquired the land here in 1853, simultaneously selling Cumberland County land held in trust for his wife Margaret Casey. By 1866–67 he is listed in the city directory as "Contractor & Builder," living at the corner of Sixth and Mulberry. There is no reason to doubt that a contractor and builder would wish to construct his own dwelling and that, given the financial means and the site, he did just that. The quality of workmanship and design here is high, indicating that Rose was probably one of the best of the Wilmington artisans. As an indication of his capability and standing as a mid-nineteenth century builder, he was one of the builders of City Hall–Thalian Hall (see fig. 51), along with John and Robert Wood and James F. Post, who was supervising architect.

A two-story frame house in the bracketed Italianate style, the dwelling is set back from the street atop a raised basement. The size of the house, its L configuration, and its finish combine with the spacious site to make it a most noticeable dwelling. By the turn of the century, when this was the residence of C. C. Covington, it was one of the best known of the Wilmington houses, one of the few pictured in the 1902 chamber of commerce publication *Wilmington, N.C., Up-to-date*. At that time its yards still covered most of the block, a picket fence surrounded the lot, and an octagonal gazebo was in the yard, as was a sizable greenhouse.

Covington acquired the property in 1872 and was in residence by 1875. He was president of C. C. Covington & Company, which he founded in 1871. The firm dealt in only three products: molasses was imported from the West Indies; flour was brought in from Grand Rapids, Michigan; and fish, locally purchased, was cured, packed, and shipped out. The company was large, well-known, and profitable.

Chestnut Street

North Water Street eastward to North Eighth

In the 1880s the New York and Wilmington Steamship Company operated from London Wharf at the base of Chestnut, an important waterfront location. Noted the *Star* on June 25, 1886, "The New York steamers will hereafter discharge and receive freight at the new shed erected near the foot of Chestnut street. This shed, by the way, is a mammoth structure, surpassing anything of the kind ever erected here."

The Rock Spring, a prominent downtown Wilmington landmark, was on the north side of Chestnut, between North Front and North Water streets. The hillside was revetted to the spring, which faced westward toward the river. Sidewalls of the below-ground spring were brick and the approach was by slate steps. Water bubbled up through the sandy spring bottom and was carried off through terra-cotta pipes. It was an old spring in 1850 and was still in use as late as 1905. Local residents went there to drink, and visiting ships frequently filled their casks from the water hole.

The Rock Spring Hotel, adjacent to the water source, achieved popularity in the nineteenth century. It was in operation by 1866, taking both its name and water from the spring.

North Front Street crosses Chestnut Street; begin 100 street numbers

HOTEL CAPE FEAR

115–125 Chestnut Street, northwest corner Chestnut and North Second
1923–25: G. Lloyd Preacher, Atlanta and Raleigh, architect; Walter Clark, builder, W. C. Watson, construction supervisor; 1938: four bay addition to the north along North Second Street

The only survivor of the city's major pre–World War II hotels, the Hotel Cape Fear (fig. 108) is a nine-story building featuring patterned brick and a heavy bracketed cornice. Essentially, the building is a column with a one-story capital, or top, a six-story shaft, and a two-story base. Ornament is used sparingly and the building makes an immediate statement—it is a hotel.

World War I brought great prosperity to the port of Wilmington. Shipping increased dramatically, and a new shipyard was established. The Orton, Hotel Wilmington, and smaller hotels and inns in town could not handle the overflow business, and there were fears that the city was being bypassed because of its lack of hotel space. On December 13, 1919, the chamber of commerce recommended construction of a major new hotel, and the *Star* announced on January 5, 1920, that its slogan would be "A new hotel in Wilmington—A new hotel in Wrightsville Beach." It was felt that the Wilmington hotel should be centrally located, near downtown and trolley-car lines, and that it should have at least two hundred and fifty rooms. The community was canvassed, May 3 was declared "Hotel Day," and by May 4 almost four hundred thousand dollars had been subscribed for hotel construction. On May 14 a site at Chestnut and North Second streets was acquired. On June 19, Kenneth M. Murchison, Wilmington and New York architect, presented plans for the hotel.

The lot was paid for, a hotel charter was adopted, and another lot adjacent to the first was purchased—

108. Hotel Cape Fear, 115–25 Chestnut Street, northwest corner Chestut and North Second streets. G. Lloyd Preacher, architect, 1923–25.

but still no hotel. Architect Murchison's plans were evidently forgotten.

As part of a revival of the hotel plan in the summer of 1922, architects were invited to Wilmington to discuss the hotel. Between June 7 and July 4, firm representatives traveled in and out of Wilmington in a constant stream. W. L. Stoddart seemed to be the architect drawing the most local interest, but it went no farther than that.

On March 2, 1923, discussions began with G. Lloyd Preacher of Atlanta and Raleigh. Preacher, a well-known hotel architect, had designed the Fort Sumter in Charleston, the Cecil, Ansley Annex, and Pershing Point in Atlanta, and the Soreno in St. Petersburg.

On October 2 the Cape Fear Hotel Corporation was organized, and Preacher's plans were examined and accepted. Walter Clark, a Wilmington builder, was awarded the construction contract. W. C. Watson, who had supervised construction of the new U.S. Custom House on North Water, was retained as construction supervisor, and on November 1, 1923, at 11 A.M., ground was broken. The *Star* enthused: "The hotel building will cost, when completed, approximately Eight-hundred fifty thousand dollars. The structure will be handsome in design and splendidly appointed throughout. It will be of reinforced concrete, fire proof. The exterior will be of brick and limestone. It will be nine stories in height. It will contain more than one-hundred rooms, a handsomely appointed dining room and lobby, also a ball room, roof garden, etc."

Concrete footings were poured on December 1, and on January 13, 1924, the *Star* boasted "We are above ground." By January 29 the second-floor slab was being poured; by March 16 the eighth-floor slab. There were then two hundred men at work daily, with a weekly payroll of some thirty-five hundred dollars.

Construction was marred by an accident on January 31, 1924, when a carpenter was killed in a fall at the site. On March 21 a storm toppled the work elevator, and it had to be reerected. On May 21 another worker was killed at the site. In spite of this bad luck, the exterior brickwork was completed and the cornice placement was begun June 7. By June 27 the exterior was completed, and the work of washing it down was begun.

J. W. Alexander, who had operated the Battery Park Hotel in Asheville, was chosen to operate the Cape Fear, and an unnamed Philadelphia decorator was chosen to design the interiors. Alexander announced on September 21 that "excepting the Battery Park Hotel in Asheville, no hostelry in North Carolina would surpass the Cape Fear." He intended to open for business on November 1.

By November 1, Walter Clark, whose construction firm was building the hotel, had disappeared, and his absence was creating numerous and annoying construction delays. Clark was declared bankrupt on November 11. What followed would have made a fine Laurel and Hardy movie script, as Alexander tried to open his hotel and creditors tried to collect from the Clark company. In one celebrated incident, furniture and furnishings began arriving for the hotel in December. The first room was installed on December 16. On December 19 the building elevators were attached by creditors, leaving Alexander with furniture for a 150-room, nine-story hotel, and no elevators.

Furnishing went on as fast as it could be accomplished under the circumstances, and before the end of the year the elevators were operating again. The first guest, a friend of Alexander, stayed in the hotel on January 7, 1925. The Hotel Cape Fear opened officially on January 10, 1925, and the economist Roger Babson was the first guest to register. The hostelry became a favorite of north-south travelers, so popular and well-known that its 150 rooms were not sufficient. Some 35 more were added in a 1938 addition.

One of the early guests of the hotel was George W. Rappleyea, who stayed in the hotel several months during 1925. A clipping from a Wilmington newspaper for May 19, 1925, noted that, "George W. Rappleyea, who at one time operated the Southport Light & Power Co., the Cape Fear Telephone & Telegraph Co. and the Southern Blue Print & Map Co., is responsible for the wave of unrest and dissatisfaction that has engulfed Dayton, Tennessee, through institution of a suit against John T. Scopes, science teacher in the Dayton high school, to determine the validity of the anti-evolution bill, passed by the Tennessee legislature." The Rappleyea suit resulted in the July 1925 Scopes Trial, in which Clarence Darrow was defense attorney and William Jennings Bryan was the prosecutor.

February 22, 1926, a newspaper reported that "over 1,000 people inspected the new Stutz automobile while it was on display in the lobby." In late 1942 the U.S. Army took over the hotel café to use as a Women's Army Corps (WAC) mess. The corps, formed in 1942, was still in its infancy, and the Wilmington unit was an early one. It was not until after June 23, 1943, that (as noted in the *Star*) repairs could be begun and the restaurant again opened to the public.

A native Wilmingtonian who spent much time at the hotel when he was a reporter for the Wilmington *Star-News* was David Brinkley. In his November 10, 1974, column Bill Reaves noted a local speech by Brinkley:

> *Toward the close of his talk he reminisced about his youth in Wilmington. He recalled when he was assigned by the* Star-News *to cover the many meetings of various civic organizations on the mezzanine of the Cape Fear Hotel. He said he became accustomed to eating the same meal five times a week, breaded veal cutlet, mashed potatoes and green peas. His favorite speech, which he heard about five times in one week, was the "Romance of Cast Iron Pipe," which lasted about two hours.*

A complete accounting of those who either stayed at, ate, or were associated in some way with events at this hotel would probably be astounding. Though the building remains, it is no longer in operation as a hotel. It is the last reminder of an era when guests arrived in Wilmington by passenger train, private railroad car, steamer, private yacht, or airplane, by automobile and even, occasionally, by chauffeured limousine.

North Fourth Street crosses Chestnut; begin 400 street numbers

RADCLIFFE-MENDELSOHN HOUSE

411 Chestnut Street
c. 1830–82

When the estate of Timothy D. Radcliffe was divided by the court of pleas in the March session of 1844, this property and the house next door, the Radcliffe-Bloom House, at 419 North Fourth Street, went to Robert S. Radcliffe, who sold 419 but kept this property. It is likely that a house was already standing here. The *Star* in "a partial list of buildings erected and improvements made during the past twelve months," published September 24, 1882, listed "Captain R. S. Radcliffe residence on Chestnut, between Fourth and Fifth streets, rebuilt in a handsome and stylish manner, but not quite completed."

Evidently the changes made by Captain Radcliffe were not drastic. The structure is a Wilmington Plain house and seems to fit architecturally into the 1830s era, its stylistic elements transitional between the Federal and Greek Revival styles. The house has a double porch on the street facade, possibly one of the elements of the 1882 rebuilding.

A later resident was Rabbi Samuel Mendelsohn, who arrived in Wilmington on February 27, 1876, to minister at the Temple of Israel, where he remained rabbi for forty-five years. He was living there when Gray noted the residence on his 1881 map.

RADCLIFFE-BLOOM HOUSE

419 Chestnut Street
c. 1850

A mid-century Plain cottage in the Greek Revival mold, this single-story-with-attic dwelling features a box cornice and a closed pediment portico with Tuscan columns fluted from waist to shoulder.

Part of the Timothy D. Radcliffe estate divided by the court of pleas in March 1844, this lot went to Robert S. Radcliffe—who maintained ownership until April 3, 1858, when he sold to Thomas E. Lawrence. Though the purchase price of $550 seems low, it is likely that the house was already standing. H. H. Bloom, a retail grocer, acquired the house in 1863.

North Fifth Avenue crosses Chestnut Street; begin 500 street numbers

WOOLVIN-WARREN HOUSE

512 Chestnut Street
c. 1895: H. E. Bonitz, architect

Window sash with colored-glass borders; roof finials; a stained-glass transom with the street number of the house worked into the design; a canopy porch with paneled posts, spindle course and turned balustrade; and a hitching post at the curb—there are few more perfect examples in Wilmington of the looks and finish of the Victorian-era house.

The *Star* noted on December 19, 1890, that "The house formerly owned and occupied by Mr. James F. Woolvin has been sold, and is now being removed to the opposite side of Chestnut street to make room for a better structure." Why Woolvin, a bookkeeper, would have waited four years to construct a new dwelling is not known, but the house is said to have been built in 1895, with H. E. Bonitz as the architect. Apparently Woolvin's marriage provided the impetus for the construction, but his bride died soon after the house was completed, and the saddened husband sold the structure.

The purchasers, Archie G. Warren and his wife Mary Cline Warren, were popular ice-cream and candy makers. They acquired the house in January 1896 and moved in almost immediately. It is still owned and occupied by their descendants.

North Sixth Street crosses Chestnut Street; begin 600 street numbers

Trees in the block of Chestnut Street between North Sixth and North Seventh streets are thriving, and nineteenth-century buildings echo each other across both sides of the block. From the standpoint of architectural quality, almost every house within the block is a fine example of its age, era, or style. Standards of upkeep are varied, but the block complex is a vivid reminder of the aesthetic quality of nineteenth century residential life in Wilmington, little changed since c. 1881.

KAHNWEILER-CHASTEN HOUSE

602 Chestnut Street
c. 1865

From an examination of the records available and a study of the exterior of the house, c. 1865 seems a workable date for its construction. The structure is a Plain cottage, with six-over-six sash, gable roof, and exterior brick chimney. The porch with Tuscan columns is probably a late nineteenth- or early twentieth-century addition.

Mina Kahnweiler of New York acquired the entire southern side of the block from William C. Bettencourt in 1863. When the property was sold in 1872 at a purchase price far greater than the 1863 price, it had shrunk to a corner lot. It is likely that this house was standing, and it may have been shifted one or more times as the block developed, each time moving closer to North Sixth on a diminished lot. If such movement did occur, it was completed by 1881, when the house was on its present site. This movement could account for the present chimneys, foundations, and exterior material, and a house older than c. 1865 may be underneath.

When Martha Chasten purchased the property in 1903, she was probably already in residence.

SHINES-BEAR HOUSE

603 Chestnut Street
c. 1867; remodeled 1882

Smaw's Wilmington city directory of 1866–67 shows Mrs. Eliza Shines residing at the corner of Sixth and Chestnut Street. In 1873 when the property was purchased by Morris Bear it was sold by D. H. Da Silva and Eliza M. Da Silva of Baltimore, Maryland. Eliza M. Da Silva was probably Eliza Shines, either builder of the house or wife of the builder. Bear worked on the house in 1882 when, on September 24, the *Star* carried "a partial list of buildings erected and improvements made during the past twelve months." Among structures listed was "Morris Bear and brothers, improvements to residence, corner of Sixth and Chestnut streets, now one of the handsomest dwellings in the city."

Morris Bear was in residence from 1873 to 1913, probably, as indicated above, with other members of the Bear family. Samuel and Fannie Bear lived here until 1916, and then Fannie Bear Hahn until 1930.

Morris and Samuel Bear, Jr., brother and son of the merchant Samuel Bear, were merchants in their own right, prominent in several firms. Morris engaged in business on North Front Street under the firm name of Morris Bear & Bro. The firm was founded about 1872 by Morris, who managed it until his death in 1889. Samuel Bear, Jr., and Isaac Bear, his brother, continued the business in wholesale dry good and notions under the name Morris Bear & Bro. Samuel Bear, Jr., was, in addition to his other interests, a director of the Delgado Cotton Mills.

A bracketed-and-vented Italianate house with pedimented roof and porch, the structure is a large and handsome Italianate dwelling. There are perhaps a dozen other houses of the type in Wilmington, several or all of which may have been built by G. M. Altaffer, who built his own home in the next block of Chestnut, c. 1870.

WESSELL-HARBERS HOUSE

606 Chestnut Street
c. 1875; remodeled c. 1890

Charles Wessell purchased the land on which this house stands on August 11, 1874. It is likely that he began construction of the house soon thereafter. The west house is known to have been completed and occupied by Wessell in 1881, as identified on Gray's map of that year. A handsome side-hall house in the late vented-and-bracketed Italianate style, it features brackets with drop pendants. The recessed east side and the spindle courses and brackets on the porches are from later in the century, c. 1890.

Wessell willed the house to his wife, Rose Harbers Wessell, who left it to her family, the Harbers.

GLAMEYER HOUSE

610 Chestnut Street
c. 1878

Henry A. Glameyer, a grocer and liquor dealer in the first block of North Water Street, purchased this property in August 1877 and was in residence shortly thereafter. After his death, the firm was carried on by his widow under the name Glameyer and Kuck.

A later resident of the house was John Theodore Runge. He boarded with Mrs. Glameyer from 1903 until his death in 1929, when the April 24 *Star* noted that he was a "pioneer wireman . . . first associated press operator in south to take copy on typewriter . . . operator more than 30 years. He was engaged at the Associated Press Bureau in Washington, D.C., for a considerable period."

A bracketed-and-vented Italianate structure, the house probably has much the same appearance that it had when constructed, except for the porch ornament, which seems to be somewhat later.

STYRON HOUSE

612 Chestnut Street
c. 1880

Charlotte H. Styron purchased the lot in 1872; in 1874 she gave it to her son, "in consideration of the natural love and affection . . . as well as for the consideration that the said Wallace H. Styron aided in paying for said land." It is likely that the house was begun soon after 1874, inasmuch as it appears on Gray's 1881 map.

A bracketed-and-vented Italianate structure, the house is basically a rectangle with symmetrical window placement. The chamfered porch posts sit atop pedestals and flare outward above the neck molding, a somewhat unusual treatment of the Italianate porch in Wilmington.

ZOELLER HOUSE

616 Chestnut Street
c. 1890

A two-and-a-half-story Queen Anne–style dwelling with a hip roof and central cross gable, the house features a hexagonal bay below the cross gable. The bay is decorated with bargeboard-bracket canopies with drop pendants. The east side is recessed one bay to allow a porch at the second level with a radiating-sun bargeboard; and the continuation of the first-story porch one bay deeper on the west than on the east.

Victor E. Zoeller, watchmaker and jeweler, acquired the lot in 1877. The Zoellers maintained ownership only to 1910. It was acquired shortly thereafter by J. H. Brunjes and his wife, who maintained ownership to the 1950s. Zoeller built the present house c. 1890.

North Seventh Street crosses Chestnut; begin 700 street numbers

CHESTNUT STREET UNITED PRESBYTERIAN CHURCH

710½ Chestnut Street
1858: Mr. Moody, builder

Although the architect of the Chestnut Street church (fig. 109) is not known, it seems likely that he was a Wilmingtonian. The manner in which the simple board-and-batten church is rendered appears to be a cross between pattern-book Carpenter Gothic and Wilmington Italianate. The bargeboards of the gable roof, the projecting entrance pavilion, originally an open portico, and the cupola are scalloped and punctuated with pendants in the Carpenter Gothic style, while all the openings are round-arched, singly or in pairs, in the Italianate manner. The simple church, set back from the street among its massive live oaks, is unique to the city and remarkably unchanged on the exterior, though the interior has been recently modernized.

The church was begun in 1858 as a result of a local religious revival, which several churches shared; the first sermon was preached in this building on October 17, 1858.

Intended by the First Presbyterian Church as a mission chapel and a thanks offering for God's mercy, it became, on November 6, 1858, the Second Presbyterian Church when fourteen persons, including one of the ruling elders of the First Church, withdrew to form the new congregation. The new Chestnut Street building was surrendered to the new church.

James Sprunt, speaking at the fiftieth anniversary of St. Andrews Presbyterian Church on November 22, 1908, reminisced about this building where St. Andrews began as the Second Presbyterian Church. His remarks were carried in the November 29, 1908, *Star* and in 1914 were reprinted in his book *Chronicles of the Cape Fear River*:

When after many deliberations and misgivings, a site for the second church had been selected between Seventh and Eighth streets, we plodded through the deep sand daily, watching the progress of the building, the total cost of which was, I think, $2,500.

The church building was erected under contract with a Mr. Moody, and the progress to completion was watched with anxious interest by the little band—a mere handful—which formed its original membership. Conspicuous among these were my father Alexander Sprunt, John C. Latta, John R. Latta, John Colville,

109. *Chestnut Street United Presbyterian Church, 710½ Chestnut Street, at MacRae Street, 1858.*

and others, all of whom have gone to their reward.

It is a remarkable fact that the exterior of the original building on Chestnut Street has not been repainted in fifty years. When it was painted after its erection, the first coat of color was sanded by the usual process in imitation of brownstone. This has withstood the exposure of half a century. I examined the exterior a few days ago and found it in an excellent state of preservation, with the exception of the pillars and front, where the paint was visibly wearing away.

When the Chestnut Street Presbyterian Church was formed on April 21, 1867, with thirty-four black members, it purchased the building from the then predominantly white Second Presbyterian Church congregation. The Chestnut Street church has served a black congregation since 1867.

110. Altaffer House, 713 Chestnut Street, c. 1870.

ALTAFFER HOUSE

713 Chestnut Street
c. 1870; G. M. Altaffer, builder

Gerald M. Altaffer, who purchased this land in early 1870 and constructed this house (fig. 110) soon thereafter, is listed in the city directory for 1894–95 as a cabinetmaker and as residing on Chestnut Street between Seventh and Eighth streets. Altaffer's profession—he is listed variously as patternmaker, contractor, or cabinetmaker—may account for the unusually fine detail and finish of the one-and-one-half-story, bracketed-and-vented Italianate cottage. The structure is similar to the two-story Shines-Bear House at 603 Chestnut Street, built about the same time, and to several other houses in Wilmington. Together, they constitute a basic subspecies within the indigenous Italianate of Wilmington. The depth of the frieze, which is bracketed and vented, and the center pediment, echoed by a pedimented porch roof, are two of the notable features of the type, as are a center entrance and a five-bay facade. The houses are square and massive, tending to the horizontal rather than to the vertical of the side-hall and most of the center-hall Italianate houses. A very few of the subspecies exist in a side-hall, three-bay plan, but exhibit the other characteristics of the Altaffer House.

According to a Wilmington newspaper, Altaffer died in 1907, and his funeral was held in his home at 105 North Seventh Street, one of several Altaffer residences listed in the city directories. Altaffer's obituary in the October 22, 1907, newspaper noted that he had been born in Rockingham County, Virginia, but came to:

Wilmington early in his life and had spent practically all his life here. By trade he was a pattern maker and for years was employed at the Wilmington Iron Works, early known as Hart & Bailey. Later he was a member of the firm of Altaffer, Price & Co., manufacturers of doors, sash, blinds, etc. The plant of the firm was destroyed by fire and the business was never resumed. After the fire Mr. Altaffer conducted a business on his own as pattern maker at which he was especially proficient.

It is possible and probable that Altaffer is responsible for much detail on Wilmington houses, especially those built by James F. Post in the later part of the nineteenth century. Post was one of the pallbearers at Altaffer's funeral.

Princess Street

North Water Street, eastward to North Eighth

During the nineteenth century, DeRosset's Wharf was located at the base of Princess Street on the south side. Later the waterfront block between Princess and Market was to become the U.S. Customs Building and Wharf with U.S. Coast Guard moorings at the Customs Wharf.

Inasmuch as the County Courthouse was located on Princess between North Second and North Third streets until the last decade of the nineteenth century, when it was moved to Princess and North Third, and the city hall and Thalian Hall, Wilmington's major theater, were on Princess at North Third, Princess Street was a major Wilmington traffic artery.

The grouping of governmental and cultural structures within a two-block area made the Princess Street blocks between the waterfront and North Third prime commercial space. This location not only brought concentrations of commercial buildings, but by the early twentieth century the docks of the Wilmington-Southport Boat Line steamers were at the base of Princess.

In addition, Princess was the major east-west street for the trolley. Cars of the street trolley companies ran out Princess Street from North Front to North Twentieth. Lines intersected or joined Princess along the way at North Ninth, North Tenth, and North Seventeenth streets.

M. C. DARBY & CO. BUILDING

114 Princess Street
c. 1880

Essentially a two-story building with basement, this brick structure is arranged so that it has two first floors: The one in the basement is approached by walking down a few steps; the other, directly above, is approached by walking up a few steps. Entrance to the basement is revetted across the front. The revetment is matched by a porch above at the first level. The building is a handsome one in the Italianate commercial style, featuring scroll-with-crest wooden window lintels and corbeled dentil cornice.

Though the builders and original tenants are not known, the structure seems to have been a favorite of realtors. In 1887, Dr. J. H. Durham had his dental offices at 114 Princess Street. J. C. Wright and Son, real estate agents and auctioneers, maintained offices here during the first decade of the century. Also in the building was M. C. Darby & Co., real estate agents. The *Star* reported the founding of the company in its July 12, 1904, edition. Its principals were Miss M. C. Darby and Mrs. Florence R. Strange, probably the only female-owned and operated firm then in the real estate field. Miss Darby had, prior to this time, been postmaster of Wilmington. In 1912, the Darby firm was developing Love Grove as one of its suburbs. The Radio Electric Company—which was, according to the December 3 *Star,* "the first exclusive radio supply store and repair shop" in the city—operated here in 1922. Another tenant was the Star Dry Cleaning and Processing Company, which was here by 1926.

MERCER & EVANS BUILDING (later Dixie Cafe)

115–17 Princess Street
before 1884

A three-story brick store that has lost its street-level facade, the building is nonetheless a handsome commercial structure, probably constructed prior to 1884, when it seems to be on the Sandborn maps.

The March 10, 1889, *Messenger* shows J. C. Mund's drug store at 117 Princess Street. By August 2, 1890, the paper has H. C. Evans selling shoes there. The *Weekly Star* of April 29, 1892, lists the Cape Fear Manufacturing Co., makers of negligee shirts, at 117 Princess, and the French Cafe must have opened there soon after or had already been in operation by that time. The *Dispatch* on July 1, 1897,

111. Messenger and Southern Bell Telephone and Telegraph Building, 121–23, 125, and 127–29 Princess Street. Charles McMillen, architect: 121–23 was built in 1906; 125 in 1902; and 127–29 in 1899.

reported that W. H. Cromm had purchased it from Steljes and Schnibbler. By October 7, 1898, the *Dispatch* reported Henry Litzgen opening a saloon and restaurant at 117, "the old stand of the French Cafe."

Mercer and Evans, which occupied 115 Princess Street in 1895, moved into 117 as well in September 1900. Prior to that, W. V. Hardin had operated a saloon at 117. A clipping from the *Morning Star* newspaper for January 1, 1901, about an early morning fire noted that "No. 115 is owned by A. J. Mercer and No. 117 is owned by A. H. Evans."

By 1903 the Dixie Cafe was operating at 117 Princess Street, later expanding to 115. Under the heading "The Dixie Cafe," the April 16, 1903, *Dispatch* announced, "Mr. John W. Batson, who for nearly five years was connected with the real estate agency of Mr. W. M. Cumming, has bought an interest in the Dixie Cafe, on Princess street, and he and Mr. A. A. Hergenrother will continue it in the future. The cafe will be run strictly first class and the service will be splendid. A number of improvements are now being made and others contemplated."

The *Star* for September 22, 1904, noted: "The Dixie Restaurant is employing true country style in announcing the hour for meals. A large bell has been erected in front of the restaurant on Princess street and when meal hour arrives the bell is rung with force."

On March 21, 1905, the same newspaper carried the following: "The Dixie Cafe has just installed a very handsome soda fountain, from which delicious, cold drinks will be served all during the season, day and night. The fountain is one of the prettiest in the city."

MESSENGER AND SOUTHERN BELL TELEPHONE AND TELEGRAPH BUILDING

121–23, 125, 127–29 Princess Street
Charles McMillen, architect; 1899: 127–29 Princess, L. H. Vollers, builder; 1902: 125 Princess, builder unknown; 1906: 121–23 Princess, Central Construction Company, Greensboro, builders

Actually a row of five buildings constructed over a six year period, the structures (fig. 111) follow a single design: late Romanesque commercial, in brick, with cast-iron storefronts. All were constructed for Morris Bear & Bros., who owned the property, financed the building, and built to order for leasing back to tenants. Architect Charles McMillen provided the design for all the buildings.

On March 12, 1899, the *Messenger,* for which the corner structure at 127–29 was built, announced construction of a:

Home For The Messenger

Plans Made for a Handsome New Brick and Stone Building for the Newspaper, Publishing, and Printing Establishment of the Jackson & Bell Company—It Will be Erected on Second and Princess Streets—Work to Commence in Two Weeks.

The proprietors of the Messenger have closed a contract with the Messrs Morris Bear & Bros., for the erection of a commodious and handsome office building, to be erected on their eligible property on the northwest corner of Second and Princess streets. . . . The Messenger Building will be a handsome structure of pretty architectural design and will be the completest and best equipped newspaper and publishing establishment in North Carolina. The plans have been drawn by Mr. Charles McMillen, the capable architect for the magnificent Masonic Temple soon to be under construction. . . .

The building is to be constructed of brick, and will front 42 feet on Princess and run back 58 feet on Second Street. The front will be constructed of Philadelphia pressed brick and will be trimmed with brownstone. The entire front of the street floor will consist of heavy plate glass windows and doors and on this floor will be the business office of the Messenger.

A full description of the uses of the various floors of the building followed. The structure featured electric and gas lighting, water on all floors, an elevator, tiled and wood floors, and Mergenthaler Linotype machines. In addition to newspaper publishing, the company also did job printing and bookbinding. The first brick for the building was laid on April 7, 1899, and the cornerstone was laid on April 25. The building was occupied by July 7, 1899, when the *Dispatch* announced: "The Messenger is now comfortably housed in its new quarters on the corner of Second and Princess streets. The building is of brick with a front of pressed brick and with brown stone trimmings. It is a credit alike to the architect Mr. Charles McMillen and the contractor Mr. L. H. Vollers."

By July 1902 the *Dispatch* reported that Morris Bear & Bros. were erecting a building adjacent to the Messenger Building. When the structure was completed in October, it was to be leased to the Southern Bell Telephone and Telegraph Company. On September 24 the paper reported that the building at 125 Princess Street was "going up rapidly." This new building followed the style of the *Messenger* Building. The cast-metal telephone-company sign still remains in the frieze of the structure.

The third part of the complex, at 121–23 Princess Street, was constructed in 1906. The *Dispatch* reported on October 8:

Handsome New Building For Princess Street. . . .

Stores on First Floor—Telephone Company has leased Second Floor.

. . . . The firm of Morris Bear & Bros. *has just awarded a contract for a new building to the Central Carolina Construction Company of Greensboro. . . . The new building is to be built of brick. The front of the building will conform to that of the building now occupied by the telephone company and it will be pressed brick with stone trimmings.*

In addition to those mentioned above, tenants at 121 Princess have included: Southerland & Weaver, 1913–16; E. Weaver, men's clothing, 1917–20; Trust Barber Shop, 1926; and deluxe Barber Shop, 1936. Those at 123 Princess have included: Carolina Building and Loan Association, 1913–19; United Realty Company, 1915–16; and L. W. Moore, Real Estate and Life Insurance, 1912. Roger Moore and Sons Co. succeeded Southern Bell at 125 Princess in 1922. At 127–29 Princess, Jackson Bell & Co. published the *Messenger* until at least 1922. H. P. Smith, a shoe dealer and repairer, opened at 127 Princess in 1924. Electric Maintenance Co., Inc., was at 129 Princess in 1926, and Futrelle's Pharmacy operated there from at least 1936 to the 1960s.

North Second Street crosses Princess; begin 200 street numbers

112. Mugge Building, 200 Princess Street, 1892–93.

MUGGE BUILDING

200 Princess Street
1892–93

Two stories with full vented frieze and castellated parapet—this structure stands alone in Wilmington. A handsome Châteauesque commercial structure with Romanesque elements, the Mugge Building (fig. 112) sits on its corner proudly. Entrance at the corner is through a recessed door beneath an oriel. The oriel forms a prominent corner tower that projects above the roof parapet. Projecting pavillions centered in the Princess and North Second facades balance the tower; they too project above the roof parapet. Cast-iron cresting atop the towers and parapet survives, as does the cast-iron column that supports the oriel. Decorative brickwork and stone abounds. Pleasingly Victorian and well detailed, the structure evidences commercial eclecticism at its best.

A *Messenger* article on September 13, 1892, reported:

The old three story shingle building which for years has stood on the southeast corner of Second and Princess streets was torn down yesterday and in its stead Mr. Carl Mugge is to erect a two-story brick building with two stores underneath. The new building will front 46 feet on Princess street and 58 feet on Second street. Mr. Mugge will have a saloon and "cafe" in the corner store room and will reside upstairs. The old building which was torn down is an old landmark but it has to give way before the march of progress.

Various tenants have occupied the building since Mugge operated his Astoria Cafe there.

BONITZ BUILDINGS
211–15 Princess Street
1906: Henry E. Bonitz, architect; Thad F. Tyler, builder

"The office of Mr. H. E. Bonitz," noted the *Star* on December 19, 1906, "Architect and City Build-

113. Bonitz Buildings, 211–15 Princess Street. Henry E. Bonitz, architect, 1906. Detail of 213 Princess Street.

ing Inspector has been removed from the I.O.O.F. building to Mr. Bonitz's own building second floor, No. 213 Princess Street. Mr. Bonitz has very handsome offices and is located more conveniently than ever before."

The two narrow buildings at 211 and 215 Princess Street are identical commercial structures; they flank the more ornate center structure at 213 Princess, with its Neoclassical Revival detail. That center building contained Bonitz's office and is identified on its facade by the legend "Henry E. Bonitz, Architect, 1894–1906." A center window stretching two stories is flanked by Ionic pilasters and topped by a keystone arch. Squares, triangles, and other tools of the architect appear as a decorative course between the second- and third-level windows. (See fig. 113.) The decorative metal cornice seems to have carried through each of the three buildings. Perhaps storefronts were also the same, with cast-iron and street-level shop windows. Portions of the storefront remain at 211 Princess. Decorative metal cornices and window lintels survive at 211 and 215 Princess.

When new, the buildings must have been striking and an excellent advertisement for the architect, who became the best known and most prolific of the turn-of-the-century Wilmington designers.

A number of other businesses or organizations occupied offices in one or the other of these buildings over the years. Arcanum Hall and Royal Arcanum were at number 213, though activity of neither is known—perhaps rightly so, since *arcanum* means secret. Other tenants at various times included the Beach Water Company, Edison Phonograph Company, Charles M. Stieff Piano Company, and E. W. Bonitz, lawyer.

North Third Street crosses Princess; begin 300 street numbers

The city hall and courthouse dominate the entrance to the 300 street number block of Princess Street. Thalian Hall and the Courthouse Annex both front on Princess Street to the east and behind city hall and the courthouse—both of which front on North Third Street.

The landscaped area, with palm and crepe myrtle, along the north side of the block before Thalian Hall, is Col. James Innes Park. Innes was a troop commander during the 1754 French and Indian Wars, during which the young George Washington served in his command. In 1783 he left a will establishing a free school, Innes Academy, to be built on this site.

THALIAN HALL (See North Third Street at Princess for the City Hall part of the building.)

305 Princess Street, north side, between North Third and North Fourth streets
1854: design, John M. Trimble of New York, architect; 1855–58: construction, James F. Post, supervising architect; Robert B. Wood, John C. Wood, and G. W. Rose, builders

Thalian Hall (fig. 114) was opened to the public on October 12, 1858. Wilmington, a city of five thousand people, had just opened a theater seating 1,500, the largest theater south of Richmond and one of the largest in the United States.

The hall took its name from the Thalian Association, an intermittently active organization that can trace its origins to the late eighteenth or early nine-

114. Thalian Hall, 305 Princess Street, November 9, 1909, during the visit of President William H. Taft. (Courtesy Lower Cape Fear Historical Society.)

teenth century. The association functioned both as a community theater and as an organization to manage theaters and bring professional entertainment to Wilmington. On this site Innes Academy operated on the second floor and the theater group on the first floor. When the city purchased the Innes land and building, one half of the purchase money went to the Thalian Association, the funds to be used in constructing a theater on the site. By 1860 the association was unable to meet its financial obligations to the city for operation of the theater in Thalian Hall, and the building was released to the city. The organization continued to function sporadically in halls in other locations, however, and after its reorganization in the 1920s, the Thalian Association reestablished a relationship with Thalian Hall that continues to this day. If the antecedents of the present-day group are taken into consideration, it must be counted one of the oldest groups of its type in the country.

The old academy was demolished, and the cornerstone for the new joint City Hall–Thalian Hall building was laid on December 27, 1855. The design dates from at least a year earlier, however, for Robert H. Cowan, who had been appointed to secure a plan for the new town hall, had evidently solicited plans and had them in hand by late 1854. The *Wilmington Commercial* for December 30, 1854, reported that plans had been drawn by John Trimble of New York. Trimble was primarily an architect of theaters. Prior to Thalian Hall, some of his theaters included the Bowery Theatre in New York of 1845, the Broadway Theatre of 1847, Tripler, or Jenny Lind, Hall in 1850, and the New York Theatre and the Metropolitan Opera House in 1854. J. C. and R. B. Wood and G. W. Rose were selected as builders and James F. Post as supervising architect, on November 1, 1855; Post's ledgers indicate that work on the building had begun by November 5. The Wood brothers, Rose, and Post were all skilled craftsmen who had previously worked in the Italianate style and had constructed highly successful and handsome buildings.

By August of 1856, when the commissioners and the Thalian Association finally signed an agreement on the theater, work must have already been underway on that section of the building. It would have been necessary to tie the walls into those of the city hall, and it is likely that construction of foundation, outer walls, and roof was simultaneous, with the Thalians responsible for the finish of the interior of the theater. By April 6, 1858, the theater interior was sufficiently finished to allow a dance recital; the *Daily Journal* reported that "The exhibition of the scholars of Mr. Frensley's dancing school took place last night at the Theatre, which was fitted up as well as the circumstances would admit."

The paper contained a relatively complete description of the theater in its October 12, 1858, edition.

The Theatre is on the Princess street or Southern side and on the Eastern end. Its whole exterior length is 110 feet; breadth 60 feet; stage 42 by 57 feet; auditorium 45 by 57 feet, and some 20 feet occupied by passages. From parquet to ceiling is 54 feet. The ceiling, which, as well as the walls and the arch of the proscenium is handsomely frescoed, is perforated by ventilators, communicating with a very efficient but decidedly uncouth looking arrangement on the roof. There is a parquet occupying the whole ground room of the auditorium with a first tier or dress circle 9½ feet above, supported on eight iron columns, and a second tier above that, supported on columns of the same character. The arch of the proscenium is nearly 30 feet in height and rather less in width, is in good proportion and adorned with suitable painting and gilding. The drop curtains, representing a classical scene somewhere among the "Isles of Greece," is by Russell Smith, of Philadelphia, as are also some two of the scenes and two or three of the wings. Mr. Smith's reputation as a painter is already established, and will suffer no loss by this specimen of his skill, which has that bright, joyous, holiday tone, suited for the position it occupies, and is withall a work of art that will bear inspection, under any circumstances.

The house is supplied with gas throughout, there being 188 burners on the stage, in the auditorium and in the passages. Under the stage there are five excellent dressing rooms, music room, green room, etc., fitted up with gas, like the rest of the building. The scenery, machinery, etc., of the stage was fitted up by, or under the management of Mr. Joseph Walker, of Philadelphia, whose work appears to have given the fullest satisfaction. The scene painting, excepting the portion done by Russell Smith, has been done by Mr. C. J. Hawthorne and other artists. We think it right to state that the beautiful drop curtain was a present to the Association from certain public-spirited gentlemen, to wit: Messrs. Don. McRae, E. D. Hall, O. S. Baldwin, Geo. Myers and L. A. Hart. The means of egress from any part of the building, in case of fire or other accident, are uncommonly ample. The provisions for guarding the property from fire were not so well posted on. We know that at a point high up near the roof, and convenient to both limits of the L, that is, to both Town Hall and Theatre, there is a large iron tank, holding very many barrels of water, and that from this a hose can be led to any point of the interior; still we think that the adoption of further precautions is called for in this respect.

As we stated at the beginning of this sketch, the plans for the whole pile of building were made in 1855 by Mr. Trimble, of New York, and adopted by the Commissioners, the chief external variation made subsequently has been in substituting the pediment end and pillars forming the front of the Town Hall, for a small portico like that at the Theatre, which was the original design. The change adds elevation and dignity to the principal front.

The contracts were taken by Messrs. J. C. & R. B. Wood for the masonry, and by Mr. G. W. Rose for the carpenter-work, etc., Mr. James F. Post being appointed superintendent. The general arrangement of the Theatre is after the plan of Mr. Trimble, but the details and their adaptation to circumstance have all been executed under the supervision of Mr. Post.

When the theater opened in 1858, it was known as Thalian Hall. By the 1860s and the dropping of the Thalian lease, it was known as the Wilmington Theater; by the 1870s, as the Opera House; and by 1902, it had become the Academy of Music. It is now once again Thalian Hall, and the theater and adjacent City Hall are listed in the National Register of Historic Places.

Interiors at Thalian have been refurbished several times: in 1871, 1881, 1895, and 1904, and in 1909 under the design supervision of H. E. Bonitz. Its interiors (see color plate 3) served as one of the sources for restoration of Ford's Theatre in Washington, D.C. Thalian Hall retained detail of the era and could be used in evolving restoration plans for the Washington theater. At Thalian Hall evidence of the arrangement of seating remained, as did such disappearing amenities as its gas lighting system and ticket boxes. In 1938 the Princess Street window openings in the theater were closed to strengthen the structure. The round-arched dropped lintels and the plastered wall treatment remain.

115. Thalian Hall, John M. Trimble, architect, James F. Post, supervising architect, 1854–58.

John T. Ford, builder of Ford's Theatre in Washington, became a theatrical talent manager when the Ford Theater closed following the assassination of President Lincoln. Many of the productions at Thalian Hall were under his management. During 1869 and 1870 he had exclusive right, and he later managed productions that appeared here under other sponsorship. One of Ford's productions at Thalian Hall was that of the D'Oyle-Carte Company performing Gilbert and Sullivan on February 9, 1881. Ford enjoyed a virtual monopoly on the production of Gilbert and Sullivan in this country.

Among actors, actresses, vocalists, orators, and others to appear in Thalian Hall were:

Marion Anderson, *contralto, April 27, 1925*
Maurice Barrymore, *father of Lionel, John, and Ethel, with* Helen Modjueska *in* Twelfth Night, *January 30, 1884*
William Jennings Bryan *on December 16, 1912, lecturing on "The Making of Man," and on June 12, 1919, lecturing on prohibition*
Edwin Forrest, *in* Richelieu, Damon and Pythian, *and* King Lear, *on October 24, 25, 26, 1870*
Edward Everett, *April 1859, lecturing on "The Character of Washington," with proceeds going to the Mount Vernon Ladies Association of the Union, then just beginning the preservation of Mount Vernon*
James Gibbons, *later* Cardinal Gibbons, *on February 21, 1871, lecturing on temperance*
Joseph Jefferson *in* Rip Van Winkle, *January 27, 1880, April 10, 1897, and March 8, 1905, and in* Rivals, *January 14, 1884*
James O'Neill, *father of Eugene O'Neill, in* A Celebrated Case *on October 18, 1892, and in* The Count of Monte Cristo *on January 2, 1902, and February 15, 1906 (O'Neill played the count more than six thousand times over a thirty-year period.)*

Otis Skinner, *with* Helen Modjeska, *in the* Merchant of Venice *on January 12, 1894, in* Prince Rudolph *on January 18, 1898, in* Rosemary *on January 25, 1899, and in* Francesca da Rimini *on February 28, 1902*
John Philip Sousa *with his own band on January 7, 1897, February 7, 1902, and in January 1908*
General Tom Thumb, *on December 14 and 15, 1868, and on May 20, 1875*
Oscar Wilde, *July 8, 1882*

In 1905, on October 10, Thomas Dixon's *The Clansman*, on which *Birth of a Nation* was based, had appeared here. It evoked much critical comment, and the *Messenger* carried an editorial the next day noting that the play hardly presented a true picture of reconstruction problems and would not prove successful as: "an instructor of the present generation. . . . While exciting and calculated to arouse an animosity between the races, it does not teach a lesson to either." In its regular review, the paper noted that though the play was presented to enormous audiences, the company was not a good one, which was probably fortunate since better actors might have made Dixon's appeals to prejudice stronger. The play returned on April 13, 1907, and February 27, 1908. *Birth of a Nation* had its first showing in Wilmington at Thalian Hall in March 1916.

Also appearing at Thalian Hall were Charles Dickens, son of the English novelist, in 1888; Richard Mansfield in 1894 and 1895; Walter Damrosch conducting the New York Symphony on April 4, 1906, and April 20, 1912; Anna Held in 1913; Fanny Janauschek in 1875, 1878, 1892, and 1896; Harry Lauder in 1919; Lillian Russell in 1910 and 1914; Edward Hugh Southern in 1912; Sybil Thorndike in 1906; Lawrence Tibbett in 1929; Maude Adams in 1916; and Agnes Morehead on October 28, 1954.

Tyrone Power spent some time in Thalian Hall while in Wilmington in 1958 and later recommended its restoration. He wrote to then Governor Luther Hodges on April 19, 1958, in support of restoration of the theater. "I wish I could adequately convey to you my surprise and delight upon entering Thalian Hall. It has been many years since I have seen anything of its kind in this country. In fact, very few such examples exist anywhere in the world. Upon inquiry, I discovered that many of the greats of the golden age of the theatre had played there. . . . It has an atmosphere and a history shared by all too few remaining theatres of its kind in this country."

Thalian Hall was extensively used by the community, and some feel that the social use of the hall by Wilmington citizens outweighs its involvement with famous outsiders. Large crowds often gathered here for purely local reasons, including recitals and local school presentations, memorial services, and community and charity meetings. The hall was undoubtedly a community center, and in that sense alone it fulfilled the vision of the local government that authorized its construction.

One of the few American theaters of its era to have survived, Thalian Hall today (fig. 115) is an important cultural and architectural landmark.

NEW HANOVER COUNTY COURTHOUSE ANNEX

Princess Street, south side, between North Third and North Fourth streets
1924–25: Leslie N. Boney, architect; Herbert C. Chivers of New York, consulting architect; U. A. Underwood, builder

The *News* for July 27, 1923, reported that Herbert C. Chivers of New York had passed the state architecture exam and would practice part-time in North Carolina. He was, said the paper, to be associated with Leslie N. Boney in designing the new courthouse annex. The *Dispatch* could report by December 4, 1924, that Boney's plans were completed and on February 6, 1925, that the cornerstone would be laid "tomorrow afternoon at 4 o'clock." On June 26 it stated that U. A. Underwood was to be general contractor for the building "of reinforced concrete construction, with clay-tile and metal lath"; the same article noted that James A. Donnelly, of Wilmington, was applying the plaster.

On November 6 the newspaper noted that "work of installing electric fixtures in the new court house started Friday and should be completed within ten days, according to the contractor, the Electric Maintenance Company. The fixtures are all of a more or less elaborate design and include costly chandeliers."

Three stories high, plus full basement and attic, the stone-faced, Neo-classical Revival building (fig. 116)—while contrasting sharply with the adjacent High Victorian Gothic courthouse (see fig. 50)—is a fine architectural statement of its era of construction.

116. New Hanover County Courthouse Annex, Princess Street between North Third and North Fourth streets. Leslie N. Boney, architect; Herbert C. Chivers, consulting architect; 1924–25.

North Fifth Avenue crosses Princess; begin 500 street numbers

BOWDEN HOUSE

514 Princess Street
c. 1859, James F. Post, architect-builder

L. H. Bowden, listed in the 1866 city directory as a timber inspector, acquired the land on which this house stands in June of 1858. The low purchase price, the fact that Bowden lived here throughout the nineteenth century, and the architectural style of the structure lend credence to the tax date of 1859 on records in the assessors office. From 1900 to 1938 or longer, it was the residence of the Boykin family.

There is a traditional connection between the house and a dwelling of Joseph Jacobs, architect of St. John's Masonic Lodge on Orange Street. Jane Jacobs, wife of Joseph, was an earlier owner of the property and may have had a home here. An older house is said to have been incorporated into the present structure built by Bowden. An additional link is provided by the fact that Bowden married Mary Jane Jacobs King, daughter of Jane Larkins and Joseph Jacobs, and widow of J. A. King. The property transfer was therefore an in-family transfer and may well have included the Jacobs house and provided the sentiment for incorporating it into the present structure.

A plain Italianate side hall–plan house, the structure is at the street side with a well-landscaped surround.

117. Manning-Cobb-Toon House, 516 Princess Street, c. 1868.

BISSINGER HOUSE

515 Princess Street
c. 1890

Charles W. Polvogt purchased land here in 1861. It was inherited by his wife, Emilie, who later married Charles F. W. Bissinger. By 1881 the family was already residing in a large house at the corner of North Sixth and Princess streets. This structure seems to have been built between 1889 and 1893, or about 1890, probably by Bissinger, a grocer and gardener, who died in March of 1893. William L. Bissinger continued in residence. He died here in 1941.

Though a vented-and-bracketed Italianate cottage, the house bears more relationship to the Italianate as practiced nationwide in the post–Civil War era than to the style as practiced in Wilmington. The hip roof and vented-and-bracketed frieze carry through, though they are not as bold as usual, and vents are covered with paired octagonal louvered covers.

MANNING-COBB-TOON HOUSE

516 Princess Street
c. 1868

Ed W. Manning, veteran of the Confederate navy and commander of the coastal steamer *General Howard,* purchased the property here in May of 1867. Construction of the house was probably begun soon thereafter.

Dr. Benjamin F. Cobb acquired it in 1872 and practiced medicine here until the end of the decade. His office, constructed in the northwest corner of the front yard about 1872, was moved to the rear of the lot in the early twentieth century and survives.

William P. Toon, a bookkeeper, purchased the property in 1880. His descendants still occupy the house.

A bracketed-and-vented Italianate cottage, the house (fig. 117) features a wide frieze with center pediment, echoed in the full porch. A picket fence surrounds the heavily planted yard. The combination of low house, high plants, and distance from the street give the dwelling an air of great mystery.

North Sixth Street crosses Princess; begin 600 street numbers

CAPT. ALEXANDER MAY HOUSE

616 Princess Street
c. 1850; c. 1895

When Captain Alexander May insured his house at 616 Princess Street on December 30, 1850, it was listed as being one-story, "of wood and new."

A vented-and-bracketed Italianate cottage, the basic plan of the house seems to remain today—with roof, frieze, and entrance with transom and three-light sidelights. The bay window to the right front, the panels below the windows, the cornerboards with applied bull's-eyes, and the one-over-one sash are from the late nineteenth century, c. 1895. Changes to the house at that time probably included the porch decoration of floral sawn brackets paneled posts with a simple balustrade.

Surrounding the yard and raising it slightly above street level is a brownstone wall. The lot is well landscaped, and street trees survive before the house.

North Seventh Street crosses Princess; begin 700 street numbers

GIBLEM MASONIC LODGE

720 Princess Street
1871–73

On August 31, 1871, the *Star* announced that it had learned that "the lot on the corner of Eighth and Princess streets, formerly known as the Burr property, has been purchased by the Colored Masons of this city, known as Giblem Lodge, and that a large three-story brick building will soon be erected thereon for the purpose of a lodge, hall, & c." On November 1, the same paper reported: "the foundation. . . laid and the building commenced"; on November 12: "The first brick . . . will be laid Tuesday morning next at 7 'clock." On December 29: the laying of the cornerstone on the previous day, December 28, 1871, was described.

The ceremonies were conducted by Grand Master J. W. Hood, assisted by Wm. McLaurin, Deputy Grand Master, Robert Simmons, S. W., James W. Telfair, J.W., and Geo. W. Price, Sr., G.C. The exercises were commenced by the singing of an Ode by the choir, after which prayer was offered by Grand Chaplain G. W. Price, Sr. The following articles were deposited in the cavity of the stone: . . . Name of architect and builder . . . a city map . . . name of the person who presented the stone, J. W. Schenck, Jr., . . . etc., etc.

The ceremony of laying the corner stone was then proceeded with, after which an address appropriate to the occasion was delivered by George W. Price, Jr. Subsequent to the delivery of the address a collection was taken up for the benefit of the building fund.

The last brick of the structure was laid on October 2, 1873, an event that the *Star* noted in its October 3 edition. Finally, on November 14, 1873, the newspaper could state, "Giblem Lodge No. 2, F. & A. A. Y. M., held its first regular communication in the new brick hall corner of Eighth and Princess streets, on Monday evening last."

One early event in the lodge and environs deserves a lengthy description. As reported in the *Star* on November 17, 1875, it was to be an agricultural and mechanical fair or exhibition. "The exhibition will take place at Giblem Lodge and on the adjacent grounds (two full lots), which have been secured for the purpose and upon which a large shed, together with a pavilion, will be erected, under which to place articles for exhibition. This will, we believe, be the first colored Agricultural and Mechanical Fair ever held in the United States, if we except the one on a small scale held here last April."

In the same paper on December 28, 1875, it was reported:

The first fair of the colored Industrial Exposition Association, and the first of the kind ever held by the colored people of this State, was inaugurated here yesterday.

A procession was formed at 12 o'clock on Third Street, headed by the Rose Bud Band, followed by the Order of Good Samaritans, the colored Masonic fraternity, citizens on foot, carriage containing the orators, & c. The Fayetteville Star Band was also in the procession. The column, which was an imposing one, marched through the principal streets, halting at the grounds, corner of Eighth and Princess streets, where the speaking took place. The Fair was formally opened by Jos. C. Hill, President of the Association, followed by prayer by Rev. G. D. Jammison, Chaplain. An address was then delivered by John H.

Smyth, orator for New Hanover county, who was followed by Congressman Elliott, of South Carolina. There was a large attendance upon the grounds and the streets adjacent during the day.

A reporter visited the different halls and found a very creditable display in each of them.

FLORAL HALL

This Hall is on the third floor of the Giblem Lodge building. Here he found a fine array of articles. . . .

AGRICULTURAL HALL

This department is on the second floor. Here our reporter found a fine display. . . .

ON THE GROUNDS

were a display of fine carriages by Jas. A. Lowrey; open top buggy by Joshua Council, Cumberland county; open wagon, by P. P. Barge, Cumberland county; fine display of pigs by Duncan Holmes; fine pig by Henry Corbett, Sampson county. There was a fine and large display in this department, including fowls, agricultural products, etc.

The *Star* for December 29, 1875, noted:

PROGRAMME FOR TODAY—*Races. Tournament. Base Ball, Shooting Matches and other amusing games will take place at the Fair Grounds outside the city. There will be a grand exhibition in Concert Hall by the Raleigh troupe of the deaf and dumb and the blind children of the Asylum.*

Mechanical and Floral Halls presented a fine appearance. There is a fine collection of minerals in the Mineral Department.

The aged lady, 116 years old, and the wonderful child, with the tail on its back, can be seen in the same hall and under the same price of admission.

In the *Star* for December 30, 1875, it was reported:

The streets in the vicinity of the Fair Grounds were crowded at an early hour yesterday morning, as usual, while there were many also inside the grounds and in the hall.

A base ball contest took place on Orange street between Sixth and Seventh, between the Sumner Club, Capt. Henry Nash, and a picked nine, Capt. Richard Stove. The scorers were Jas. E. King and W. H. Howe. The picked nine scored 6 and Sumner's 5.

The important feature of the day was the Tournament which took place on Eighth, between Market and Princess streets. A number of knights in appropriate costume entered, and some very fair riding was done. It was estimated that there were between two and three thousand people on the grounds during the progress of the tournament. The Tournament Ball was to take place at City Hall last night. In addition to our city Rose Bud Band the Fayetteville and Charlotte bands were present on the grounds during the day and discoursed very excellent music.

The *Star* for December 31, 1875, reported:

The first Fair of the Industrial Exposition Association closed yesterday, winding up with a ball at Giblem Lodge at night. The Fair has in all respects been a successful one, and the officers and members of the Association should feel a commendable pride in the fact, thus demonstrated that the colored people of this State, and of this section particularly are so well versed in the useful and important pursuits of life, and that they have thus come forward and assisted and encouraged the Association in this their first grand exposition.

The attendance upon the Fair has been been very large from the first, while a proper respect for good order and demeanor has marked each day's proceedings.

Though the fair may have been repeated, it is unlikely that any future exhibition had the impact of this first one.

For a time the lower level of the lodge building served as a city market for the Third Ward. The space was rented for the city by February 10, 1889, according to the *Star* for that day. On February 14, the *Messenger* reported the stalls rented, and on March 13, the addition of a fish market. The market was a success, as the *Star* had reported on February 21, 1889: "Giblem Lodge market is in full blast, and the citizens in that part of the city are reveling in steaks, roasts, etc., and are highly pleased with the convenience the new market affords."

Though somewhat altered, the stucco-over-brick Italianate/late Greek Revival Giblem Lodge building retains its exterior architectural character.

Market Street

Cape Fear River eastward to Ninth Street

In an east-coast port, one expects the city to face east, or at least northeast or southeast. The fact that Wilmington does not live up to this expectation makes orientation difficult for a visitor. Market Street, which begins at the Cape Fear River and runs inland, actually points almost directly eastward, and the traveler who follows it inland arrives at the Atlantic Ocean instead of the expected interior of the state.

One also expects, especially if the approach to Wilmington is through the flat coastal plain, to find level areas and a topographically uninteresting city. Instead, the city is built on bluffs along the eastern bank of the river and is quite hilly in places. Market Street, descending some five blocks to the river, reaches the western edge of a basin that rises to the east, north, and south. In the 1974 National Register of Historic Places Nomination Form for the Wilmington Historic District, architectural historian Janet Seapker has written:

In the midst of the pine barrens and swamps which surround the city, Wilmington has an oasis quality about it. The semitropical climate fosters the hardy growth of live and water oaks, palms, azaleas, magnolias, and oleander. The town is set on a bluff which forms the eastern bank of the Cape Fear River. The grid plan laid out in 1733 and clarified in 1743 remains intact. A market and wharf at the intersection of Market and Front streets marked the center of the town. The north-south streets, with the exception of Water (authorized by the General Assembly in 1785 to be cut through) and Front streets, bear numerical indentities; named streets run east from the river. Market and Third streets [and Fifth Avenue] are broad thoroughfares, each being 99 feet wide rather than the 66-foot standard used for the other streets. In 1757 a visitor to Wilmington observed that "... the Regularity of the Streets are equal to those of Philadelp[hi]a."

Cape Fear River

For many years the commercial and actual center of Wilmington was at the base of Market, where it joins the Cape Fear River. (See fig. 118.) The municipal docks were here in the eighteenth century, continuing in use into the nineteenth and the present century. The steamer *Wilmington*, which provided service down river in the late nineteenth century and early in this century, docked here. For many years Coast Guard cutters and other boats docked to the immediate north, and the Coast Guard still maintains dock facilities here. It was from this point that a ferry operated across the river, connecting Wilmington to the countryside on the western bank of the waterway. The city did jump the river in its development, but it grew mainly eastward. Its port developed northward and southward, and the city remains on the eastern bank of the Cape Fear.

Waterborne commerce is still an obvious feature of the river. Foreign ships frequent the waters of the Cape Fear. The fireboat *Atlantic IV* ties up here. There are tugs to the south, and the *U.S.S. North Carolina* dominates the western bank of the river. From this point, there is still a fine awareness of the maritime past of the city.

Water Street crosses Market

A distinctly urban-commercial character is exhibited in the first block of Market. Structures are of uniform scale and density, two to four stories in height, and compatible in material and style. All were built for retail or wholesale commercial use and take one of two basic forms: either a commercial version of Wilmington's favored Italianate style characterized by eyebrow windows or cast-iron covered vents at the roof frieze level, or a flat, commercial-brick or masonry front ornamented with cast-iron window caps and other decorative detail.

118. The foot of Market Street looking southeast from the Cape Fear River. The First Presbyterian Church on South Third Street is seen in the center, with the small domes of the St. Mary Church on South Fourth Street just to its right.

In the first block, almost every structure fits into one of these styles, and there are architecturally no unimportant or uninteresting buildings—though some have been remodeled unmercifully and without regard to original fabric and detail.

ANTI-GERM INDIVIDUAL CUP FOUNTAIN

Market Street at Water Street
1915

An excellent example of cast-iron street furniture of the late nineteenth and early twentieth centuries, this fountain is part of the significant collection of fountains, statues, horse troughs, and commemorative markers that remain in Wilmington.

Located first in the median of Market Street at North Fourteenth Street, the fountain has been moved to the median at the intersection of Market and Water streets, adjacent to the Waterfront Park. It was originally presented to the "school children of Wilmington" through the "generosity of Miss Annie M. Dore, Arlington, Mass." The cast-iron fountain provides drinking cups in a splayed shell near the top of the shaft, and at the base are troughs for animals.

No maker's mark is visible, though the name "Anti-Germ Individual Cup Fountain" and "Pat. S106943—1111507" appear on a small plaque. The fountain has a molded base, a rectangular shaft, and a cap with molded egg-and-dart cornice. A relief plaque above the drinking area depicts a horse in profile, while another plaque depicts a draped lady.

PEDEN BUILDING

4 Market Street
c. 1880

Structures to the north of this block were destroyed by fires in 1819, 1827, and 1846, and there were other frequent and disastrous fires in the area. On this site the 1866–67 city directory indicates that William N. Peden operated the Clarendon Bar. This structure, built before 1884, has served various uses, which may have included use as Peden's bar, since he maintained ownership of the structure until 1889. In 1872 John G. Bauman operated a grocery and liquor business here, evidently renting from Peden. The present structure, believed built about 1880, may also have been rented by Bauman. In 1889 the city directory shows Register & Company, clothiers, at 4 Market Street. Among the early twentieth-century tenants were H. Moore and E. R. Ammons. Moore was a grocer and was here in 1900; Ammons, here by 1906, applied that year for a liquor license.

An adaptation of the vented Italianate, the building features eyebrow windows in the brick frieze instead of the more traditional vents.

SOL BEAR & BROS.; LATER SAMUEL BEAR, SR. & SONS

18 Market Street
c. 1868

The Bear enterprises began in the block shortly after 1866, when three brothers opened a dry goods store at 19 Market. By late 1868 they had moved across the street and opened a store offering "Ready-made clothing & gentlemen's furnishing goods—Hats and caps—Boots and shoes," according to their advertisement in the September 24, 1868, *Star*. They operated as Sol Bear & Bros., advertising in 1876 that they had been "established 1850." The brothers—Sol, Samuel, and Marcus—continued in joint business until 1882, when Samuel and his wife Henrietta acquired "the lot on which the brick store known as No. 18 Market St. now stands." There they operated Samuel Bear, Sr., and later Samuel Bear, Sr. & Sons. They were wholesale grocers, by 1906 also offering iron safes for sale. The *Morning Star* reported on October 17, 1908, "The three-story brick wholesale grocery store of Samuel Bear & Sons, No. 18 Market St., was gutted by fire. The buildings adjoining were damaged by water and smoke." The fire does not seem to have greatly damaged the Market Street facade.

A brick building with vented frieze, the structure acquired a new metal cornice, metal window lintels, and other decoration soon after Samuel Bear acquired it in 1882. Though the street-level storefront is gone, the form remains, and the building above this level is a superbly ornamented commercial structure.

SALOON OF HARRY WEBB; LATER SOL BEAR & CO.

20 Market Street
before 1869

Improvement—The building on Market Street, adjoining the store of Messrs. Sol. Bear & Bro., and formerly occupied by Mr. H. Webb as a saloon, having been purchased by the former gentlemen, is by them being thoroughly overhauled and repaired, from top to bottom, and an addition of several feet to its length. When completed it will be one of the handsomest stores in the city, and from the 1st of October will be occupied by Mr. A. T. Robinson, as a dry goods store.
*[*Star*, October 3, 1869]*

Evidently, within a short time the need for expansion of the Bear dry-goods store led to the cancellation of Robinson's lease, for from about 1870 to 1882, 18 and 20 Market Street were jointly operated as Sol Bear & Bros. Sol Bear & Co., dry-goods merchants and merchant tailors and later "rectifiers and wholesale liquor dealers," operated independently here after 1882.

The E. L. Mathews Candy Company, wholesalers of their own brand and of others, were occupants of the building by 1911. Mathews manufactured a general line of sweets, including stick and penny candies, but was best known for peanut and coconut specialities.

Though the cornice is now gone, along with some window sash and the street-level storefront, the vented commercial structure maintains its cast-iron grills, an enticing reminder of the rest of the once-handsome facade.

HANCOCK AND DAGGETT; LATER M. W. DIVINE & CO.

23 Market Street
c. 1890

Built for Hancock and Daggett, wholesale and retail dealers in paints, oils, builders' materials, and the like, the store and the Hancock and Daggett firm were acquired by M. W. Divine in 1896. Divine had engaged in a like trade across the street, and he merged the two firms using the Hancock and Daggett location. In the *Messenger* on January 22, 1896, he advertised "Divine & Chadbourn—paints, oils, glass, sash, doors and blinds. The store was formerly 'Daggett's Old Stand.' " Operating by 1902 as M. W. Divine & Co., the firm was described in a chamber of commerce brochure as "the largest concern of the kind in this section of the south."

The four-story brick building features brownstone pilasters and lintels. Lintels are decorated with a central floral crest and dropped ends with triglyphs, below which hang floral-patterned drop pendants. At the base of each window is a brick sill and brick panel, below which is a decorated brownstone sill. Even with street-level storefront and sash and cornice changes, the structure remains a superior example of late nineteenth-century commercial architecture in Wilmington.

Front Street crosses Market; begin 100 street numbers

To the north, recent mall development has introduced plants and landscaped areas to the commercial street. Hitching posts and other bits of period street furniture have been reintroduced. To the south, the street is far starker—without trees and landscaping. Some earlier lamp standards with blue and white street markers survive in the area.

Overall, the intersection of Market and Front streets is an excellent place to view the commercial architecture of Wilmington—indeed, from this point there is a fine depth of such architecture visible, constructed from about 1850 to the present.

Near the northeastern end of the block was the Carolina Hotel, later the Bonitz Hotel, a hostelry that was visited by many of the famous. Henry Clay was entertained there in 1844. The Hungarian revolutionary and patriot, Lajos Kossuth, was a guest in 1852. The *Daily Journal* reported on April 12, 1852:

Gov. Kossuth, the distinguished orator and the lion of the day, arrived here yesterday morning on board the steamer Gladiator *from Charleston, and took lodging in the Carolina Hotel. He is accompanied by his lady and suite. His arrival here was rather unexpected, and consequently no preparation had been made to give him a public reception. He visited St. James Church in the morning, and after the exercises had closed, returned to his quarters at the hotel, where a large number of citizens had now congregated, all anxious to get at least a "bird's eye view" of the Magyar Chief. At about one o'clock, a number of gentlemen were admitted into his apartment and introduced. He left this morning in the 8 o'clock train for the north.*

Certainly there were many others as well, inasmuch as the hotel adjoined the St. John's Masonic Hall—then the major meeting place and auditorium in town, and scene of many entertainments prior to the construction of Thalian Hall and frequently thereafter as well.

Though there has been a good deal of recent demolition on the eastern end of this block to the north, the streetscape to the south remains essentially undisturbed vintage urban architecture.

G. W. HUGGINS, SILVERSMITH

105 Market Street
prior to 1884; remodeled 1912

Thomas W. Brown, local silversmith and craftsman, established a jewelry store on this location in the first half of the nineteenth century. His business eventually involved William S. Anderson and George W. Huggins. Huggins acquired control of the firm in 1884, when the September 3 *Star* announced, "Mr. George W. Huggins has opened a jewelry store in the stand formerly occupied by Messrs. Brown & Anderson, on the north side of Market, near Front Street, which has been neatly fitted up for him." He remodeled the building in 1912. It was at that time that the present storefront was added. The *Dispatch* for December 9, 1912, reported the reopening: "Tomorrow is the day of the thoroughly remodelled jewelry store of Mr. G. W. Huggins—well-established, reliable and substantial—to be formally opened to the patrons and public. To this delightful event all persons are most cordially invited." When Huggins moved to Princess Street, no. 125, in 1941, the *Star* for August 3 carried the following history of the firm:

The story of the George W. Huggins concern goes back to 1865, at the close of the Civil War. Then a young man, George W. Huggins, just returning from the war, went to work for the firm of Brown and Anderson, the first jewelry establishment in Wilmington. Brown and Anderson made most of their silverware, and many pieces can be found in the homes of Wilmington's oldest residents. The present firm of Huggins has in its possession the old anvil upon which much of this silverware was made and also it has the regulator clock which hung in the original Brown and Anderson establishment and was purchased in England for a hundred dollars in gold.

George W. Huggins entered the jewelry business as a watchmaker and established his first firm in the window of his brother James' grocery store on Market street in 1870. Quality and service were two of the first policies adopted. . . .

In 1872 George W. Huggins started a number record of every watch repaired by his jewelers. Today that number stands at approximately 85,000, which shows that the firm has repaired more than a thousand watches a year, a record of service that any institution should be proud of.

In addition to a general line of jewelry, watches, and silverware, the Huggins firm was the official watch inspector for both the Atlantic Coast Line and Seaboard Air Line railroads—in an era when trains were important and expected to run on time. In discussing the Atlantic Coast Line arrangement, the *Star* for February 12, 1888, stated: "Mr. Geo. W. Huggines has been appointed inspector of watches of employees of the Atlantic Coast Line, in accordance with the new system recently adopted by the company. His business is to examine at stated intervals the watches of division superintendents, train dispatchers, conductors, baggage masters, . . . and yard masters, and all watches found to vary thirty seconds in a month will be condemned." Special inspectors and watchmakers were maintained for this work, which required checking watches every two weeks and examining and cleaning them every three months. One of these was W. A. Whitney, who joined the firm just after the end of the Spanish American War in 1898 and retired in 1941 as watchmaker and inspector of railroad clocks and watches. The Huggins firm was also contacted many times to keep the courthouse clock in working order.

A rusticated masonry building, the Huggins structure has an unusually ornate facade. Though the storefront has been changed, the cornice entablature plaque, "1870—G. W. Huggins—1912," survives.

119. I. L. Greenwald Building, 108 Market Street, c. 1880.

I. L. GREENWALD BUILDING

108 Market Street
c. 1880

A wonderfully ornamented three-story commercial structure, this building (fig. 119) is almost intact, with the exception of some cornice simplification. The street-level cast-iron storefront is a rare survival. Showcase windows with glass panels above are at street level. The center entrance, with glass transom, is recessed with show windows to either side. Portions of the iron pilasters with applied floral decoration remain.

The original use of the building is uncertain, though it is said to have contained a drugstore. The store was still occupied by I. L. Greenwald in 1902, when it was advertised as being for rent. By 1905 "The Only Restaurant" advertised its specialty, "Quail on Toast," in the December 1, *Star*. In 1908 the Wilmington Pawn & Loan Office was also at 108 Market and advertised "Money to Loan" in the *Star* for September 4.

AHRENS BROS., WHOLESALE DRUGGISTS

110–12 Market Street
c. 1906

The 1885 city directory lists 110 Market Street as the Sutton Boarding House, a use that continued as late as 1899, when Ahrens offered for rent the boardinghouse at 110 and 112, known as the old Sutton House. Ahrens then demolished that structure, replacing it with the present building.

Ahrens Bros., wholesale druggists, was established in 1906 and moved into its new building here shortly afterward. By 1912 the firm was manufacturing and marketing a patent-medicine line under the A.G.A. label, after Adolph G. Ahrens. Their A.G.A. specialities included: "Liver Pills, Nervine Bone Linament, Female Tonic, Chill Tonic, Hair Oil, Headache Tablets, and 'Po-La-Staff' for keeping flies and biting insects from off stock. All of these are made from private formulas and are valuable and dependable specifics."

Ahrens Bros. continued in business until about 1934. For the rest of the decade an A & P food store operated from the building, followed by a series of uses until the present.

Pilasters and windows survive on the building facade. Though both the roof and storefront cornice have been simplified, the building remains a noticeable and attractive commercial structure.

ST. JOHN'S MASONIC HALL

127 Market Street (now numbered 125 Market)
1841; remodeled 1907: R. H. Brady, contractor

The second structure to house St. John's Masonic Lodge, this building is one of three surviving Gothic Revival structures of its era. The other two, St. James Episcopal Church, 1 South Third Street (see fig. 52), and St. Thomas the Apostle Church, 208 Dock Street (see fig. 137), retain their Gothic facades and detail. The Gothic origin of the St. John's Masonic Hall building is still noticeable in the brick battlemented sides, though one must rely on earlier photographs for the lancet-arch windows and other facade detail. The structure was refaced in 1907, the *Star* for May 22 noting that a "permit was issued to Contractor Brady for remodelling the three-story brick building on Market Street formerly used as a Masonic Temple. The cost will be $4,500."

The *Messenger* for May 4, 1899, carried an article concerning the placing of the cornerstone in the new Masonic Building on North Front Street. In regard to this building, the writer stated, "The cornerstone of St. John's Hall, which was laid on St. John's Day, December 27, 1841, was opened yesterday and the copper box and its contents were removed after considerable difficulty. It took two men two days to find the cornerstone and it was reached with great difficulty. It was in truth the cornerstone, for it was at the very bottom of the northeast corner of the building, several feet below the level of the earth." The cornerstones from this building and from St. John's Lodge on 114 Orange Street (see fig. 144) were both opened, and their contents were placed in the cornerstone of the North Front Street building.

The hall itself must have been a handsome room, above commercial uses on the first two floors of the building. A *Star* article on October 8, 1871, indicates a well-appointed room. "The Masonic fraternity of this city, after frescoeing, repainting, recarpeting and otherwise improving their Lodge Room on Market Street, by which it has been made attractable and altogether one of the handsomest halls in this city, have recently formed a choir, which with their splendid organ, furnishes delightful instrumental and vocal music for their meetings."

The hall saw considerable community use. Notices in the newspaper indicate balls and other public entertainment, including lectures open to the public. Professional entertainers also used the hall. An advertisement for "The Tremane Brothers-and Mr. J. G. Pierson, of New York" in the *Star* for November 13, 1869, indicated that they would present "three of their popular entertainments" at the "Masonic Hall." The advertisement boasted "They are the finest Troupe of Vocalists before the public." Professor J. F. Rueckert advertised on February 24, 1875, in the *Star,* "one of his charming vocal and instrumental concerts at Masonic Hall . . . assisted by Mlle. Oristorio LiFrama, the talented Belgian dramatic and operatic vocalist."

Well-known political figures were also often entertained here. Henry Clay on his 1844 trip to Wilmington stayed at the adjacent Carolina Hotel. The *Chronicle*, as relayed by Sprunt in his *Chronicles of the Cape Fear River, Being Some Accounts of Historic Events on the Cape Fear River* (1916) reported that the hotel and the Masonic lodge were jointly used for an April 9 entertainment of the Clay party: "The rooms were beautifully decorated, the refreshments choice, the supper in refined taste and order, the music inspiring, and a hilarious spirit reigned throughout the well filled apartments." On May 6, 1847, at eleven in the morning, the visitor was Daniel Webster. Sprunt quotes the *Commercial* article of May 8 as reporting that "At the Masonic Hall Mr. Webster made a short address to the many citizens who had assembled to pay their respects to him." A visitor in 1849 was ex-President James K. Polk, and Sprunt quotes the *Commercial* for March 8, 1849 as noting the party consisted of "Mr. Polk, and Lady and niece," who announced, "at 12 o'clock Mr. Polk and suite would be happy to see their fellow citizens at the Masonic Hall, and accordingly, at that hour hundreds repaired thither and offered their salutations to our distinguished guests." This short list, covering only five years in the 1840s, would seem to indicate that there were probably many other distinguished visitors as well.

Among other commercial enterprises that used the Masonic Hall building were S. R. Bunting, who advertised in the October 17, 1868, *Star* "an entire and complete stock of Fresh Groceries for Family Use, also the finest liquors, wines, wooden ware, tin ware, hardware, hats, tobacco, pens, ink, paper." Cowan & Metts and W. P. Oldham were in the building in 1869. J. E. Willson and J. B. Huggins operated here in the late nineteenth century, and in the early twentieth, the Wilmington Grocery Company.

South Second and Market Street, southwest corner

Here stood the City Hotel, where Gen. U. S. Grant was a visitor in 1865. The *Dispatch* for December 1, 1865, announced his arrival—and departure: "General U. S. Grant arrived here early yesterday morning and, like a sensible man—having traveled all the night before—took a bed in the City Hotel and went to sleep. Having no special business with him, we did not see him; but we learn that, after resting an hour or two, he got up, washed his face and hands—just like other folks—ate his breakfast, and at twelve o'clock started for Charleston." The Civil War and the fall of Wilmington was still enough in the minds of Wilmington citizens to insure that there would be no public welcome.

Second Street crosses Market; begin 200 street numbers

At the eastern end of the block, on the northwest corner of Market and South Third streets, stood the brick DeRosset House, where John C. Calhoun stayed during the visit of President James Monroe to Wilmington on April 12, 1819.

When Henry Clay visited Wilmington on April 9, 1844, he was entertained in Capt. Samuel Potter's house, just west of the DeRosset House and on the same side of Market Street. Clay addressed the crowd from the porch of the house, as did ex-Governor Dudley of North Carolina.

COOPERATIVE SAVINGS AND LOAN BUILDING

201 Market Street
1959; Charles Boney of Leslie N. Boney, Architect, architect

In striking contrast to nearby historic structures, this two-story rectangular building in the Miesian style is faced with black opalescent granite and tinted-glass curtain windows fitted into a smoked brass grid. Before the entrance, a sidewalk sculpture (Roy Gussow, sculptor, 1959) features two stylized parabolic curves of sharply edged chromium, which hover together to simulate flight.

The Memorial Water Garden (Garvin Faulkner, landscape designer, 1972) to the east of the building features tile screens, statuary, plantings, and water. Crushed stone paving and plant borders are used within the garden, which is enclosed by a high iron fence of lance design.

BURGWIN-WRIGHT HOUSE

224 Market Street
c. 1770

The Burgwin-Wright House is the largest and most pretentious of the few Georgian-style houses

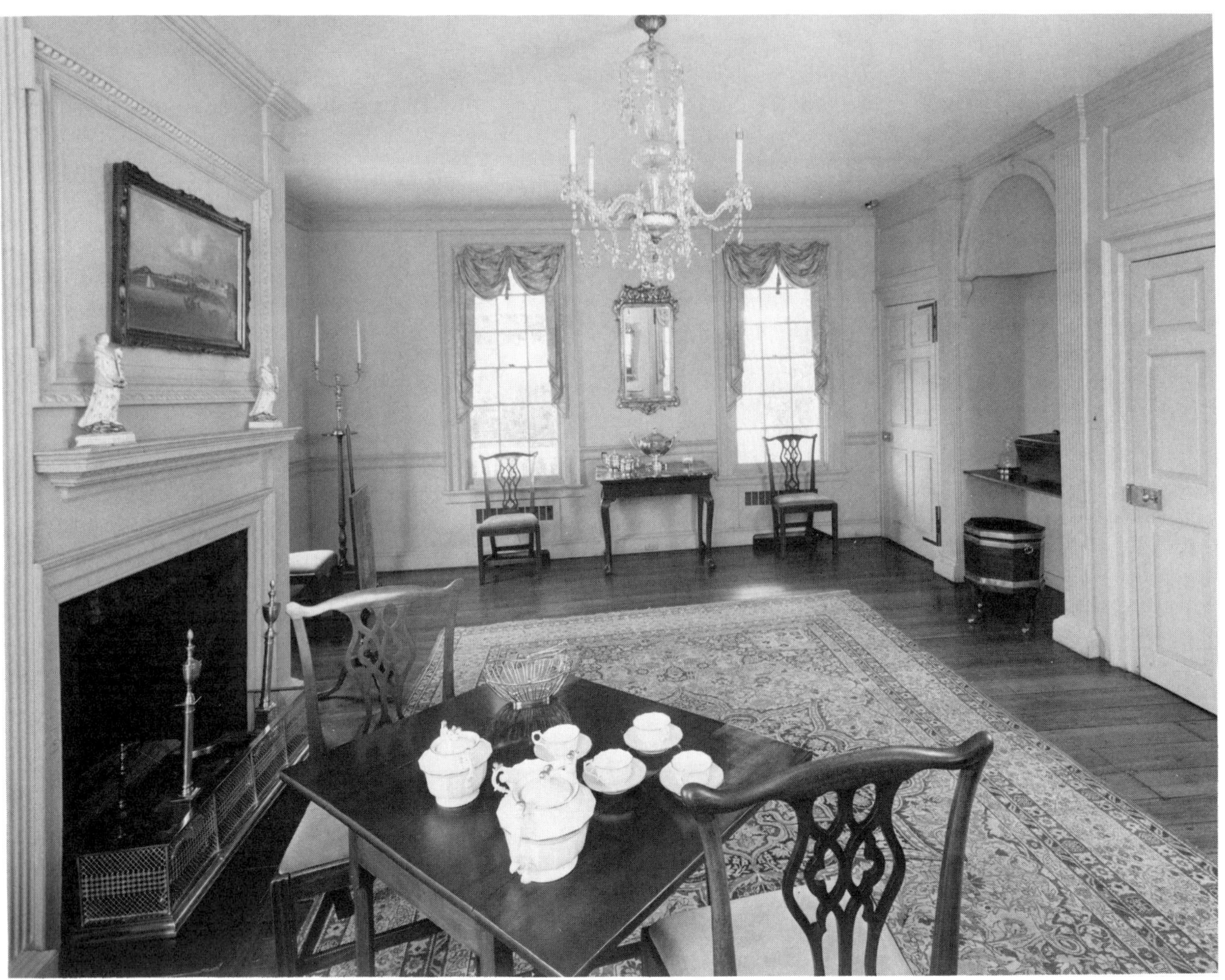

120. Burgwin-Wright House, interior; 224 Market Street, c. 1770.

known to survive in Wilmington. The frame house is two-stories over a raised masonry basement. Its most notable features are the front and rear double piazzas covered by extensions of the main structure roof. (See color plate 6.) To accomplish this, the gable roof is multiplaned—breaking just below the ridge to allow porch roofing as an integral part of the main roof but at the lesser pitch of the lower plane. Much of the Georgian detail of the second-floor interior survives, including door and window surrounds, mantels and paneled overmantels. (See fig. 120.)

Now operated as an historic house museum, the dwelling is state headquarters of the National Society of Colonial Dames of America in the state of North Carolina. Open to the public on a regular basis, the house features period furnishings. Outbuildings and garden are included in the tour.

In 1744 the justices of the county of New Hanover purchased this lot for the construction of a jail. C. J. Sauthier shows the "gaol" at this location on his 1769 map of Wilmington. According to local tradition, it was a masonry building, incorporated into the foundations of the present house.

John Burgwin, lawyer, merchant, and real-estate entrepreneur, purchased the lot in the late 1760s. A subsequent purchase in 1771 of a lot to the south indicated that that lot was between another dwelling and the house then occupied by Burgwin. Because of Sauthier's map and the stylistic evidence, 1770 seems likely as an approximate construction date.

Another local tradition holds that Lord Cornwallis and some of his staff occupied the house during the Revolutionary War when British troops were in Wilmington. The tradition is strong enough so that one of the popular names of the house is Cornwallis House. There seems no doubt the building was used by the British at the time, though the commander was likely billeted elsewhere.

Burgwin was absent from the dwelling during several of the revolutionary years, either abroad or at some of his other landholdings. In 1799 he sold the property to Judge Joshua G. Wright, in whose family the property remained until 1869. The Colonial Dames have owned the house since 1937.

Third Street crosses Market; begin 300 street numbers

On November 9, 1909, President William Howard Taft greeted the white school children of Wilmington and New Hanover County at this corner. He later greeted black school children from the steps of St. Stephen A.M.E. Church on North Fifth Street.

Dominant features to the south within the block are the St. James Church complex at South Third Street and St. James Cemetery at South Fourth. To the north the Peoples Savings and Loan Four-Dial Post Clock, though new, is a welcome piece of street furniture, harking back to an earlier era when such clocks were quite common.

121. George Davis Statue, center of Market Street at Third Street. F. H. Packer, sculptor, 1909–11. The spires of the First Baptist Church and St. John's Evangelical Lutheran Church are on the left; a tower dome of Temple of Israel is on the right.

GEORGE DAVIS STATUE

Center of Market Street, just east of the intersection with Third
October 14, 1909: cornerstone laid; April 20, 1911: statue unveiled (Frank Packer, sculptor)

Though most of the center plaza and street trees of the block are gone, the Davis statue (fig. 121) remains to reintroduce Market Street as a major planned and landscaped thoroughfare. From this point west to the river, the street is stark indeed; even the two gardens in the preceding block are set back from the sidewalk. From this point east—up the hill—Market Street once more assumes its place as Wilmington's main street. Street plantings are part of this atmosphere, as are the center plazas, but it is items of civic sculpture such as this statue, that are the most noticeable reminders. Three of them—the Davis statue, the Harnett Obelisk (Market east of Fourth Street), and the Kenan Fountain (Market and Fifth Avenue, fig. 127)—come in rapid succession. The rejection of recent state highway department and traffic engineer proposals to remove these is a continuation of the good planning and design that located them here in the first place.

Most architectonic of the Wilmington memorials, the Davis statue represents cooperation between the sculptor and the architect, and a superb knowledge of place.

The nationally known sculptor Frank Packer designed this and several other works in Wilmington. He worked with Daniel Chester French on, among other projects, the seated Lincoln in Henry Bacon's Lincoln Memorial in Washington, D.C. Though the architect is unknown, the pedestal was carved by the Gorham Company of Providence, Rhode Island.

Davis, a lawyer, was born in New Hanover County and spent most of his life (1820–1896) in Wilmington. A Whig who had supported Henry Clay, he was a delegate from North Carolina to the 1861 Peach Convention in Washington, D.C. Called by the Commonwealth of Virginia and presided over by ex-President John Tyler, the convention attempted to find some way to insure the preservation of the Union. When North Carolina finally seceded—her neighbors to the north and south had already done so—Davis was one of two delegates-at-large to represent North Carolina in the Confederate Provincial Congress. After formation of a Confederate government, he was elected one of the North Carolina senators.

Davis became attorney general of the Confederate States of America in January 1864 and held that position until April 1865 and the close of the war. Arrested and imprisoned, he was freed by President Andrew Johnson's general amnesty, returned to Wilmington, and practiced law.

The Davis statue was erected by the Cape Fear chapter no. 3, United Daughters of the Confederacy.

Fourth Street crosses Market; begin 400 street numbers

HARNETT OBELISK

Center of Market Street, just east of the intersection with Fourth Street
1906: M. G. Delahunty, Philadelphia, designer and builder

This commemorative obelisk on its stepped marble base was erected by the North Carolina Society of the Colonial Dames of America and actually honors "colonial heroes of the Lower Cape Fear." It mentions the "hundred and fifty men who made the first armed resistance in the American Colonies to the oppressive stamp act of the British Parliament February 19, 1766." Cornelius Harnett (1723–81), "patriot and statesman," is mentioned by name: therefore the Harnett Obelisk.

The cornerstone for the marker was laid in mid-April 1906, the *Dispatch* reporting on April 14 that the ceremony would "take place Friday morning and the Society of the Cincinnati will attend the ceremony, which will be a beautiful one." The monument arrived in Wilmington in November 1906. The *Star* for November 10 said, "Mr. M. G. Delahunty, the well known designer and builder, of Philadelphia, is in the city a guest at the Orton. Mr. Delahunty is in the city in connection with the monument which the Colonial Dames will erect to Cornelius Harnett." The same paper, on November 18, called Delahunty "the desiner" and continued:

[He] has been here the past week with a corps of skilled workmen engaged in putting up the monument and enough is already seen to give the impression that it is going to be a very handsome memorial.

The base of the shaft is seven feet square and the height of the entire structure will be thirty feet. . . . The monument is of the best Vermont Barre granite and is very pretty. It was finished sooner than expected and is by all odds the handsomest of the several monuments that Delahunty has erected in Wilmington.

Cornelius Harnett (who has been called the Samuel Adams of North Carolina) was born in Wilmington and was an early supporter of the rights of the colonists. The first member of the provincial assembly of the state from Wilmington, he was appointed in 1773 to a House of Commons committee to inquire into English encroachment on the rights and liberty of the colonists. At the first meeting of the North Carolina Provincial Council on October 18, 1775, Harnett was elected its president—in effect making him Revolutionary governor. His activities and ideas had become so well known to the Crown by 1776 that when General Henry Clinton, on board his ship in the Cape Fear River, issued a proclamation of amnesty to all persons who would obey his orders and lay down their arms to end the "wicked and unprovoked rebellion" then in progress, he noted pointedly "except Cornelius Harnett and Robert Howe." Clinton's forces landed and burned Howe's plantation, though Harnett was not at the time within British reach.

On April 12, 1776, the provincial council authorized North Carolina delegates to the Continental Congress to vote for Independence and chose twelve persons to serve as a council of safety for the state. When that council met in Wilmington on May 14, 1776, Harnett was chosen its president. On the twenty-second of July the Declaration of Independence reached the council, then meeting in Halifax. They resolved to circulate the document and cause it to be publicly proclaimed. August 1, 1776, was set for that purpose in Halifax. At noon on that day, from a stage in front of the courthouse, Cornelius Harnett read aloud the words of the Declaration of Independence, publicly endorsing establishment of a new nation.

Harnett served in the Continental Congress as a North Carolina member from 1777 to 1780. In 1781, while lying ill near Wilmington, he was captured by a British raiding party and taken to Wilmington, where his death occurred in captivity.

Harnett's dwelling on the northern edge of the city has disappeared. His grave is in St. James Cemetery, just across the intersection at Market Street and South Fourth.

122. Mary Jane Langdon House, 408 Market Street. E. W. Brown, architect, 1870.

MARY JANE LANGDON HOUSE

408 Market Street
1870: E. W. Brown, architect, Alfred Howe, builder

On August 10, 1870, the *Star* carried the following: "Mrs. Langdon is having a very handsome residence erected on the lot owned by her which is next east to the corner lot and the site of the building owned by Mrs. Langdon and destroyed by the fire of '66." The construction contract for the house built by the widow Langdon (fig. 122) survives, identifying E. W. Brown as architect. The twenty-six page contract for construction, which included specifications for the house, was drawn up and signed by Alfred Howe, a black builder. Nothing is known of Brown and not very much of Howe insofar as his background is concerned. (See northeast corner of South Third Street at Queen [301 Queen Street], Alfred Howe House.)

Langdon heirs remained owners of the property until 1958, although in 1875 the corner of their lot had been sold for construction of the Temple of Israel. In 1958 the Langdon House was sold to the First Baptist Church. The house is one of two major area preservation projects that the church has fostered, along with the preservation of its own significant sanctuary building.

A frame, two-story structure, the Mary Jane Langdon House is in the vented-and-bracketed Italianate mode. The major difference from many of its stylistic counterparts is its porch, which is framed and has a deep arched frieze above column caps. Howe described the porch as "of neat and handsome appearance, with proper shaped roof, with gutter formed in the cornice and supported by four tasteful & ornamental pillars or columns in front, and half antae in the rear; to have neat siderails with turned balusters, and to have entrance steps in front of easy ascent, supported or flanked by neat side buttresses."

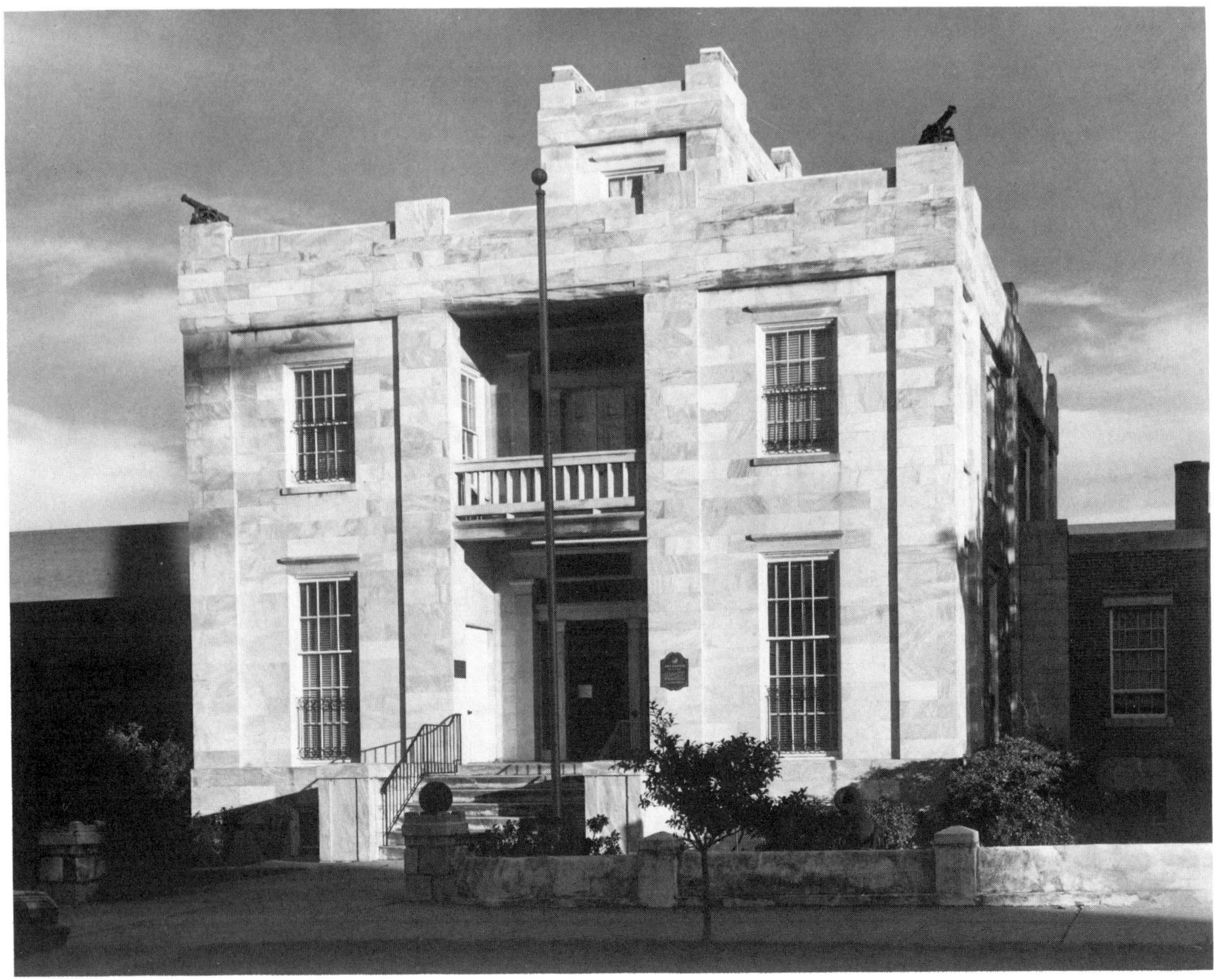

123. John A. Taylor House, 409–11 Market Street, c. 1847.

JOHN A. TAYLOR HOUSE (Former Wilmington Public Library)

409–11 Market Street
c. 1847

John A. Taylor bought the lot here, running from Market Street to Princeton Street from the three sons of Mary Jane Toomer Walker and James Walker in July of 1845. Taylor was evidently in residence by 1850, when the census lists him as here and having real estate valued at $40,000. A businessman, he operated a ferry across the Cape Fear River, owned a steamer called the *Calhoun*, and was active in railroad and other transportation enterprises. He evidently had the funds to construct such a dwelling and did so between 1845 and 1850—probably about 1847.

An unusual Classical Revival residence, both in design and in finish, the structure (fig. 123) is of pressed brick and the facade is marble veneered. A two-story building with recessed center bay and center tower, the dwelling has an unadorned roof parapet and plain pilasters. It presents an oddly austere facade to the street, very unlike a residence. Perhaps the absence of gardens in the approach and of the street trees that once tended to soften the severity of the house, accounts in part for the strong impact of this facade on the viewer.

Ellen Bellamy, who with her family and other relatives took Christmas dinner with the Taylors here and often visited, described the house in the late nineteenth century this way in an account she wrote.

> *The house was wonderful, not only handsome on the outside with marble trim, but beautifully furnished. The grounds were equally beautiful. There*

5. Zebulon Latimer House, interior, 126 South Third Street, 1852.

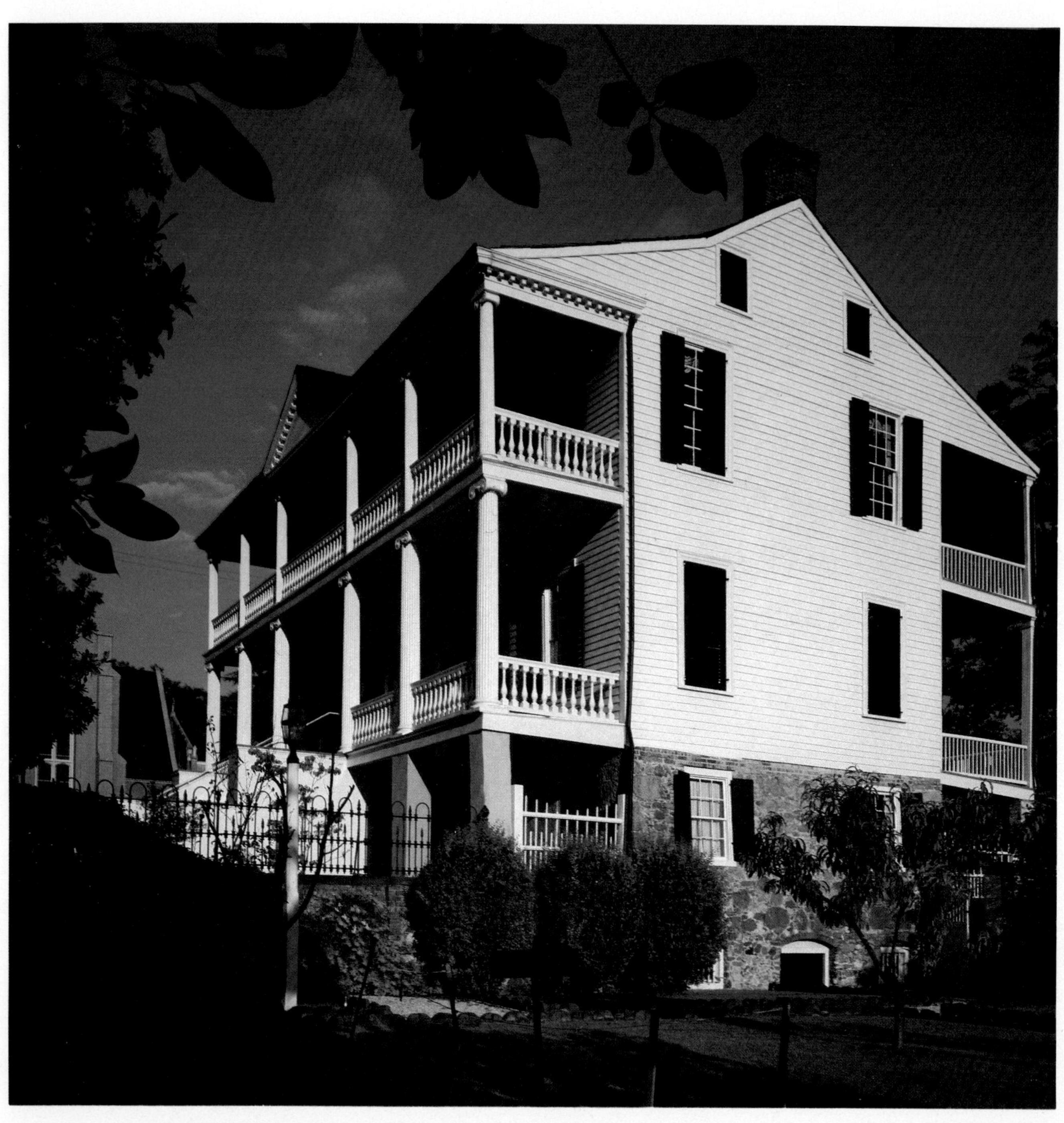

6. Burgwin-Wright House, west end, 224 Market Street, c. 1770.

was a wall around the yard with an iron rail on top and a large iron gate at the entrance. On either side of this wall was a hedge with tall hedges at the entrance. When you opened that iron gate you went into grandeur. Inside the hedge were laid off flower beds. The front yard was divided from the back, and on the western front there was a green house. They had a gardener, Mr. Lamb, whom Uncle Taylor brought from Ireland. He had entire charge of this beautiful green house. Afterwards he became a famous florist here in Wilmington. The lot ran from street to street. The back yard was as pretty as the front. It was laid off with broad curved walks and a circle in the middle was surrounded by roses of all descriptions. In the middle of the circle was the cistern. In the Northwest corner of the lot were the stables.

In the backyard proper there was a tremendous brick house used as servants' quarters. Underneath the first floor was a store room and smoke house. . . .

Going from the front yard into the house were marble steps. The basement was a little underground and very attractive, where the dining room was. . . .

There were some urns in the yard in each bed. I remember when the house had to be sold Mother said to Mrs. Taylor, "You should take one of those urns to the cemetery" whereupon she said "No Liza, I can't do it for they go with the house." [Ellen Douglas Bellamy, Back with the Tide *(Wilmington: privately published, 1940), p. 461.]*

Taylor died in 1873, and by 1876 the estate was in financial difficulty. The house had to be sold at public auction and was bought by Charles Stedman for $500. Stedman, who has been a major in the Confederate forces and was later a congressman, maintained ownership until 1891, when it was again auctioned. A January 22, 1891, advertisement in the *Star* described the house and property as: "that truly superb and costly Residence in Marble and Pressed Philadelphia Brick, containing twelve rooms, with out-buildings of brick, upon east [*sic*] side of Market between Fourth and Fifth street, having a frontage of 130 feet with a depth of 195 feet more or less, with the perpetual privilege of a 10 feet Alley, leading to Princess street."

The Wilmington Light Infantry bought the house in 1892 and used it as an armory until at least 1951. During that period the cannon atop the front corners of the roof parapet were set in place. In 1951 the Wilmington Light Infantry deeded the building to the city to be used as a library. Voters approved a bond issue to renovate the building and add a section to the rear in 1954, and the Wilmington Public Library was dedicated on July 16, 1956.

MARTIN-HUGGINS HOUSE

412 Market Street
1870: James F. Post, architect and builder

One of a small number of French Second Empire–style houses that remain in Wilmington, the Martin Huggins House (fig. 124) is the only one built in that style that has not been changed. A two-story frame box with concave mansard roof, the massive quality of the plan is notable, especially since the house was built during the era when the style was at its height nationwide. The porch, almost full, follows the typical Wilmington Italianate canopy, or concave, form. As used here, it is a perfect echo of the prominent mansard roof.

James F. Post's ledgers identify him as the author and builder of this house, and the Wilmington newspapers confirm the date. A notice in the May 18, 1870, *Star* stated, "Mr. A. Martin has a fine wooden structure going up on his lot in the burnt square, Market Street."

Alfred Martin, a commission merchant with a store at 3 Dock Street in 1866–67, was also in business with B. A. Hallett on Eagles' Island. There they manufactured rosin oil, naptha, varnish, pitch, and turpentine. After 1868 Eugene A. Maffitt, famous Civil War blockade-runner and Martin's son-in-law, joined in the business. The 1875 city directory lists Martin as in residence here and as a commission merchant and manufacturer of naval stores.

Martin had retired by 1889, and late that year, he sold the house to George W. Huggins. The *Star* listed the sale in its December 3 edition and called the house "one of the most desirable private residences in the city."

Huggins was a jeweler who had worked with the firm of Brown and Anderson before establishing his own firm in 1870. He later acquired control of the Brown and Anderson firm, taking over its business in 1884. (See 105 Market Street, G. W. Huggins, Silversmith.)

124. Martin-Huggins House, 412 Market Street. James F. Post, architect, 1870.

CAROLINA APARTMENTS

420 Market Street
1906–07: R. L. Shape, architect; H. E. Bonitz, supervising architect

The *Messenger* chronicled the beginning of the destruction of the buildings at the corner of Market and South Fifth on April 2, 1906, "preparatory to building the six-story apartment houses to be erected by the Carolina Apartment Company." (See fig. 125.) A contract for construction had been signed by July 30, according to the *Dispatch*.

The contract for the erection of the new apartment house to be built by Mr. Thomas H. Wright and others on Fifth and Market Street has been awarded to the Central Carolina Construction Company, of Greensboro, and work on the new structure will be commenced within the next 30 or 40 days.

The plans for the building were drawn by Robert Louis Shape, of New York, and the architect is Mr. L. K. Motz, also of New York. The supervising architect will be Mr. H. E. Bonitz, of this city, who will give his personal attention to the erection of the new apartment house.

Mr. Shape is one of the leading architects of New York city, having charge with Mr. George B. Post, of the erection of the New York Stock Exchange building, which will cost five and one half million dollars and the New York City College, which is to consist of six or seven buildings, the total cost of their erection being seven million dollars.

A six-story building of brick in Flemish bond with darkened headers, the apartment house is one of only two major apartment buildings constructed downtown before the 1960s. The other, the Cape Fear Apartments at 426 South Third Street, was not built

125. Carolina Apartments, 420 Market Street, looking southwest across the Kenan Memorial Fountain. R. L. Sharpe, architect, 1906–7.

until 1911. The Carolina Apartments is matched in height and bulk by only a few other buildings in the commercial area. On this site it is fortunately balanced by the massive First Baptist Church, immediately across Market, and by the imposing Bellamy Mansion, diagonally across the intersection.

The twelve-bay facade features five sets of paired windows with single windows in the end bays. Windows on the first level, on each end, and above the entrance have stone sills and stone lintels with keystones. Stone is also used in the string course that divides the base from the second story, in the water table, and in the monumental entrance, marked by a stone balustrade supported by massive scroll brackets. Two huge wrought-iron carriage lanterns light the entrance. Balconies, with wooded floors and ornate balustrades, were features on the upper floor apartments. The balustrades remain, though the floors have been replaced by iron grilles and the balconies joined by an exterior fire escape of iron. Originally wooden ladders were supplied.

Other facades of the structure are marked by center open arches that rise five stories, providing light and ventilation for interior apartments.

The building has had many distinguished tenants. One current resident is the artist Claude Howell, who was born in the building and has lived there all of his life.

FIRST BAPTIST CHURCH

421 Market Street
1859–70: Samuel Sloan, Philadelphia, architect

Sloan, who later designed the North Carolina governor's mansion in Raleigh and who died in that city, provided designs for two Wilmington churches. It was the design of the First Baptist Church (fig. 126) that brought him to Wilmington, where he was later commissioned to design a new building for the First Presbyterian Church. That structure burned in 1924. The First Baptist Church still stands, very little changed and a fine example of Sloan's design and engineering ability.

A massive asymmetrical structure, the church epitomizes the affluence of pre–Civil War Wilmington. Constructed of brick, with stone accents, the design features double towers, one at each corner of the facade. The towers, unequal in height, are crowned by attenuated broach spires. Doors are in wide pointed arch openings, while lancet windows occur in twos and threes.

Ornament on the facade remains only in the foliated capitals of engaged columns flanking the entrance and in corbels that support the molded hood molds of windows near the eastern entrance. All hood molds were once supported by corbels; the brick stages of the towers were accentuated by projecting pinnacles of brick and by gable finials; the spires themselves were decorated with heavy designs in the patterned slate sheathing of the tower-roof faces. Though the building has been stripped of exterior ornament and now appears quite severe, it remains a superb Gothic Revival building in the Early English Gothic mode.

Pews, galleries, gallery grills, and the circular ventilators in the ceiling—all heart pine—remain on the interior from the original building. The church bell was presented on December 4, 1871 (shortly after

126. First Baptist Church, 421 Market Street. Samuel Sloan, architect, 1859–70.

the dedication of the church), by George R. French, who had sent the bell from the Front Street Baptist Church to Boston for recasting. A new organ and chandeliers were installed in 1890, and during the ministry of the Reverend Calvin Blackwell, 1898–1903, "new improved art windows were placed in the church." The glass is handsome, especially some of that in the front entrance stairwells. This probably remains from the earlier glass.

Baptists had organized in Wilmington prior to October 1, 1808, and were worshiping in a building by 1826. The map drawn by T. E. Hyde in that year shows the two-story Baptist Church as one of the major buildings of the city. This c. 1825 building seems to have been used by the Baptist congregation over the years, though they did not acquire title to the land on which the building stood until 1851. Since the Baptist Meeting House—which still stands (at 305 South Front Street; see fig. 34) and is now known as Baptist Hill—is distinctly Italianate in character, it is probable that it was remodeled about 1851, after the congregation acquired title to the land. The Baptist Meeting House congregation, reorganized on April 13, 1833, used the Front Street building until at least 1864. Then they moved to the city hall, where they worshipped until the present building was dedicated on May 1, 1870.

Land was purchased here on February 1, 1858, during the ministry of the Reverend John L. Prichard. Prichard had come to Wilmington in 1856 with the understanding that the congregation would build a larger and better house of worship. His *Memoirs*, published in 1867, state:

> *Towards the close of 1857 they began to consider the matter in earnest and early in 1858 a lot on the corner of Fifth and Market streets was purchased. In the fall of this year Mr. P., with one of the deacons of the church [George R. French] visited Richmond, Baltimore, Washington and other cities, examining models and consulting architects, with the view of securing the best plan for their new edifice. In February 1859 the subscription list was opened, and pledges to the amount of $10,000 secured the day.*

The congregation then had two hundred forty-two members, including those who were slaves, paupers, or wards of the church. The church records indicate that, "On April 18, 1859 the building committee recommended that a Mr. Sloan of Philadelphia be the architect and that the church be modelled after the Fredericksburg Church. The model finally decided upon was Early English Gothic with two towers, a high tower and a lower one." Though French and the Reverend Mr. Prichard may have liked the Fredericksburg church, built in 1854–55, Sloan seems to have had other ideas, and as the discussion above indicates, the model finally accepted was evidently Sloan's own and has little relation to the Fredericksburg church. The size and finish of the new church must have seemed magnificent to the small Wilmington congregation, and it is a tribute not only to the ability of Sloan as a designer and engineer, but to his ability as a promoter. The structure has an unusually broad and horizontal facade, though the peak of the gable actually is quite high. The effect is created by the broad slopes of the roof and the placement of the towers at the corners of the facade. The western tower is a smaller version of the soaring eastern one. The eastern spire, which reaches 197 feet above the street, is said to have been the tallest church spire in the United States when completed, and from those checked in major American cities, I see no reason to dispute that claim. The tower's base is brick. Buttresses are forty-six inches at the base, almost 4 feet thick, and walls are thirty-eight inches, more than 3 feet thick. Red heart pine and dowels were used in the roof construction. Slate was used as the roofing material. It is said that John Hanby, an architect and builder who later lived next door to the church on North Fifth Avenue, came to Wilmington to construct this spire, brought here because of his special knowledge and because of the construction problems created by the extreme slenderness, or attenuation, of the towers. The eastern spire, completed and sheathed before 1865, was used as a lookout by Confederate forces and later by those of the Union.

In an average wind the 197 foot tower sways from eight to twelve inches, and in a strong wind the swaying can be easily observed from the street. It has withstood several hurricanes, the most severe being Hurricane Helene in 1958, when the tower withstood winds of 135 miles per hour.

With Sloan's plan in hand and enough money secured to begin work, the excavation was begun in late 1859. The entries for 1860–61 in Dr. Prichard's *Memoirs* (1867) provide a poignant account of construction progress and the emerging Civil War.

> *1860. May 4th—Walked to church. The workmen are laying brick. The walls are rising. Yet I hope to see them rise.*
>
> *July 19th—Went to church. Saw the door sills, which had just arrived in the steamer "Parkersburg." "I delight in the stones thereof. . . ."*
>
> *July 21st—They have raised the window frames on the west side of the church. I was so glad to see it.*
>
> *Aug. 3rd—Left home on a trip to secure funds for the building our church edifice.*
>
> *Aug. 15th—Went to the new church—it has grown some. But, O, I feel so sad at the thought of the troublous times. Lord shall the work cease? O let it*

not, I pray Thee! . . . I feel profoundly the importance of the crisis in political matters. O God, forsake us not. Give us men for the times.

Dec. 21st—Walked round by the church. At work on the west side, turning arches over the windows. . . . Heard cannon firing at the news of the secession of South Carolina.

1861. April 13th—Fort Sumter bombarded all night! Everybody is excited. War has commenced; when will it end? Sumter surrendered unconditionally by Major Anderson, commander! Great rejoicing in Wilmington, flag raising & c. The windows on towers of our church raised to-day. So glad.

April 22nd—Companies from West and South concentrating—Went on the roof of our new church.

June 11th—Walked to the church. Front gable nearly done. Lord, I thank Thee for this, and will trust Thee for the rest.

July 30th—Went to the new church—upon the tower, & c. The doors and windows are being closed and the lumber piled.

The Steamer *Kate* ran the blockade into Wilmington in July of 1862, bringing cargo from Nassau and, it was eventually conceded, yellow fever. Initially, the fever and death were mainly among the poor, and it was not until September 13 that an epidemic was conceded. The Reverend Mr. Prichard had sent his family to Richmond on August 12, but chose to remain in Wilmington himself to minister to those who were ill and to their families. The minister at St. James Episcopal and the priest at St. Thomas the Apostle Catholic also remained, and all three died of yellow fever. Initially no body counts were kept, and it is impossible to tell how many of those who fled the city eventually died elsewhere. The Reverend J. D. Hufham, who edited Prichard's memoirs for their 1867 publication, gives some figures that make the horror that enfolded the city comprehensible.

For several days the railroads and the high-ways leading from the city were crowded with families seeking safety in flight. . . .

. . . for the week ending October 3rd, 267 cases and 82 deaths were reported. The following week there were 395 cases and 40 deaths. This falling off in the mortality led the people to believe that the disease had culminated; but their hopes were rudely dashed to the ground when the following week footed up 431 cases and 102 deaths, and the week after 194 cases and 111 deaths. Here the pestilence seemed to have spent its force and rapidly declined: the next week to 116 cases and 40 deaths; then to 47 cases and 30 deaths; then to 21 cases and 21 deaths; the number constantly growing smaller till the fever disappeared. These statistics included only the white persons who died in Wilmington. Many who fled, bore the seeds of the disease with them to the places of refuge and there died. The negroes were spared at first, almost universally, but towards the close the mortality was greater among them than among the whites.

The Reverend Mr. Prichard's death left the church without the strong figure who had spurred it to acquire ground, architect and building. The Civil War was in full swing, and the status of the city, which was becoming a major Confederate port, was something less than normal. It was not until after the war that the congregation could turn to finishing the interior of the building that they had begun. Finally on May 1, 1870, the completed building was dedicated.

R. H. Brady repaired the slate roof of the church in 1896, and remodeled and enlarged the education section to the rear of the church about 1906. About 1910, granolithic sidewalks were placed around the

127. Kenan Memorial Fountain; center of intersection of Market Street and Fifth Avenue. Carrere and Hastings, architects, 1921. Carolina Apartments can be seen in the background.

128. Kenan Memorial Fountain, detail.

church, the roof was reslated, and the vestibule floor was tiled. The new education building was built in 1920. L. H. Vollers was the builder. The structure was first used on January 1, 1922.

Fifth Avenue crosses Market; begin 500 street numbers

The Kenan Memorial Fountain is at the center of this intersection, the only street crossing in Wilmington where landscaped center plazas appear in all radiating streets. With the First Baptist Church, the Bellamy Mansion, and Carolina Apartments as architectural foils and the fountain as a centerpiece, this is easily the most impressive intersection in the city, visually exciting and of immense architectural importance, in spite of overhead wires and traffic lights.

KENAN MEMORIAL FOUNTAIN

Center of intersection, Market Street and Fifth Avenue
1921; Carrere & Hastings, architects

A gift to the city from Wilmington native William Rand Kenan, Jr., the fountain (figs. 127, 128, and 129) was intended for the dual purpose of beautifying the city and memorializing Mr. Kenan's parents, William R. Kenan and Mary Hargrave Kenan.

Water, emanating from a festooned limestone bowl, splashes into a circular pool surrounded by secondary fountains arrayed with sculpted turtles and fish. Another section of the fountain, at street level, was removed in 1953, after State Highway Commission traffic engineers recommended that "in the interest of public safety," the entire fountain be removed and the intersection cleared. The move was resisted, though the fountain was lighted and reduced in size.

Benches in the Fifth Avenue center plazas and limestone walls in the Market Steet center plazas are a part of the fountain design, tying it to the location and visually extending it across the intersection.

One of the most important pieces of architecture in the city, the fountain was designed by Carrere & Hastings of New York, designers of such landmarks as the New York Public Library and the old Senate Office Building and old House Office Building in Washington. The *Dispatch* for June 16, 1921, stated that the fountain was sculpted and then erected in New York, was dismantled and shipped to Wilmington by train, and was then reerected on site here. The parts required some thirty carloads, according to the *Dispatch* article.

129. Kenan Memorial Fountain, at night.

130. Bellamy Mansion, 503 Market Street. Rufus Bunnell, architect, James F. Post, supervising architect, 1859.

BELLAMY MANSION

503 Market Street
1859: Rufus Bunnell of Vermont, architect;
James F. Post, supervising architect

An architectural maverick, the flamboyant Bellamy Mansion (fig. 130) combines elements of the Greek Revival, Italianate and Classical Revival styles in an extravagant eclecticism unmatched elsewhere in Wilmington. The frame house, essentially a two-story box, is set above a high raised basement, its shallow pedimented gable roof crowned by an ornately decorated cupola.

While the house itself is large, its mass is increased

two-thirds by the two-story porch carried around three sides of the house on colossal free-standing Corinthian columns. The entablature is ornate, as is the heavily carved center entrance set in a segmental-arched surround (fig. 131). Windows are of varied forms—Palladian, arched, and trabeated—and ornate balconies occur at the second level.

The house is set well back from the street on a large corner lot, and its massiveness is emphasized by large magnolias, a sizable yard with tropical plants, and a cast-iron fence perched atop a high brick base. The fence, probably cast in Wilmington by Hart & Bailey iron works, is identical to the fence at 111 South Third Street, the site of L. A. Hart's now-demolished house, and to that used before the Bailey House at 219 South Third Street.

Though the carriage house has disappeared, its entrance from North Fifth Street is still discernible. The two-story brick servants / slave quarters and privy / necessary survive in the northeastern rear corner of the lot. (See fig. 132.) Cistern and charcoal filtration systems also survive, along with a dairy cooling room adjacent to the cistern.

Though other Wilmington dwellings may deserve to be called mansions, only this house acquired and kept that popular name; it seems always to have been called Bellamy Mansion.

Nothing is known of the Vermont man, Rufus Bunnell, who is credited with the design of the house, though his name seems to have been associated with the house for a very long period of time. James F. Post, the supervising architect, is certainly Wilmington's preeminent architect / designer, and it is likely that much of the finish of the structure, if not the basic design, are Post's. There certainly are similarities in massing and complexity of design elements with the city hall facade at 102 North Third Street, where Post was also supervising architect. Whatever the evolution and authorship of the design, this street corner must have been one of the most exciting in town in 1859-60, when this house was being completed and the First Baptist Church, directly across North Fifth Avenue, was being started. The two structures, both on the Wilmington heights, were certainly focal points of the developing city.

The mansion was built by Dr. John Dillard Bellamy, a physician who also had extensive landholdings and slaves outside the city. During the era of construction of the mansion, he was a director of the Bank of Cape Fear, of the Wilmington and Weldon Railroad, and of a number of other firms and business organizations.

131. Bellamy Mansion, entrance detail.

Though the house was occupied by the Bellamy family before the Civil War, they spent much of the war period inland, with only Dr. Bellamy in residence here. During that time the cupola of the house was often used as a lookout, especially during the December 1864 and January 15, 1865, battles of Fort Fisher. From the latter date to February 22, 1865, when Wilmington fell to the Union forces, the Bellamy cupola and the Baptist Church east spire are said to have been constant lookout posts.

After the fall of Wilmington, the mansion was used by federal forces and served as headquarters for, among others, Gen. Joseph Hawley. A native of North Carolina, Hawley studied at Hamilton College, was admitted to the bar, and in 1857 became editor of the *Hartford Evening Post*. He was present as a Union officer at the first battle of Bull Run and was breveted major general in 1865. He was later governor of Connecticut, a member of the U.S. Congress, and U.S. Senator from Connecticut. The Bellamy family returned to the mansion after it was evacuated by its Union occupiers. During the 1870s and 1880s Woodrow Wilson frequently visited here with the young John D. Bellamy, who

132. Bellamy Mansion slave quarters and necessary, 1859.

seems to have been Wilson's best Wilmington friend. Bellamy later served in Congress.

Ellen Douglas Bellamy, daughter of the builder, continued to live in the mansion until her death. Her memoir, *Back with the Tide,* was published in 1940. She wrote her few pages, beginning in 1937, as a reply to *Gone with the Wind,* which she felt to be a less than accurate account of a Southern family during the Civil War and its aftermath.

The house is now owned by a family foundation.

WILLIAM JONES PRICE HOUSE

514 Market Street
c. 1855

William Jones Price, a physician, acquired in 1854 the property on which this house (fig. 133) stands; it remained in Price family ownership until 1934. (See 101 North Seventh Street, the Captain Joseph Price House.) John De Witt and his family, from Chicago, were early twentieth-century residents of the house, which they rented from the Price heirs. De Witt was supervisor of mail and express traffic for the Atlantic Coast Line Railroad.

Typically Italianate in form and arrangement, the house deviates from the Wilmington mode in its ornamentation and decoration. The entablature is not bracketed and vented, and the porch is more evocative of the Stick style in its components than of the era during which the house was constructed. Indeed, the porch, raised over a full basement, may be a later refinement.

On a tree-shaded lot with cast-iron fence at street side, the house has been occupied by the Wilmington Chamber of Commerce since 1968. It is one of a

133. William Jones Price House, 514 Market Street, 1855.

large number of buildings in Wilmington preserved by civic, religious, and governmental use.

Sixth Street crosses Market; begin 600 street numbers

SAINT PAUL'S EVANGELICAL LUTHERAN CHURCH

603 Market Street
1859–69: H. Vollers, architect; James F. Post, supervising architect; 1907–8 addition: Joseph Schad, builder

Church records indicate that in June of 1859 H. Vollers submitted a plan for a Gothic church, sixty-five by forty feet with a vestry room in the rear thirty by sixteen feet. The plan was adopted, and a building committee, of which H. Vollers was a member, was instructed to proceed with the construction of the church. The ledgers of James F. Post reveal that he was given the job of superintending the building, and it is probably he who is responsible for the finish of the structure. When the church was being completed ten years later, the *Star* of January 20, 1869, reported, "The woodwork of the church is under the immediate supervision of Mr. Jas. F. Post, much of it being of an intricate nature and requiring consumate skill in architecture to execute." On August 20, 1869, the *Star* noted "The elegant edifice erected under the supervision of the skilled architect Mr. J. F. Post, is now completed." Vollers was still a member of the congregation and had his own construction business, though he does not seem to have challenged newspaper reports crediting the work to Post.

Both St. James Episcopal, 1 South Third Street (fig. 52), and St. Thomas the Apostle Church, 208 Dock Street (fig. 137), preceded Saint Paul's in the Gothic Revival style. While St. Thomas is a pleasing vernacular structure that seems to owe much to St. James, Saint Paul's does not seem to owe anything to either of the two earlier Gothic Revival buildings. St. James seems to have been stuccoed initially, but as with St. Thomas, Saint Paul's was built as a brick building, and was later stuccoed. It is now a rusticated stucco structure, punctuated by pilasters that separate lancet windows. The pedimented facade features a center tower, square in section and topped by pinnacles and an elongated octagonal spire with cross finial. The lancet entrance, with echoing window above, is in the tower.

A mission of the North Carolina Lutheran Synod was established in Wilmington in 1858 in response to the large number of German settlers who had come to the city in the 1840s and 1850s. The *Lutheran Observer* of June 6, 1858, reported a visit to Wilmington—where the writer was surprised at the size of the German population, which numbered "between four and five hundred, a large portion of which are Lutherans manifesting a strong attachment to the church of their fathers." Saint Paul's was organized on May 31, 1858, a constitution was adopted March 27, 1859, and the congregation was received into the North Carolina Synod on April 30, 1859.

The cornerstone for this church building was laid on September 6, 1859. By the end of 1860 the walls were up, the steeple was completed, and the roof was covered with slate. The congregation hoped to have the church completed and dedicated at the May 1861 Synod, to be held in Wilmington. During 1861 the lecture room to the rear of the santuary was far enough completed to allow divine service and Sunday school, but the North Carolina Synod meetings had to be held elsewhere. The Lutherans, as well as the Baptists, had not foreseen the Civil War, and both church buildings remained only partially completed until after that conflict.

The Reverend John H. Mengert (later a missionary to India), who had come to Wilmington to establish the mission and had preached in German to his flock, remained with the church until the fall of 1863. Though ministers visited periodically, there was no regular minister again until 1869.

The unfinished church building was occupied by military forces at the close of the Civil War and suffered such damage that the congregation, which was without a minister, debated sale of the property. In July 1866, with the assistance of the Reverend G. D. Bernheim, the decision was made to keep the building and complete it.

Before work was resumed in 1868, the congregation desperately sought means for completing the building. The bilingual congregation found two committees necessary, as noted by the February 28, 1868, *Star*: "The congregation of this Church met at the residence of Mr. L. Vollers yesterday afternoon, for the purpose of devising means to finish their Church edifice on Market Street, which began in 1859, and the operation upon which was suspended by the inauguration of the war. Two committees had been appt'd some time ago, one to wait upon the German citizens and the other upon the American citizens."

The finished structure was dedicated on August 22, 1869, and was described in the *Lutheran Visitor* by the Reverend L. Muller of Charleston:

The writer, who is himself engaged in the erection of a church, and tolerably well acquainted with ecclesiastic architecture, was greatly surprised at the taste, churchliness and beauty of this edifice. Although only sixty-five by forty-five, it has nevertheless a handsome steeple. It is built of bricks and covered with slate laid down in cruciform pattern. The outside could hardly be simpler. The beauty consists in its admirable proportions. The style is Gothic, which we insist is the only legitimate style for German churches, and the interior presents the most elegant church that we have seen this side of the ocean. The pulpit, the altar, the pews, the gallery, only over the vestibule, the lofty ceiling laid off in panels, and the massive roof timbers all in pure Gothic style, are of southern yellow pine, not painted, but varnished. The wood has been so judiciously chosen and carefully selected, that it surpasses in appearance the richest maple. The red cushions and carpeting made an admirable contrast.

But the windows! Also pure Gothic double windows, with rhombs above for emblems—how charming! The light-grey glass with black arabesques and shadings, edgings of blue, red, yellow, and green, emblems in kitehead, such as the bible, the cross, the crown, the baptismal fount, the cup, the lamb, the dove, stars, and eyes—it is magnificent.

The bell for the church (fig 134) had already been installed. On July 30, 1868, the *Star* had reported:

The bell for the new Lutheran Church arrived here yesterday, per the "Wm. P. Clyde," and will probably be put into position this week. It comes from the foundry of Jones & Co., Troy, N.Y., weighs 1,038 pounds and bears upon it the following inscription:

134. Saint Paul's Evangelical Lutheran Church, bell, 603 Market Street, 1868.

Presented by
Adrian & Vollers
Wilmington, N.C.
1868
"I to the church the living Call,
And to the grave do Summon all."
Saint Paul's Evangelical Lutheran
Church.

> *The work on the church is being pushed to rapid completion. Stained-glass windows are expected for it in about two weeks, although they are not quite ready to put them in.*

Evidently it was almost a year after the installation of the bell and the stained-glass windows before the building was ready for dedication.

The Reverend Mr. Bernheim became full-time minister to the congregation on December 29, 1869. He saw the large parsonage on North Sixth Street completed in 1871, and in 1873–74, the brick exterior of the church was stuccoed. The *Star* described the contemplated work in its November 18, 1873, edition, and the nearly completed work in its February 12, 1874, edition:

> *The edifice is to be stuccoed with what is known as Portland Cement, which when dry, will present a greyish white appearance while the windows and door caps will be made to resemble brown stone. The stuccoing will be laid off in large blocks to represent stone. Mr. Henry Schmidt* [sic]*, late of Hamburg, Germany is the contractor who has had an experience of 15 years in working this Portland Cement in Germany, Sweden and in this country.*

> *The work of stuccoing the Lutheran Church, under the management of Mr. Henry Smyth* [sic]*, has been about completed. . . . The stuccoing is made to resemble blocks of light grayish stone, which has a fine ef-*

fect, the artistic skill displayed reflecting much credit upon Mr. Smyth, the contractor.

Bernheim remained as minister until 1881, spending time writing, editing Lutheran publications, traveling, and operating Saint Paul's School, which he founded.

Extensive work was accomplished on the interior of the church in 1890, as detailed by the May 31 *Star*:

Saint Paul's E. Lutheran Church, which has been in the hands of the painters and decorators and other skilled workmen for several weeks, will be opened for services tomorrow, to be conducted by the pastor, Rev. F. W. E. Peschau; the morning service at 11 o'clock in English and the evening service in German.

Extensive improvements have been made in the interior of the building. A new ceiling, of native pine, in panels, finished in oil and varnish, has been put in, and the walls have been handsomely frescoed, both in the vestibule and the church.

In the church proper the decorations show a bronze border, beginning at the floor, trimmed with black and gilt tracings and above a row of tiling extending around the inside of the building. The mid-walls are handsomely frescoed in buff, with frieze work of dark blue above. The ceiling is exquisitely panelled in dark colors, harmoniously and beautifully blended.

The council room in the rear of the church is done in grey "paperine," with the walls mottled brown, and the furniture has also been rejuvenated and new matting placed on the floor.

The work has been done entirely by home artists, and will compare favorably with any. Mr. E. V. Richards was the designer, and the painting was done by R. L. Hutchins.

The Church Committee superintending the work outlined above consists of Messrs. L. Hansen, A. Smith and J. D. H. Klander.

Electric lights will be placed in the church next week, similar to those in use in the First Presbyterian Church.

During 1907–8 the church was enlarged and the sanctuary refurbished. Joseph Schad was the builder. This work involved the addition of one enlarged projecting bay to the sanctuary, changing the church from a simple to a basilica plan.

The church organ, a Moeller from Hagerstown, Maryland, was installed in 1917. In 1920 ten stained-glass windows were installed to join the four already in the church—possibly some of those installed in 1868. In 1937 the interior of the church was once again renovated, this time by the Rambusch Decorating Company of New York, though much of the 1890 stenciling by Richards was retained.

The church building (see color plate 2) is not only a handsome reminder of the wealth and importance of the German community in nineteenth-century Wilmington but a superb example of the craftsmanship and capability of hometown artisans and designers, including H. Vollers, James F. Post, and E. V. Richards.

Seventh Street crosses Market; begin 700 street numbers

HOWELL HOUSE

702 Market Street
c. 1896

One of the classical Italianate houses, with low hipped roof, bracketed-and-vented entablature, and side-hall plan, Howell House nevertheless has a Greek porch that features fluted columns with Corinthian capitals. It is a handsome and noticeable house, especially because of its corner location, which presents one full side to the viewer.

GILCHRIST HOUSE

708 Market Street
c. 1895; remodeled 1913: Alex. Morton Emerson, Boston, architect

Essentially a straightforward Queen Anne–style house with patterned shingle gables and multipaned dormer windows, it is the iron cresting of the roof and the superb Stick-style porch, with stick brackets, posts with applied decoration, and turned balustrade, that are the most noticeable features of the dwelling. The house is large and, since it sits almost on the street, most imposing.

About 1895 the older house already on the property was either demolished or incorporated into the present structure. William Gilchrist, a commission merchant and president of the Acme Manufacturing Company, acquired the dwelling in 1913. Gilchrist retained Alex. Morton Emerson to design alterations

135. Gilchrist House, 708 Market Street, c. 1895; 1913.

and additions for the structure. Emerson's drawings, dated May 15, 1913, and listing his office address as 40 Central Street, Boston, partially survive in the Lower Cape Fear Historical Society Archives. It was Emerson who brought the house to its present finish (fig. 135).

GRANT-WRIGHT HOUSE

712 Market Street
c. 1853

Tax records indicate a construction date of 1853 for this house (fig. 136), and from stylistic evidence, there seems no reason to doubt that date.

The Carpenter Gothic style is relatively rare in Wilmington. The George Cameron House at 512 Surry Street (fig. 165) and the Chestnut Street United Presbyterian Church at 710½ Chestnut Street (fig. 109) are the only other Wilmington structures that approach this cottage in the quality of their sawn-wood decoration. Wave-pattern bargeboards drip from house, dormer, and porch eaves. Porch posts are sawn in a geometric pattern. The floor-length windows on the street facade are a concession to the Italianate style, but the quality of the sawn work, the gable roof, and the end-to-the-street configuration clearly label the cottage as Carpenter Gothic.

It is likely that James Grant built the house and maintained ownership until 1869. In that year he sold the property to William E. Wright, who is listed in the Wilmington city directory of 1877–78 as a carpenter and as living in this house. Wright may have been responsible for the sawn woodwork, applying it either because he liked it or because it was good advertising for his skills.

Wright sold the property to Mrs. Walker Meares in 1878, and it has been in the Meares-Lovering

136. Grant-Wright House, 712 Market Street, c. 1853.

family since that time. The dwelling is often called either the Lovering Cottage or the Meares-Lovering Cottage.

WALKER TAYLOR HOUSE

714 Market Street
c. 1898; Henry Bonitz, architect

Built for the Walker Taylors, the house was the couple's home until 1937, when Mr. Taylor died. Mrs. Taylor continued to occupy the house until 1946.

A Queen Anne design by local architect H. E. Bonitz, the dwelling also displays Neoclassical Revival elements. These are particularly notable in the five-bay porch with projecting central pavilion, Tuscan columns, turned balustrade, and dentil cornice. The interior brick chimney with corbeled neck and brick panels, and the complex slate roof with cresting and finials, gable ornaments, shingled pediment and multistage octagonal tower are typical of the Queen Anne style. At street level, the arrow-motif cast-iron fence on a brick-wall base and the fleur-de-lis cast-iron entrance gates survive.

PERDEW HOUSE

718 Market Street
1910

W. E. Perdew, a merchant and president of Perdew-Davis Hardware Co., held the same office with the Peoples Building and Loan Association and with the Independent Ice Company. The Perdew family maintained ownership of this property until 1946.

In the Neoclassical Revival mode, the house features full porch with Tuscan columns, turned balustrade, dentil cornice, and balustraded roof. The hip roof of the main structure, with modillioned cornice, contains a hipped dormer. Sash in the dormer and in other windows is multipaned.

Eighth Street crosses Market; begin 800 street numbers

NATIONAL GUARD ARMORY; NEW HANOVER COUNTY MUSEUM

814 Market Street
1935–37: H. C. Linthicum, Raleigh, architect; Works Progress Administration, builder

In a modified late Gothic Revival style, the armory is typical of buildings constructed during the 1930s as part of the Franklin D. Roosevelt administration public works program.

The verticality of the structure—especially of its window bays, which alternate casement windows and stucco panels—and the crenelated sides and recessed planes of the facade are notable features of the structure. At the apex of the entrance pavilion is a shield with a female figure and the date "1936."

On September 15, 1935, the *Star* headlined "Wilmington May Get Two Armories; They Are Among 47 for State Which Have Been Approved by Project Division." The article continued:

Each armory would be of brick or concrete. H. C. Linthicum, Raleigh architect in charge of the plans, said work on the structures should start within four weeks.

Each armory will cost about $24,000 it is figured.

Included in the 47 armories sought for this state are ones for Company I, 120th Infantry, and Headquarters battery, 252nd Coast Artillery, both local national guard units.

It was learned last night Captain W. H. Kelly, commander of the battery, has submitted plans for a two-story building with the hope they will be accepted in order to allow construction of an armory on property owned by the unit on Market street near Ninth. The plot is said to be too small for the one-story type now planned by the state organization.

Evidently the two-story building was accepted by Linthicum, or modified by him, for the armory constructed was two-stories high. The *Star* continued the chronicle of construction in its May 8, 1936, edition:

Carpenters formerly employed by the WPA and who have returned from jobs outside the county will be given special consideration in the matter for reassignment if they will contact W. M. Hibbs, WPA engineer, at his office in the basement of the courthouse, he announced yesterday.

Mr. Hibbs said he needs approximately 20 carpenters at this time for work on the national guard armory on Market Street.

"If the purchasing division of the Works Progress Administration (WPA) will place material at my disposal immediately the armory building will be completed and roofed over by June 30," Mr. Hibbs said.

"Unless the materials are placed here, however," he said, "it will be impossible to complete the armory in the specified time."

Completion of the building does not mean completion of the armory, but the construction of the shell and roof.

Men are now engaged thirteen hours a day, 20 days a month, he said, working in two shifts.

By May 14 the paper could report that work on the armory was "progressing rapidly" and that it was being leased to the Cape Fear Artillery, Headquarters Battery, 252nd Coast Artillery, North Carolina National Guard.

The building was designated for use by the Wilmington–New Hanover Museum, now the New Hanover County Museum, in the late 1960s, and after a renovation period to adapt the structure, it was opened in April of 1970. A museum had begun in 1897 in the Wilmington Light Infantry Building, the John A. Taylor House—further west on Market—but its contents were transferred to Raleigh in 1918. In 1929 the collection was returned to Wilmington, and the New Hanover County Museum was housed in the courthouse on North Third Street (see fig. 50). In 1962, with increased support from the county government, the museum acquired a full-time director. The museum has several permanent collections and an ongoing special community and educational schedule.

Dock Street

Cape Fear River eastward to South Eighth

In his book *The Life of Woodrow Wilson,* Josephus Daniels notes that the young Woodrow Wilson rode his bicycle through downtown Wilmington and swam in the Cape Fear River at the foot of Dock Street. Certainly many other Wilmington youth did the same over the years.

Dock Street evidently gained its early name from its connection with the river and docks at waterside. During the nineteenth century important landings, including Hall & Pearsall's Wharf to the north and Ice House Wharf to the south, were located at its foot.

The street still maintains its association with the river. The J. W. Brooks Warehouse to the north on South Water Street is a major waterfront building, as are others in the area. Dock Street actually goes to the river with no trees or beach intervening. Docks survive and tugs tie up here, along with an occasional fishing boat, presenting not only a fine picture, but some idea of riverborne commerce and the importance of the port of Wilmington.

The block between South Water and South Front streets is a study in the use of paving brick for Wilmington streets. Near the river, brick is predominantly "Reynolds Block," blending into "Catskill Block" near the center of the block and ending with "Southern Clay Mfg. Co." brick near Front Street. "Pebbles Block," used in patching, appears throughout.

THE ST. THOMAS THE APOSTLE CHURCH

208 Dock Street
1845–47; Stuccoed 1858; 1870: J. C. and R. B. Wood, builders

Evidently, the unknown architect of St. Thomas (fig. 137) drew inspiration from both St. James Episcopal Church, 1 South Third Street (fig. 52), and St. John's Masonic Hall at 125 Market Street. All are Gothic Rivival in style (St. John's has been refaced), featuring lancet arch windows, brick construction, and crenellations that follow the roof line and project above it. St. Thomas is a vernacular copy of St. James, but without a tower. In place of the tower, the builders of St. Thomas introduced a massive central gable and lancet arched window of three lancet units.

The *Chronicle* announced on October 29, 1845, that the church was to be built. The *Commercial* of July 17, 1847, noted that dedication and consecration were planned for July 28. The building was stuccoed in 1858.

In 1870 the church was extended to its present dimensions. All stained glass seems to be late nineteenth century. Changes in the interior of the church in 1933 and great damage by a fire in November 1968 have made it difficult to determine early or important interior components.

Bishop England of the diocese of Charleston, S.C., credited with establishing Catholicism in North Carolina, visited Wilmington regularly from 1821 to 1843. Father Thomas Murphy, the first full-time priest in Wilmington, was appointed in January 1845. Murphy supervised the construction of the church and shepherded the young congregation through the difficult Civil War era. During the yellow fever epidemic of 1862, he remained in Wilmington to minister to its victims and contracted the disease, of which he died. He was one of three clerical victims, as the ministers of St. James Church and the First Baptist Church also died of yellow fever contracted after they had remained to minister to the sick. Father Murphy is buried beneath the floor of this building.

In September of 1849 Father Murphy baptized Maria Cenna Jones in this church. A slave, she is believed to have been the first black Catholic in North Carolina.

Father James A. Corcoran succeeded Murphy as priest at St. Thomas. In 1869 he was the only American among one hundred theologians called to Rome to help prepare for the Vatican Council to be held in late 1869 and early 1870. It was the first

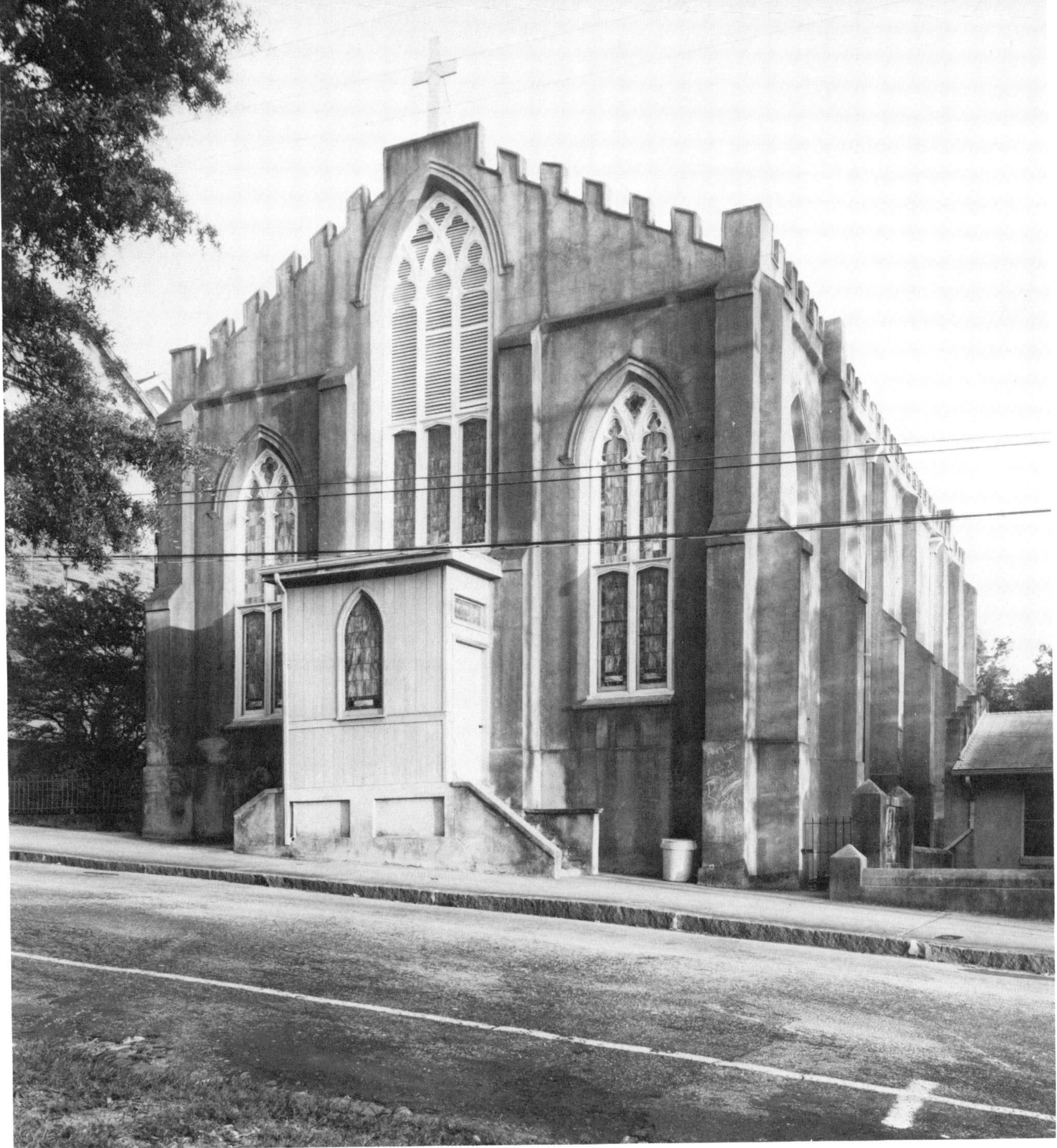

137. The St. Thomas the Apostle Church, 208 Dock Street, 1845–47; 1870.

such council in some three hundred years—since the last ecumenical council had concluded its work at Trent in 1563.

Also attending the council was Father James Gibbons, at age thirty-six the youngest bishop in the assembly. He was then vicar apostolic of North Carolina, with St. Thomas as his procathedral. This was surely an unusual and high-level representation for any church; for one this small it was astounding.

Gibbons arrived in Wilmington in October 1868 and on November 1 was installed at St. Thomas as bishop and vicar apostolic of North Carolina. He immediately busied himself with the affairs of his diocese—traveling, writing, and, at the same time, concentrating on St. Thomas.

Extra land adjacent to the church had been purchased before Gibbon's arrival, and almost immediately he began the search for a teaching order that might provide assistance in Catholic schooling. In August 1869 he turned to the Sisters of Our Lady of Mercy in Charleston, and on September 20, three nuns arrived in Wilmington. On October 11, 1869, they opened the Academy of the Incarnation for girls and by January 3, 1871, had begun a parochial school under the patronage of St. Peter. They were the first teaching sisters in the state, and these two schools, the first parochial schools in North Carolina. The area became so identified with the church and the schools that for years the section was known as Catholic Hill or Piety Hill.

During late 1869 and until October 1870, while James Gibbons was in Rome at the Vatican Council, a twenty-four by forty foot extension of the church to the rear of the older structure was completed. It was intended as the bishop's residence, and Gibbons moved in immediately after his return from Rome.

In October 1871 St. Thomas's School opened in the basement of the church with twenty boys. Another October 1871 event was the reception of the first young lady of Wilmington and the diocese as a candidate for the Sisters of our Lady of Mercy. Bishop Gibbons preached the ceremony on October 15. On August 29, 1872, Gibbons was appointed Bishop of Richmond but was not relieved of his duties as vicar apostolic of North Carolina. On October 6, he preached his last regular sermon as bishop at this church. He traced the history of the church and noted that wherever he had been, even during the year in Rome, his "heart was in North Carolina and in Wilmington." He noted that while there were actually forty Catholics in Wilmington when Father Murphy arrived in 1845, there were four hundred in 1872. In the four years since Gibbons had arrived in North Carolina, the number of priests in the vicariate had increased to eight, and two parochial schools had been established—as had a number of churches and missions. Above all, the total number of Catholics in North Carolina, fourteen hundred, had doubled.

Gibbons moved from Wilmington to Richmond, then to Baltimore. There, on May 18, 1886, he received the notification that he had been elevated to cardinal. He returned again to St. Thomas and, on July 16, 1888, preached in the small procathedral as James Cardinal Gibbons. He visited the church only one more time, in 1912 when he returned to Wilmington to dedicate St. Mary's Pro-Cathedral on South Fifth Street. That visit must have been one of nostalgia, especially since the Wilmington church was so associated with the cardinal's rise to national and international renown.

No small part of Gibbons's fame stemmed from his book *Faith of Our Fathers*, which became a best seller. The idea for the volume grew out of his work with non-Catholics and converts in North Carolina, and the first draft chapter was written at St. Thomas's, in the quarters to the rear of the Sanctuary, while James Gibbons was visiting in Wilmington early in 1876. Gibbons's book has passed through edition after edition and is said to be among the most widely read books on religion in the English language. By 1917 Cardinal Gibbons was able to report that the volume had gone through eighty-three revisions, and by that time, some 1,400,000 copies had already been sold. The work is still in print and is selling well in many languages—working toward three million copies in sales, having passed the two million mark in 1952.

The little church of St. Thomas also produced Father Thomas Frederick Price, Wilmington native and son of Alfred L. Price, an early Catholic convert and publisher of the Wilmington *Journal*. Price was the first native Catholic priest in North Carolina, ordained in St. Thomas on June 20, 1886. Price distinguished himself as co-founder of Maryknoll Fathers, a group established with the assistance of Cardinal Gibbons, who had given Price his first communion in St. Thomas, confirmed him, followed his career closely, and knew of his zeal and interest in missions. The Maryknoll organization, formed in 1911, became the Catholic Foreign Mission Society of America. The Maryknoll Seminary opened at Ossining-on-the-Hudson, New York, in September 1912. Price died but seven years later, while a missionary in China. Gibbons survived him by only a year and a half.

One well-attended event at St. Thomas was the funeral of Rose O'Neal Greenhow, October 2, 1864. Mrs. Greenhow had been responsible, as a resident of Washington, D.C., for notifying the Confederate forces at Manassas of the time of march and the strengths of the Union forces moving against them at the outset of the Civil War. After the transfer of much vital information to the South Mrs. Greenhow was arrested as a Confederate spy, imprisoned for a while, and escorted south. Her book *My Imprisonment* concerned her experiences in Washington and made her an international celebrity, well enough known to be received by both Napoleon III and Queen Victoria on her 1864 trip to Europe. She drowned on September 30, 1864, when, on returning to this country, she left the blockade runner

Condor, which had run aground trying to run the Union blockade into Wilmington. Fearing Union patrols, Mrs. Greenhow asked to be set ashore, and, weighed down by two bags of gold, she drowned when her small boat capsized. She was buried with the full honors of a hero, her St. Thomas funeral attracting great crowds.

After the opening of St. Mary's in 1912, St. Thomas became the black Catholic church for Wilmington. After a fire here in November 1966, the two congregations merged at St. Mary's. Since that date St. Thomas's has not served an active congregation.

South Third Street crosses Dock

From the corner of Dock and South Third Streets there is a particularly fine vista in both directions along Third Street. To the south it is a boulevard with street trees, center plaza, statuary, and well-maintained homes. In the foreground the First Presbyterian Church dominates the view.

To the north along Third Street, there are impressive buildings in the first block, and beyond Market the courthouse and City Hall are well-known landmarks. There are no center plazas, no street trees, and no street furniture to the north, however. Unfortunately, expanses of asphalt have been substituted for the greenswards that can be viewed to the south.

South Fifth Avenue crosses Dock; begin 500 street numbers

Vistas to both the north and south along Fifth Avenue offer immense trees, a planted center strip, street furniture, and fine residential structures on both sides of the street and give an exciting example of the well-developed urban residential avenue. This area of South Fifth is certainly one of the visual joys of the city.

NORTHROP HOUSE

504–6 Dock Street
1896–97: Joseph Silvey, builder

The *Star* for August 22, 1897, noted that since August 1896 a number of residences had been erected in Wilmington. Among them, one on "Dock between Fifth and Sixth, for Mr. W. H. Northrop, Sr., by contractor Joseph Silvey" was listed. The Northrop House was evidently this one, though it seems to have been occupied by Samuel Northrop, general manager of S. & W. H. Northrop Lumber Co., who died here in October 1909. It is logical to assume that lumber and millwork from the Northrop Company would have been used.

A fine Victorian era structure, the two-story dwelling is frame with a hip roof. The roof terminates in a gable projection to the northwest front and in another gable atop the octagonal bay window on the western facade of the house. Because of the projecting wall to the right front, the house has two facade levels, though the full porch has but one. The single-plane porch against a multiplaned facade is an unusual treatment.

LARKINS HOUSE

517 Dock Street
c. 1852

Gray's 1881 map of Wilmington lists the house shown in figure 138, and its quarter-of-a-block lot, as the residence of William Larkins. The Wilmington city directory for 1866-67 lists William Larkins's residence as "cor. Dock & 6th." The house is now situated second from the corner, another house having been built beside it. The *Star* of July 27, 1868, reported that Larkins's residence, "corner of Dock and Sixth streets," had been entered by a robber.

The legal records concerning the house are not particularly helpful in determining a construction date. The property was acquired by Timothy L. Guess in 1844. His daughter Belinda married William Larkins, and the property passed directly to her at Guess's death in 1857. The house seems to have been standing then. It is likely that it was built as a farmhouse, and then expanded, with the sawn work added, around 1880. The earlier roof exists beneath the present one. Larkins is listed in the 1883 and 1885 directories as a cashier at the First National Bank and in the 1889 directory as a rice planter. He died in 1891.

In 1903 Belinda Larkins, a widow, sold the property to Samuel Behrends. Behrends, from Hanover, Germany, moved to Wilmington from New York City. A merchant, he established Behrends Furniture Store, located on Front Street at Dock. He died in 1928, but the property remained in his family until

138. Larkins House, 517 Dock Street, c. 1852.

1972—it was owned by only two families between 1844 and 1972.

A bracketed-and-vented Italianate house, the dwelling has intricate sawn woodwork. Windows are capped with pierced, crested cornice caps. The vents in the frieze are covered with sawn panels and a sawn course of stylized Acanthus leaves runs around the house beneath the eaves.

Evidently it was a slow news day in November 6, 1874, when a *Star* reporter wrote: "The residence of Mr. Wm. Larkins, corner of Sixth and Dock streets was entered last night, while the family were at tea, and six hats taken from the rack. . . . Six hatless individuals, including four of our ministerial friends, are in attendance at the Baptist Convention here."

MARTIN-CROUCH HOUSE

520 Dock Street
before 1880; 1889

A two-and-a-half-story frame Victorian-era house with gable roof, the dwelling (fig. 139) features shingles in the pediment, a wide-eave overhang, and molded cornice. The three-bay porch, on two planes, is the highlight of the otherwise plain house. Particularly fine, this porch has an open quatrefoil course atop posts with applied ornament, linked by a sawn balustrade.

The house was the home of Alfred Martin who died here in 1897. In his September 2 *Dispatch* obituary, the paper noted:

> *Mr. Alfred Martin, one of Wilmington's oldest and most highly respected citizens, died at the residence of his son, Mr. W. A. Martin, 520 Dock street, last night in the 85th year of his age. Mr. Martin was born in Virginia, January 14, 1812, but shortly afterward his family moved to Guilford county, this state, to live. In early manhood, he removed to Wilmington. Prior to the Civil War he formed a copartnership in the naval store business with Mr. R. G. Rankin. He continued in this business until 1887. Mr. Martin served two years as mayor of the city and was one of the town commissioners during 1862.*

The house seems to be on the Gray 1881 map, and there is no stylistic reason to doubt that it predates 1880. On the other hand, the *Messenger* for March

139. Martin-Crouch House, 520 Dock Street, before 1880; 1889.

9, 1889, notes under "New Building" that "Mr. E. S. Martin is building a handsome residence on Dock, between Fifth and Sixth streets." Perhaps this is when the porch reached its current configuration. E. S. Martin was also a resident of this house at that time, and died here in 1920. He was evidently a well-known orator and astronomer. The *Weekly Star* for October 22, 1886, noted his unanimous selection as orator "upon the occasion of the celebration of the centennial anniversary of the reorganization of the Grand Lodge of North Carolina. . . . Mr. Martin is a student both of North Carolina and of Masonic history."

On July 29, 1897, the *Star* noted, "In connection with the eclipse today it may be mentioned that Mr. Eugene S. Martin of this city, has next to the largest telescope in the state owned by an individual." Later, the *Dispatch* of March 27, 1914, printed the following: "Eugene S. Martin, Esq., who is probably the best informed man in Wilm. on things astronomical, has presented to the High School a handsome astronomical telescope, five feet in length, and with an aperture of five inches. The instrument will be mounted on the top of the High School building."

After E. S. Martin's death, the house was sold in late 1921 to Dr. Auley McRae Crouch, Sr. Dr. Crouch and his two sons, Drs. George Crouch and Frederick Crouch, all pediatricians, practiced from this house.

South Sixth Street crosses Dock; begin 600 street numbers

DANIEL LENNOX GORE HOUSE

604 Dock Street
prior to 1880

Daniel L. Gore is listed as resident at 604 Dock Street for the first time in the 1883–84 city directory, though in the 1881–82 directory his residence is listed as "6th, corner of Dock" probably 604 Dock. The house certainly appears on the 1881 Gray map, so it must have been built by then. Gore purchased the property in 1877; prior to that time, none of the property owners are listed in the directories as residents at this address.

140. Smith-Gore House, 608 Dock Street, c. 1830.

Daniel Lennox Gore was in Colonel Hinsdale's regiment during the Civil War and was involved in the first battle of Fort Fisher. In Wilmington he "went into business with his cousin W. I. Gore. From 1867–77 they operated a concern known as Gore and Company. In 1877, Gore went into business by himself. By 1900, the business had become incorporated. During his life he was actively connected with a number of large enterprises. He was president of Marlboro Cotton Mills of McColl, S. C. and of Great Falls Manufacturing Co. of Rockingham Co., N.C." (*Star*, February 16, 1925).

Gore lived at 604 Dock Street until his death in February 1925, when he left the property to his wife. The family had extensive land holdings in Brunswick County, according to an obituary for Gore in the *Star* on February 16, 1925. One sale of Gore land, reported in the *Dispatch* on July 10, 1912, was recorded as a "$250,000 Land Deal" and involved the sale of twenty-seven thousand acres of land situated near Hamlet. It was evidently part of the real estate that provided the basis for the considerable Gore fortune. The house remained in the Gore family until 1942.

The house is a fine bracketed Italianate dwelling with raised wooden panels instead of the usual vents. The canopy porch is typical of the Wilmington Italianate.

SMITH-GORE HOUSE

608 Dock Street
c. 1830

In the absence of historical documentation, it is difficult indeed to date a house such as this. Stylistically, the Smith-Gore House (fig. 140) seems in the mainstream of the Greek Revival elsewhere and, in Wilmington, one of the Wilmington Plain houses. The gable roof, plain band frieze, porch with square posts and simple balustrade, windows with molded architrave, and center entrance in the five-bay facade, with four-light transom and four-light sidelights, all would indicate a pre-1850 date.

The property was part of the considerable land of Miles Costin, which came to James C. Smith through his marriage to Mary A. Costin, Miles's daughter. Smith, who graduated from the University of North Carolina in 1852 and married Miss Costin in 1853, was a commission merchant. He died in New York in January 1889, but his widow seems to have continued in residence, maintaining ownership until 1890, when the Gore family, who resided next door, purchased the property.

John Homer Gore, Jr.—who died with his brother-in-law, William M. Brewer, in an accident on the Cape Fear River in late 1904—lived here. Gore and Brewer were buried side by side in Oakdale after a double funeral from this house on December 13, 1904, in what the *Star* called the "Last Scene of One of the Saddest Tragedies Wilmington Has Ever Known." The house remained in Gore family ownership until about 1960. Among its occupants was William Bryant Cooper, who was lieutenant governor of North Carolina from 1921 to 1925. He resided here from 1932 until 1959.

The iron fence is atop a brick wall with brownstone cap. Brownstone posts with pyramidal caps are used. At the entrance, the wall curves into the entranceway, which is approached by broad steps. Gates have a ball and circle motif. The cast iron marked "Valley Forge," is probably late nineteenth century.

HYDE HOUSE

621 Dock Street
before 1880

Property on which this house stands was acquired by William Hyde in August 1857 and remained in the Hyde family until August of 1890. The house appears on the Gray map of 1881, so that it was present during Hyde ownership of the property.

A vented-and-bracketed Italianate dwelling, the structure appears from style—especially the entrance and the full-length windows of the first level—to be earlier in the era rather than later. The two-over-two sash and replaced porch frieze seem to date from after 1890, or post-Hyde ownership.

South Seventh Street crosses Dock; begin 700 street numbers

W. J. PENNY HOUSE

721 Dock Street
c. 1870

A vented-and-bracketed Italianate dwelling, the Penny House seems to remain substantially as built. The facade on two planes, wide frieze and well-detailed L-shaped canopy porch give the house an imposing presence.

William J. Penny, a dry-goods merchant, and his heirs maintained ownership until 1907. It was acquired in that year by W. H. Pemberton.

Cottage Lane

South Third Street between Dock and Orange Streets; one block east to South Fourth

Alleyways into the interior of blocks were a necessity in preautomotive urban areas. While dwellings or other types of structures were built on the perimeter of the block and faced outward to avenues or streets, block interiors were less orderly, inclining toward mazes of pedestrian or carriage ways off the alley. These offered access not only to the service and servants' entrances, but to gardens, stables, carriage houses, exterior kitchens, necessaries (or privies), servants' or slaves' quarters, and many other types of outbuildings. Taken together, these buildings often constituted sizable villages on the interior of blocks.

Though in most cases block interiors were de-

141. Hart Carriage House, 309 Cottage Lane. James F. Post, architect, c. 1852. Wiley-Williams Cottage, 311 Cottage Lane, c. 1845, is in the right center.

pendent on the larger structures that fronted on the streets, there were occasionally houses fronting on the alleys, normally called alley dwellings. In some cases, as here, the alley and the dwellings on the alley had been raised above the common status—Cottage Lane implies something more than Cottage Alley might.

The lane seems to have had its present name since at least 1851, and once contained more buildings than it does at present. The 1866–67 Wilmington directory lists the following with a Cottage Lane address: residence of James C. Perry, machinist; school operated by Mrs. C. O. Perry; residence of Wm. A. Williams of the firm of Wm. A. Williams & Son; residence of W. Burkhimer, harbor master; residence of Gerald M. Altaffer, patternmaker for Hart & Bailey; and residence of Robert C. Dudley, insurance agent, with whom Edward Dudley, clerk for Wm. L. Berry, and John Dudley, clerk for Oscar G. Parsley, boarded. Daniel Morrell was listed as having a school at the corner of Fourth Street and Cottage Lane, and Levi Hart, of the Hart & Bailey Iron Works, as living at the corner of Third Street and Cottage Lane. This meant that not only were portions of the Hart and Morrell dwellings on Cottage Lane but portions of their gardens, yards, and outbuildings as well.

It is now difficult, except near South Fourth Street, to visualize the enclosed alley, with its large numbers of dwellings and other structures. Although the residences that originally abutted the lane at its South Third Street entrance have been demolished, their walls and fences survive, flanking the slight incline that is the entrance to the lane. The iron to the south, around the yard of Levi Hart's house, is earlier than that to the north and much more ornate. It is believed to be a Wilmington product, manufactured by the Hart & Bailey Iron Works. Of the four fences of this type in Wilmington, one is also around Bailey's yard.

From the interior of the block, and visible from the Lane, two of Hart's outbuildings survive. The Hart Wine House is a two-story, hip-roof, frame building to the north and rear of the brick Hart Carriage House.

HART CARRIAGE HOUSE

309 Cottage Lane
1852: James F. Post, architect / builder

In addition to building the carriage house, Post carried an 1852 entry in his ledger for repairing Hart's stable and his fence. The present Hart fence is probably later, and the stable does not survive. The carriage house still stands, however. Two-story, brick, with projecting parapets on the gable ends, it combined carriage and equipment storage with quarters. Such utilitarian structures are often quite pleasing in their architectural character, but, because they are secondary structures, they generally do not survive. The continued presence of the Hart Carriage House (fig. 141) is especially felicitous, both because of the building's associations and use and because it anchors a portion of the northern side of Cottage Lane.

Acquired by the First Presbyterian Church in 1965, the carriage house was leased to the Junior League of Wilmington in 1967–68. It has been adapted for use as Junior League headquarters to provide both office and meeting space.

WILEY-WILLIAMS COTTAGE

311 Cottage Lane
c. 1845

When Elizabeth Wiley insured her one-and-a-half-story house (fig. 141) in 1851, she noted that it was made of wood and "five or six years old." It was also listed as being on the north side of Cottage Lane—not only further identifying the existing structure as the one being insured, but indicating that the alley was known as Cottage Lane at least as early as 1851. Mrs. Wiley deeded the property to her brother-in-law John Williams in 1853, but probably continued in residence. The house remained in Wiley-Williams ownership until 1967.

A later resident of the cottage was the artist Elizabeth A. Chant. She came to Wilmington in 1922 and rented the cottage and the Hart Wine House, using the wine house as her studio and school. There she painted, conducted classes, and welcomed and sat for fellow artists. Among local students who studied with Miss Chant are Margaret Hall, Claude Howell, Henry J. MacMillan, and Hester Donnelly, all well-known artists. (See Crockette W. Hewlett, *Two Centuries of Art in New Hanover County* [Durham, N.C.: Moore Publishing Company, 1976], for narrative, examples of work or portraits, and biographies of all of the above.)

Miss Chant is said to have been a delightful eccentric, fond of designing her own clothes and of describing herself as "Wilmington's resident Druid." Her influence on the arts, through her accomplishment as an artist and a teacher and as a founder of the Wilmington Art Association, was tremendous.

Orange Street

South Water Street eastward to South Ninth Street

In 1880 Lippitt's Wharf was located at the base of Orange Street, along with multiple other businesses. One of these was the Orange Street Grist Mill, located in a large two-story brick building with its own wharves. In the late nineteenth and early twentieth century, City Market, the major town market, was located near Orange Street at 120-122-124 South Front Street, between South Water and South Front

142. Smith-Anderson House, 102 Orange Street, c. 1740 and later.

streets. The trolley lines of the Tidewater Power Company ran up Orange Street between South Sixth and South Ninth streets. The car barns of that company, demolished in 1976, were on South Ninth at Orange.

South Water Street crosses Orange Street

From the base of Orange Street, the Cape Fear River, with tugs at their Water Street moorings and with rotting boats and pilings on the opposite side of the river, provides picturesque views. Also visually exciting is the stone wall along Stonewall Alley to the south and in the middle of the block, now part of the Wilmington Iron Works complex. Said to be made of ballast stones from sailing vessels, the wall is of incalculable age, but certainly pre-1850.

South Front Street crosses Orange Street; begin 100 street numbers

Every house on the south side of Orange Street within this block is historically and architecturally important and survives within an urban context of street trees and shaded, quiet sidewalks; the north side of the block is bare, however, without echoing buildings. It is an important early block, especially since two of Wilmington's Georgian style buildings are here at 102 and 114 Orange (see figs. 142 and 144). The other two structures, one (110 Orange) a dwelling from the Greek Revival era and the other (104 Orange) an office from the mid-century, are equally important. Together they are an excellent example of the architectural heritage of the city during the first century of its growth.

SMITH-ANDERSON HOUSE

102 Orange Street
c. 1740, with later alterations

Wilmington is reported to have consisted of sixty dwellings in 1758. A year earlier Peter Du Bois had described those dwellings as "in general very good. Many of Brick, two and three stor[i]es High with double Piazas w[hi]ch make a good appera[nce]" The Smith-Anderson House (figs. 142 and 143) fits the description very well and was certainly one of the houses standing in 1757 when Du Bois wrote the above.

Though somewhat altered, the early configuration

143. Smith-Anderson House, photograph of etching by Louis Orr from an advertisement in Print Connoisseur, *vol. 5 (1923), pl. 23. (Courtesy of New Hanover County Public Library.)*

of the house is discernible. Of brick laid in Flemish bond, the dwelling rises two and one half stories. The house plan, a center hall with two rooms on the east and one room and a porch room—now filled in, but detectable in changes in brickwork—on the west, seems to be unique among surviving buildings in Wilmington. The triple-hung sash of the second-level windows is also unique. The iron balconies on which these windows footed were not removed until after 1910. The house seems to be the oldest surviving structure in Wilmington. Built about 1740 in the Georgian style, the dwelling was altered in the Greek Revival era and again later.

Edward Mitchell, a planter, acquired the lot on which the house stands in 1738, paying just twenty-four pounds for the two lots. When he sold the one on which this house stands to John Smith in 1744, just six years later, he sold it for two hundred fifty pounds, the increase in price probably indicating the presence of a substantial house.

When Smith transferred the property to his daughter Elizabeth Bailey in 1772, he specified that should she die, the property would revert to him, though agreeing that it should continue in the possession of her husband James Bailey "until all expenses with interest be fully paid which James Bailey shall expend in furnishing and improving the house now standing." The property finally passed from Smith family ownership in 1799.

The Anderson family acquired its first interest in 1829, when Alexander Anderson began buying property in this location. When he died in 1844, he owned the entire northwest corner, or one fourth of the block. The property was divided between his two sons Edwin A. and James Anderson. When James applied for insurance in 1849 on the house he occupied at 110 Orange Street, he listed E. A. Cushing as residing in this brick house. Dr. Edwin A. Anderson later lived here, as shown in the 1867 Wilmington directory. A well-known local physician whose office was located next door to his residence, Dr. Anderson died in 1894. The property remained with his heirs until 1910.

DR. EDWIN A. ANDERSON'S OFFICE

104 Orange Street
c. 1845

A small L-shaped board-and-batten structure, the office is in a style one would expect to have been used in the mid-nineteenth century, though its construction date has been estimated as late as about 1870. The structure was standing in 1881, when it was listed on the Gray map. Dr. Edwin A. Anderson, who had served as a surgeon in the Confederate army, was by that time using the building as his office.

The small building has served various uses since the 1890s, including offices for the Wilmington–New Hanover County American Revolution Bicentennial Association. The structure seems also to have been something of a nomad. Moved from its original site sometime between 1889 and 1893 to a site to the rear of the Smith-Anderson House at 203 South Front Street, it was moved back to its Orange Street site in the 1960s.

HOGG-ANDERSON HOUSE

110 Orange Street
c. 1825

A transitional house embodying Federal and Greek Revival elements, this is a two-and-a-half-story, frame, gable-roof structure with dormers. A spoke-and-post wood fence atop a brick wall surrounds the yard. A house of this type and style would be much more at home in New Bern than in Wilmington, where it stands almost alone as a house type.

Built by John Hogg, a merchant, the property passed to Alexander Anderson, along with the brick house at 102 Orange Street (see fig. 142) in 1829. His son, James Anderson, a merchant, seems to have moved into this house almost immediately and remained at least into the 1870s.

For a time in the twentieth century the house was used by the Salvation Army as a home for women. The *News-Dispatch* reported on April 1, 1925, that the building was to be dedicated to that purpose on the following Thursday.

ST. JOHN'S MASONIC LODGE–ST. JOHN'S ART GALLERY (NOW KNOWN AS ST. JOHN'S MUSEUM OF ART, INC.)

114 Orange Street
1803–5: Joseph Jacobs, architect; Benjamin Jacobs, builder

On January 25, 1803, Peter Carpenter deeded to Anthony Toomer "Most Excellent Grant Master of the Grand & Royal Chapter of Jerusalem commonly called the Royal Arch," and Gilbert Geer the "Worshipful Master of the St. John's Lodge No. 1, of Ancient York Masons," the land on which the present building stands. The cornerstone for the lodge building (fig. 144) was laid on June 12, 1804, and the building was occupied in 1805. An item in the lodge minutes in 1826, noting a tribute to Benjamin Jacobs, who had died, states that Jacobs was "builder of our first home." Benjamin and Joseph Jacobs came to Wilmington from Hingham, Massachusetts, in 1800, and according to the *Cape Fear Recorder* of September 30, 1829, Joseph Jacobs designed the building that his brother built.

In 1810 Peter Carpenter noted in his will his desire that "Mr. Wilkinson, the brick layer, should run a brick wall ten feet high around the Lodge in the town & that the cost thereof should be defrayed by my executors." The fence with its excellent Flemish Bond brickwork survives and is rare not only for its survival but even more so for our ability to date it so exactly and to assign to it the name of the bricklayer.

On the interior, an allegorical overmantel from the Masonic use of the structure survives. (See color plate 4.) Covered over at some point, it was rediscovered in 1913 when the building was being repaired. The *Star* reported on July 25, 1913:

> Masonic Emblems Found. *Recently a number of Masonic emblems were uncovered on the walls of the late Mr. Thomas W. Brown, 114 Orange Street. The walls were being stripped, preparatory to placing another design of paper, by Mr. T. P. Dorsey, who is a Mason and recognized the emblems as being those of his own order. He cleared away the paper, carefully so that the dimmed emblems over the mantle could be seen.*
>
> *Besides the emblems there are other evidences of the lodge room of a hundred years ago. In the door of an anteroom is a peep-hole such as seen in the doors of lodge rooms of the present time. In another room where it is presumed that candidates were prepared for the trying ordeal of being initiated are seen evidences of where fixtures were attached to floors.*

Evidently the murals were covered over again and did not resurface until 1943, when the building was again being redecorated. Artist Claude Howell was responsible for the restoration of the mural. It depicts, in an arched surround, a landscape with smiling sun. This is flanked by shields with Masonic symbols. The arch keystone contains the eye and within the arch the motto "Holiness / to the Lord." Drapery fringes provide a border around the arch.

The *New Bern Herald* of February 2, 1809, gives an indication of both the date and the artist for the mural, probably only a surviving part of a larger decoration. One "Mr. Bellanger," who was considering moving to New Bern from Wilmington and was advertising for work, noted that among his skills were profiles, miniatures in ivory and glass, portraits, and "Ensigns and Masons Aprons elegantly executed at various prices." The heading for the advertisement identifies Mr. Bellanger as "Profile-taker, Painter and Lodge's Decorator, Residing in Wilmington, N.C." Bellanger's assertion that he was "Lodge's Decorator" in a city where there was only one lodge, and where there seems to have been no other artist capable of doing the work, must be taken at face value. Bellanger could have accomplished the mural, and other, now-lost lodge decoration c. 1808.

The building passed out of Masonic and into private ownership in 1825 and became a dwelling. Thomas W. Brown purchased it for a residence, and the structure remained in his family until 1943.

Frame additions to the rear of the brick structure

144. St. John's Masonic Lodge–St. John's Art Gallery (now St. John's Museum of Art, Inc.), 114 Orange Street. Joseph Jacobs, architect, 1803–5.

probably date from more than one era, but all are likely to have been made before 1849. In that year Thomas W. Brown, a watchmaker, silversmith, and jeweler, applied for insurance on August 25, noting that his residence was, "Located on Orange Street between Front and Second. Building *OLD* and made of bricks; addition of wood and nearly new; no scuttles in either building. Main 2 stories, 40 × 20; Piazza in rear 12 feet wide with room at each end; shingle roof; a cooking stove in basement with pipe entering chimney well secured. The addition is 2 stories, 18 × 17 feet on south east corner; 1 chimney and 2 fireplaces; stove used in room in winter, pipe in the chimney well secured." Brown's residency stretched from about 1828 until his death in 1872.

For a time during the World War II era, the building housed a restaurant called St. John's Tavern. Since 1962 it has been the home of St. John's Art Gallery, St. John's Museum of Art, Inc., a southeastern North Carolina cultural center.

One major exterior change took place in the building about the time it changed from Masonic lodge to residence, about 1825; the original entrance was at ground level, but changes in the level of Orange Street, as it was graded and improved, moved the entrance above the street to the second level, the entrance used today.

Documentation on St. John's includes not only Masonic records, but a number of graphics. Included are sketches of Wilmington by the architect Henry Bacon. Bacon, who grew up in Wilmington, drew St. John's in April 1887.

Though built during the era when the Federal style was popular, St. John's is Georgian in style. It is built of brick, the facade is laid in Flemish bond, and it is two stories high with a hip roof. A stucco belt course runs across the five-bay facade. Significant exterior elements that survive include windows

145. Fanning House, 208 Orange Street, c. 1845.

and sash. The present entrance is from the Federal era, mixing the Georgian and Federal styles on the exterior just as they are mixed on the interior. Basically, however, the eras are distinct, and the structure remains a good architectural study of design and artisanry in early nineteenth-century Wilmington.

South Second Street crosses Orange Street; begin 200 street numbers

Within the block and to the south there is a good collection of outbuildings viewable from the public way. At Hoskin Alley two brick carriage houses, with quarters above, are in full view. Both were built

7. Fifth Avenue United Methodist Church, detail of stained glass, 409 South Fifth Avenue, E. V. Richards, stained-glass artisan, 1889–90.

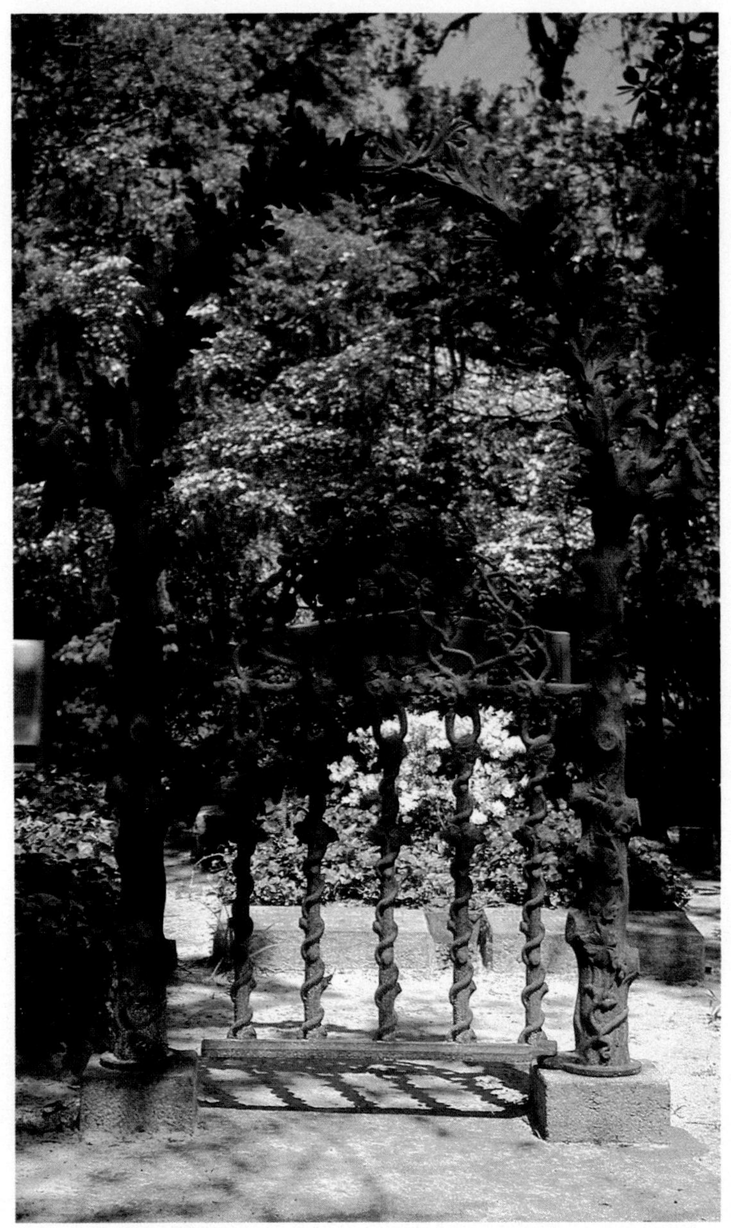

8. Oakdale Cemetery, C. Stemmerman iron, 1868.

around 1882, concurrently with the houses they served. At the entrance to the alley, the full-blown brick carriage house serving the Henry G. Latimer House at 203 South Third Street (fig. 65), with fine finish and cupola, was entered directly from Orange Street. Slightly to the south, the other brick carriage house, serving the Edward Latimer House, was entered from the alley. Further southward along the alley and on its west side, one sees a frame carriage house with vertical board-and-batton siding on the second level.

Hoskin Alley still leads into the interior of the block. Such alleys were common in pre–twentieth century Wilmington and served the interior of almost every block. Servant and trade entrances to most houses were off such alleys and most outbuildings gained access from these alleys. These included carriage houses and stables. Though most alleys have been closed because of disuse, rights-of-way normally remain.

Almost directly across the street from the Hoskin Alley entrance to Orange Street is the servants quarters at 215 Orange Street for the Zebulon Latimer House at 126 South Third Street (see fig. 62 and color plate 5). Two stories high and of brick construction, the quarters has a double porch across the facade.

Trees within the block and on other Orange Street blocks as one proceeds eastward add much to the urban character and feel of the street.

FANNING HOUSE

208 Orange Street
c. 1845

A three-story bracketed Italianate house, the structure (fig. 145) features stucco over brick, diminution of fenestration, and a Greek entry with transom and sidelights. The wide roof overhang is supported by rafter extensions and brackets. Below the frieze is a row of eyebrow windows—diminutive and directly above the windows of the two levels below. In later houses of the style, these windows advanced into the frieze and became vents. Standing high above the street, this is a handsome early-Italianate house, well landscaped and planted.

Phineas W. Fanning purchased the property on which the house is located in 1839 but, due to financial reverses, was not able to begin construction until c. 1845. Fanning came to Wilmington from Massachusetts, where he was born on Nantucket Island. He first supported himself as a merchant; later became editor and publisher, along with partner Thomas Loring, of the *Wilmington Free Press*, a weekly newspaper; and finally occupied himself as a painter, especially as a sign painter. One of the Fanning enterprises was reporting in the *Daily Journal*, December 12, 1851: "Wood & Fanning has a new Ominbus. It is the first and an indication of approaching city-hood."

The house passed from Fanning's ownership in 1852, and by 1886 it had been purchased by Joseph Newman, a dry goods merchant. During the later part of the nineteenth century it was rented by the family of Claude H. Dock, who operated a turpentine distillery on Eagles' Island, across the Cape Fear River.

Partially burned about 1972, the house has been revitalized and is once more a private residence.

South Third Street crosses Orange Street;
begin 300 street numbers

Good views up and down South Third Street at this corner allow ample enjoyment of the landscaped boulevard—with center plazas, statuary, other street furniture, and plants. Though most of the trees on South Third Street are small and recently planted replacements for earlier trees, those in the 300 block of Orange Street are ancient and worth notice. Within the block the First Presbyterian Church complex at 121 South Third Street (see fig. 60) dominates the northern side of the street.

LANGDON HOUSE

314 Orange Street
c. 1810

Built by Richard Langdon shortly before his death in late 1810, the house (fig. 146) is one of the Wilmington Plain houses with Federal massing, finish, and detail. Not only does the house fit within the stylistic era of c. 1810 construction, but the fact is supported by documentary evidence. Langdon's wife Jane married Samuel R. Jocelyn on January 19, 1812. Jocelyn later acted as agent and trustee of the University of North Carolina. In 1816, in a court order to recover debts to the university for which Jocelyn had signed, a sheriff's deed refers to the "house and lot" on Orange Street, so evidently the house was standing by that year.

Acquired by Samuel Russell in 1829, the property

146. Langdon House, 314 Orange Street, c. 1810.

remained with his heirs. In 1859 his sons Joseph B. and Henry P. Russell applied for insurance on the property, describing it as "Made of wood and in good repair, has scuttle and ladder; house 16 × 30; 2 stories, 2 chimneys and 4 fireplaces."

The Russell Brothers were merchants—trading under that name. A later resident was Samuel G. Northrop of the firm of Northrop & Cumming.

RANKIN-ORRELL HOUSE

318 Orange Street
c. 1897

Outstanding among the Queen Anne houses of Wilmington, the Rankin-Orrell House (fig. 147) is a full-blown example of the style. It features a variety of window and roof forms, porches, balconies, shingled wall surfaces, and an octagonal tower, all arranged in typical asymmetrical fashion. The house today retains its stained glass and its trim.

The house was constructed in 1897 by Napoleon Brown Rankin and his wife, Mary Ella, who purchased the lot (which at that time included the house at 314 Orange Street) in 1885. The couple lived in the older house while the new dwelling was being built.

In 1924 the property was acquired by Thomas R. Orrell, who immediately deeded it to his mother, Virginia B. Orrell, as her residence during her lifetime. The property remained in the Orrell family until 1969.

South Fourth Street crosses Orange Street, begin 400 street numbers

HILL-BOLLES HOUSE

409 Orange Street
c. 1885

Acquired by Mary M. Hill in 1870, the property passed to Hannah P. Bolles in 1888. The house is not on the 1881 Gray map, but is on the 1893 Sanborn map. A construction date around 1885 therefore seems logical. The *Evening Dispatch* of August 5, 1899, noted, "The residence of Mr. R. E. Smith, at No. 409 Orange Street, is being handsomely re-

147. Rankin-Orrell House, 318 Orange Street, c. 1897.

painted. It is the residence formerly occupied by Mr. H. A. Whiting." By 1901 Mrs. B. O. Stone was in residence; by 1932 Mrs. Nellie Noyes Bolles, whose funeral was held here on April 14, had been in residence some years.

A Stick style house, it is a frame, two-and-a-half-story structure with complex roof and multiplaned facade. There is a wide roof overhang supported by cut brackets. Areas of shingle and of siding appear on the facade, as does intersecting stickwork. Windows are outlined with stick architraves. The porch has reeded posts and an arcaded stick balustrade. The various dormer and gable forms, semicircular stained-glass transom, and hexagonal bay add touches of the Queen Anne style.

GORE HOUSE

410 Orange Street
1875

Rachel Ann Gore, wife of William Iredell Gore, a merchant, purchased the property on which this house stands in 1871. According to the *Wilmington Morning Star* of August 27, 1875:

During the early part of the year Mr. W. I. Gore commenced a 2½ story frame house on the lot adjoining his then residence on Orange street, near Fourth. This building was completed and occupied by Mr. Gore in June last, and is now one of the prettiest places in the whole neighborhood. Having vacated his old house, Mr. Gore has lately proceeded to tear it down and build a neat two-story dwelling in its stead. Work on this structure is being pushed, and when completed it will be occupied by Major J. H. Hill. Mr. Gore is entitled to considerable credit for his enterprising efforts to improve and beautify his surroundings.

The Gore family occupied the dwelling until at least 1935, when Julia Gore died here. Her January 7 obituary in the *Star* noted that the funeral was to be from the residence and that she had lived there for the last sixty-five years, having come to Wilmington with her family in 1870. William Iredell Gore's funeral was held from the residence on June 28, 1903. The *Dispatch* for June 29 carried this obituary:

Mr. William Iredell Gore, one of the oldest and most highly esteemed citizens of Wilmington, died Saturday night at his home on Orange Street. For years he was one of the leading business men of the city and took a prominent stand in the commercial development.

Deceased was born at Little, S.C., Dec. 25th, 1829 and engaged in the wholesale grocery and commission business. During his career here he was associated at different times with Mr. D. L. Gore, Mr. Albert Gore and Mr. M. J. Corbett. He sold out to Mr. Corbett several years ago.

Mr. Gore enlisted in 1861 as second lieutenant in the Waccamaw Light Artillery. His record was the best. The funeral was conducted yesterday afternoon from the late residence No. 410 Orange Street.

A vented-and-bracketed Italianate structure, the two-story frame-house facade is on two planes. The three-bay projecting plane is pedimented, with echoing pediment on the porch roof. It is one of a small number of Italianate structures with this facade feature, all constructed in the early 1870s and probably having some connection with G. H. Altaffer as builder or designer.

The H. B. Eilers Carriage House and servants quarters at 417 Orange Street was built around 1852, concurrently with the construction of the Eilers House, 124 South Fifth Avenue (fig. 90).

South Fifth Avenue crosses Orange Street; begin 500 street numbers

As at other intersections of east-west streets with Fifth Avenue, there are good vistas of this major boulevard in both directions. This area seems to have been called Little Fayetteville. The *Star* for March 31, 1868, mentioned the title and noted:

Within one hundred yards of the corner of Fifth and Orange streets, there are now living about forty former inhabitants of Fayetteville. It is emphatically a Fayetteville settlement, and affords a striking evidence of the large number of persons who have, since the war, removed from that town to Wilmington. The senior editor of the "Star" was, we believe, the pioneer in this movement, having commenced preparations for a removal as early as June, 1865; and he little thought then that, in his new home, he would so soon be surrounded by such a number of his old neighbors and friends.

At the close of the war, every indication was favorable to the impression that Wilmington was not only destined to be the commercial metropolis of N.C. but one of the most flourishing cities of the Atlantic coast.

WOODBURY-LILLY-HOGGARD HOUSE

504 Orange Street
c. 1854

A frame, two-story, bracketed-and-vented Italianate house, five bays wide with center pavilion, the dwelling was probably constructed late in the ownership of the site by James S. Green, who held it from July 1816 to May 1854. The other possibility is that it was built early in the ownership of Daniel P. Woodbury, who maintained ownership from 1854 until 1879, when it passed to Catherine E. Lilly. Gray's 1881 map shows the center block of the house already standing and labeled E. Lilly. Edmund Lilly, Catherine's husband, was a merchant and cotton buyer in the firm of Lilly and Brothers. The Lillys made the first of the additions to the house after 1881.

The Lilly family maintained ownership until 1919, when John T. and Virginia E. Hoggard purchased the house. The Hoggards immediately sold a half interest to John F. and Cottie O. Miller. According to the *Star* of June 24, 1919, Dr. John T. Hoggard and Dr. J. F. Miller intended to open a hospital in the house. It would, the article stated:

> *be immediately converted into a modern hospital. The institution will be known as the Wilmington Hospital. Every device of a well equipped hospital will be installed in the building when completed, and each department will be under the supervision of resident physicians trained in that particular branch of medicine or surgical science. The institution will be private but open to the practice of any physicians of the city who wish to make use of its equipment. The location of the new hospital is regarded desirable by the physicians interested. It is there that the city elevation reaches its highest point, and it is in a quiet residential section of the city, centrally located and easily accessible from any part of the city. Plans have been drawn by architects and construction of the additions contemplated will begin within a few days. Each of the 50 rooms for patients will have a private bath. The addition will be fire proof, brick construction.*

Work was accomplished, but evidently not in brick and not to the extent planned. The hospital did open, but seems to have been known as St. John's Sanatorium. Evidently the Millers resided at the house. The 1921 city directory lists Mrs. Miller as superintendent, and lists both her and Dr. Miller as residents of 504 Orange Street.

The sanatorium was in operation until 1924. In 1927 the Hoggards regained full ownership of the property, and after reconversion of the house and its additions from hospital to residence and doctor's office, they moved in. Dr. Hoggard maintained offices in the southwestern corner of the structure until he retired about 1948. He died in 1965.

Hoggard, who had been with Teddy Roosevelt's unit in Cuba during the Spanish-American War and had served as a doctor overseas in France in World War I, was a prominent Wilmington educator. He has been called the "Father of Wilmington College," now the University of North Carolina at Wilmington. He was one of its founders, served as its second president, and was chairman of the trustees until his death. He also served as chairman of the local school board for some twenty-five years. Both a high school and a building at the college bear his name. Mrs. Hoggard continued to live at this address until her death in 1967.

BISHOP'S RESIDENCE

510–12 Orange Street
c. 1905

One of the fine Neoclassical Revival houses in Wilmington, the Bishop's Residence (fig. 148) is a two-story brick structure with slate-covered roof, quoins, and a brick water table. The colossal portico with paired Ionic columns, molded cornice, dentil course, slate-covered pediment, and oval window with keystone and tracery is the main feature of the house. The other, the entrance, can be viewed fully between the paired columns of the portico. The monumental entranceway has a heavily molded cornice, a dentil course, and sunburst medallions over Ionic pilasters, a five-panel double door, and mullioned transom. Narrow vertical windows flank the door. At the second level is a window flanked by smaller round-arched windows. The center opening gives onto a balcony with turned balustrade supported by acanthus scroll brackets. The whole is sited back from the street on a large lot.

The Episcopal Diocese of North Carolina purchased this property from James Green about 1870, and by 1873 Bishop Atkinson of the diocese was in residence, utilizing the dwelling that was already on the property. Bishop Watson lived here from the time he became bishop in 1884 until his death in 1905. At the annual convention of the diocese in June of 1905, it was decided to tear down the existing dwelling and construct the present one at a price not to exceed eleven thousand dollars. By July 10, Thomas D. Meares, chairman of the committee, was advertising for removal of the old house. Construction of the new building was begun soon thereafter, but was not completed until 1908, at a cost of $15,048.94. Robert Strange, who had become bishop in 1905, lived in the William Rand Kenan House, 110 Nun Street, before moving here in 1908. He died in 1914 and was succeeded by

148. Bishop's Residence, 510–12 Orange Street, c. 1905.

Bishop Thomas C. Darst. Darst lived here until he retired in 1945, and he was succeeded in residence by Bishop Thomas H. Wright, who lived here from 1945 until the structure was sold in 1966.

WILLARD HOUSE (now Bynum-Willard House)

520 Orange Street
c. 1853; c. 1895

This Italianate house (fig. 149) is one of three in Wilmington that follows almost exactly the elevations, plan, and ornamentation for the "Cubical Cottage in the Tuscan Style" given by A. J. Downing in *The Architecture of Country Houses,* published in 1850. Built on a side-hall plan, these stuccoed brick dwellings are two-story with low hip roofs supported by brackets. Window surrounds are like those Downing called "Italian." He recommended that the verandah be allowed to be overgrown with grape or other vines. Here, the foliage and decoration is of permanent cast-iron in the form of trellises that carry a canopy roof. The Edward and Henry Savage House at 120 South Third Street (fig. 59) and the MacRae-Dix House at 108 South Third Street (fig. 58) are look-alikes for this house; several others are markedly similar.

There is an addition, with stained glass, to the east, probably built late in the nineteenth century. The glass reflects the iron of the porch through its use of grapes and grape vines. The sidewalk of stone is from the same late nineteenth-century era, as is the "Stewart Iron Works, Cincinnati, Ohio," fence that surrounds this corner property. A sizeable lot and good landscaping add to the illusion of country grandeur that Downing had intended for a house in this style.

Albert A. Willard moved to Wilmington in 1865 to operate a shipping business. He owned 520 Orange Street until his son, Martin S. Willard, bought it. Martin Willard was chairman of the New Hanover County Commissioners for many years, served one term in the state legislature, and was president of the Carolina Insurance Company. The family sold the house in the late 1950s.

149. Willard House (now Bynum-Willard House), 520 Orange Street, c. 1853; c. 1895.

South Sixth Street crosses Orange Street; begin 600 street numbers

SKINNER HOUSE

611 Orange Street
c. 1891

A massive Queen Anne structure with seven facade bays on two planes, the house (fig. 150) is frame with a three-bay projecting cross gable. Sawn barge-boards, gable ornaments in the Stick style, patterned shingle in the gable ends, and a superb porch with center entrance pavilion and clipped corners with entrances are features of the facade. A spindle course is full on the porch and arched over the entrances. Turned posts flanked by brackets and an arched openwork balustrade are used.

The house is a striking example of the Queen Anne style, its position above the street adding to the illusion of grandness and size. The yard slopes from the house to the brick wall with rounded cement top that contains it at the sidewalk and entrance drive.

Emily J. Skinner acquired the property from E. G. Whitney in 1885. Evidently by March of 1891 the house was under construction for Emily and Samuel W. Skinner, who mortgaged the property

150. Skinner House, 611 Orange Street, c. 1891.

to the Wilmington Homestead and Loan Association. It was certainly completed by 1898, when it is shown on the Sanborn map.

Capt. S. W. Skinner was owner of Skinner's Marine Railway, on the site of Cassidey's shipyard at the foot of Church Street.

The property remained in Skinner-family ownership until 1929, when R. R. Stone purchased it. The next year he transferred the house to his son, Harriss Stone, who resided there with his family for a number of years.

McLAURIN HOUSE

619 Orange Street
c. 1867

On December 2, 1867, Mary Dickson wrote her brother John McLaurin a four-page letter ending with: "I understand you have got into your house long since. I presume you feel quite at home in it now." Inasmuch as the city directory for 1866–67 lists John McLaurin of Moffit Bro. & Co. as residing on Second between Ann and Nun streets, with Hugh W. McLaurin, bookkeeper for E. Murray & Co., boarding with him, it seems likely that McLaurin built the cottage at 619 Orange Street in 1867 after the text for the directory had already been prepared.

The *Messenger* for September 26, 1894, noted, "Mrs. W. M. Parsley will open a school for small children at the residence of Mr. John McLaurin, 619 Orange St., on October 8th."

The cottage, in the Wilmington Plain style, sits well back from the street, still maintaining its large lot. Only a single story high, the frame structure features a porch beneath the main gable roof. It has three open bays to the east, which are closed to form a room on the west.

Photographed by Frances Benjamin Johnston in

the 1930s for the collections of the Library of Congress, it was one of the very few Wilmington buildings so honored. Miss Johnston evidently was taken with its quaintness and picturesqueness.

South Eighth Street crosses Orange; begin 800 street numbers

The western half of the 800-number block of Orange is a collection of substantial two-story late-Victorian-era dwellings built in 1905 by Furney J. Gooding. All have fine detailing. The *Star* reported Gooding's purchase in its February 2, 1905, editions and noted that he proposed "to build a large number of modern residences on the site." Evidently that was accomplished during the year, for the paper carried the following on December 4, 1905:

A committee representing the property owners of the St. James' block which is bounded by Orange and Ninth and Ann and Eighth streets, and on which seven new buildings have been recently erected, and another is now under way, will present a petition to the Board of Aldermen asking for streets around the block to be improved.

The petition will ask the board to improve the four streets surrounding the block, by macadamizing, and establishing curb lines, laying stone curbing.

The sidewalks around the block will be laid by the owners by the property and will be, very likely, of concrete.

The property on "St. James" block, when all the buildings and residences are erected will represent a valuation of between $70,000 and $100,000 and will be one of the prettiest residence sections in the city. The property owners are very hopeful that the Board of Aldermen will see fit to grant the improvements desired.

When the block is completed, which will be early in the summer of 1906, there will be twenty-four residences thereon, each costing from $2,000 to $3,500. The block will be supplied with artesian water. In the center of the block will be an open court, 30 × 160 in size, which will be planted with shrubbery and flowers.

The property had been the site of St. James Home, operated by the Sisters of the Good Shepherd. The home was begun in 1870 to assist "every poor woman in the city, and for those mothers who are prevented by continued illness from giving their children proper attention or the mothers who are compelled to leave their children during the day to earn a livelihood." The home burned in April of 1896, according to the *Messenger* of April 5. An article in the *Star* on March 15, 1905, sheds some light on the St. James institution.

There was filed for record in the office of the Register of Deeds at the Court House yesterday morning an old instrument of date March 29th, 1867, conveying from the lamented Dr. Armand J. DeRosset and wife to the vestry and wardens of St. James' Episcopal church, in this city, the property known as the "O.A.N. Grounds," which was recently sold by the vestry and wardens of the parish to Mr. Thomas P. Bagley, and over which sale it was at first thought there would be a legal controversy. The old deed describes the property as "all those lots or parcels of land, between Orange and Ann and Eighth and Ninth streets, being the whole of Block No. 133." and the conditions of the gifts to the church are set forth in the following language:

"That the said parties of the first part, for the purpose of aiding in the establishment of a Home for Indigent Widows or Orphans, or in the promotion of any other charitable or religious object to which the property hereinafter conveyed may be appropriated by the party of the second part in further consideration of $1 to them in hand paid, etc."

As it is understood that the proceeds of the recent sale are to be used in the work of the Chapel of the Good Shepherd, Sixth and Queen streets, the opinion has been given that the recent sale is in full compliance with the conditions under which the property was given to the church by the lamented Dr. DeRosset.

ST. JAMES STREET DWELLINGS

Orange Street, center of block between South Eighth and South Ninth streets
c. 1885

Gray's 1881 map shows the St. James Home established on the south side of the street, within its own block. Across the street to the north, the block is largely undeveloped except for standing structures at the northeast corner of Orange and South Eighth streets. No alley or street runs through the block. Today, in the center of the block on the north side,

151. St. James Street dwellings, center of block between South Eighth and South Ninth streets off Orange Street, c. 1885.

opposite the former site of the St. James Home, St. James Street runs north-south from Orange Street to Dock Street. It is but a block long, as are Gore's Alley, Magnolia Street, and Jasmine Street to the east, all of roughly the same late-nineteenth century development era and all maintaining some of their earlier character, though St. James Street seems to be the most complete.

This almost unknown street is important because of the collection of nineteenth-century cottages along its perimeter, and because it evidences interior uses of the block. St. James Street is paved with asphalt paving block, and nine houses front on it. All are frame, one-story, plain houses, containing a room or two. Those at numbers 107, 113, and 117 St. James Street have gable roofs parallel to the street. Those at numbers 108, 110, 112, 116, and 118 have gables perpendicular to the street. The house at 121 St. James Street (fig. 151) is a bit more complex, with its L shape, shingle decoration, and larger porch. All the structures are directly on the street and have porches and gardens to the sides and rear. There were previously more houses in the block, and it was once much more crowded then at present.

What the block evokes today is a three-dimensional picture of the type of surroundings in which a substantial part of the city's population lived in the nineteenth century. These houses could have been constructed at any time in the century and would have looked essentially the same. Their purpose was housing, basic and unadorned.

152. Chandler's Wharf, riverfront; Ann Street at South Water Street, 1977–78, with collection of earlier buildings and vessels.

Ann Street

From South Water Street eastward to South Ninth Street, the Cape Fear River is at the foot of Ann

South Water Street enters Ann Street from the north

CHANDLER'S WHARF

2 Ann Street
1977–78: attraction with infused houses and ships

Chandler's Wharf (figs. 152, 153) conceived and developed by Thomas H. Wright, Jr., takes its name from the ships' chandlers—outfitters and provisioners for ships—who were such a fixture of the nineteenth-century Wilmington waterfront. On a five-acre site, between the bluff and the Cape Fear River, are several nineteenth-century houses moved from other parts of Wilmington, a nautical museum and a collection of ships. Belgian paving block, picket fences, wooden boardwalks, warehouses, loading docks, and a wharf lined with barrels and tobacco hogsheads are used to recreate the atmosphere of the post–Civil War and early twentieth-century waterfront. During that era Wilmington was North Carolina's largest city, the world's leading exporter of tar, pitch, and turpentine, and one of the largest cotton exporters in the world. The Chandler's Wharf

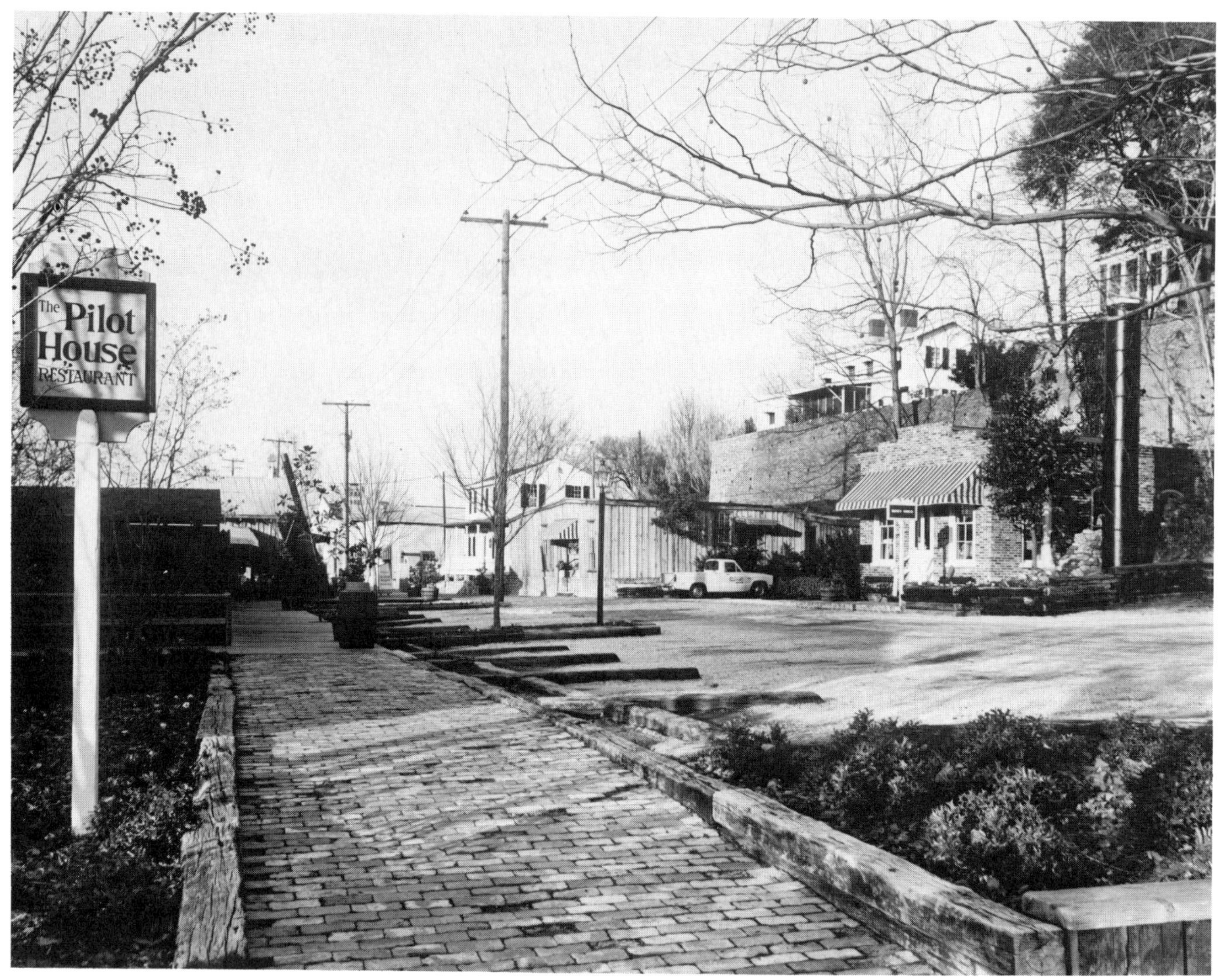

153. Chandler's Wharf, with restored buildings, 2 Ann Street, 1977–78.

area simulates the crowding, clutter, and excitement of the Wilmington waterfront. Open to the public on a regular basis, the area offers dining and shopping. Admission is charged for the ship museum, for tours of the harbor and for the ferry to the U.S.S. *North Carolina* Battleship Museum across the river. Tours and ferry are aboard the *Captain J. N. Maffitt*, built in 1944 in Portsmouth, Virginia, as a "liberty launch" for the U.S. Navy.

Among the other vessels at the wharf is the *John Taxis*, built in 1869 and believed to be the oldest existing wooden tugboat in the country. The 1937 two-masted schooner *Harry W. Adams*, a 147 foot sailing vessel was built by Smith and Rhuland of Lunenburg, Nova Scotia. A type that operated along the Atlantic coast for a long period, this ship was built for cod fishing during the season and freight during the off season. Other craft include the *Geneva May*, a 1908 skipjack designed for oyster dredging in Maryland and North Carolina; the *Edward M*, a handmade 1920 craft constructed of five logs; *Miss Santa*, a twentieth-century shrimp boat built in Wanchese, North Carolina; and the *Eugene Wasdin*, built in 1926 for the Public Health Service, used as a boarding tug at quarantine stations and also used in Boston, Marcus Hook, Charleston, and Hampton Roads.

Several buildings, moved from other parts of the city, are also incorporated into the complex. Just to the left as one enters is the Reston-Richardson House, a two-story weatherboarded house built c. 1853, and moved to this site in 1977 from 720 Orange Street. The c. 1885 Iron Works building was built by Robinson and King, a naval stores producer and storer, and used after 1910 by the Wilmington Iron Works. It was moved from the South Water Street block to the north, which is still occupied by the Wilmington Iron Works, and was reconstructed on this site. Across from the Iron Works building is the Craig House, moved to this site from 505

154. Edward P. Bailey House, 313 Ann Street, 1879–80; c. 1910.

Wooster Street. It was the home of William E. Craig, a merchant who operated a cooperage on the present Chandler's Wharf site until 1883. The house was sold in 1891 to John C. Davis and was moved to Chandler's Wharf on May 11, 1977. To the right of the entrance are two other turn-of-the-century cottages, once threatened with demolition. They were moved from South Third Street. The five buildings serve varied uses, from offices to restaurant.

South Third Street crosses Ann Street; begin 300 street numbers

EDWARD P. BAILEY HOUSE

313 Ann Street
1879–80; remodeled c. 1900

Though this structure (fig. 154) is a French Second Empire–style house, remodeling placed a gable

155. Ann Street between South Fourth and South Fifth streets, Southern Clay Manufacturing Company pavers.

and a shingled frieze before the earlier roof. The mansard survives, however, and can be seen to the sides and rear of the house. An early entrance and some early sash also survive, but the porch and most windows are from the turn-of-century remodeling, as are the frieze and the false front gable.

The porch with its ship's wheel brackets is the most notable feature of the house. Turned posts and applied floral decoration in the entrance pediment and the end panels of the porch are fine stylistic elements, helping to tie the house to Wilmington's Queen Anne style of c. 1900.

Built on the John C. Bailey lot, this structure was sited to the rear of an old house standing at the northeast corner of Ann and South Third streets. John C. Bailey probably lived there while building his own house to the north on South Third Street. Edward Bailey acquired the older house and corner lot from John C. and Elizabeth A. Bailey in June of 1879. He is identified in the deed as "their nephew" and given the property for "Five dollars and love and affection." Edward likely already lived in the old house, and must have begun construction of the new house at 313 Ann almost immediately. He seems to have been in residence there by September 12, 1880, when the *Star* reported a fire in the old house, owned by E. P. Bailey, but occupied by Robert Houston. Edward P. Bailey maintained residence at 313 Ann until his death in 1904. The Bailey family business, acquired by Edward, was the Hart and Bailey Iron Works. The firm evolved into the Wilmington Iron Works, with Edward P. Bailey as president. A major Wilmington firm, the iron works fabricated in metal and wood everything from fences and architectural ornament to ships. It is probable that architectural detail on this house was produced by the firm.

South Fourth Street crosses Ann; begin 400 street numbers

156. Tileston School, 400 Ann Street. John A. Fox, architect, James Walker, supervising architect, 1871–72; later buildings in the complex to the left and right.

This block of Ann Street, with its "Augusta Block" and "Southern Clay Mfg. Co." brick pavers (fig. 155) and stone curbs is dominated by two structures, St. Mary's Rectory and Tileston School.

TILESTON SCHOOL

400 Ann Street, between South Fourth and South Fifth Streets
1871–72: original building in center of block, John A. Fox, Boston, architect, James Walker, supervising architect, Strausz and Rice, builders; 1910: center part of Ann Street annex, J.F. Leitner, architect; 1919: wing and stair halls to south of original building, H. E. Bonitz, architect, R. H. Brady, builder; 1937: wings to Ann Street annex, Leslie N. Boney, architect; 1950: gymnasium addition and conversion into a junior high school

Opened in 1872 as Tileston Normal School, the school (fig. 156) has borne several names, including Wilmington High School. Today, as Tileston School, the entire complex of 1871–1937 buildings and a newer post–World War II gymnasium are utilized.

On July 1, 1871 the *Star* reported:

We were shown yesterday by Messrs. Strausz and Rice the plans for the new building soon to be erected on the commodious lot, corner of Fourth and Ann streets, for the use of Miss Amy M. Bradley as a Normal School. The ground floor will contain four rooms, capable of seating forty scholars each. The two front rooms will be 26 ½ by 34 feet, and the two back rooms 28 by 34 feet in dimensions. The front passage, with stair cases, will be 11 feet wide and the back passage 8 feet wide. Each of the rooms will contain a platform constructed so that the teacher can overlook the whole school.

On the second floor will be the Exhibition Hall, covering the entire dimensions of the building, which will be 68 feet front and 72 feet deep and will be capable of seating a large number of persons. In the back part of the hall a large and convenient stage will be located with ante-rooms in the rear, and a handsome bay window overlooking the back portion of the lot. In front there will be recitation rooms, which can be thrown open so as to seat a portion of the audience during an exhibition. The building will be furnished with all the modern improvements for ventilation or heating the various rooms and will be surmounted by a handsome cupola 8 feet square by 11 feet high. The front view, judging by the plans, will present a very handsome appearance, as also those of the sides and rear. The building, taken altogether, will be one of the finest school edifices in the state.

It will be named for the father of Mrs. Hemenway, of Boston, the generous lady to whose liberality this community is indebted for the important educational advantages which it has enjoyed to such a large extent for several years past.

The plans to which we are indebted for the above particulars, which are exceedingly well executed, were drawn by John A. Fox, Esq., of Boston.

Indeed, the plans should have been well drawn, for Fox was an important Boston architect who worked with the firm of Ware and Van Brunt before opening his own office. He designed the Boston Museum of 1871 and a large number of town halls and other public buildings. (The 1883 *Information and Statistics Respecting Wilmington, North Carolina* lists James Walker as the architect. He was probably the local architect who supervised construction.)

Mary Tileston Hemenway of Boston financed the construction of the 1871–72 school and for twenty years paid for its operation. Her maiden name, Tileston, was given to this school; her married name, Hemenway, to a school on North Fifth Avenue. Amy Morris Bradley, a New Englander who came to Wilmington at the end of the Civil War, served as principal of the school and maintained a cottage in the southwest corner of the lot at South Fifth. She occupied the cottage until her death in 1904, and though attempts were made by former students to save the small house, it was destroyed sometime between 1910 and 1915.

Funds for Tileston ceased in 1891, before Mrs. Hemenway's death in 1894. The school remained a part of her estate. A lease on the property was obtained from the Hemenway heirs in 1897, and Tileston reopened as Wilmington High School. In 1901 the property was deeded to the city of Wilmington. The 1910 and subsequent additions were constructed by the city.

Many Tileston students have become well-known at the city and local levels and several have gained even wider renown. Henry Bacon, who graduated with the class of 1884, gained worldwide fame as architect of the Lincoln Memorial in Washington, D.C. Bacon designed a number of other important buildings and a series of monuments and memorials with such sculptors as Daniel Chester French, Augustus Saint-Gaudens, and James Earle Fraser.

Though Thomas W. Wilson, later President Woodrow Wilson, seems never to have been a full time student at Tileston, he did study there in 1875, after leaving Davidson and before entering Princeton. During the same year Wilson played baseball with the Light Foot Baseball Club. In the margins of his geography textbook (now part of the Wilson Papers at the Library of Congress), young Wilson included a roster of the team—he was second baseman—a diagram of the field, and words for team cheers.

Over the years the Tileston Upper Room, the exhibition hall of the plans, gained a wide reputation. Not only was it used for graduation and various school functions but also for public meetings and dramatic presentations.

For a number of years the Thalian Association used the Upper Room, and Tileston students also presented entertainment there. One student presentation on May 11, 1878, was described by the *Star* as a "beautiful drama in three acts, entitled 'The Cricket on the Hearth. . . .' " Professional groups also appeared in the Tileston Upper Room. On May 2, 1880, the *Star* headlined "Hartley-Denck Combination,"

Last Appearance! Tileston Upper Room! Monday Evening—May 3. Messrs. Hartley and Denck will give their third and last entertainment as above, when another brilliant programme will be rendered, including "Horatius," "Jennie McNeal," "Punch, Brothers, Punch" and the choicest musical selections, the whole concluding by particular request, with "Artemus Ward's Panorama," which is identified with Mr. Hartley's readings throughout England and the

157. Tileston School, bas-relief panel, c. 1910.

United States. To commence at eight o'clock. Admission on this occasion twenty-five cents."

Though the interior of the Upper Room was remodeled in 1941, it still retains a coved ceiling and fine ceiling ventilators. The *Star* for August 6, 1941, noted that W. A. Simon was doing the work, which included "replacing the old plaster ceiling" and constructing a new stage with modern proscenium arch. It is likely that the full history of the Upper Room is an important and impressive one, rivaling in its community and social use that of Thalian Hall.

The original two-story, brick, Italianate building of 1871–72 still stands to the south, or rear, of the on-street complex, in the center of the block. Much of the facade to the superb building is obscured by the annex, but the cornerstone can still be seen on the northeast corner. It was placed November 30, 1871, with full Masonic ceremonies. Alfred Moore Waddell was the orator.

Tileston's original building has no stylistic counterparts in the city. A majority of the other surviving Italianate buildings are residences or narrow commercial structures. Tileston has a low hip roof with brick dentils and wooden corbels. The segmental arched four-over-four double-sash windows are set in ornate brick arch surrounds with stone keystones, drop lintels, and sills. Basement grills, set in brick arches, are cast iron in elaborate foliar patterns. Much important detail survives, including the later Majestic coal chute.

Newer portions of the building, along Ann Street, were built in two parts. The center section of the Neoclassical Revival structure, with its three-bay pedimented portico, was built in 1910. The columns now have no heads though the pilasters retain their Ionic capitals. Documentary photographs indicate that the column capitals were also Ionic. The recessed additions at either end of this structure date from 1937 and follow the style of the 1910 structure.

The 1919 southern annex, the stair halls and rear or southern, section of the original building, blends well with the 1871–72 structure, though the difference in brick is most noticeable.

Several plaques survive on the walls of the various parts of the building, and while these are notable it is the bas-relief sculptures that are unusual (fig. 157), reflecting the interest of the school administration and students in the arts. At least four different bas-reliefs are in the Annex and three in the southern annex. All seem to date from the early twentieth century. Two are dated 1909 and 1913. Two have

158. St. Mary's Rectory, 401 Ann Street, 1911–12.

casting marks—"Cavroni & Bros, Boston." Their themes are either cultural or patriotic. While largely unnoticed today and uncatalogued, these plaques and bas-reliefs constitute a fine collection of civic sculpture and ought to be so regarded.

Near the southeast corner of South Fourth and Ann Streets, within the school grounds, is a massive live oak tree. It is said to have been one of the early eighteenth-century boundary markers for the town and the scene of political and other gatherings. Its size and beauty leave little doubt of its age, and it is certainly one of the great trees of Wilmington and the surrounding area.

ST. MARY'S RECTORY

401 Ann Street
1911–12: Rafael Gustavino (Jr.), architect

A two-story structure with wide roof overhang and exposed rafters, St. Mary's Rectory (fig. 158) has a brick first story with stucco at the second level. It was probably designed by the younger Rafael Gustavino to blend with the St. Mary Church, which it serves. The rectory's size and bulk are notable, as is its use of materials and derived Spanish style. It is an excellent foil for the Neoclassical-Revival Tileston School annex, which dominates the southern side of the block.

South Fifth Avenue crosses Ann Street; begin 500 street numbers

The two blocks of Ann Street from South Third Street to South Fifth Avenue are good examples of Wilmington street development, with vistas from Ann Street along each of the three streets. Relatively narrow, South Fourth Street is typical of Wilmington's streets. Residences hover close to the street, and trees meet overhead. Surfaces are often, as here, still of paving brick. South Third Street and South Fifth (with its grand name of Avenue) are the city's north-south ceremonial streets, extremely wide with developed center plazas and landscaped sidewalks. Only these two streets and Market Street (on an east-west axis) are so divided. The center plazas, along with plants, fountains, and street furniture were added in the 1880s.

In the decades after World War II, Third Street became a major automotive artery through Wilmington, and most of its trees and much of its landscaping disappeared. North Third Street is now bare, and South Third Street has also suffered, though the center plaza, some street furniture, and plants remain. A program of replanting street trees was recently undertaken. In sharp contrast, South Fifth Avenue offers vistas from Ann Street in either direction of a well-developed nineteenth-century street with center plaza and trees meeting overhead to form a canopied boulevard.

The site of the Union School (1856–86) on the north side of Ann Street is now filled with structures either built on or moved to that site after demolition of the school building in 1923. The name is remembered, however, in the Union Baptist Church at Ann and South Sixth streets—a building that may have been constructed as part of the Union School complex and later converted to religious use.

WILMINGTON PLAIN HOUSE

507 Ann Street
c. 1830

One of the structures moved to the old Union School site is this early nineteenth-century house, built in a transitional style with both Federal and Greek Revival elements. It is obviously the oldest structure in the block, its age evident in its nine-over-six, small-paned sash, flush raking cornice, molded box cornice, low-pitch gable roof, and the interior chimney and side entrance with transom and sidelights in a one-story ell to the east. In most other houses of this type, the ell is a porch—as it is at the Dubois-Boatwright House, 14 South Third Street (fig. 54)—rather than enclosed space as it is here.

The house was moved from Ann and South Fourth Streets, where it was sited slightly to the west of the present St. Mary's Rectory. On that site the dwelling was either a residence or part of a residential complex. After 1869 it was part of the Academy of the Incarnation, which opened on October 11 of that year. When the buildings were being demolished in 1910–11 for construction of the present St. Mary's complex, this dwelling was spared. After the Union School property was made available (c. 1915), the house was moved one block up Ann Street, across South Fifth Avenue, to its present site.

Nun Street

Cape Fear River eastward to South Seventh Street

Nun Street runs into the Cape Fear River. There are no barriers, just a curious "Dead End" sign at the point where street and water join. A popular boat landing, the base of the street offers superb views across and up and down the river. To the north are Chandler's Wharf (1978), tugs, docks, and the Wilmington waterfront; to the south are old wharves and new port; to the west are rotting wharves and boats; and to the east, the river bluff.

The bluff here is quite precipitate and the climb from the river to South Front Street a steep one. Houses on the west or river side of South Front Street require high retaining walls to maintain their position on the bluff. (See fig. 159.) A crenellated stone wall behind the Dudley Mansion continues in brick farther south. The upper part of the Dudley wall is said to have been extended upward by James Sprunt just after his 1895 purchase of the house. The corner towers and some of the other wall decoration have since been removed.

Extensions of the Dudley Mansion wall can be seen in a variety of stone cuts and types. A stepped brick wall with stone topped posts and a stone pyramid is to the south. To the north, behind the Hon-

159. Retaining wall, Nun Street at Cape Fear River.

net House is a stone and brick wall of a different character.

These retaining walls are all quite architectonic, exhibit good artisanship, and are a fixture of the Wilmington waterfront.

South Front Street crosses Nun Street; begin 100 house numbers

WILLIAM RAND KENAN HOUSE

110 Nun Street
c. 1870; remodeled c. 1910

Constructed for W. R. and Mary Hargrave Kenan, this is the house where their four children were born. Kenan, a Confederate veteran, lawyer, and merchant, was born in Kenansville, N.C., and settled in Wilmington after his graduation from the University of North Carolina following the end of the Civil War.

William Rand Kenan, Jr., was born in this house on April 30, 1872, and spent his childhood here before leaving to study at the University of North Carolina. A scientist, he pioneered research on calcium carbide, earning his own fortune before inheriting much of the Henry Flagler estate from his sister. At his death in July 1965, Kenan left an estate worth more than one-hundred million dollars.

Jessie Hargrave Kenan, second of the Kenan children, was also born and grew up here. She married Joseph Clisby Wise in the First Presbyterian Church at 9:20 P.M. on Thursday, June 16, 1892. According to the *Messenger*: "reception followed at the home of Captain Kenan, Nun Street. The couple left on midnight train for a northern tour." The midnight train may have been the deciding factor in the unusual wedding hour. Mrs. Wise also inherited part of the estate of her sister Mary Flagler. Mrs. Wise returned to this house to live c. 1910 and maintained residence until 1916, when she sold the dwelling to T. Edward Sprunt.

160. W. A. Dick House, 113 Nun Street, 1900–1901.

Mary Lily Kenan, third of the Kenan children born here, married Henry M. Flagler in 1901. Festivities took place in this house the night before the wedding. The Flagler party traveled to Wilmington from New York by special train and, after an overnight in Wilmington, went by train to Magnolia, North Carolina. From Magnolia the wedding party drove to Liberty Hall, the Kenan home in Kenansville, where the couple were married. Flagler, founder of the Florida East Coast Railroad, was a major Florida developer and is credited with being chiefly responsible for the growth of Florida as a winter playground. He was an early associate of John D. Rockefeller and a founder of Standard Oil. Among his wedding presents to his wife was one million dollars. His enormous estate was left to Mary Lily Kenan Flagler at his death in 1913. She ultimately shared it with her siblings, upon her death.

The last Kenan child, Sarah Graham Kenan, who was born here on February 17, 1876, married her cousin Graham Kenan. A major philanthropist, she later returned to Wilmington, where she lived on Market Street, next door to a house occupied by Jessie Kenan Wise.

The Nun Street house seems originally to have been a bracketed Italianate structure with two street planes, constructed c. 1870. The handsome Neoclassical Revival remodeling was undertaken by Mrs. Wise c. 1910.

Between eras of Kenan family occupancy, Episcopal Bishop Strange lived here. The *Star* of September 2, 1904, noted that: "It is understood that

161. Hansen House, 114 Nun Street, c. 1882.

the handsome Kenan residence on Nun Street, between Front and Second, has been rented for Bishop Strange and he will occupy it after the first of November."

W. A. DICK HOUSE

113 Nun Street
1900–1901

"Contractors say," noted the *Dispatch* of May 15, 1900, "that this weather is especially favorable to their work. They are pushing building operations vigorously. Carpenters began work today on the handsome new residence to be erected for Mr. W. A. Dick on Nun Street between Front and Second."

A Neoclassical Revival structure, the Dick House (fig. 160) may be the earliest of its genre in Wilmington. It is a frame temple with a colossal Ionic portico. The centrally located door is Palladian. The units are separated by Ionic pilasters and the recessed door is flanked by engaged Ionic columns. A leaded fanlight and patterned sidelight are set within a molded architrave with paneled reveals.

The 1902 city directory, the first to show William A. Dick residing at 113 Nun, lists him as chief passenger clerk, Atlantic Coast Line Railroad. Within the year he joined the firm of Dick & Reilly, "Successors to D. O'Connor, Real Estate and Insurance and Notaries Public, Established A.D. 1869" with

162. Schonwald House, 116 Nun Street, before 1880.

offices at 110 Princess Street. In 1910 he was listed as real estate broker, notary, and agent for the Southern Building and as secretary and treasurer of the Cape Fear Club. Dick died in 1922. His wife, Nellie Draper Dick, continued to live in this house until her own death in 1947.

HANSEN HOUSE

114 Nun Street
c. 1882

The house (fig. 161) is not on Gray's 1881 map, but appears on the Sanborn map in 1889. Since Ludvig Hansen purchased the property in 1881 and Louis Hanson did not sell it until 1903, it seems logical to assume that Hansen built the house. In the 1885 city directory, he is listed as in residence at 114 Nun Street. There has long been confusion over the name, but both Hansen and Hanson are correct, depending on the era of use. On May 23, 1901, the *Star* carried the following: "Mr. L. Hansen has posted notice at the Court House that he will make application to the Clerk of the Superior Court for an order empowering him to change his name from 'Ludvig Hansen,' his true name, to 'Louis Hanson.' Mr. Hansen asks for the change, as the notice sets forth, because he has become a citizen of the U.S.A. and intending to make this the country of himself and family, he wishes to Americanize the name."

A vented-and-bracketed Italianate house, the structure is given a Steamboat Gothic appearance by the central tower above the canopy porch, and by the sawn-wood floral decoration of the porch frieze. The paneled decoration of the tower, with its parabola-shaped windows and its weathervane, give the house a distinctive character.

SCHONWALD HOUSE

116 Nun Street
before 1880

A bracketed-and-vented Italianate house (fig. 162) with canopy porch, the structure was standing at the time Gray accomplished his 1881 map. It may have been standing as early as 1853, when Sarah Ellis sold the property to Henry P. Russell. She had acquired it in 1834, paying $1,000 for a considerably larger lot than the one she sold in 1853 for $2,000. It is possible that Sarah and her husband, Charles D. Ellis, built the house during that period, though this has not been established. Evanda O. Toomer acquired the property in 1874, Andrew Smith in 1879, Martha C. Mebane in 1888. Eda E. Sneed assumed ownership in 1894, and Carrie and J. T. Schonwald in 1902. Schonwald, a physician, the son of a famous Hungarian doctor, and an author of medical treatises, is listed in the 1903 city directory as in residence. A resident after the turn of the century was Charles E. Hooper, the nationally known hotelier who operated Wilmington's The Orton Hotel.

The double entry doors, each having four panels with rounded-arch panels above, are heavily molded and typical of the Italianate style. A heavy cable molding separates them. The porch, with its turned spindles and posts resting on paneled bases, was likely constructed at a later time. The spindle course—especially the arched section over the center bay—is both distinctive and handsome.

ELLIS-DULS HOUSE

120 Nun Street
c. 1860

Sarah Ellis acquired the lot in 1834. That purchase included the property next door at 116 Nun Street, which the Ellis family sold in 1853. They maintained ownership of this corner property until 1871. From stylistic evidence, the house was probably built around 1860. It was standing by the time Gray drew his 1881 map.

J. W. Duls bought the house in 1886 and lived there until 1915–16. Duls was a merchant selling groceries, cigars, and tobacco from his store at 114 South Front Street.

A vented-and-bracketed Italianate house with a canopy porch, the dwelling has a five-bay facade with center entrance door topped by a transom and flanked by sidelights. A brownstone wall with capped posts surrounds the slightly elevated front yard.

South Second Street crosses Nun Street; begin 200 street numbers

BEERY HOUSE

202 Nun Street
c. 1853

One of the largest and most imposing of the vented-and-bracketed Italianate houses in Wilmington (see fig. 12), the Beery House is three stories beneath a hip roof with center cupola. Full-width two-tier porches appear on the front and the rear of the house. The front porch has an advanced central bay supported by paired posts, to compensate for the center pavilion of the five-bay house. The entrance is approached by splayed, tiered steps. There is diminution of fenestration from the full-length first-floor windows to the small sash at the third level.

Benjamin Washington Beery, who built the house, is listed in the 1866–67 city directory as "shipbuilder." His firm was Cassidey & Beery Shipyard, on South Water Street between Nun and Church. Not only could Beery walk to his business, but he constructed his home so that, from the cupola, he could keep an eye on the shipyard and on river commerce in general.

Beery went privateering early in the Civil War on a vessel fitted at his own expense, but soon abandoned the personal enterprise to return to his shipyard on Eagles' Island. He constructed several Confederate ships, including the steamer *Yadkin*, the ironclad *North Carolina*, and a number of launches.

W. A. Northrop of the firm of Northrop and Cumming was a later resident. The 1885 directory shows Northrop and W. M. Cumming, who was bookkeeper for the firm, in residence here. A major Wilmington firm, Northrop and Cumming's activities revolved around their steam and planing mills. Inasmuch as Gray's 1881 map shows this as the home of W. A. Cumming, it is probably safe to say that the house was the residential headquarters of the Northrop and Cumming empire. The firm owned or occupied more real estate at the time Gray accomplished his 1881 map than any other Wilmington commercial enterprise listed.

KING-THORPE HOUSE

209 Nun Street
c. 1890

Not on the 1889 Sanborn map, the house appears in its present configuration on the 1893 map, with the exception of the pedimented porch projection over the entrance steps, which was constructed between 1910 and 1915. Mary and Charles King acquired the property in 1872 and maintained ownership until 1904, when it was sold to the Wilmington Towing and Construction Company. By 1905 W. B. Thorpe, president of the company, is shown in the city directory as in residence. Thorpe's firm later changed its name to W. B. Thorpe and Co., Inc.

During the period of King occupancy, the house seems to have been something of a Wilmington social center. The *Messenger* noted, on May 29, 1892, in an advertisement: "Amateur Performance, THE MOUSE TRAP. To be presented at the residence of Mrs. Chas. H. King, corner South Third and Nun streets, on Tuesday evening, May 31st, at 8:30 o'clock. Admission 25 cents. Refreshments served at usual prices." On September 30, 1899, the *Dispatch* reported that the house was decorated. "The residence of Mr. C. H. King, on Nun street between Second and Third, is handsomely decorated today in honor of the hero of Manila. Three portraits of the Admiral, showing him at three different stages of his life, look out from as many windows. They are draped in red, white and blue, and the general effect is very fine." Adm. George Dewey, the Spanish-American War hero, was then being touted for president, a cause that the Kings evidently supported. The causes of the family were not just theatrical and political, however. The *Star* on June 9, 1900, noted that, "A number of children will give a delightful lawn party at the residence of Mrs. Chas. H. King, 209 Nun Street, for the benefit of the starving in India. Refreshments will be sold."

A full-blown Queen Anne house, this is a two-and-a-half-story frame dwelling with a complex roof and a center, projecting cross gable. The gable features a decorated bargeboard, patterned shingles, and a multipaned lancet window. A porch runs across the facade at the first level, terminating at the east end in a two-story octagonal tower with pointed roof and finial. The tower, open at the second level, is enclosed on the first and surrounded by the porch.

DUNCAN CLARK HOUSE

210 Nun Street
c. 1840; 1890–92

Duncan Clark, a native of Greenock, Scotland, died in Wilmington on November 13, 1850, leaving to his wife Mary his dwelling house on Nun Street. Clark had acquired the land on which this house stands in 1829, presumably without a house, so he must have constructed the nucleus of the present house sometime between 1829 and 1850. Since the will in which the dwelling is mentioned was written in 1845, the house must have been standing by then. An approximate date of 1840 has been used to cover the period of construction. It was Clark's heirs who sold a portion of their land to Benjamin W. Beery, who constructed his house next door at 202 Nun Street.

The configuration of the original Clark House, said to have been remodeled about 1893, would probably have been Wilmington Plain house. With its cross-gable roof and fine porch, the house is an architectural puzzle from the exterior.

South Fourth Street crosses Nun Street;
begin 400 street numbers

WILSON HOUSE

413 Nun Street
c. 1891

Though this house was not here when Gray completed his 1881 map and the purchase price in 1891 of the lot does not indicate the presence of a house, the structure is stylistically older than the records seem to indicate. It is a vented-and-bracketed Italianate house, with side-hall plan and full-length windows on the porch. This contrasts with the somewhat later vented-and-bracketed Italianate house next door at 411 Nun Street, which by its first-level windows and trim would seem to have been built later than this house.

Alexander M. Wilson, a steamboat captain, acquired the property from Sally Burgwin in March of 1891 and maintained ownership until September 1901, when he sold to Sterling F. Craig. The house was certainly built before 1901, and it is probable that Wilson either constructed it about 1891 or moved the house to this site from another location.

South Fifth Avenue crosses Nun Street; begin 500 street numbers

CHADWICK-KING HOUSE

513 Nun Street
1888

Though Gray's 1881 map shows a house at this site, it does not seem to be the present house, since David N. Chadwick purchased the property in 1887 for just $250. It was Chadwick who erected the present dwelling, as noted in the *Messenger* on March 8, 1888: "Mr. David Chadwick is erecting a handsome residence on Nun Street, between Fifth and Sixth streets." Chadwick, who operated a saloon at 15 Market Street, was in residence by 1892, when (according to the June 23 *Messenger*) the funeral of his infant son was held at the residence on Nun Street.

The S. M. King family were later residents in the dwelling, by the early twentieth century.

The house is one of a small number of vented-and-bracketed Italianate structures that is also pedimented. This one, however, has a canopy porch without a pediment, whereas most of the other pedimented Italianate dwellings have a porch that echos the pediment of the hip roof. The house is possibly associated with G. M. Altaffer as contractor and builder.

South Sixth Street crosses Nun Street; begin 600 street numbers

GREGORY CONGREGATIONAL CHURCH

609 Nun Street
1880; S. B. Weston, builder

A capsule history of the church complex was included in the *Catalogue of the Teachers and Pupils* published by the Gregory Normal Institute in 1897.

The American Missionary Association began its work among the Freedmen of Wilmington, April 3rd, 1865. Mr. Longley, the first one of its teachers on the ground, issued a call for a mass-meeting of the colored people, to take measures for the establishment of schools.

A corps of eight teachers at once opened day schools in as many different churches. In a short time the number of teachers reached fourteen, and other schools were opened for women, and night schools for both sexes.

The next year an orphan asylum was opened at Middle Sound, eight miles from Wilmington. The most of the children were afterwards provided with good homes in the West. This branch of the mission was abandoned in 1870.

Sunday School work was instituted the day previous to the day-school work, and since then mental and spiritual instruction have gone on hand in hand.

In 1869 the School Board of Wilmington began to co-operate with the Association in sustaining free schools, and continued to do so until 1873, when the local authorities concluded to discontinue further co-operative school work, and to establish a school of their own.

This led to the re-organization of the schools, and to the establishment of the Williston Academy and Normal School, the academic department of which was open to receive students in October, 1872. Since that time the name has been changed. For a short time it was called the Memorial Institute. The School has for the past thirteen years been known as the GREGORY INSTITUTE, named in honor of Hon. James J. Gregory, of Marblehead, Mass., to whose Christian liberality is chiefly due the present group of buildings—the Church, the School and the Home.

The Church is a neat brick building, 72 by 36, and was built in 1880. The Teachers' Home is a substantial brick structure of three stories, and was built in 1881.The School House is a commodious wooden building of two stories, flanked by two wings, each 54 by 16 feet, having a front of 116 feet, with room for 350 pupils. It was completely remodelled in 1881.

The Church has had, since its organization in 1876, seven pastors—Rev. Henry Black, whose pastorate lasted three and one-half years; Rev. D. D. Dodge, thirteen years; Rev. Mason Noble, one year; Rev. G. S. Rollins, three years; Rev. Wm. E. Skelton, five months; Rev. Frank W. Sims, four years, and the present pastor.

Among the lady principals of the School were Miss Roper, Miss Auld and Miss Chandler. In 1882 the present course of study was adopted, when Rev. Wm. H. Thrall filled the position of principal for two years, who was succeeded by the present principal, an interim of two years having been filled by Prof. F. T. Waters.

Since the establishment of the work in this city, the Association has expended more than $140,000 in the *cause of education, of which sum about $30,000 has been paid in as tuition by pupils.*

The land on which the church stands was purchased in 1868 by the American Missionary Association, and a church was probably built soon thereafter, along with the wooden school building. The American Missionary Association, a Congregational group from New England, was active in providing schools and meetinghouses for southern blacks, providing teachers and ministers as well as funds.

Under "Improvements," the *Star* reported on May 12, 1881:

A fine three story brick building is going up on the same lot upon which the new Congregational Church stands, which was recently dedicated . . . and is intended as a residence for the teachers employed in what is known as the "New Hampshire Memorial Institute," a large and flourishing school for colored people, located on the corner of Seventh and Nun streets, in the charge of Rev. D. D. Dodge. This building, which is now used both as a school house and dwelling for the teachers, is to be remodelled and made into a first-class school edifice. The funds for these important improvements, it is understood, are to be supplied by the same parties in Boston—Mr. J. J. Howard Gregory and others—who donated money for the erection of the splendid Congregational Church building referred to. Mr. S. B. Weston, the builder of the latter, is also the master mason in charge of the construction of the dwelling. These improvements bring a good deal of money into our midst, to say nothing of the moral and intellectual advantages involved.

In its next edition, for May 13, the *Star* apologized to Mr. Gregory for stating that he was from Boston, noting instead that he was from Marblehead, and added: "In this connection we would state that a bell was received for the church yesterday as a donation from the same gentleman, bearing the inscription 'The North to the South, in Sympathy and Love.' "

The teachers' residence to the east of the church has recently been demolished, though its retaining wall and steps are still extant, as are some of its magnolia trees. The frame school building has also disappeared, but the brick church still stands. Though the entrance, flanking windows, and approach have been modified, the structure remains a handsome late Gothic building, its tower being especially attractive when viewed from the east across the open greensward that marks the former site of the teachers' residence and school building.

Church Street

Cape Fear River eastward to South Fifth Avenue

The Cassidey shipyard and later the Skinner shipyard (1906), the Cape Fear Machine Works (1911), and Broadfoot Iron Works (1921) were located at the base of Church Street on the river. It was at the Cassidey shipyard that the Confederate ironclad *Raleigh* was constructed and launched in 1864. It was also here, at either the Broadfoot or the Cape Fear machine works, that many of the sewer and water covers on streets in Wilmington were manufactured. As one walks through the city, these two manufacturers' names—along with that of the Wilmington Iron Works—appear frequently.

Water Street theoretically cuts through here from the north, though the block between Nun and Church seems never to have been a thoroughfare. It was for a long period of time traversed by a railroad track, however, and much waterborne commerce was transferred to and from the trains that used the Water Street–Surry Street tracks.

Church Street was graded into the river as early as 1872, when the *Star* reported on January 19 that Church Street "from the water front to the river is to be graded immediately so that the fire engines can reach the water without difficulty." On January 28 the paper reported that the city force was "engaged in making a dock at the foot of Church Street," which rises rather steeply from the river.

163. Cassidey-Harper House, 1 Church Street, 1828; c. 1910.

CASSIDEY-HARPER HOUSE AND CASSIDEY SHIPYARD SITE

1 Church Street
c. 1828; c. 1910

James Cassidey purchased two lots on the north side of Church Street in 1828. Both ran from Front Street to the river. Evidently he began building his house almost immediately. A ship carpenter, he was involved with the shipyard at least by 1837, for during the late 1830s he borrowed heavily and mortgaged his property to the limit. Since he is not known to have been involved in any other enterprise, the funds must have been for the shipyard, with most of the monies involved in construction of facilities here.

In 1846 James Cassidey, "Proprietor," advertised in the October 8 *Commercial*: "Wilmington Marine Railway. This establishment has been in operation several years and is prepared to take up the largest vessels that come into this port. Steamboats over 400 tons have been taken up frequently. Attached to the yard is a blacksmith establishment and foundry." On November 21, 1846, the same newspaper reported: "Launch: This morning the French Barque 'Harve Martinique' was launched from Mr. Cassidey's Marine Railway; she was copper bottomed, and glided into the water most beautifully, and sat upon the bosom of the water with all the majestic grace of a swan." By the time of the publication of the 1866–67 city directory, the firm was listed as "Cassidey & Beery (James Cassidey & Benjamin W. Beery) Ship Builders South Water, bt. Nun and Church." Their full-page advertisement in the same directory notes that "Having every facility at our command, we are prepared to execute all orders in our line promptly."

James Cassidey died in 1866, as that advertisement was being run in the directory. He was seventy-four years old and left the house to his daughter, Ann Elizabeth Cassidey Munds. Ann had married the Reverend James Theus Munds, who had died in June of 1863. Mrs. Munds was listed in residence here by Gray on his 1881 map. Capt. James Thomas Harper was a later owner.

The shipyard certainly continued in operation. In 1874 the *Star* reported the February launching of a pilot boat: "The new pilot boat 'Nellie B. Neff' was launched yesterday at the foot of Church street, for Messrs. Piver and Sellers of Smithville [Southport].

164. Georgian-style coastal cottage, 6 Church Street, late eighteenth century.

The boat is a handsome little schooner. She measures 42 feet in length over all, 13 feet beam and 5 feet hold. Good judges say she will be a swift sailer."

The Cassidey-Harper House (fig. 163) still stands, a notable Federal era dwelling. Sash, beaded siding set both lapping and flush, and fine six-panel doors survive, as does other detail. The house now has a gambrel roof that has often been pointed to as the only early gambrel in the area. The Sanborn maps show a two-and-one-half-story house on the site in 1904 and while the house is the same in area and outline plan on the 1910 maps, it is a two-story dwelling. The change in height may reflect the installation of the gambrel roof c. 1910, and this corresponds with oral history. Since dormers in the gambrel must be depended on to light the second story, the change from two and one-half stories was a basic one. If the house had a gambrel roof before, it was changed to its present level and type. If it did not, then the house was simply given a more twentieth-century Dutch Colonial look. Since the chimneys and present roof are new, they offer no obvious exterior evidence useful in dating the building, except to indicate a twentieth-century origin for chimney stacks and roof.

Of major interest is the fact that the unusual gambrel end of the house faces the river and has double entrances with some surviving doors as well as a two-level porch with closed pediment and square posts.

Whatever the date of the gambrel roof, the house is a fine one and the setting truly beautiful. The house maintains its relationship to the river and to the location of the industry that supported its early owners.

GEORGIAN-STYLE COASTAL COTTAGE

6 Church Street
late eighteenth century

One sees here (fig. 164) the rear of the house. It faced an earlier road, long gone, which meandered southwestward on the opposite side of the house. The structure, although maintaining its original facade in what is now the back yard, has probably kept the present orientation to Church Street since the early nineteenth century. The orientation of the original entrance facade leads one to believe that the house is earlier than late eighteenth century, and the robust character of the Georgian interiors, along with Georgian exterior detail buttresses that belief. (St. John's Masonic Lodge, 114 Orange Street (Fig. 144), is also quite Georgian, however, and it was not constructed until 1802.)

The documentary problem with this house is compounded by the fact that it seems to have been constructed for rental or tenant use and not for owner occupation. Archibald Maclaine purchased the property at a sheriff's sale in 1772, the first breakup into lots of this block, and gave it to his son-in-law George Hooper by will in 1790–91. George Hooper—brother of William Hooper, one of the North Carolina signers of the Declaration of Independence—was a merchant operating as George Hooper & Co., and construction of the house was certainly within his means. In 1821, in the division of George Hooper's estate, the property passed to his son, Archibald Maclaine Hooper. Archibald was a lawyer and writer who also seems to have been an absentee owner. He disposed of the property in 1828 to William G. Beatty. Beatty began an era of owner occupation. The lot and house passed through several owners until 1859, when it was purchased by James Darby, and the property remained in the Darby family until the mid-twentieth century.

The structure is a handsome Georgian-style raised coastal cottage. Houses of this style characteristically have a story and a half above a raised basement, with stylistic elements that are Georgian in character. The house type appears in several coastal areas. On the earlier entrance facade, the full-length porch stands on piers above a full basement, with dormers in the wide gable roof above. The survival of this type of house in Wilmington, is unusual, and it has an amazing number of early architectural features and detail.

South Fourth Street crosses Church Street; begin 400 street numbers

"Southern Clay Mfg. Co." pavers (see fig. 155) continue in use.

ROBERT H. BRADY HOUSE

408 Church Street
c. 1890; R. H. Brady, builder

On August 20, 1895, the *Dispatch* carried an advertisement: "R. H. Brady, Contractor and Bricklayer, is thoroughly competent to take contracts and do all kinds of work in the bricklaying line. Give me a trial. R. H. Brady, 408 Church Street." Brady, who dwelt in the house at this address, evidently also maintained offices at his dwelling site. He later operated as Brady & Simon, Builders and Contractors, until the partnership was dissolved in 1925. He continued work until 1934, when, at the age of seventy-five, he finally retired. He died here in 1936, but members of the Brady family continued in residence until 1980.

No complete list of the buildings constructed by Brady has been compiled, but he worked frequently with architects H. E. Bonitz, J. F. Leitner, Charles McMillen, and B. H. Stephens, among others, on both residential and commercial projects. Some of his contracts included: tiling the vaults in the New Hanover County Courthouse on North Third Street at Princess (fig. 50), 1897; repairing the roof of the First Baptist Church, 421 Market Street (fig. 126), in 1899 and enlarging the Sunday school there in 1906; remodeling The Orton Hotel, 109–17 North Front Street, in 1906; constructing the Consolidated Market and Fire Engine House no. 3, at 602–6 North Fourth Street (fig. 74), in 1907; remodeling the interior of City Hall, 102 North Third Street, in 1909; building the Bijou Theatre at 223 North Front Street (see fig.29) in 1912; adding the southern annex to Tileston School, 400 Ann Street (fig. 156), in 1919; and constructing many other residential and commercial buildings listed elsewhere in this study. Few did more to shape the physical face of Wilmington than Brady during his some fifty-five years as a builder.

The house seems to have been a Wilmington Plain house, three bays wide—perhaps with Italianate touches, as the floor-length windows of the first-floor facade indicate. The house appears on the 1898 Sanborn map with a typical Italianate configuration and porch across the front. The 1904 map shows the porch extended around the east side of the house. By 1915 the house had been enlarged and reached its present configuration. The cross-gable extension over the porch to the east, without fill of the porch at the first level, is an unusual treatment.

Surry Street

Church Street southward to Castle

Surry Street is now but one block long and is paved with asphalt block. Granite curbing appears to the east, but to the west the street is edged with Belgian paving block. Blowing sand has covered this in places and street edges are pleasantly undefined.

Surry Street was opened by an act of the legislature c. 1785. By 1895 a street railway was under construction along Surry. As completed, the railway was essentially a continuation of the railroad spur that ran down Water Street from the Union Depot area at Front Street and Campbell Street to industries south of Castle Street along Surry Street.

The docks of the Clyde Steamship Co. line of New York, Wilmington, and Georgetown steamers were on the riverfront at Castle and Surry streets. The station of the Wilmington, Onslow & East Carolina Railroad was at Surry and Queen streets. The first train from Wilmington to Jacksonville, N.C., along the line ran on January 29, 1891, according to the *Star* of January 31, 1891, and regular service was begun on February 4 according to the *Star* on February 3.

Gasworks were located at Castle and Surry streets as early as 1881. By this century these had evolved into the Tidewater Power Co. gas and power plant. The street was generally industrial and commercial to the west between Surry Street and the river, residential to the east.

Surry Street is essentially a southward continuation of Water Street, developed in the nineteenth century. Though Water no longer cuts across the waterfront between Ann and Church, the street and its rail line once traversed the entire waterfront.

GEORGE CAMERON HOUSE–NEWKIRK HOUSE

512 Surry Street
c. 1800; late nineteenth century; 1976

This is the only survivor of the Wilmington Federal-era houses to have a tripartite configuration and one of the few Wilmington houses to have such abundant sawn-wood embellishment. From its character the decoration seems to date from the late nineteenth century. The house (fig. 165), with its three-part plan and well-chosen site, would be attractive without the decoration. With its frosting, it is lifted to unique.

George Cameron acquired the property on which the house was built in July 1800, and the deed from George Hooper contains the legal phrase "together with the wharf, buildings and all other improvements." When Henry Toomer transferred the same property to Hooper in 1793, the deed had mentioned a dwelling. Cameron is known to have had a two-story dwelling on his lot, for when he sold to Peter A. Hollman in 1814, he sold the land "together with a two-story house thereon." The transfer noted that the dwelling faced Surry Street. Enough design evidence survives to indicate that much of the two-story center section and one-story wings of the house can be dated to George Cameron's era, c. 1800—indicating that this was the two-story house he sold in 1814. This seems also to be the property described in an 1819 "For Sale" notice in the *Cape Fear Recorder*: "Two lots, bounded by Church Street on the north, and by Captain Cameron's possessions on the south, extending from Front Street to the River. The improvements thereon being a wharf the full bredth of the lots and a commodious dwelling house." Evidently Peter Hollman then occupied the commodious dwelling. When Hollman finally did sell to James Cassidey in 1826, he described the property as the lot "on which said Hollman lives."

During much of the twentieth century the house has been known as the Newkirk House after Catherine and H. H. Newkirk, who purchased the dwelling in 1910.

Recently the house suffered varied misuse and neglect. By the early 1970s it was being used for storage, as a construction shack, and as a workshop by the Wilmington Housing Authority. In 1973 when the authority announced plans for its demolition,

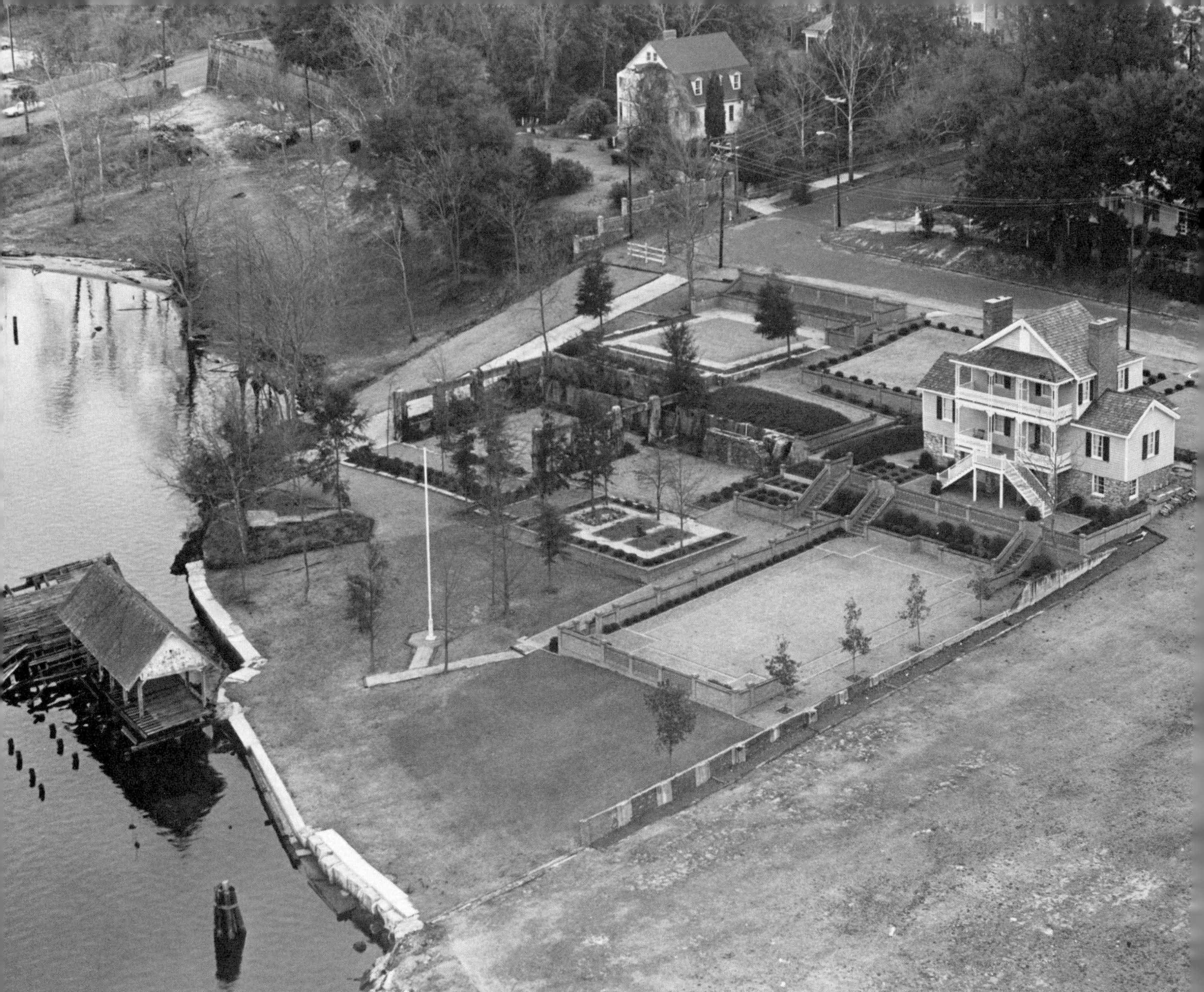

165. George Cameron House–Newkirk House, 512 Surry Street, c. 1800, with 1 Church Street in the upper center.

the house was acquired for one dollar by the Historic Wilmington Foundation, was moved west across the street from its old site to the present site, and was placed on a new foundation. The new lot, the moving, and the foundation added a considerable amount to the initial one-dollar investment. In October 1974 George Jones of Industrial Sales Corp., Inc., purchased the house and lot and began work. Interiors of the structure have been adapted, while the exteriors, now renewed, retain the basic form and trim they had when the house was moved.

Around the house, landscaped grounds have been developed as a public park under the direction of Landscape Architect Richard Bell. The gardens have brick retaining walls, brick walks, and brick lattice walls, as well as treated wood used for containment. Azaleas, hollies, gardenias, and various evergreens are used. Some are planted in borders, some naturalized and some on berms. Trees on the site when it was acquired have been kept, as have the foundations of the Cape Fear Machine Works/Broadfoot Iron Works. These early twentieth century remains are being integrated into the park, as are the remains of the company dock—pilings, wharf, and wharf covering of strong square posts with shingled roof. These structures are vestiges of a fine block history summarized by Bill Reaves in his October 10, 1974, "Inside Old Wilmington" column in the *Morning Star*:

During the Civil War this land was the site of the Cassidey Shipyard, which was noted for building large wooden sailing vessels and occasionally a war vessel. In 1866–67 it was the property of James Cassidey and Benjamin Beery, who operated the shipyard jointly. They also operated a marine railway or dry dock there for some years. Down the street near Castle was the works of the Wilmington Gas Light Company and in the same block George C. Preston operated a soap factory.

Around 1877–78 the shipyard was operated by F. A. L. and H. C. Cassidey and R. G. Ross, who built many fine and large wooden sailing vessels and some smaller craft. Beery severed his connection with the Cassideys and moved to the foot of Wooster Street where he conducted a similar business. In the 1870s at the foot of Church Street was located also J. D. Stanley and Company, manufacturer of pine wood oil, tar, railroad and ship paints.

About 1883 Samuel W. Skinner came into the picture, having purchased the property from the Cassidey brothers and the shipyard business continued to thrive there. In 1884 J. D. Stanley sold his paint and tar business to L. Hanson, who continued in the same line of business. Adjacent to this property was located S. & W. H. Northrop, who operated a saw and planing mill. Very handy for the shipyard operation.

Louis H. Skinner inherited the shipyard business from Samuel W. Skinner and continued in operation there until 1913–14. In earlier years (1900–02) another factory was in operation on Surry Street between Castle and Church—the Shuttle Block Manufacturing Company, owned by Lindley A. Wheedon or Weedon.

In 1913 the Skinners sold out their business, with Louis Skinner joining the Builders Supply Company on Chestnut Street. The Church-Surry Street site became the home of the Cape Fear Machine Works, manufacturers of boilers, etc. This company was operated by C. W. Worth and remained there until 1919. Other officers of this company were Bernard O'Neill and James A. Springer.

In 1919 the Broadfoot Iron Works was opened for business at this location, with William G. Broadfoot and James H. Hughes as officers of the company. Robert E. Tapp later joined this company. In the 1940s W. G. Broadfoot served as vice consul for the Norwegian Royal Vice Consulate located at the Iron Works office.

In 1955 all that was left at this site was a warehouse of the old ironworks. Operating from this property was the Ocean Tile and Glass Company and the Atlantic Glass Company.

On the waterfront at this spot many old-timers will remember the famous presidential yacht "Mayflower" which remained docked there until it finally was dismantled.

The old craft had much history attached to it, having been used by many Presidents of the United States as a pleasure craft. It was a floating palace. Royalty had been entertained on the mahogany and glass vessel.

One of the visual surprises of the city is from the wharf here on the water. To the north, the riverfront with its ragged configuration of pilings, various uses, and natural bank is visible. Tugs are tied up in the middle foreground and in the distance large ships are docked. To the left the superstructures of the U.S.S. *North Carolina* can be seen above the trees of Eagles' Island. It is the Wilmington skyline, however, that is the star of the view. The ships of Chandler's Wharf, the Brooks Warehouse in brick, the stone Lennon Building (the former U.S. Customs House), the Masonic Building, and the Murchison Building dominate the scene. One gets the idea from the view that this is a city, intensely developed on a river hill or bluff. Within the area, one sees buildings visibly climb the river bluff.

To the south one sees the lumbering operation across the river and a fine view of the new state-highway vertical-lift bridge. Such bridges are a distinct engineering type. This one is frequently seen in operation as ships enter or leave the upper harbor. Parts of the petroleum storage facilities at the upper part of the new port are also visible.

The George Cameron House park provides a chance to experience the river, both as a reason for the city's existence and for its present beauty and relationship to the existing city. This opportunity and the chance to experience the past through the remnants of the iron works and the renewed George Cameron House make the park a prime piece of urban open space.

Streetcar Suburbs Introduction

Prior to 1900, Market Street extension or road was a pleasant country thoroughfare through undeveloped, relatively high and wooded land past the Wilmington National Cemetery toward the coast. By 1863 it was the Topsail Sound Plank Road, but was not constantly maintained. To the north along Princess extension was the New Bern road running northeast. The Wrightsville Turnpike, a shell road, branched off Market Street near its present intersection with South Seventeenth. It seems to have been the major route to the beach for many Wilmington residents.

Traveling eastward today from the Cape Fear River along Market Street, one passes from the eighteenth century through the nineteenth century to the city of the present. East of Thirteenth Street in the areas near Market Street, the city is almost exclusively twentieth century.

The present Winoca Terrace—*Winoca* derives from *Wi*lmington, *No*rth *Ca*rolina— area (North Thirteenth, North Seventeenth, and Princess streets and Oakdale and Pine Forest cemeteries form the Winoca Terrace boundaries) had already been mapped by 1870. With the growth of Oakdale Cemetery in the 1850s, the Winoca Terrace area between the cemetery and downtown Wilmington was an obvious site for expansion, though development and use of the name *Winoca Terrace* seem not to have occurred until half a century later.

Out Wrightsville Avenue, astride the Mineral Springs Branch, the Delgado Cotton Mills and Delgado Mills Village were constructed in 1899–1900. Ground was broken on June 1, 1899. By September several houses in the village had already been occupied and by November boilers were being installed in the mill. The *Star* for April 15, 1900, reported more than one hundred houses built and occupied.

The electric cars of the Tidewater Power Company streetcar line ran from the downtown waterfront out Princess Street to Seventeenth and then on Wrightsville Avenue by Delgado Mills out of the city and to the coast, crossing Wrightsville Sound and terminating at Lumina Pavilion at Wrightsville Beach. Downtown Wilmington and more distant areas were also available to residents through the trains of the Wilmington and New Bern branch of the Atlantic Coast Line Railroad which crossed Wrightsville Avenue at the mill.

Closer to downtown, Winoca Terrace residents also had a direct trolley line to downtown Wilmington via Princess Street. As the Carolina Heights area (bounded by North Seventeenth, North Twentieth, and Market streets and Bellevue Cemetery) developed, it was served by a spur up Princess Street to North Twentieth then to the National Cemetery entrance on Market.

Carolina Place (bounded by Market Street, Gibson Avenue, Burnt Mill Creek and Wrightsville Avenue) was served by a line from South Seventeenth Street which continued on Perry Street and across on South Twentieth Street to Metts Avenue. Carolina Court (bounded by South Seventeenth Street, Wrightsville Avenue, and Castle Street) was served by the main line down South Seventeenth Street which also served Manhattan and Bronx between Carolina Court and Delgado Mills Village. (Brooklyn was in another section of town astride North Fourth Street north of the railroad tracks.)

These developments were streetcar suburbs in the truest sense of the phrase. The electric cars made both suburban living and downtown work and shopping economical and quick. Development along the corridors the cars served was rapid. Some development was already underway by the 1870s, when streets were laid out in the area that became Winoca Terrace. The *Star* of February 6, 1875, reporting changes in the Wilmington and Sea Side Railway Company, noted that there was a car line on Red Cross Street that offered access to Oakdale Cemetery. This line would have served the Winoca area. After the horse-drawn trolleys were electrified, the number of lines into the area increased until it was efficiently serviced by cars of the Tidewater Power Company Electric Railway.

The Carolina Heights and Carolina Place developments are fairly typical of early twentieth-century suburban development in Wilmington. Both used the traditional grid street pattern of the city, though in Carolina Place, Wrightsville Avenue cuts diagonally across on one boundary, creating odd-shaped lots.

The two developments seem to have been planned for different clients. Carolina Heights is laid out along the named streets. Large lots cut halfway through the block to service entrances through the center of the block off the numbered streets. Carolina Heights houses always face the named streets, and no dwellings were allowed on numbered streets. Carolina Heights deed restrictions required, among other things, that a minimum amount be expended in constructing a house.

In Carolina Place blocks were more intensely developed, and houses were smaller, crowded more closely together, and constructed on all streets.

Though the blocks to the south of Market between South Seventeenth and South Twentieth streets are in Carolina Place, they were developed in accordance with Carolina Heights rules, thus protecting the grand houses that would be built north of the thoroughfare in Carolina Heights. Today the traveler notices the differences in the developments when he passes South Twentieth Street. The large houses and lots to the west of Twentieth Street along Market Street are typical of Carolina Heights, while those to the east along Market are more typical of Carolina Place.

Initial development in Carolina Heights was concentrated on Princess Street between Seventeenth and Eighteenth streets. In Carolina Place early development was along Wrightsville Avenue and Perry Street. These were the areas nearest the streetcar lines and with direct access to downtown.

On November 8, 1908, a reporter for the Wilmington *Star* wrote that: "The work going on at Carolina Heights probably embraces the most forward step Wilmington has taken in a long time and those behind the enterprise are deserving of the highest commendation for what has been and is being done. It is a most splendid illustration of the fact that progress is still the watchword for Wilmington and that the city is growing in spite of the cry of panic and hard times."

On April 18, 1909, the paper reported "marked activity during the past several weeks in Carolina Place property." In 1909 at least seventeen lots were sold in Carolina Heights; at least eight, in Carolina Place. By 1913 the activity had reversed, with at least nine sales in Carolina Heights and thirteen in Carolina Place.

The *Star* had reported in its November 8, 1908, article that Carolina Heights promised "in the very near future to be not only Wilmington's most fashionable but one of its most delightful suburbs." On March 25, 1913, the paper headlined: "Further Development In Wilmington's High Class Suburbs—Carolina Heights," noting that "a large force of men was put to work yesterday making still further improvements in the undeveloped portion of Carolina Heights, possibly Wilmington's highest class and most succcessful suburbs."

Mary Bridgers, an heiress of Col. Robert R. Bridgers of the Atlantic Coast Line Railroad and other railroads and businesses, was the major developer of the Carolina Heights area and the blocks along Market Street from Seventeenth to Twentieth streets. She actively pushed development of the new suburb, and her presence and money attracted other wealthy and prominent builders.

DeRosset Development Company handled sales in Carolina Heights; the American Suburban Corporation, those in Carolina Place. The Heights had a full-time architect/engineer as well, Burett H. Stephens, who came to Wilmington from Chicago in 1906. In addition to his duties as overall architect of the development, he also designed many structures built there and in other parts of Wilmington. Stephens seems to have intended the 1700 block of Market as a buffer between Carolina Place and Carolina Heights: an open public and landscaped part of the Carolina Heights development most visible from the streets and streetcars.

Mrs. Bridger's religion was reflected in the Christian Science church she planned and built to the south of Market in the 1700 block. The 1908 Stephens plan, published in the *Star* on November 8, showed tennis courts behind the church to the south and a landscaped park with fountain to the west. Across the street it shows three houses planned or under construction. As the block ultimately developed, the church and two houses were built to the south and four houses to the north. Today only two houses survive on each side of the block.

The four houses in the 1700 block of Market, all imposing early twentieth-century structures, comprise the "Market Street Mansions" area, listed in the National Register of Historic Places. In full-blown Neoclassical and Colonial Revival styles, the block recalls the confident wealth of the pre–World War I era. Built and occupied by railroad and commercial magnates or heiresses, the four homes convey the gracious mode of living of the early twentieth-century affluent resident of the Wilmington suburbs.

Ideals of the times—an intense interest in modern conveniences and sanitation combined with an honest respect for the grandeur money could buy—are embodied in these four homes and their surroundings. They sit on immense lots, balanced across Market Street. Both houses at the beginning of the block are in the Georgian Revival style, both at the end of the block in the Neoclassical Revival style; yet all four are individually treated and distinctive.

Market Street, which divides Wilmington along its east-west axis, is lined by live oaks whose branches meet to form a canopy over the street. At street level the intervals between curb and sidewalk also contain palm and azalea. A high brick wall fronts Market Street on the north, broken only by an arrow-shaft, cast-iron fence, and gates. This wall is common to the two mansions north of Market. The homes across the street sit far back in naturally landscaped lots.

The 1700 block is remarkable not just for the character of its houses and landscape material but for its survival. There are no intrusions, and it still presents an early twentieth-century face to the viewer, changed only by the increased size of the trees and the increased traffic on Market.

In these streetcar suburbs, individual houses provide a casebook sampling of styles contemporary in the early decades of this century. Georgian Revival, Neoclassical Revival, Shingle style, Spanish Colonial Revival, all the manifestations of the Bungaloid style, and other styles coexist in their early street setting. Some buildings follow national stylistic trends closely; others are more whimsical and innovative. These dwellings range from the mansions of the super-rich to the simple houses provided for workers by a paternalistic cotton mill.

The area seems today to be part of a continuous city whose suburbs are miles beyond. However, tree-lined streets, stylistic diversity, individually constructed houses, as well as the amenities of surrounding land, gardens, and pleasant indoor-outdoor living, remain as evidence of suburban development in a more self-confident and individualistic era.

Market Street

From Thirteenth Street eastward to Twentieth

Market Street came by its name naturally. The city market was located in the street at its intersection with Front Street. It marked the center of the city, dividing it into northern and southern halves. The location and use demanded an important street, wide and well developed.

Streets that crossed Market Street, though they may not have marked official city limits, effectively marked development limits. Early in the nineteenth century, that limit was Fifth Street. By 1869 and the Civil War, Thirteenth Street was the general boundary; by 1870 it was Seventeenth Street; by the turn of the century it was Burnt Mill Creek, just east of Twentieth Street.

In the 1300 and 1500 street-number blocks, Market Street is still wide, with well-developed median and planted sides. Live oak, azalea, crepe myrtle, and gingko, some festooned with Spanish moss, remind the traveler that all of Market was once planted in this manner.

166. New Hanover County High School, 1307 Market Street. Leslie N. Boney, architect, 1919–25.

Thirteenth Street crosses Market; begin 1300 street numbers

NEW HANOVER COUNTY HIGH SCHOOL

1307 Market Street
1919–25: Leslie N. Boney, of W. J. Wilkins & Co., architect

This massive building and the adjacent Trinity United Methodist Church at 1403 Market Street are the only full-scale examples of the use of glazed tile in Wilmington structures.

In 1914 the County Board of Education began acquiring land in the 1300 blocks of Market and Princess streets for school construction. Land acquisition was completed in 1919; cornerstone for the new school was laid in 1920; the first classes were held in the completed center block in 1922; and the wings were completed in 1925.

Two stories over a full basement, the sand-colored brick structure (fig. 166) is banded horizontally in courses of glazed tile. The projecting central entrance pavilion is echoed by blind wings that also project. The windows and entrance in the center pavilion and the two-story banks of double windows in the recessed area are set in monumental glazed-tile panels.

The central doorway, approached by flanking triple-unit stairs to a platform with cast-iron lamps and a central stair leading to the entrance, has a heavily molded lintel surmounted by cherubs holding a globe. The lintel is supported by acanthus brackets that frame the "New Hanover High School" plaque. A grapevine relief, also used elsewhere, surrounds the door. The window above the entrance is surmounted by a cartouche flanked in relief by cornucopias and open books. Egg-and-dart courses, slash-and-rosette courses, and continuous rosette courses are used in the horizontal decorative bands.

At least three students who studied at the school have gained national and international reputations. Claude Howell, Wilmington artist and former teacher at the University of North Carolina, Wilmington, studied here. David Brinkley, ABC newsman and writer, who has won a great many broadcasting awards, also studied here. A fellow student of Howell was the writer Robert Ruark, who died in 1965. Ruark's 1957 *The Old Man and the Boy* was autobiographical, concerning his childhood in Wilmington and the surrounding area. Among his other works, *Horn of the Hunter,* 1953; *Something of Value,* 1955; *Poor No More,* 1959; *Uhru: A Novel of Africa,* 1962; and *The Honey Badger,* 1965, are the best known. Sonny Jurgensen and Roman Gabriel are among the well-known athletes who studied here.

To the rear of the school building on Princess Street is the New Hanover High School Gymnasium, 1930–40, Leslie N. Boney, architect. Though this utilitarian building is almost two decades younger than the school building it serves, its textured brick walls and decoration are a pleasant and compatible addition to the education plant by the same architect. Two tiers of windows are flanked by recessed entrances, each with granite architrave decorated with scroll brackets, cornucopias, and cartouches. A stone water table serves as a common lintel for the windows. Above them, a granite stringcourse is decorated with laurel wreaths and rosettes of dogwood, echoing the glazed-tile stringcourse of the school building.

Brogden Hall, the physical education and classroom building constructed in 1954, was designed by the firm Boney established, Leslie N. Boney, Architect. The striking pedestrian bridge that crosses Market Street in front of Brogden was constructed by Miller Construction Company in 1975–76, John R. Oxenfeld, architect.

WORLD WAR I MARKER

Market Street at South Thirteenth Street
1922: J. Maxwell Miller, sculptor; J. Arthur Limerick, Co., caster

A stone slab with molded cornice and shoulder, the marker stands on the front lawn of the high school. A bronze plaque on the front depicts a female warrior in low relief. She is draped, wears a helmet topped by an eagle, and carries a shield, held at arms length, in her left hand. In her right hand she holds a laurel branch to her breast. The marker with its patriotic decoration and inscription is typical of its post–World War I era.

According to the *Dispatch* of May 7, 1922, "The handsome and imposing bronze statue for the soldiers' memorial has reached Wilmington, coming direct from J. Arthur Limerick company, who made the cast from the model by Miller, the well known sculptor, and it is a thing of beauty." The marker was unveiled on May 20 of that year, Memorial Day. It had been funded through contributions raised by Wilmington/New Hanover County public-school students and the chamber of commerce. Senator Pat Harrison of Mississippi gave the dedicatory address.

In reporting the dedication, the May 20, 1922, *Star* suggested it was "erected at this spot in the hope and belief that it will be a constant inspiration to the school children of the county to make their lives worthy of the heroic deed."

PEMBROKE JONES PLAYGROUND GATE

Market Street at South Fourteenth Street
1925: R. H. Brady, builder; Wilmington Iron Works, caster

Though the playground is now little more than an open field with tennis courts and portions of the entrance and most of the fence are missing, the brick-pillared gate with its fine iron arch is a good example of locally produced ironwork. The grillwork is quite substantial, though it seems to be a delicate filigree, composed of geometric and foliar patterns. It was cast by the Wilmington Iron Works.

In announcing work on the new arch, the *Dispatch* wrote on April 29, 1925: "The arch will be paid for out of the Pembroke Jones fund. It will measure 15 ½ feet from center of the two columns and will be of pressed brick and concrete. The columns will be three feet square. The structure will be ornate and in complete accord with the high excellence of the other equipment at the playgrounds, which is declared to be one of the most modern in the entire country."

North Fourteenth Street enters Market; begin 1400 street numbers

TRINITY UNITED METHODIST CHURCH

1403 Market Street
1920–21: Leslie N. Boney for W. J. Wilkins & Co., architect, O. G. Gully, contractor; education building, 1945–48: Lynch, & Foard, architects, Gillette Miller, builder.

The Neoclassical Revival church building displays an obvious kinship to the New Hanover County High School building—both were designed by the same architect, and they were constructed simultaneously.

The monumental portico of the temple-form structure, reached by two flights of steps, employs pressed metal, wood, and tile. Fluted tile columns with Corinthian capitals support the closed pediment of tile, wood, and pressed metal. The columns are linked by a wooden balustrade, and the pediment contains a tile wreath with cross in a foliage bed. The heavily molded metal cornice is supported by acanthus modillions and a dentil course.

Begun in August 1889 as the Market Street Sunday school, the church evolved into the Market Street Methodist Mission in November 1889 and into the Market Street Methodist Church in May 1891, adopting the name Trinity in 1907. The first meetings of the group were held in the Giblem Lodge at North Eighth and Princess streets, but the congregation soon moved to a structure at Ninth and Market.

As the city expanded westward, the congregation decided to move into the developing area and acquired this land. The first services were held in this building on December 4, 1921.

HARGROVE BELLAMY HOUSE

1417 Market Street
1921–22: Northrup & Obrian, Winston-Salem, architects; Northeast Construction Company, Winston-Salem, builders

Sited on the interior of a large lot that stretches between Market and Princess streets, the house presents two facades to viewers, though the Princess Street front is almost hidden behind a high brick wall with cast-iron entrance gate. The Market Street facade of the two-and-a-half-story Georgian Revival house is clearly visible, its entry is a projecting center pavilion with closed pediment. The molded cornice with dentil course that forms the base of the pediment continues around the structure. The recessed entrance door with paneled reveals is surmounted by a swan-neck pediment with an urn and swags. A dentil course and pilasters with acanthus support the entablature.

Hargrove and Sarah Bellamy acquired the land on which the house was constructed, beginning in 1920 and making subsequent purchases to bring the lot to its present size.

HOLLOWAY-SCHAD HOUSE

1419 Market Street
c. 1905

Oldest of the surviving houses along Market Street in the area, this structure bridges the stylistic gap between turn-of-the-century Victorian-era houses closer to downtown Wilmington and the more contemporary early twentieth-century styles found in the rest of the area.

An L-shaped frame dwelling with narrow siding, simple corner boards, wide cornice frieze, and hipped roof, the house features a simple porch with turned Tuscan columns and a turned balustrade. Stone, used in chimneys, foundation, steps, and retaining wall at street level, and multipaned and patterned sash add to the earlier feel of the house.

Built by E. L. and Cammie Lord Holloway, the house was sold to Joseph Schad in 1910. Schad, a local builder, added an ell and made interior changes. From Munich, Germany, Schad came to Wilmington to build the Bridgers House at South Third and Dock streets. He remained after that house was completed to become a builder.

ST. ANDREWS–COVENANT PRESBYTERIAN CHURCH

1416 Market Street
1917: sanctuary; 1921, Kenan Memorial Building: K. M. Murchison, New York, and James F. Gause, Wilmington, architects, and Rhodes and Underwood, builders; 1957: additions to Kenan Memorial Building

In a late Gothic Revival style, all three buildings within the church complex (fig. 167) are of stone so well matched in style and color that the individual

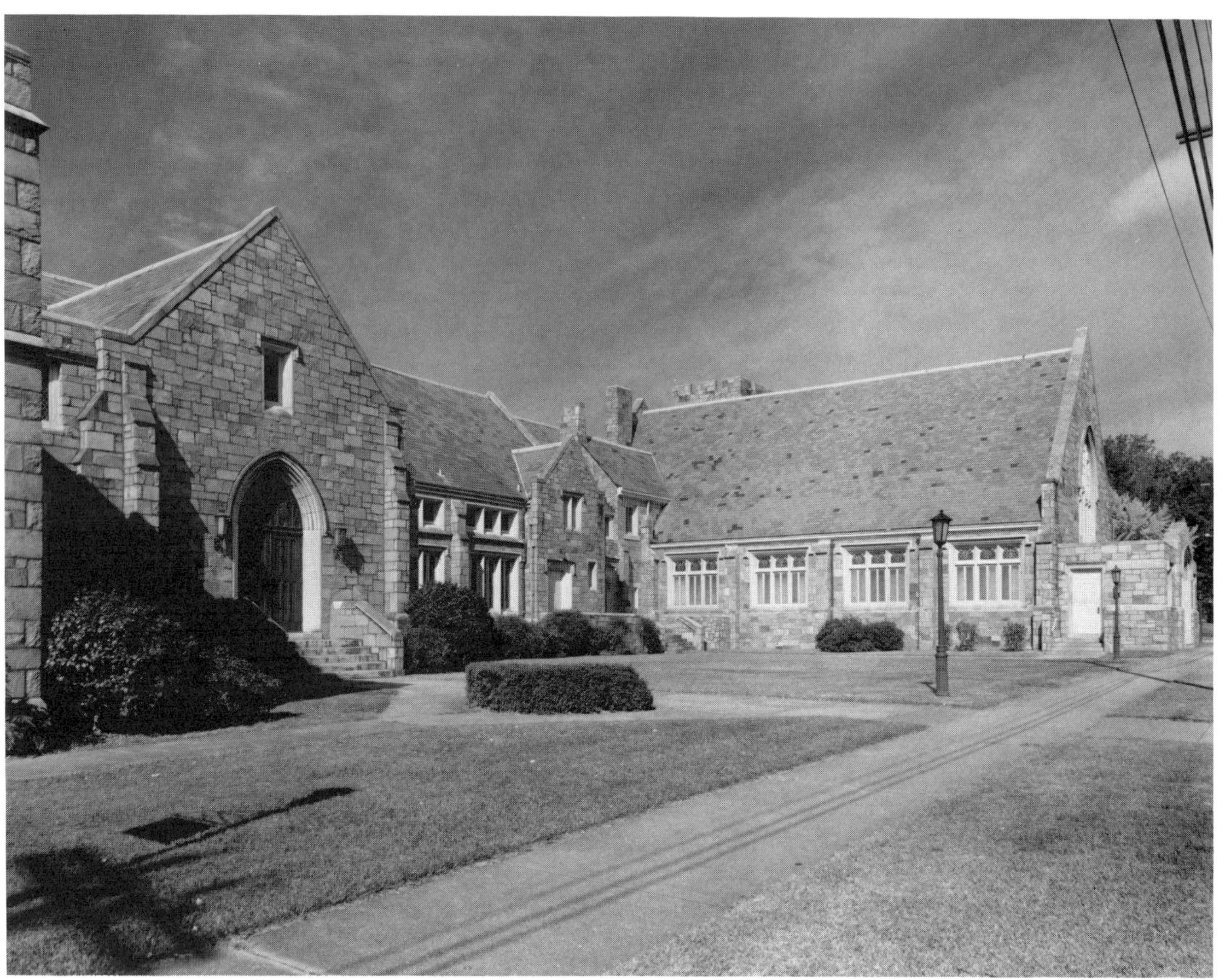

167. St. Andrews–Covenant Presbyterian Church, 1416 Market Street (Fifteenth Street entrance). K. M. Murchison and James F. Gause, architects, 1917–21.

parts are almost indiscernible. Window and other openings are in a variety of English Gothic forms. Stained glass, bells, cornerstones, and some furnishings from earlier buildings have been incorporated into the present structure.

The published church history indicates that the Ginkgo (Ginkgo biloba) trees along Market Street in front of the sanctuary were planted in 1918–19; they were brought from China to Wilmington by Presbyterian missionaries and given to the congregation for planting here. They are unusual for Wilmington.

Construction of the complex was begun by the Church of the Covenant, which was organized officially in January 1918, just after completion of the sanctuary. The congregation was established by the First Presbyterian Church, which had acquired land here in 1911 to serve residents of the expanding area.

St. Andrews, a much older church, was also an offshoot of First Presbyterian. Organized as Second Presbyterian Church in 1858, the congregation worshipped in a frame structure on Chestnut Street at McRae Street. The church adopted the name St. Andrews in 1888 and constructed a building at 520 North Fourth Street (see fig. 73). Both buildings are still standing.

The Church of the Covenant and St. Andrews merged in 1944, adopting the combined names of the two congregations and utilizing the buildings of the Church of the Covenant.

Among the famous ministers who have preached here was Peter Marshall. The *News* for September 20, 1940, noted that he would speak here every afternoon at 3:30 from November 11 to 15.

168. Saint Paul's Episcopal Church, Market Street at North Sixteenth Street. 1927–28; 1936; Lynch and Foard, architects, 1956–58.

Fifteenth Street crosses Market Street; begin 1500 street numbers

Market Street blocks between Thirteenth and Sixteenth streets give a rare glimpse of the street at its pre–World War II best, when it was a well-landscaped and planned ceremonial street offering entry to and exit from the city that it divided into northern and southern sections. Market Street was bordered by some of Wilmington's best dwellings, business houses, and public buildings.

Sixteenth Street crosses Market Street; begin 1600 street numbers

SAINT PAUL'S EPISCOPAL CHURCH

16 North Sixteenth Street
1925: master plan for construction between Market and Princess; 1927–28: construction of present parish house; 1936: enlarging and remodeling of the rectory; 1956–58: construction of new church building, Lynch and Foard, architects

The rough stucco, brick, and stone exteriors of all three parts of the complex (fig. 168) show evidence of construction in accordance with the 1925 master plan. Gothic forms predominate in the nave and chancel, especially in the wood and stain of trusses and furnishings and in the stone floors. The baptismal font and the stained-glass windows over the altar and main entrance are from an 1888 building on South Fourth Street. Pews and other interior furnishings were manufactured by Page Furniture Company of Albemarle, North Carolina.

Saint Paul's Parish was formed under the guidance of Bishop Thomas Atkinson, who presided at the first vestry meeting on June 9, 1858. The congregation worshiped in buildings at Fourth and Orange streets until 1914, when it moved to the present site,

169. Bluethenthal House, 1704 Market Street. James F. Gause, Jr., and James B. Lynch, architects, 1917.

acquired in 1912. The original brick church facing North Sixteenth Street was found to be structurally unsound, and in 1938 all church activities were moved to the parish hall. That structure remained a multipurpose building for nineteen years; on Whitsunday 1958, the first service was held in the present church building.

Seventeenth Street crosses Market Street; begin 1700 street numbers

BLUETHENTHAL HOUSE

1704 Market Street
1917: James F. Gause, Jr., and James B. Lynch, architects

A brick, two and one-half story, Georgian Revival house with gable roof, the structure (fig. 169) sits far back from the street on a large lot. The entrance to the house is particularly well detailed. Centrally located in the five-bay facade, it is composed of an open pediment above a round-arched entrance with flanking sidelights.

Begun March 22, 1917, and occupied that year, the house was built by Herbert and Janet Weil Bluethenthal. Mr. Bluethenthal was a prominent local businessman, and Mrs. Bluethenthal was an active social welfare leader.

EMERSON-KENAN HOUSE

1705 Market Street
1908: Burett H. Stephens, architect; 1909: remodeled and finished, J. F. Leitner, architect; 1923: remodeled by Thomas Hastings of Carrere and Hastings, architects; 1931: remodeled by Leonard Schultz, architect

170. Emerson-Kenan House, 1705 Market Street. Burett H. Stephens and James F. Leitner, architects, 1908–9; Thomas Hastings, architect, 1923; Leonard Schultz, architect, 1913.

Begun by Mary Bridgers, major developer of the area, the house was reported completed by the *Star* of November 8, 1908. Burett H. Stephens, Mrs. Bridger's architect and the overall architect for Carolina Heights, probably drew the plans. It seems likely that work on the house was finished by Thomas Emerson, president of the Atlantic Coast Line Railroad who purchased the house in January 1909 and was its first resident. Emerson retained J. F. Leitner as his architect to finish the house.

A massive two-and-a-half-story brick structure, the house (fig. 170) is three oversized bays wide and nine deep. The hip roof features semicircular headed dormers, and there is a full entablature with dentil and acanthus modillion cornice. The central three-bay entrance portico is supported by colossal Corinthian columns. This is flanked by single-story porches supported by Tuscan columns. The west side features a porte cochere; the east side, an elliptical domed solarium.

171. Bridgers-Brooks House, 1710 Market Street. Burett H. Stephens, architect, 1910–11.

The house sits amid a large lot enclosed by a brick wall. Its formal landscaping and lawn treatment contrast sharply with the naturalistic treatment of the Bluethenthal House directly across the street at 1704 Market Street (fig. 169). Like the Bluethenthal House, which incorporated the site of the Christian Science Church into its grounds, the Emerson-Kenan House includes the sites of two other houses in its present grounds. One, a later house, was on the corner of North Seventeenth Street; the other, also a c. 1908 house, was in the center of the block.

After Emerson's death in 1913, the Emerson-Kenan House was rented to Lyman Delano, executive vice-president of the Atlantic Coast Line. In 1923 the house was purchased by Sarah Graham Kenan of St. Augustine, Florida. It was she who brought the house and grounds to their present size and state, retaining first Thomas Hastings and later Leonard Schultz to accomplish architectural changes.

Mrs. Kenan, a native Wilmingtonian, was the widow of James Graham Kenan and a wealthy heiress as the sister of Mary Lily Kenan Flagler Bingham, widow of Henry Morrison Flagler—who was cofounder of the Standard Oil Company and developer of Florida's east coast.

A noted philanthropist who gave heavily to various causes, especially education, Mrs. Kenan died in 1968. The house was deeded to Wilmington College, now the University of North Carolina at Wilmington. Since May of 1969 it has been the residence of the chancellor of the university.

BRIDGERS-BROOKS HOUSE

1710 Market Street
1910–11, Burett H. Stephens, architect (probable)

The dwelling (fig. 171) is approached by a heavily shaded circular drive where massive trees allow only

172. Holt-Wise House, 1713 Market Street. Burett H. Stephens, architect, 1908–9.

tantalizing glimpses of the house, a frame Neoclassical Revival dwelling. The low hip roof is just visible atop the monumental balustraded portico. Three oversized bays wide and four deep, the house carries a full entablature. The entrance facade is dominated by a full-width portico of a colossal Roman Doric order, topped by a paneled solid balustrade. The wide columns and the massive entablature, whose bulk is increased by the balustrade, give the house an air of powerful solidity.

Construction was started by Mary Bridgers, the developer of this area. She died on November 10, 1910, from a fall at this construction site. J. W. Brooks purchased the property and completed the house. Mildred Hutaff acquired the house in September 1936.

HOLT-WISE HOUSE

1713 Market Street
1908–9, Burett H. Stephens, architect and builder

A two-and-a-half-story frame structure, the house (fig. 172) is three oversized bays wide and five deep, with a hip roof and transverse gables. It carries a full entablature with dentil cornice, and on the front facade, displays a full-width portico, supported by a colossal Ionic order. Each side facade is treated with a one-story porch, also supported by Ionic columns and surmounted by a balustrade. The front portico breaks out at the center bay, where it is supported by paired columns and topped with an identical balustrade. Extending from the porch on the east facade and treated in the same manner is a porte cochere. The garages and servants' quarters stand to the rear, nearer Princess Street.

Edwin C. Holt purchased land here in May of 1908 and began construction in November. Jessie Kenan Wise, widow of Joseph O. Wise, purchased the house in 1916.

Mrs. Wise, a native of Wilmington, was the daughter of William Rand Kenan. She was an heiress of Mary Lily Kenan Flagler Bingham—as was her sister Sarah Graham Kenan, who later purchased the Emerson-Kenan House next door to the west at 1705 Market Street (fig. 170). After Mrs. Wise died in 1968, the house was deeded to Wilmington College, now the University of North Carolina at Wilmington, to be maintained as a memorial to her.

Nineteenth Street crosses Market Street; begin 1900 street numbers

CARR HOUSE

1901 Market Street
c. 1910, Burett H. Stephens, architect

This two and one-half story Shingle-style house is brick on the first level, shingled on the second. The roof is a complex hip with slab chimneys and low dormers. The dwelling features a shingled pent separating the first and second levels, a recessed bay with cast-iron grapevine surround and balustrade, a one-bay double-window projection that is shingled, and a hexagonal oriel with shingle roof. The three-bay porch on the left front has a molded cornice and a plain frieze atop rough fieldstone posts.

J. O. Carr, one of the early builders in Carolina Heights, purchased the lot from Mary Bridgers in 1908 and began construction. Carr occupied the house until his death in 1949. His widow, Susan Parsley Carr, continued in residence until her death in 1964. The house passed from Carr ownership in 1965. Carr, a Wilmington lawyer, was a member of the state legislature and headed the North Carolina Education Commission in the 1920s. He came to Wilmington in 1899 and maintained a law partnership with Judge George Rountree as Rountree & Carr until 1930. Carr was president of the Wilmington *Morning Star* in the 1920s, chairman of the New Hanover Board of Education in 1909–16 and 1927–31, and in 1932 a member of a state commission to rewrite the North Carolina constitution.

HINTON HOUSE

1919 Market Street
1912–13: John F. Leitner, architect

In an eclectic Mission style, the house is a two-and-a-half-story brick structure with tile-covered hip roof. The roof overhang features carved rafter projections. Shaped curvilinear parapets project above the roof at both ends of the facade, which is decorated with brick panels and stringcourses. The center porch has a brick parapet and both wood and brick columns. At ground level the porch continues across the facade as a brick terrace enclosed by a low brick balustrade.

Also on a lot acquired from Mary Bridgers, this dwelling was constructed by Joseph Hatch Hinton, local hotelier, banker, and developer. The *Star* noted on February 6, 1913, that "Mr. and Mrs. Jos. H. Hinton have moved into their handsome new home, 20th and Market streets, Carolina Heights. They have one of the most beautiful and comfortable homes in the entire state."

Hinton began his hotel career as manager of Wilmington's Hotel Purcell, moving in 1888 to the new Orton Hotel, which he purchased in 1906. He was also involved in the construction of the Seashore Hotel in Wrightsville Beach and in the development of Kure Beach and Sunset Park.

Twentieth Street crosses Market Street; the entrance to the Wilmington National Cemetery is just beyond on the north side of Market Street (see "Cemeteries and Parks")

North Fifteenth Street

Market Street northward to Oakdale Cemetery

North Fifteenth Street is fairly typical of streets in the Winoca Terrace development. It is relatively narrow, but its collection of architectural styles and fine structures is impressive. It is probable that more houses than indicated were architect-designed: some built for individual clients, others from published architectural plans.

The street is a major approach to Oakdale Cemetery from Market Street, and as such is an important and visible urban street.

North Fifteenth Street begins at Market Street

YARBOROUGH HOUSE

20 North Fifteenth Street
1916

Street-level retaining walls with pilasters and three tiers of steps approaching the dwelling and porch, all of the same brick as the house, indicate the manner in which this brick residence was planned for the site. Elements of building and setting echo each other in materials and plan.

One of the largest of Wilmington's Bungaloid-style structures, this one-and-a-half-story house with wide, low, clipped gable roof maintains the roof overhang and exposed rafters of the style. The gable roof parallel to the entrance, low dormer, and deep porch—each with shed roof—are design elements found also in many smaller bungalows nearby.

W. C. and Bertie Hanson Yarborough purchased this large corner lot in 1915. Late in 1916, the *Star* reported on October 15, "Winoca Terrace is another suburb in which building is now quite active. Mr. W. C. Yarborough is building a beautiful modern brick home at 15th and Princess streets which will cost $4,000." Except for a kitchen that was modernized in 1965, the residence remains essentially as constructed.

Princess Street crosses North Fifteenth Street; begin 100 street numbers

STRUNCK HOUSE

101 North Fifteenth Street
1922–23

The paired Tuscan columns of the porch, tripled at the corners, are repeated on the wide side porch, whose flat roof evokes a trellis with larger and more elaborately carved rafter projections than those of the main porch.

A frame Bungaloid-style structure with wide roof overhang, the house features massive bracket-braces, as well as carved and shaped rafters. Another of the bungalow types, the house has a high gable roof that covers the porch beneath a single plane. The gable dormer is prominent and extends over the porch.

Mr. and Mrs. E. P. H. Strunck purchased this Winoca Terrace lot in 1920 and were in residence by late 1923. The house is little changed.

Chestnut Street crosses North Fifteenth Street; begin 200 street numbers

SCHNIBBEN HOUSE

211 North Fifteenth Street
1919–20

Of all the Bungaloid style houses in the area, this one is closest to the western Stick-style bungalow. It has a cross-gable plan with two broad gables. The wide overhang features exposed rafters. In the gables, overhangs have carved bargeboards and prominent laminated joists that project beyond the roof line—evocative of the pueblo construction of native Indians and the Spanish settlers in the southwest.

173. Emmett H. Bellamy House, 1413 Rankin Street. Clarence Shepherd, architect, 1930.

While presenting a distinctly Bungaloid single-story facade to North Fifteenth Street, the house manages a full two stories to the rear. As with many bungalows, smallness is an illusion created by the lowness and flatness of the roof. Though many bungalows are not as well planned and detailed as those at 20, 101, and 211 North Fifteenth Street, the style was used by many Wilmington builders between 1910 and 1930.

This structure seems to have been built by Louis Lipinsky, who acquired the lot in 1919, constructed the house, and sold it to Martin and Matilda Schnibben in early 1920.

Rankin Street crosses North Fifteenth Street; begin 400 street numbers

EMMETT H. BELLAMY HOUSE

1413 Rankin Street (Rankin Street at North Fifteenth Street, southwest corner)
1930: Clarence Shepherd of Ohio, architect

In a Spanish Colonial Revival style, the house (fig. 173) displays a variety of bay openings in its entrance facade—no two are alike. Houses in this style often present an asymmetrical appearance along with textured stucco walls, low tile roof, wide roof overhang, carved rafters, and entrance lanterns. The cast-iron lanterns, and the interior mantels of this house were custom made from architect Clarence Shepherd's design by Florentine Craftsmen of New York.

The large landscaped yard and plants native to this

area, including palms, help the design bridge the gap between its west coast origins and its east coast site.

Emmett H. Bellamy, a local attorney who served in the North Carolina Senate, built the house and lived there until his death in 1952.

HICKS HOUSE

410 North Fifteenth Street
1928: William D. Brinkloe, architect; J. T. Ritter, builder

The roof gives this house its individuality. While the structure is two stories to the rear with a relatively short roof plane, the elongated front plane swoops down to below the first-floor ceiling level. On the right the wide roof overhang is pierced to allow a double window; on the left it flares upward to form an eyelid, the shingle of the roof following the gentle curve of the projection.

The house is covered with narrow wooden siding that laps at the corners. The same siding is used beneath the eaves overhang, which has been steamed and fitted to the curve of the roof above the eyelid window.

Off center to the south, the entrance consists of a door and a tier of five casement windows above a single sill. To the south of this a trellis support for a vine reaches from the ground to the eaves, helping create the illusion of a thatch-roofed, vine-covered cottage in the English countryside. Indeed, the plans for the house are said to have been patterned after Ann Hathaway's Cottage.

Glasgow and Helen Russell Hicks acquired the Winoca Terrace lot here in 1927, and with the help of their builder, they adapted published plans by architect William D. Brinkloe. Except for a 1939 boiler room and 1944 den, the residence is as constructed.

The entrance to Oakdale Cemetery is just beyond the Hicks House and Cemetery Office (see "Cemeteries and Parks")

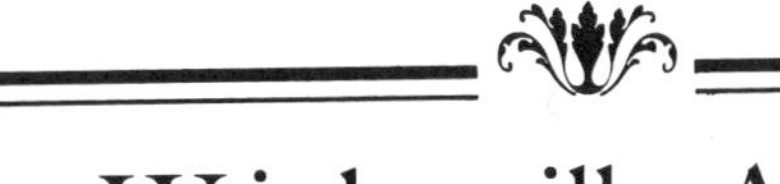

Wrightsville Avenue

From South Seventeenth Street southeastward to the 2200 block of Wrightsville Avenue

A narrow, gently curving street, Wrightsville Avenue predates twentieth-century development of the area. As the Wrightsville Turnpike, it was a nineteenth century route to Wrightsville Beach. After 1899 and construction of the Delgado Cotton Mills at the intersection of Wrightsville Avenue and Wooster Street the turnpike became a major connector to Market Street and the downtown waterfront and commercial area, evolving into Wrightsville Avenue.

Buildings to the northwest of Wrightsville Avenue are in the Carolina Place development, while those across the street are in the Carolina Court development. Generally, Carolina Court did not develop as fully or as early in the century as Carolina Place.

The oldest structures in the area are along Wrightsville Avenue. Surviving turn-of-the-century houses are generally recognized by their irregular plans, hip or complex roofs, and sawn or turned wooden detail—brackets, gable ornaments, spindle courses, balustrades.

In the post-1915 era the bungalow superseded the Victorian cottage. Bungalows normally have gable roofs, are single story, and are without sawn or turned ornament. The 1700 and 1900 blocks of Wrightsville Avenue are an excellent example of the popularization of the Bungaloid style, proving its adaptability for dwellings to fit almost any pocketbook.

The porch was a feature of both the pre-1915 and the post-1915 houses of the area. An integral part of the dwelling, it was an indoor-outdoor room where the family relaxed, observed street life, and talked with neighbors. Its evolution from highly decorated Victorian gingerbread to utilitarian space and porte cochere is one of the interesting studies of these three blocks.

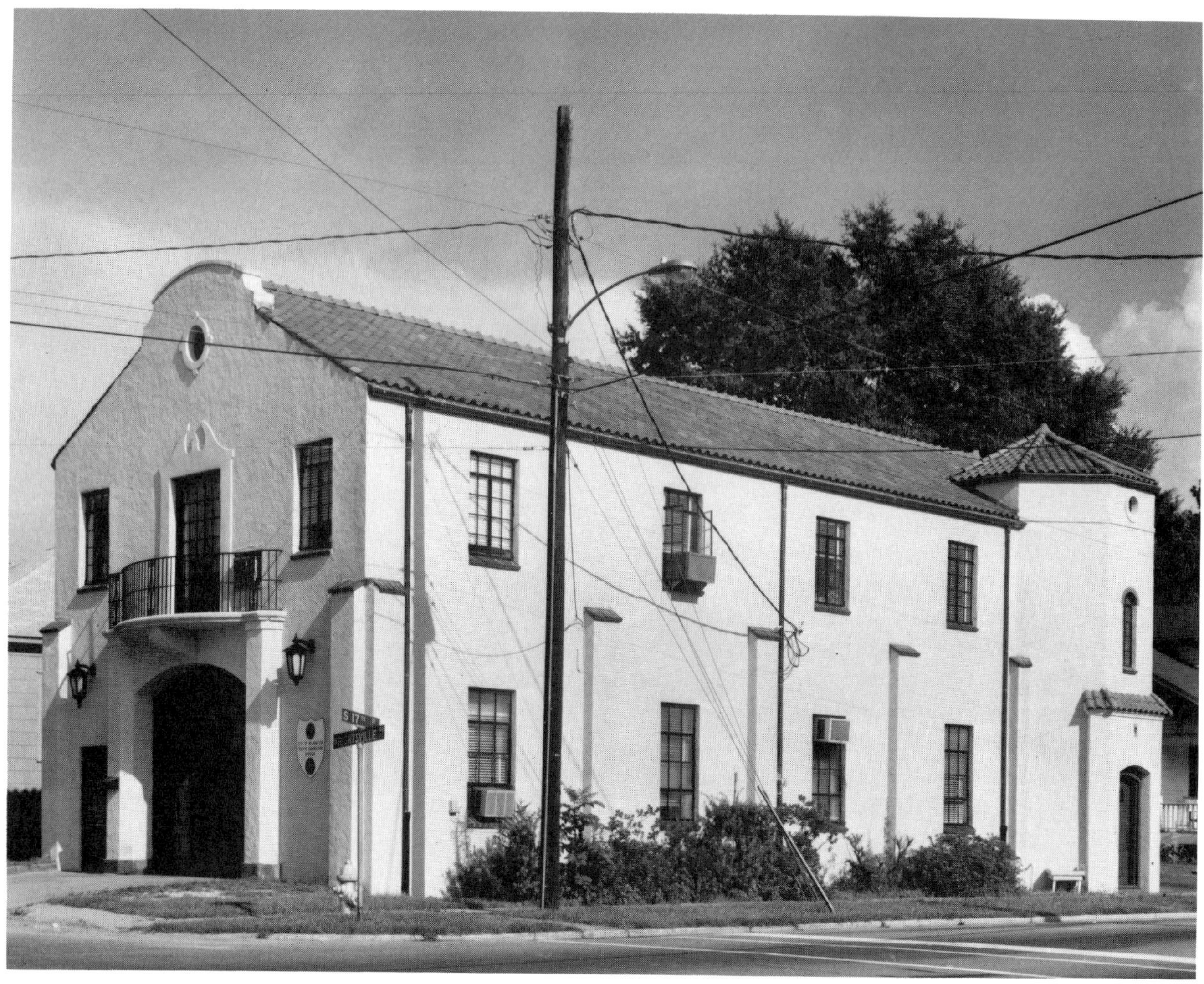

174. Fire Station no. 5, 1702 Wrightsville Avenue. Lynch and Foard, architects, 1931.

Wrightsville Avenue begins at South Seventeenth Street

FIRE STATION NO. 5

1702 Wrightsville Avenue
1931: Lynch and Foard, architects; U. A. Underwood, builder

In the Mission style with stucco walls and tile roof, the station (fig. 174) continued a Wilmington tradition of well-designed municipal structures. The plain plaster walls, the low-pitched roof, the semicircular arch with balcony above the vehicle entrance, the gable parapet, and the tower are all hallmarks of the style.

Though no longer serving as a fire station, the building is still maintained and used by the city.

DELGADO MILLS, OFFICE AND HOUSE

Beyond Gibson Street astride Wrightsville Avenue
1899–1900: Zachary and Zachary of Raleigh, architects and builders

The 1899–1900 mill village was part of a complex that originally consisted of mill, engine room, boiler house, dye house, bleachery, storage warehouses, company town, company store, school, post office, and church.

A mineral spring on the site where the mill and its attendant structures were built made the area a popular picnic spot. It was also the site of considerable Civil War activity. In the Confederate entrenchments thrown up to protect Wilmington from possible land invasion from the east, Hobson's and Miller's batteries were on the site of the mill village by 1863.

175. Delgado Mills office, 2231 Wrightsville Avenue. Zachery and Zachery, architects, 1899.

The gun emplacements, trenches, and fortifications survived the war and were a well-known attraction. During 1875 John D. Bellamy and the young Woodrow Wilson, son of the minister of the First Presbyterian Church, often came here. "Mr. Bellamy remembers vividly reading aloud Scott's *The Pirate* with young Wilson. They would walk over to what was called in those days Delgado Mills, which had been a camp for Confederate troops during the war. There were fine trees about and the young men would lay on the mounds which had formerly covered the ammunition magazines and take turns in reading aloud" (Ray Stannard Baker, *Woodrow Wilson, Life and Letters, Vol. 1, Youth, 1856–1890* [Garden City, N.Y.: Doubleday, Page & Co., 1927], p. 79).

It was this site that was chosen for the Delgado Mills. The *Messenger* of May 30, 1899, reported "The site for the Delgado Cotton Mills, Wilmington's $250,000 cotton factory, to be erected at the mineral spring, on the shell road, in the southeastern suburbs of the city, presents a busy scene these days." By September 6 the same newspaper could note that: "Quite a village has already grown up around the mill. Forty neat one and two story cottages, with from three to five rooms, have been erected and already fifty or sixty people are residing on the grounds. In the course of a month twenty-five or thirty families, who are to furnish help for the mill, will be settled around the mill. Some of the mill hands are already on the grounds."

The *Dispatch* for November 8, 1899, reported: "The house for Superintendent Reid is nearing completion, and sixty or more of the cottages for operatives will soon be ready for occupancy. It is learned that the company will build a church near the mill, use of which will be given to all the denominations."

176. Delgado Mills Village house, 2149 Dexter Street. Zachery and Zachery, architects, c. 1899

By April 15, 1900, the *Star* could headline "At Delgado Village—Thriving Little Town Gradually Settling down after Its Hasty Establishment" and report:

A visitor to the new Delgado village to the southeast of the city would now be surprised to find the remarkable signs of progress evidenced upon every hand and to note what changes have been wrought by the establishment of the big cotton manufacturing enterprise there. The cottages, of which there are more than a hundred, are now well nigh filled with a contented set of operatives, who are much pleased with the new location. The Mineral Spring affords a copious supply of good water and situated on the shell road and on the Wilmington Seacoast railroad, the people find easy approach to the seaside resorts and are promised in the very near future excellent school and church advantages.

The company store in the village brings the operatives near to market and it is already doing a splendid business. "The hours of labor in the mills are very reasonable," remarked a resident of the village yesterday, "and the people who have collected from all parts of the State to the new factory are beginning to feel at home. Of course a number of contentious persons naturally found their way here with the two hundred and more new operatives who came, but we have succeeded in weeding these out and are now pleased with the new surroundings."

The mill starts up in the morning at 6 o'clock with forty minutes for dinner at noon and the day force "knocks off" at 6:30 in the evening. On Saturdays the operatives are given a half holiday that they may visit the city, beaches or other places.

A new post office will soon be established there, and Delgado will be the most thriving suburb of the city.

Parts of Delgado Mills Village survive. Though efforts were made in the early 1970s to save the brick mill building with its four-story tower and use it adaptively, they failed, and the building was destroyed. With its destruction the city lost one of its most significant early industrial structures and one of considerable architectural distinction.

The loss was not complete, however, for the Mill Office (fig. 175) (1899: Zachery and Zachery, architects and builders, John D. Long, contractor for the brickwork) survives at 2231 Wrightsville Avenue. A two-story brick structure of Darlington Brick Works brick, it is pleasingly Victorian, with a complex roof and fine sawn gable and porch ornament. Now used adaptively, the office is a significant reminder of the quality construction of the Delgado Mills complex.

Dwellings of several sizes constructed for the mill employees also survive. The largest houses along Wrightsville Avenue included the house built for Superintendent Reid. The well-detailed and ornamented houses at 2149, 2153, and 2157 Wrightsville Avenue represent the largest and most ornate of these dwellings. Slightly smaller and less ornate structures such as those at 2105, 2135, and 2145 Wrightsville Avenue represent the status of an employee at the second level of the mill hierarchy.

The major part of the village is to the northeast along Dexter and Fowler streets between Delgado, Newton, and Kent streets. Dwellings range from medium-size houses along Dexter Street at Kent (see fig. 176, 2149 Dexter Street) to single-room homes or duplexes of one room each along Fowler Street at Delgado. Some of the houses are constructed of vertical board and batten, but most are covered with horizontal siding. One unifying feature appears in almost all mill houses—ventilators in gable ends and in cross gables are sawn in a whirling floral pattern.

This company store survives, as do some of the recreational facilities constructed by the mill for village inhabitants. The school and the church are now gone, but the survival of residential villages of this type may be rarer than the survival of the mills themselves.

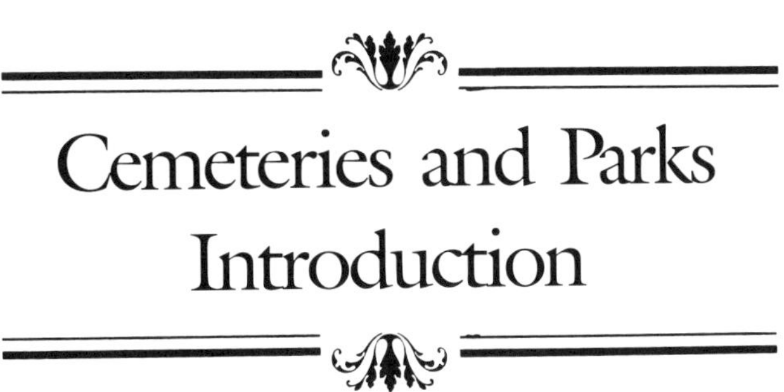

Cemeteries and Parks Introduction

Wilmington is well known for its parks and gardens, and most tend to identify Greenfield Lake, Airlie, and Orton as the city's best. Indeed there is every reason to be proud of these three remarkable attractions, but there is another quite different park area near downtown that usually escapes mention.

Stretching in a crescent from North Thirteenth and Harnett streets on the northwest along Burnt Mill Creek to Metts Avenue on the southeast are a series of cemeteries and public parks that offer a wide variety of cultural, natural, and environmental experiences. Cypress and marsh plants abound in the naturally landscaped area of Mary Bridgers Park and Wallace Park, while azaleas and other blossoming plants are in Bulluck Park. Azalea and camellia are in Oakdale Cemetery where dogwood, redbud, magnolia, oleander, and gardenia vie with the azalea for showiness.

The Civil War history of the area, an extremely important era in Wilmington, is embodied in the Confederate cemetery within Oakdale Cemetery and in Union graves within Wilmington National Cemetery.

Other facets of Wilmington history also come into focus within the cemeteries: yellow fever as a nineteenth century killer can be graphically understood in the public yellow fever area in Oakdale. The taste and wealth of area families is reflected three dimensionally in funerary monuments and landscaping of family plots.

The racial, ethnic, and religious heritage of the area is also recorded here. Nineteenth century Jewish settlers in Wilmington established a Hebrew Cemetery in Oakdale, while later Jewish immigrants started another burial place near the B'nai Israel synagogue. Masons, Odd Fellows, Woodmen of the

World, King's Daughters and Sons, and others claim their own space, where they repose side by side within marked plots. The names of the places where Wilmington's German inhabitants were born offer an excellent geography lesson. In Pine Forest Cemetery, Wilmington's minority black history is laid out before the visitor in the graves of former slaves and free blacks, doctors, servants, educators—all brought together by one common denominator.

Landscaped cemetery-parks and perpetual-care areas located outside of cities began as business ventures, first in France and then England. By 1831, with the establishment of Mount Auburn Cemetery near Cambridge, Massachusetts, they had moved across the Atlantic. The movement won quick acceptance, and with the establishment of Laurel Hill in Philadelphia in 1836 and of Greenwood in Brooklyn in 1838, the American cemetery movement had begun. By the end of the decade it was a national movement. Within fifteen years many of the country's great landscaped parks and outdoor sculpture gardens—cemeteries all, and Oakdale Cemetery, chartered in 1852, among them—had been established.

Such areas offered space, a landscape plan, and professional care. Funerary art—which prior to the time had been the exclusive preserve of the super rich and the powerful and had not been possible in most crowded in-town or churchyard cemeteries—flowered. Design in cast iron and stone, sculpture, tombs in popular architectural styles, and the practice of landscape gardening all entered a period of ascendancy.

Constant streams of visitors, especially on weekends and holidays, attended the new cemeteries to stroll, to sit and enjoy the outdoor art of landscape and landscape plants, to look at the monuments, and to meet others similarly engaged. For the Victorian, who often had more family in the cemetery than at home, weekly visits were a matter of course, with flowers, books, and picnics taken along. The *Star* reported on October 28, 1874: "We are glad to learn that the work of grading Miller Street is progressing finally and that there is a prospect of a fine drive to 'Oakdale' on an early day. This is a much needed improvement, as at present, a ride or a walk to the Cemetery is an undertaking of no little magnitude. With a good drive and good sidewalks, visitors to our beautiful 'city of the dead' will have cause to be thankful."

By 1903 access was considerably easier, and the flow of visitors greater. The *Dispatch* announced on May 7: "The C. R. L. & P. Company announces that on Friday and Saturday of this week cars will leave Ninth and Princess for Oakdale Cemetery every ten minutes from 2 to 7 p.m. Next Sunday cars will be run to the cemetery from Ninth and Princess every ten minutes from 9 a.m. to 7 p.m."

In spite of the parklike setting, the landscape architects and craftsmen did not allow their contemporaries to forget the purpose of the cemetery. Symbolically weeping plants were developed and used. Weeping willows and other trees with weeping varieties were featured. These real plants often shaded plots where lifelike representations of them appeared on iron cemetery gates and on carved stones. In Laurel Hill and other cemeteries the weeping varieties of trees were pointed to with pride. None of the earlier cemeteries could approach the Wilmington cemeteries in such symbolism. At Oakdale, for instance, Spanish moss made every tree a weeping variety—nature as a Victorian-era landscape gardener.

The cemeteries were economic and political successes. Formed and supported by important men with wealth and influence, they became immediately popular, aided, not surprisingly, by town ordinances that forbade burial within the city limits. The new cemeteries became virtual monopolies.

Within this area of Wilmington and contiguous to each other are five cemeteries and three parks that, although twentieth century in origin, embody nineteenth-century ideals of naturalism and upkeep. Together they are prime cultural documents of the area's past, prime open space usable in myriad ways, and superb landscape gardens and arboreta. They are at the same time excellent outdoor sculpture gardens and museums. They are, in short, the very essence of nineteenth-century culture and taste.

Oakdale Cemetery

North end of North Fifteenth Street
1852–55: L. Turner, surveyor

Oakdale Cemetery evolved from a meeting early in 1852 of several prominent Wilmington businessmen to discuss a new burial ground outside the city limits. Their discussion covered the cemetery movement elsewhere and the sanitary and health considerations of continuing to bury within church and private burial grounds. A committee was appointed to locate a suitable spot and to secure a charter from the state. The charter was adopted as Chapter 175 of the 1852 *Laws of North Carolina*:

Whereas, public sentiment in the town of Wilmington, in accordance with the enlightened experience of populous cities and towns elsewhere, is opposed to the interment of the dead amid the bodies of the living, not only for sanitory [sic] *but for other obvious reasons; and whereas, experience hath also shown that it is desirable to have public burial grounds, subject to such laws, rules and regulations as will insure to the living the continued protection of the remains of their dead, and the decent preservation of the grounds by securing them in perpetuity to the object of their dedication; and whereas, several citizens of Wilmington are desirous to purchase a tract of land for the purpose of establishing thereon a public cemetery, and for the reasons above stated, wish an act of incorporation, and the object being deemed worthy of encouragement; therefore . . . Armand J. DeRosset, Jr., Edward Kidder, Platt K. Dickinson, William A. Wright, Oscar G. Parsley, Dugald McMillan, John A. Taylor, John L. Meares, Charles D. Ellis, Henry Nutt, Stephen D. Wallace, John McRae, James Cassidey, Stephen B. Polly, and George R. French, and their successors, be and they are hereby created a body politic and corporate by the name and title of the "Proprietors of the Wilmington Cemetery."*

When and how the cemetery came to be called Oakdale is not known, but the reason for the name is obvious. It was high land bounded on three sides by stream valleys, where there were massive live and water oaks. The first located use of the name is in volume 13 of *Occident* (1855), where the dedication of the Hebrew Cemetery at "Oak Dale" is reported. There are other references to the cemetery as *Oak Dale*, but the general usage, especially in Wilmington newspapers, seems to have been *Oakdale*. Finally, on March 4, 1901, the state legislature amended the 1852 charter in part, so: "that Section 1 of said chapter one hundred and seventy five of the private laws of one thousand eight hundred and fifty-two be amended by striking out the words 'Proprietors of the Wilmington Cemetery,' in line eleven of said section (printed laws) and inserting in lieu thereof the words 'The Oakdale Cemetery Company' the object being to change the name of said corporation." Thus in 1901 the name by which the cemetery seems to have been known all along became official and legal.

The 1901 amendment to the charter also allowed the cemetery corporation to enter into perpetual-care arrangements. While the company had always been responsible for overall care and upkeep, individual lot owners had generally cared for or made arrangements with the company or some other custodian for care of individual plots. The first perpetual-care agreement of Oakdale dated from 1870, when the national perpetual-care movement was still in its infancy.

By 1877 the company had reached a general agreement on perpetual care, and the first "Perpetual Care Contract" was made with W. H. McDade for his lot, no. 41 in section H. After some trial and error, it was decided that the amount necessary for perpetual care would return, at five percent per year, the funds necessary to meet the annual cost of maintenance. Perpetual-care agreements originally worked out in such cemeteries as Oakdale are today common practice.

Initially, sixty-five acres were acquired for the cemetery. Enough land had been added to the original cemetery to bring the acreage to one hundred by World War II. With the opening of the Annex Extension in 1945 and the Memorial Garden in 1950, the acreage increased to over one hundred twenty-eight.

The original sixty-five acre area was bounded on three sides by creeks, and a 1911 *Historical Sketch* published by the cemetery noted that "Nature seemed to have moulded the ground for that purpose, and left it for man to beautify."

L. Turner was commissioned to survey the cemetery and lay it out. Almost immediately, sections A through H were laid out and mapped. Turner may also have been involved in designing the landscape plan for the grounds. Another possibility is that Charles Quigley, the first superintendent, was involved in landscape design of the grounds.

Certainly, as the 1911 brochure indicates, the topography of the site was the determining factor in the plan. The graceful circles, crescents, and other carefully shaped sections indicate a plan carefully based on the site, sound principles of landscape architecture, and nineteenth-century cemetery design. It does not seem possible for a plan as complex as Oakdale's to have evolved without a landscape architect, but no evidence has yet been found to suggest an identity, unless that designer was Turner or Quigley.

On December 5, 1854, lots were sold at public auction for a minimum price of fifty dollars per lot. Most brought ten to forty dollars more than the minimum charge. After the sale the company declared the cemetery open for burials, and the city followed in 1855 with an ordinance that forbade interments within the town limits. The first burial within Oakdale came on February 5, 1855, when Annie DeRosset, six-year-old daughter of the president of the cemetery company, Armand J. DeRosset III, was interred.

Landscaping seems to have begun almost immediately, probably under the direction of superintendent Quigley. The best of the forest oaks were left on the site, as were other trees, but an infusion of landscape plants was also begun. Certainly dogwoods were among the first plants cultivated here, and by 1860 camellias were being planted. The earliest of these, set on the Munds lot, have been destroyed, but the Sarah Frost variety planted near the old summer house (now also destroyed) still flowers, as does the c. 1895 Elegans Variegated variety on the Woolvin lot. For both azalea and camellia, Oakdale is one of the state's best gardens.

The original entrance to the cemetery seems to have been from the south, off Rankin Street at either Fourteenth or Fifteenth streets. Before the Miller Street (Campbell) entrance could be opened, the creek had to be bridged. George Franklin, a black contractor, built the bridge in February and March of 1868. From that time until well into the twentieth century, the main entrance to Oakdale was from Miller at North Thirteenth.

A lodge was built there in 1871. The *Star* for March 21 reported that the new lodge was "rapidly approaching completion." On May 1, 1874, the paper noted that "the work of erecting the summer houses . . . has been commenced and one of them is nearly completed." On May 5 it noted that the last coat of paint was about to be applied and on March 1, 1876 that new clay and marl walks in Oakdale were "much more serviceable than formerly, when the sand proved such an impediment to feet and pleasant locomotion."

In 1896 James F. Post was retained to design a new gate and lodge. The original stone lodge with mansard roof was a handsome structure, but it was demolished after the main entrance to the cemetery was moved in 1915 to North Fifteenth Street because with the changed entrance, the lodge no longer served its intended purpose. It and the 1870s summerhouses were viewed as upkeep problems that drained the company of needed capital. Nothing remains of the summerhouses. Stone from the lodge now forms an outer wall around the Willetts plot, and the cornerstone to the Post-designed lodge is in the yard before the present cemetery office at the North Fifteenth gate to the cemetery.

Portions of the entrance designed by Post remain. At least three of the stone posts are in place and remains of other posts lie just outside the cemetery and across the creek—a sad fate for the work of one of Wilmington's best known architects, James F. Post. His obituary in the July 16, 1899, *Messenger* had suggested: "Indeed there is barely a street of our city that does not bear evidence of his taste and skill. If no monument is ever reared to his memory, the beautiful brownstone lodge at Oakdale cemetery, designed and built under his supervision, will be a lasting testimonial of his useful career." Alas, no monument has been erected, and the lodge is gone, the entrance gates almost gone.

Oakdale received much more attention in the nineteenth century than it does now, and its press was nothing short of incredible. One *Star* writer on January 7, 1872, concluded a long article on Oakdale by requesting readers to "go and see for themselves what has been done and is now doing to add to the beauty and adornment of a cemetery which can already compare favorably with the handsomest in the country."

Nor were the accolades all local. On May 3, 1874, the *Star* reprinted an article by W. J. Woodward in the New York newspaper *The South*. Woodward concluded his account: "Oakdale is indeed a most fitting place for the home of the dead—no sound of work or play—no clatter of wheels—solitude reigns—all the consolation which can be gained from sympathy in nature can be secured here, which are the qualities that could serve its purpose. It is now beautiful, but is destined at no distant day to become wonderfully beautiful." On May 16, 1878, the *Star* reprinted the following from Col. John D. Cameron of the Hillsboro *Recorder*:

The new cemetery, Oakdale, is one of the most beautiful of all the attractive spots which modern taste and sentiment have prepared for the repose of the dead. Nature has done much in providing appropriate accessories, broken grounds not to be looked for in a country as flat as this, fine trees, appropriately hung with funeral moss, and washed by a dark winding stream whose black waters are suggestive of the dark gulf between life and death every mortal is doomed to pass. And everything that taste and skill and unremitting care and work could do to adorn and beautify has been done. Winding walks and drives, margined with evergreens and bright with the richest of flowers and redolent with the most fragrant of odors, almost banish the suggestion of mortality, obtrusively brought to mind by the shafts of costly monuments.

Still, on September 17, 1880, the *Star* lamented "our citizens should feel pride in our cemeteries, especially 'Oakdale' which is regarded as one of the handsomest south of Baltimore, and yet very few visitors to our city, we opine, are ever informed of this lovely spot or urged to take a look at it."

For those who did go to look, the cemetery had, by 1888, "between three and four miles of main avenues or drives within the enclosures, besides a great number of walks for pedestrians, where carriages cannot be used."

It is not really possible to separate the individual monuments from the setting and from the overall effect. Oakdale terrain is extremely hilly, marked by knolls encircled and laced with winding paths and carriage ways. The live oaks, draped with Spanish moss, form dark canopies over magnolia, dogwoods, and camellia. Foliage is dense, and the overall "picturesque" atmosphere suggests a medieval ruin. Individual family lots that rise above the paths are generally entered by stone steps marked by the family name. Most lots are well defined, either outlined by a low stone wall or by a cast-iron fence. These openwork cast-iron fences are in either the rustic or the Gothic mode. Delicate wire chairs or vine-patterned cast-iron settees often furnish the grave area. Grave markers are in a variety of shapes and styles, including Egyptian obelisks, Gothic pinnacles, stone floral bouquets, simple slabs, cast-iron crosses, and massive stone mausoleums.

Atop a hill, towering over all other markers, is a monumental bronze soldier standing on a pedestal—The Confederate Monument (fig. 177). "A Monument to our Dead" headlined one Wilmington newspaper on May 14, 1868:

Subscriptions are now being circulated in our city, with the intention of raising a sufficient amount of money to enable the Memorial Association not only to place a suitable fence around the Memorial lot, in the Cemetery, but eventually to erect an appropriate monument over the remains of the Confederate dead, who are sleeping their last sleep in the lot. Just and fitting it is that all honor should be shown to our gallant lost ones—never will their names be forgotten until the Southern heart has ceased to thrill at the recollection of our glorious past—an event which can never happen. In regard to the monument we have only to submit one word—Let it be of North Carolina granite. *Let not those sacred graves be desecrated by the erection over them of marble from the Northern land—better, far better and far more appropriate would it be to place there the roughest hewn post of Carolina wood than noble stone which ever came from a Northern quarry, or was chiseled by the hand of a Northern sculptor. We deem it little short of desecration to do it. . . . We would feel proud to contribute our humble*

177. Oakdale Cemetery. Confederate Monument, William Randolph O'Donovan, sculptor, 1872.

mite to place over the loved ones a granite stone cut from our own quarries, but may our arm be blasted the day that we subscribe one cent to enrich any Northern man by the purchase from him of a memorial monument for our Southern dead.

By July 28, 1869, the Ladies Memorial Association, responsible for the Confederate plot and the plan for a monument to the Confederate dead, was reported by the *Star* to be soliciting contributions but to have "no plan for a monument . . . definitely decided upon." Perhaps, on that basis, the writer of the 1868 article did subscribe. If so, he may later have wished to reclaim his contribution, for northern artisans were indeed involved in the finished product.

A capsule history of the undertaking was in the *Star* on May 10, 1879. The lot, according to the article:

was generously donated by the Oakdale Cemetery Company to the Ladies Memorial Association, who removed to the same the remains of four hundred and sixty-seven Confederate officers and privates who together braved the exposures of the camp, endured the fatigues of the tiresome march and faced the dangers of the battle field, and who now together fill honored graves, wet by tears and hallowed by the offerings of Sympathetic hearts.

Soon after the lot came into the possession of the Memorial Association [December 15, 1867] it was enclosed with a beautiful iron railing, and on the 10th of May, 1872, the monument was unveiled in the presence of interested spectators, and memorial address being given by Maj. C. W. McClammy, and Col. J. J. Hedrick acting as Chief Marshall.

The Monument, consisting of a BRONZE STATUE OF A CONFEDERATE SOLDIER *and medallion likenesses of our great chieftan* [sic], *Robert E. Lee and the christian soldier and hero, Thomas Jackson, was designed by Mr. O'Donovan of Virginia and executed by Maurice J. Power at his National Art Foundry in New York, while the granite which forms the pedestal was furnished from a North Carolina quarry by Lineham.*

Maurice J. Power and his National Art Foundry were undoubtedly Northern, and the sculptor's office was in New York. The granite was from a North Carolina quarry, however, and the sculptor was, as identified in the article, "of Virginia." William Ran-

178. Oakdale Cemetery. Hebrew Cemetery gate, 1855.

dolph O'Donovan was born in Preston County, Virginia, in 1844, although he later established a studio in New York. O'Donovan was a nationally known sculptor, noted for his portrait busts and bas reliefs. Securing his services for the Wilmington work indicated the intent of the Ladies Memorial Association to secure the best.

The monument was a conspicuous piece of art and gained wide attention. The *Star* for May 3, 1874, reprinted W. J. Woodward's description of a visit to Oakdale, written for the New York newspaper *The South*:

On an elevated mound was a pedestal whose base was granite, and die and cornice marble, probably ten or twelve feet high. On the base of this pedestal the simple inscription "To the Confederate dead" and on the front and rear faces of the die bas reliefs in bronze of Generals Lee and "Stonewall" Jackson. Poised on the pedestal, a bronze figure some six feet in height, representing a Confederate in full dress uniform and in the position of "at rest." This monument looks modest, yet nothing could be more grand. It is perfect, and the position it occupies is very appropriate.

The monument was indeed then much more grand than it is now, for it faced the cemetery entrance. One entered the gates and began the even climb to the hill where the marker stood, all the while under the gaze of the soldier atop his pedestal. Something of the effect can be recreated by going to the base of the hill and turning at the Masonic plot toward the monument, but with the change in entrance and the destruction of James F. Post's stone gateposts, iron gate, and mansard gatehouse, the surprise and frame of the approach were lost. The Ladies Memorial Association later merged with the United Daughters of the Confederacy, Cape Fear chapter

179. Oakdale Cemetery. Marshburn plot fence, 1857.

number 3. The monument, fence, and landscaping of the plot are still well maintained by that group.

A fine introduction to the cast-iron of Oakdale, the fence around the Confederate plot seems to have been erected c. 1870, but there is much earlier dated iron in the cemetery. Among the best is the delicate iron arched gate to Hebrew Cemetery (fig. 178) with the legend "Opened March 6, 5615—1855." The iron fences of the French and Murphy plots are from 1856, while those around the Meares and Marshburn plots are dated 1857. The Marshburn fence (fig. 179) is a vining grape; the others are in several designs from vining oak to much more classical motifs. The Meares gate has an arcaded design with clustered columns and foliar decoration. Within the iron of the Marshburn gate two lambs lie beneath a weeping willow tree. The Stemmerman iron, c. 1868, (see color plate 8) is yet another notable example of the fine cast iron at Oakdale.

Undated fences worth noting include the lyre fence of the Peden plot, the fence with stone posts and chains of the Martin plot, and the fence of the Stevenson plot. Iron furniture includes finely detailed chairs in the Van Amringe and Solomon plots; a cast-iron grapevine settee in the Bailey lot; and the woven wire settee made by "Howard and Morse, New York" in the Mohn lot. Furniture designs include grape, ivy, and oak leaves along with fern and other organic designs. Found in the yellow fever area are the Sarah King cast-iron cross and the Agnes Slick cast-iron cross with its trefoil ends. Miss Slick died February 8, 1866, and the crosses probably were made around that date. The cemetery is the best place in the state to study the mid-nineteenth century use of cast-iron and the number of designs available. It is likely that much of it was locally cast by Hart & Bailey/Wilmington Iron Works.

The yellow-fever area, 1862, with its few markers and open character, and Hebrew Cemetery, with

180. Oakdale Cemetery. Duncan Cameron marker. c. 1790.

crowded markers and enclosing fence, are two of the large special-use graveyards within Oakdale. A Chevra Kadisha was organized in 1852 for proper burial rites for the Jewish dead in Wilmington. On March 6, 1855, they dedicated the Hebrew Cemetery portion of Oakdale, with Rabbi Isaac Loeser of Philadelphia officiating. In 1894 James F. Post's account books show that he was paid for laying out walks in the section. As already mentioned, its cast-iron fence and gate have no counterparts in Wilmington. The delicacy of the workmanship of the arch and the massiveness of the "Hebrew Cemetery" marking are in sharp contrast.

Among the more interesting stones within the section is that to Arthur Bluethenthal. It features a brass palm frond atop a low flat-topped stone with a Lafayette Flying Corps symbol on the face. Ironically, that emblem featured not only an American Indian headdress but a swastika as well. Bluethenthal was the first Wilmington man killed in World War I. He had joined the American Field Service as an ambulance driver on May 16, 1916, and subsequently the Lafayette Flying Corps. He was killed in action on June 5, 1918. Bluethenthal, a sergeant and pilot, was in an air battle when killed. The Wilmington airport was named Bluethenthal Field in his honor. His story was also included in the 1958 movie *Lafayette Escadrille*.

The Meyer-Bear mausoleum, with massive granite walls and brass door, is a fine monument. It was erected by Meir's Marble and Granite Works, a Wilmington firm, in the early twentieth century. Curbing and stonework in the Rheinstein and Bluethenthal lots, 1900, is by Tucker Bros., also a Wilmington firm.

Another of the special-interest areas is the Masonic plot, near the old entrance to the cemetery. The area contains what is probably the oldest marker in the cemetery, that of Duncan Cameron (fig. 180), erected about 1790 by his "surviving parents." Cameron, who seems to have been from Greenock, North Britain, and to have been a cooper, died December 7, 1790, at the age of twenty-two. The fantastic sandstone marker is carved with Masonic emblems, and it ranks with the best of the existing Wilmington stonework/sculpture. It was undoubtedly carved in England and is more evocative of an English country churchyard burial ground than one on this side of the Atlantic. A Wilmington newspaper for November 27, 1909, carried news of the discovery of the Cameron marker:

While excavating yesterday afternoon for the new residence to be erected by Mr. Frank L. Huggins on the vacant lot at the east side of Fourth, between Market and Dock streets, several workmen unearthed a tombstone. The stone bore an inscription and was buried about a foot and a half beneath the surface level. The stone is about five feet in length and three feet wide. When found it was lying in a horizontal position about two feet below the ground.

The inscription on the stone is as follows and it is perfectly legible with the exception of one or two words: "In memory of Duncan Cameron, . . . to Malcolm Cameron; Cooper in Greenock, North Britain, Who Died Dec. 7th, 1790, Aged 22 Years. To Whose Memory this is Erected by his Surviving Parents." The monument is a slab of brown-stone. On the reverse side there is the Latin inscription, "Sit Lux et Lux Fuit." Translation of the Latin is "Let There be Light and There was Light."

The bones of deceased were found lying beneath the stone. These were carefully collected and will probably be re-interred in consecrated grounds. . . . The place where the stone and bones were found is just across the street from the present St. James Church graveyard. One citizen stated today that he remembered when there was a dozen or more tomb-stones in close contiguity to the one uncovered yesterday afternoon by the workmen.

The bones were subsequently reburied in Oakdale with Masonic ceremony, and the marker reerected.

Edward Bishop Dudley's monument, octagonal on a granite base, is one of a large number of signed markers in Oakdale. It is marked "R. E. Launitz, New York." Dudley, who died October 30, 1855, was the first elected governor of North Carolina.

"Gaddess, Baltimore" was the carver of the Edward Swift DeRosset marker. It is a round arched stone with a naturalistic floral bouquet and a rifle. DeRosset died December 30, 1861. The stone carries the legends "Aged 17 years, Only a Private," and "Faithful until death."

A somewhat better known Civil War casualty, and hardly a private, is also buried at Oakdale. Rose O'Neil Greenhow's marker is a stone plaque with a cross atop. Mrs. Greenhow—who at the beginning of the Civil War lived in Washington across Lafayette Park from the White House—gathered information on Union troop movements and plans and passed it along to Confederate forces across the Potomac from Washington, D. C. Later arrested, Mrs. Greenhow was expelled from the Union and became a European celebrity. She was drowned while leaving a ship in September 1864 off Fort Fisher. The ship had run aground while attempting to penetrate the blockade of Wilmington, and Mrs. Greenhow left it to avoid possible Union capture. Bags of gold strapped around her body are said to have caused the drowning. Her funeral was held in the St. Thomas the Apostle Church, and the stone erected here bears the notation "a bearer of dispatches to the Confederate Government."

Paddison, Pretlow, and Anthony are names in one family plot, unique because it contains nine identical grave markers that were erected from the 1860s to the 1970s. Stones are upright and have rounded tops and scroll sides. Erected in a straight line, their bearing evokes a sense of order and military precision that is not shared by the surrounding cemetery.

A number of the Oakdale markers were sizable enough and obvious enough to rate large amounts of newspaper space. One of these was the marker to Dr. J. Francis King, erected in September of 1880. Dr. King, born in Beaufort, was a Confederate surgeon who settled in Wilmington in 1865 and built a large and devoted practice. In ill health, he left Wilmington on August 13, 1879, to travel to Saratoga, New York, to recuperate. He remained there until October, when he went to New York visiting various hospitals, doctors, medical colleges, etc. He died at 1 Washington Square in December 1879. The *Star* described the monument erected to his memory in its September 12, 1880, edition:

The erection of the monument to the late Dr. J. Francis King, heretofore alluded to, has been completed. It is of blue granite, from Columbia, S.C. . . . On the front panel is a record of birth, birthplace, age and death of Dr. King; and on the right and left sides appropriate inscriptions, one of which is "Erected by His Friends and Patients as a Tribute of Their Respect." It is a handsome monument, and attests the high esteem in which the deceased was held by his many friends in the community.

The marker was erected under the supervision of John Maunder.

Maunder was also the artist for the Zebulon Latimer marker. Its erection was noted by the March 8, 1883, *Star*: "A large and handsome monument has been erected in Oakdale Cemetery, over the remains of the late Zebulon Latimer, of this city, Mr. John Maunder, the Wilmington marble artist, who was employed to put it up, having completed the work yesterday morning. It is of the finest Maine granite, highly polished, of the moslem style, weighs about 17,000 pounds, and is about eight feet high, while the bottom base is seven by four feet in diameter."

The Murchison plot, with its well-developed site and several monuments, is typical of the large lots and monuments maintained by the most affluent of the Wilmington families. The Murchison monument was erected in 1883. A Wilmington newspaper noted the construction in its June 15, 1883, issue:

We had the particulars on Saturday, but delayed noticing the fact, of the erection of a magnificent monument in Oakdale Cemetery to the memory of the late Capt. David R. Murchison, formerly one of our most prominent business men and leading citizens, the finishing touches to which were given it on Saturday afternoon. It was made of the finest Connecticut granite, at the establishment of Mr. James Sharkey, near the entrance to Greenwood Cemetery, Brooklyn. It came on the steamer Regulator, *and was successfully transported from the steamer to the cemetery grounds by Mr. Michael Carroll, for which he received the sum of $100. The base of the monument measures 6 feet 6 inches square and rests upon a foundation consisting of 207 ½ feet of solid masonry, which was built by the Cemetery Company, under the direction of Superintendent Donlan. There are twenty-four separate pieces in the monument, and it stands twenty-two feet high from the level of the surface, being surmounted by the statue of "Hope" in the person of a lovely female figure, resting upon the representation of an anchor, the figure being 6 feet 6 inches in height. There is not a flaw to be discovered in the monument, and everything about the figure, including eyes, hair, features, drapery, etc., is completed and faultless. The bottom base, which (as we stated) measures 6 feet 6 inches square, weighs 4 ½ tons; the second base bears the family name in large raised letters with polished faces; while base No. 3 has polished faces, with the inscription on the north face, engraved in raised letters, "DAVID R. MURCHISON, Born December 5, 1837; Died February 28th, 1882." Then comes the "Die." with four polished columns with carved bands, the corners surmounted by handsome carved cups. . . .*

This, we understand, is the second monument of its particular kind designed in this country. It is all American work, and one year was consumed in its construction; the total cost as it now stands being about six thousand dollars. It arrived here Tuesday, the first stone was put upon the wharf Wednesday, and was up and complete Saturday afternoon.

The lot, which is to be beautiful by the addition of all the modern improvements, is beautifully located, being almost on a line with and south of the Confederate monument, with a fine open back view.

The monument—which weighs 38,000 pounds—is no doubt the handsomest one in the State.

The Abbie E. Chadbourn marker was also the handiwork of the Tucker firm. Under the heading "A Handsome Monument," a Wilmington newspaper reported its erection in its December 22, 1880, edition:

Mr. George Chadbourn has recently erected to the memory of his lamented wife, the late Mrs. Abbie E. Chadbourn, one of the handsomest monuments to be found in Oakdale Cemetery. It is of the style known as cottage monuments and was built at the marble works of Mr. H. A. Tucker, at No. 310 North Front Street. The entire monument is of granite, that for the base and cap having come from Biddeford, Me., and that for the die from Quincy, Massachusetts. It is eleven feet in height, and is four by six feet at the base. The base and cap are dressed plain but the die is polished, being ornamented at the ends and sides by polished columns which are surmounted by beautifully carved Corinthian caps. The top of the monument is surmounted by an urn which is beautifully polished and handsomely carved.

The plain marker to the memory of Mauger London and his family was the work of a New York firm. On January 23, 1901, the *Messenger* identified the firm and described the marker:

Mr. L. T. Coykendall, of New York, of firm of Presbrey & Coykendall, designers and manufacturers of monuments and mausoleums, is here to superintend the erection of a sarcophagus monument on the lot of Mauger London, in Oakdale Cemetery, where the prominent lawyer and citizen lies buried with the members of his family.

Messrs. Presbrey & Coykendall have the contract to erect this monument, and it has arrived here by steamer and is now being transferred to the cemetery. It will be placed in position probably by tomorrow.

The monument is a very handsome one, but of plain design, in keeping with the well known wishes of Mr. London. It is made of the very finest Barre, Vermont, granite, and will be mounted on a granite die with four polished sides. The monument itself will be six feet in height, its length will be five feet six inches, and its breadth three feet six inches.

On the face of the monument in raised polished letters is this simple inscription: "Mauger London, 1812–1894."

On February 6, 1907, the *Star* reported the erection of the marker to Col. Thomas S. Evans: "Mr. Harry E. Rupprecht, expert monument designer of Washington, D.C. is in the city and on yesterday superintended the erection in Oakdale Cemetery of a sarcophagus memorial to the memory of the late Col. Thomas S. Evans, the former well known marine lawyer of Wilmington and one of the city's prominent citizens. It is a handsome granite design, five feet in height."

In the Bacon family plot, both the family marker and the marker to the architect Henry Bacon (fig.

181. Oakdale Cemetery. Henry Bacon marker. 1924.

181) are after designs by Henry Bacon himself. It appears they both derive from his 1880s drawing of the "The Tomb of Publius Varius," at Assos, Turkey. Bacon's drawing, signed "Henry Bacon, Del." was included in the report on the *Investigations at Assos* . . . , part 1, published in 1902 by the Archaeological Institute of America. The report was edited for publication by Bacon's brother Francis, who was a member of the expeditions. The large, upright family stone erected in 1919 was designed and commissioned by Henry Bacon. His own 1924 marker, a smooth stone stela with a delicately cut palmate top and a bead and reel border, is plainly incised "Henry Bacon/1866–1924/The architect of the Lincoln Memorial at Washington." The design of this marker is said to have been patterned after a drawing found on his desk following his death. It is almost identical to a drawing of his of a stela on the Troad, now in the Boston Museum of Art, but it also closely resembles a stela in the Assos drawing. On a visit to the cemetery (with daughter-in-law Virginia Jennewein) Carl Paul Jennewein noted that while working with Picirille Brothers, New York, he had carved the Henry Bacon marker. Jennewein's work is internationally known.

Several other markers are also finely designed and carved. Across the cemetery from the Bacon plot is the 1918 grave of George Trask, Sr., and his wife Emma Borneman. The headstone is long, low, and rectangular. In square panels at the ends are finely detailed engaged cabbages. The center portion of the monument is a rectangular projecting marble slab. It is decorated by the single word *Trask* and by a carved stalk of corn with detail of the tassel and silk of the two ears clearly visible. The cabbages and corn memoralize the truck-farming endeavors of the Trask family. Beginning in the 1880s, the family were pioneers in establishing the area as a truck-farming center, with lettuce, cabbage, corn, and other vegetables shipped by rail and water to consumers in the north.

Near the Trask marker, stairs leading up to the family plot where Thomas Edward and Amanda Nutt Parsley Sprunt are buried are labeled "T. E. Sprunt." Their grave is marked by a large, flat marble base above which stands a tall Greek marble slab. Anthemion antefix crown the marker at apex and corners. In high relief, within a hollow of the slab face is an angel draped in flowing clothing, her body resting in the fold of her wings. The flowers in her arms, and her face, hands, and feet are in extraordinary detail. The sculptor was Frank H. Packer, a pupil of Saint-Gaudens who also worked with Daniel Chester French on the seated Lincoln in Washington's Lincoln Memorial. This early twentieth-century monument is one of three Wilmington markers by Packer. The George Davis statue on Market Street (fig. 121) and the Confederate Memorial on South Third Street are also his work.

182. Oakdale Cemetery. Murchison mausoleum. K. M. Murchison, architect, c. 1898.

Several fine mausoleums deserve mention. Among these are the Moran crypt, reveted into its hillside; the Pembroke Jones brick mausoleum with its Neoclassical Revival massing and detailing; the Vollers tomb with its stained glass; the Murchison mausoleum (fig. 182), and the Bear mausoleum.

The Murchison mausoleum was described in the April 11, 1898, *Dispatch*.

The mausoleum for Colonel K. M. Murchison which has been in process of construction at Oakdale cemetery for some time, has been completed and formally turned over to the owner by the contractors.

The mausoleum is the first of its kind ever constructed here and naturally excites much interest.

The exterior is constructed entirely of Mt. Airy granite and the interior of North Carolina marble, highly polished, and the floor of Mosaic tiling.

It is 15 feet 10 inches by 21 feet and is 22 feet high.

The floor of the mausoleum is several feet above the ground and spacious steps lead to it.

Arched above the doorway, is chiseled the name in block letters, "Murchison" and above the door surmounting the tip is a large cross set in scroll work. On the four corners are scroll ornaments or antefixes. Surmounting the rear is a large plain stone cross. A small window of marble is set in the rear wall, . . . stained glass lights and stained glass windows ornament the front door. Inside are twelve catacombs of marble made to receive twelve caskets.

The work will compare favorably with any of its class in any of the northern cemeteries and reflects great credit on the builders, Messrs. H. A. Tucker & Bro., the contractors.

Col. Murchison stated that he wished only North Carolina stone used in its construction which was complied with and Mr. Tucker states that no finer effect could have been obtained with any other stone. It is a beautiful design, and great ornament to the cem-

etery and cost over $10,000. Col. Murchison's son, Mr. K. M. Murchison, Jr., was one of the designing architects.

K. M. Murchison, Jr., later gained fame as a New York architect and either designed or consulted in the design of several Wilmington buildings.

Among the well-landscaped plots are the Kenan plot—Mary Lily Flagler Bingham is interred here—with its stone steps and landscaped surround and its 1937 cross/stone for the Wise family. The Bulluck plot, a landscaped garden with walls, benches, entrance gates, flagstone walks, dogwood, and azalea, is another of the fine landscaped areas.

The Graham Kenan plot is perhaps the epitome of such areas. It is a well-manicured Neoclassical Revival lot surrounded by a stone balustrade and retaining wall to the back. Shrubbery hides the lot from the passerby, but the entrance stairs that curve up the terrace from the sides opposite the mausoleum provide a provocative peek. The marble tomb has a molded cornice, egg-and-dart and dentil courses, and a crossetted architrave over the entrance that is topped by a cherub relief and a panel enclosing the name "Graham Kenan." The mausoleum facade is also decorated with classical courses and Ionic engaged columns. Two urns flank the doorway. The shield on the marble door is of blank metal and reads "Viva ut Vivas." This may be translated "he lives so that you may live." Opposite the mausoleum and on the entrance side between the two stairways is a stone bench with reverse scroll arms and a curved back. The bench, which sinks into the foliage behind it, has the inscription "The tree is known by its fruits and the noble family by a noble man." Paving before the bench is in a radiating pattern. The lot provides a marked contrast to the rest of the lots at this intersection. A hugh live oak shelters the crossroads and the overgrown Zebulon Latimer lot that lies opposite, with its blocklike stone coffin, is more typical.

Other markers that ought to be mentioned include the one for Augusta Endicott who "died July 7, 1847," with its Gothic marble pinnacle on a molded base; Annie DeRosset, the first grave in the new cemetery in 1855, with a lamb on her tombstone and a rose on her footstone; the Susan Wright marker, with a log draped in garlands and set in a pile of stones; the Van Bokkelen marker, with its stepped octagonal base, carved octagonal column, and faced urn; the tall monument for J. A. Springer, with engaged columns, wreath, and urn decoration; Joshua G. Walker marker with its high rounded arch; the Harriet Taylor grave, outlined in stone to indicate the bed in which she sleeps; and the R. Lewis Litgen obelisk.

Oakdale is more than an outdoor museum, for it displays a history of North Carolina design awareness, taste, and devotion to art that is unmatched elsewhere.

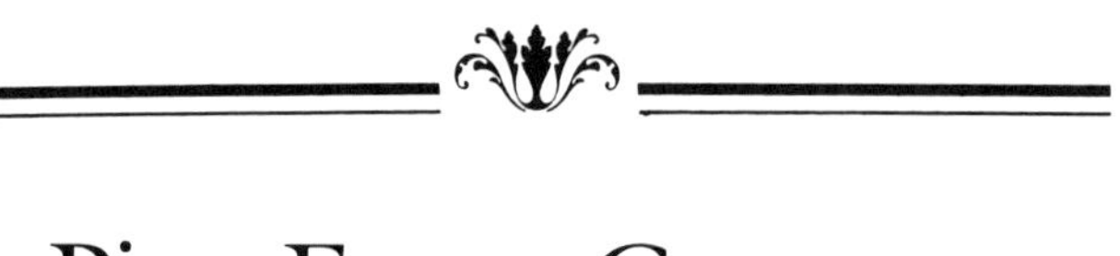

Pine Forest Cemetery

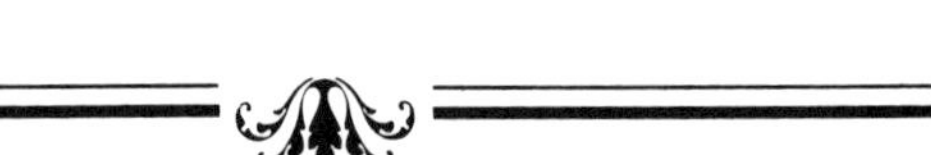

North end of North Sixteenth Street
1860–69

In 1860 the commissioners of the town of Wilmington purchased fifteen acres adjacent to Oakdale Cemetery for use as a black burying ground. It had been illegal since 1855 to bury within the city limits, and it is likely burials had already begun in the area purchased. Stones from the 1840s and 1850s are common at Pine Forest and may have been transferred here.

When black Representative G. W. Price introduced a bill in the North Carolina House in 1869 asking for incorporation of a Wilmington cemetery, it was with the Pine Forest property in mind. The bill passed, and the burying ground was incorporated as chapter 150 of the General Assembly Acts of 1868–69. The act noted that Duncan Holmes,

Owen Berney, David Sadgwar, William Kellogg, James Green, Solomon Nash, Henry Taylor, Alfred Hargrave, Hezekiah Reid "and their associates . . . are hereby constituted body politic and corporate by the name and style of the Pine Forest Cemetery Company, and . . . may acquire, take and hold a lot or tract of land containing not more than twenty acres for the purpose of establishing a burial ground at or near the City of Wilmington."

Though the act of incorporation does not identify the company as a black organization, it is clear from subsequent events that the purpose of the incorporation was to allow the Pine Forest Cemetery Company to take over the previously purchased black city cemetery. The company soon petitioned the city for a deed. The *Star* reported on November 30, 1869, that the petition had been referred to the mayor. No immediate action seems to have been taken. On September 6, 1870, a correspondent for the paper wrote:

> *The city authorities, we learn, are soon to make a deed to the Trustees of Pine Forrest* [sic] *Cemetery of the land purchased for that purpose in 1860, and it is expected that the improvements on the grounds will commence at once. There is no reason why this cemetery should not vie with Oakdale in beauty and adornment. We suggest a plan for its improvement, which we have heard is frequently adopted in the New England states. That is, let those who are unable to give money, give one, two or three days labor, as they can best afford. In such a case* labor *is* money, *and counts just as good as cash. We say to our colored people that respect for the dead and a well kept Cemetery are unmistakable signs of civilization and cultivation.*

The newspaper seems to have been campaigning for transfer of the deed. On August 26 it had railed against the condition of Pine Forest, noting that it was "in a most deplorable condition. The lots are overgrown with wild flowers and stubborn weeds and the entire grounds are fast becoming subject to their control." Evidently both the writer and the Pine Forest trustees saw black ownership as one way to insure adequate care for the area.

When the ground was finally deeded to the Pine Forest Company in 1871, the property was described in the deed as:

> *Beginning at an old stake on an old mill dam being the south east corner of Oakdale cemetery . . . thence along said old dam . . . till it strikes the mill creek thence up the creek with the meanders thereof to a point due east from the mouth of a small branch or ravine, thence west across the marsh of said creek to the eastern outlet or mouth of said ravine thence westwardly with the meander of said ravine to its source on or near the Old Race track, thence west . . . to a stake . . . containing 15 acres.*

A considerable amount of work would have been necessary to put the series of mill dams, races, ponds, creeks, marshes, and ravines into usable cemetery form. Evidently that work was undertaken in accordance with a plan for the trapezoidal site, for on January 14, 1872, Pine Forest Cemetery secretary Joseph E. Sampson advertised in the *Star*: "if any one have found or seen the Plan of the Grounds of Pine Forest Cemetery they will confer a great favor on many interested person by leaving it with the Secretary."

One immediate problem for the company was access to the cemetery. Initially this seems to have been by Miller Street to Oakdale Cemetery, then through Oakdale to Pine Forest. In 1875 the city opened North Seventeenth Street to the cemetery from Market Street, but it remained a hazardous route. It was not until 1888 that a plank walk was finally advertised from North Fourth Street along Red Cross [Rankin Street] to Pine Forest.

The Pine Forest Company attracted the interest and cooperation of the black community, and many prominent blacks were associated with it. In addition to Sampson, John G. Norwood and Charles E. Cleapor, among others, served as secretaries. Members of the board of directors at various times were Alfred Howe and other members of the Howe family, Duncan Holmes, Alexander Price, Sandy Moore, James K. Cutlar, Edward Dickson, J. P. Green, Joseph J. Jones, Lewis LeGrand—all before 1885. Later boards were composed of equally prominent citizens.

In addition to sale of lots and use of donated labor as recommended by the *Star*, the trustees also tried other means of raising money. One suggested activity, aimed specifically at funds for erecting a lodge or chapel at Pine Forest, was a concert by choirs of the black churches. The suggestion was reported in the *Star* on November 24, 1875. Considerable progress on the cemetery was evidently made. In the 1883 publication *Information and statistics respecting Wilmington, North Carolina, being a report by the*

President of the Produce Exchange presented to its members, April, 1883, James Sprunt called Pine Forest "well situated and carefully attended." The *Star* for April 15, 1884, noted that "Pine Forest (colored) cemetery now has a nice lodge in its midst." In 1888 a writer for the paper reported that "there is a commendable neatness and taste manifest in the care of the grounds."

The cemetery was evidently an intensely used one, though figures on its use are difficult to obtain. In 1877, one year for which they are available, there were 242 Pine Forest burials. Of these, 103 were adults, 121 were children under twelve, and 18 were stillbirths.

Today's entrance to Pine Forest is through a 1938 iron spiral archway, supported on brick pillars. Frequently the Pine Forest Cemetery name, worked into the iron arch, casts shadow detail that transfers the name from the arch to the street. A plaque on the gate reads "Pine Forrest *[sic]* Cemetery, Inc., 1861–1938, Board of Directors, K. T. Boland, Pres., C. T. Wright, Sec., L. C. Middleton, Treas., J. W. McRae [and] W. A. Green, custodian, N. C. Taylor, Thos. Sweet."

Sections of brick-paved roads survive in several parts of the cemetery, as does some good cast-iron. The iron includes the well-detailed settee in the Gilmore plot; the "Cincinnati Iron Fence Co. Inc." fence, early twentieth century, around the Jas. E. Howard plot; the iron fence with open posts and fine workmanship around the Thos. Rivera plot; and the narrow plot surrounded by iron fence with delicate woven wire and finial topped posts of the plot of Eva Wilson, 1891, and Jacob Scott, 1881.

There are several "sweep yard" plots, with the sand raked or swept clean, and also a number of graves decorated with conch shells. Perhaps the best of these, combining both a sweep yard and shell decorations are graves in the "Lott *[sic]* of P. C. Smith." Such grave decorations are shared by a number of North Carolina coastal settlers and by many residents of Appalachia, as well as by residents of such faraway Pacific areas as Guam and American Samoa.

There are many excellent trees in Pine Forest, including sizable long leaf and other varieties of pine. The magnolia tree in the Yarborough plot is one of the largest and most magnificent of its species in the area. The gardenia and other plants in the Fisher plot are notable, as are the azalea and magnolia in the Lofton plot; the azalea in the Pearsall plot; the camellia in the Cox-McRae plot; the dogwood in the Green plot; and the red cedar in the Moody plot.

Among the notable blacks buried at Pine Forest is John E. Taylor, deputy collector of customs for the Port of Wilmington. Taylor also operated a local shoe store. Dr. James Francis Shober, who died on January 6, 1889, is also at Pine Forest. Shober, born in Salem, North Carolina, in 1853, graduated from Lincoln University in 1875 and received his M.D. degree from Howard University Medical College in 1878. He was the first black physician in the area, an elder of the Chestnut Street Presbyterian Church, and an influential community leader. Dr. James B. Dudley, a Wilmington native who attained national fame as an educator and was president of North Carolina College in Greensboro, is buried here, as are several members of the Howe family, who were contractors and builders. Alfred Howe was a member of St. Mark's Episcopal Church, 220 North Sixth Street (fig. 99), and aided in its construction. In the late nineteenth century he was a sought-after local builder, constructing such dwellings as the Mary Jane Langdon House, 408 Market Street (fig. 122). The Alfred Howe plot has a marble marker in the center of a well-kept area that identifies A. Howe as having "died Oct. 6, 1892, aged 74 years." The original stone to Howe is now almost buried, as are several other older stones in the plot, which is surrounded by granite posts with metal pipe fencing. Valentine Howe, Sr., was also a member of St. Mark's. When he died in 1905, his firm was constructing the annex to James Walker Hospital (now demolished), a major building contract. He was a member of the North Carolina legislature, captain of the Cape Fear Fire Engine Company, president of the State Firemen's Union, alderman of the Fifth Ward, an Odd Fellow, and a Mason.

One of the finest stones in any of the Wilmington cemeteries is that to Charles Wingate (fig. 183), "who departed this life Nov. 20th, 1862, Aged 36 years." The stone is deeply carved on a heavily molded base. The legend is carried on a scroll surrounded by a border of dogwood flowers and leaves. The rear is carved as well and contains a tribute from Wingate's wife Margaret:

I could weep when I think of those joys that are past.
I could weep when I think that those joys could not last.
But hope sends a vision that's gentle and fair,
And bids me look upward and cease to despair.

183. Pine Forest Cemetery. Wingate stone, 1862.

Among the naturalistic markers, the rustic stone tree over the grave of Lucy Robinson is notable. Erected in 1896, the marker has permanent ferns growing around its base and a stone dove perched on one of the tree limbs.

One of the more interesting markers is that of a family pet. It is a block of marble with a carved stone dog atop. It bears the legend: "Jip Jones, Born Sep. 23, 1890, Died May 18, 1901. This was the only dog we know that attended church on Sunday. He was loved by everybody who knew him."

Among the folk markers, the cast-concrete marker with its cross and wreath erected to E. D. Mosley is a fine piece of folk art. Its legend reads "In memory of Farther [*sic*], E. D. Mosley, Mother, Carrie Mosley, made by E. Mosley, Son of above names."

Thomas R. Mask, M. D., who died in 1911, is buried in a large corner lot with a tall, round, cone-topped marker. Stone posts, a chain fence, and a cast-iron settee are featured. The Whiteman plot with its stone surround and clean-swept surface has an early-twentieth-century urn-topped marker on a stepped base. Maggie Whiteman, 1912, John H. Whiteman, 1917, and Hester Whiteman, 1902, are all memoralized by the impressive marker. Charity and Thomas Rivera are remembered by a tall obelisk on a pedestal over a stepped base.

Fine symbolism is used on many of the markers. Eddie, son of Jane Fleeming, who "died Nov. 2d, 1870" has a marker (fig. 184) with inverted torches and a broken rose, both signifying death. The grave of Laura Elizabeth Nixon, 1930, is surrounded with marble sides, foot, and head—the bed in which she lies in death. The headboard bears the epitaph: "The grave itself a garden is where loveliest flowers abound." The 1889 stone to Hattie E. Wescott features a deeply carved sheaf of wheat, a symbol for life. There is perhaps no better symbolism in any of the area markers than that on the stone to Lorenzo

184. Pine Forest Cemetery. Fleeming marker, 1870.

Bow Kennedy, "Born 1881, Died 1889." The eight-year-old-Kennedy is memoralized by a carved rose in bud, its stem bent, leaves drooping, and bud withered without opening.

Many of the markers also provided the dead with permanent garlands of flowers. The deep carving of the flowers on the Lydia Harriss stone, 1855, gives them a vibrance and vigorousness that almost equals that of the Wingate stone. Another of the finely carved stones with flower and scroll surround is that of Priscilla Burney, also 1855. The carving on the 1844 marker to Jane Howe, daughter of Anthony Howe, is outstanding, as are the carved wreaths encasing the single word *sacred* on the Margaret Hale stone, 1862, and the draped stage on the Minerva Green marker, 1870. The Joanna Rourk marker, 1889, features oak leaves and acorns.

It is likely that many of the 1840–60 stones were made by one stonecarver. Though none are signed, many of the cited ones have similarities in the quality of the symbolism and the depth and accuracy of the carving.

Some of the stones contain biographical information. The marker "Sacred to the memory of Solomon W. Nash who departed this life June 25, 1846, aged 67 years . . . " has a long inscription, difficult to decipher but part biographical. Prince Leeboo, who died December 23, 1858, at the age of seventy-two was "a member of the M.E. Church and a class leader for many years and died in the faith." Rev. W. H. Banks, who died April 9, 1881, was "pastor of Ebenezer Baptist Church for 16 years." The stone of Rachel Freeman, 1930, was erected "In sacred and loving memory of one whose life was dedicated to the elevation of Humanity." One imagines that Mrs. Freeman was a tireless worker for dignity and equal human rights.

If these words do indeed refer in some way to civil rights or to race, they may be the only references to the subject on stones in this cemetery. No mention of slavery or free Negroes was found on any of the stones here, though such references are quite common in black cemeteries. There is perhaps a reason why the information on the stones is so bland. It may have evolved from cemetery policy or from some other sense of community. However it happened, it is an interesting and unusal aspect of a black cemetery that contains pre–Civil War graves, as well as a large number of graves from the war period and immediately after.

Bellevue Cemetery

North Seventeenth Street and Princess Place Drive
1876–78

When the Bellevue Cemetery Company filed incorporation plans in 1872, the incorporators noted that their purpose was to enable persons: "chiefly those of limited means, to secure a proper and suitable burial place for their dead; to have such cemetery properly disclosed and ornamented with shrubbery and evergreens and to keep it so beautiful as to render it a fit burial place for the families of those who may become stockholders of the shares of the company or the purchasers of lots therefrom."

That aim was not accomplished immediately. "It is desired," a Wilmington newspaper noted on April 25, 1876: "that all subscribers to the capital stock of the Bellevue Cemetery Company will meet at the Second Baptist Church this evening, prepared to pay the first installment due upon their stock. This is a new cemetery, which is about to be established for the benefit of persons of limited means. It is to be located on a ten-acre tract of land. The laying out of the cemetery grounds is expected to be commenced tomorrow."

Evidently the cemetery was begun at that time, though its charter was not received from the North Carolina legislature until January 26, 1877. That document stated in very explicit terms the reasons for the new cemetery. Its preamble reads: "Whereas, in the city of Wilmington, the means for interring the dead in a manner adapted to the present enlightened public sentiment is very limited, except it be attended with expense too great for men of moderate means to sustain; and whereas, it is the desire of this class of citizens to afford their deceased relatives, friends, and all other persons, a place of burial."

Oakdale had been developed from 1852 as a burial place for the prominent and well-to-do citizens of Wilmington. When the city adopted an ordinance in 1855 to prohibit burials within the city limits, even the bodies from church cemeteries were disinterred and removed to Oakdale. Though St. James Cemetery located on the Southwest corner of South Fourth Street and Market Street, was not removed, burials there ceased.

Lots at Oakdale had sold well, expensive monuments were erected, and it was a virtual monopoly. This was a major reason for establishing Bellevue, for many of the incorporators of the new cemetery—with names such as Manning, McEachern, Bellamy, Taylor, and Canady—would hardly have been considered of moderate means.

Land for the burying ground was acquired by The Bellevue Cemetery Co. in June of 1876 from William A. Wright and Eliza Ann Wright along the north side of the old New Bern Road (Princess Place Drive) and west of Burnt Mill Creek. The 15½ acre site abutted Pine Forest Cemetery and included the area where Green's Battery of Confederate troops had been stationed during the Civil War. The earthwork entrenchments thrown up by the battery must still have been obvious when the area was purchased, though they were soon leveled for the new burial ground. Reminders were unearthed with some frequency, however, for even as late as January 16, 1909, the *Star* reported that a grapeshot dug up at Bellevue was on display in the office of the paper and was "quite a curiosity."

It seems unlikely that Bellevue was professionally designed. It was laid out with considerable attention to detail, however, and with knowledge of cemetery design. Some of the design could have evolved from Oakdale, some from the knowledge and desires of the founders. The surveyors may also have been responsible. The *Star* for June 8, 1876, noted that: "The new Bellevue Cemetery will be open in about a week. It has been surveyed by Messrs. James & Brown. We learn that it will be fenced in immediately, and that lots costing from $30 to $40 will be for sale. The first fifty lots laid off will be for the use of stockholders, when the remainder will be disposed of to the public."

Landscape design in Bellevue seems to have been dictated by topography. The cemetery lodge is at the center and highest point in the area on part of a spine of high land that runs from the entrance northeastward. Land slopes from this to both the southeast and the northwest, and the sections follow this natural slope.

The date of the first burial at Bellevue is not known, but by early 1878 the cemetery had evidently been in use for some time. The *Star* reported on April 16, 1878, that "Bellevue cemetery is assuming quite a handsome appearance, considerable improvements having been made in the grounds." On June 27, it reported that Seventeenth Street was being graded, cleared of roots and stumps, and "will be overlaid with clay ballast, so as to make it hard and compact like Market Street. This improvement is made with special reference, on the part of the authorities, to the convenience and accommodation of funeral processions en route for Bellevue, which have heretofore found the street in question rather a 'hard road to travel.' "

The cemetery lodge, c. 1900 (fig. 185), is the only such surviving structure in the Wilmington cemeteries. Frame, on a brick foundation with overhanging, finial-topped roof, the octagonal structure is an enclosed gazebo with six-over-six sash on seven sides and the entrance door on the eighth. The structure is a fine example of its type.

Among plants originally used in Bellevue were orange trees. The *Star* for October 25, 1904, noted that oranges of a bitter-sweet variety grown quite extensively on the coast of Florida were ripening on a tree at Bellevue. On October 6, 1905, the paper again reported that the tree was bearing. The orange trees have since either died or been removed.

Today Bellevue has no wall, is exposed to street traffic on two sides, and its character retains little of the quiet landscaped park of 1888. The plan, and a significant collection of monuments survives, as do many plants, including arbor vitae, magnolia, gardenia, oleander, azalea, and dogwood. Several massive oaks probably predate the cemetery and were retained when it was laid out. Sizable cypress survive near Burnt Mill Creek. Of the other natives, the spiderwort, naturalized gladiolus, black-eyed Susan, and asparagus are most noticeable. The asparagus, brought into the cemetery in flower arrangements,

185. Bellevue Cemetery. Lodge, c. 1900; Bagley plot.

has sown itself throughout the area, sending up succulent spikes in the spring, which mature to tall showy branches with red berries. In more carefully tended surroundings the asparagus would be checked; here it runs rampant.

Far simpler than Oakdale, Bellevue has little iron work, though the Everitt plot is surrounded by a fine 1887 fence. There is also some tubular iron fencing with iron planters atop iron posts. The undated marker to Mary J. King is a cast-iron cross. The gravestone erected over the grave of Mable Isla Gore in 1898 seems to be unique in the Wilmington cemeteries. It is the only fully developed cast-metal marker located.

Overall, Bellevue markers are simple. There is an angel here and there, but almost no other statuary. In the Bagley plot an angel on one knee prays for an infant who died in 1869 (see fig. 185) and in the Benton plot one is shown comforting an infant, though the 1922 grave is that of a fourteen year old. A cast angel marked Lorena S. Golden, 1899, is fine nineteenth-century folk art.

The 1884 marker for Stephen H. Morton, topped by turned Tuscan columns that support an open vaulted arch with stone cap and urn, and the John S. McEachern marker of 1889 are the largest and most impressive in Bellevue. McEachern was one of the founders of the cemetery and served as secretary/treasurer of the company until his death. Longtime president of the Bellevue Cemetery Company, and another of its founders, John D. Bellamy, Jr., is buried at Oakdale.

Several impressive Woodmen of the World stones are in the cemetery, along with other naturalistic markers. Among the best are the 1887 Bagley marker and two Smith markers of 1898. The Bagley marker (see fig. 185) is more than six feet tall, depicting a truncated tree, as if it had been struck and its top severed by lightning. Stone fern grows from its base, and stone moss covers part of the bark. A section of the upper portion of the tree, fallen in position for a footstone, has a hole in the trunk containing a stone bird nest with two stone eggs. The monument is signed "F. O. Gross, 381 Wabash Avenue, Chicago." The superb 1887 Thomas H. Smith marker is also by Gross. Nearby, the Mary Catherine Smith 1889 marker has a parchment plaque hanging by a rope from a tree limb, all in permanent stone. The stump of a smaller stone tree is the foot marker. Rustic stone planters fashioned to resemble tree limbs are at several places within the cemetery.

Bellevue abounds with the graves of fallen veterans, including at least one hundred and thirty-five Confederates who saw service during the Civil War. It was also a frequent burial place for sailors who died while their ships were in port in Wilmington. Many graves are evocative of the maritime importance of Wilmington as an international port. They include that of the German Conrad Freytag of the steamship *Hohenfels,* who drowned March 16, 1934; the Englishman John Smallwood, who died suddenly aboard the S.S. *Hay Green* on November 13, 1889; the Irishman J. Cards from the steamer *Foxtown Hall,* who drowned May 25, 1913; and many more.

Bellevue also has its share of whimsical and enigmatic grave markers. These include the combined stone of twin brothers B. L. and C. T. Grant, who died within eight months of each other in 1920, at age forty-five. The stone notes that:

As twins to mortal life we came.
As twins we rest together.
As twins we hope to rise again,
As twins with Christ forever

Closer to the entrance is the plot of the Whatsoever Circle of the King's Daughters and Sons. A simple monument in the center is surrounded by more than twenty graves—some marked, some unmarked. The *Star* reported the unveiling of the monument with appropriate ceremony on August 11, 1909, but gives no clue to the origin or the membership of the Whatsoever Circle.

Charles Williams Stewart, born 1869, and William Elmer Stewart, born 1901, who were father and son, rest beneath a single stone. The Stewarts became folk heroes after killing two police officers during a raid on their distillery in Brunswick County. Many claimed the Stewarts had been hounded by the officers and provoked into the killings. In spite of their folk-hero status, both were electrocuted in North Carolina's Central Prison in 1925.

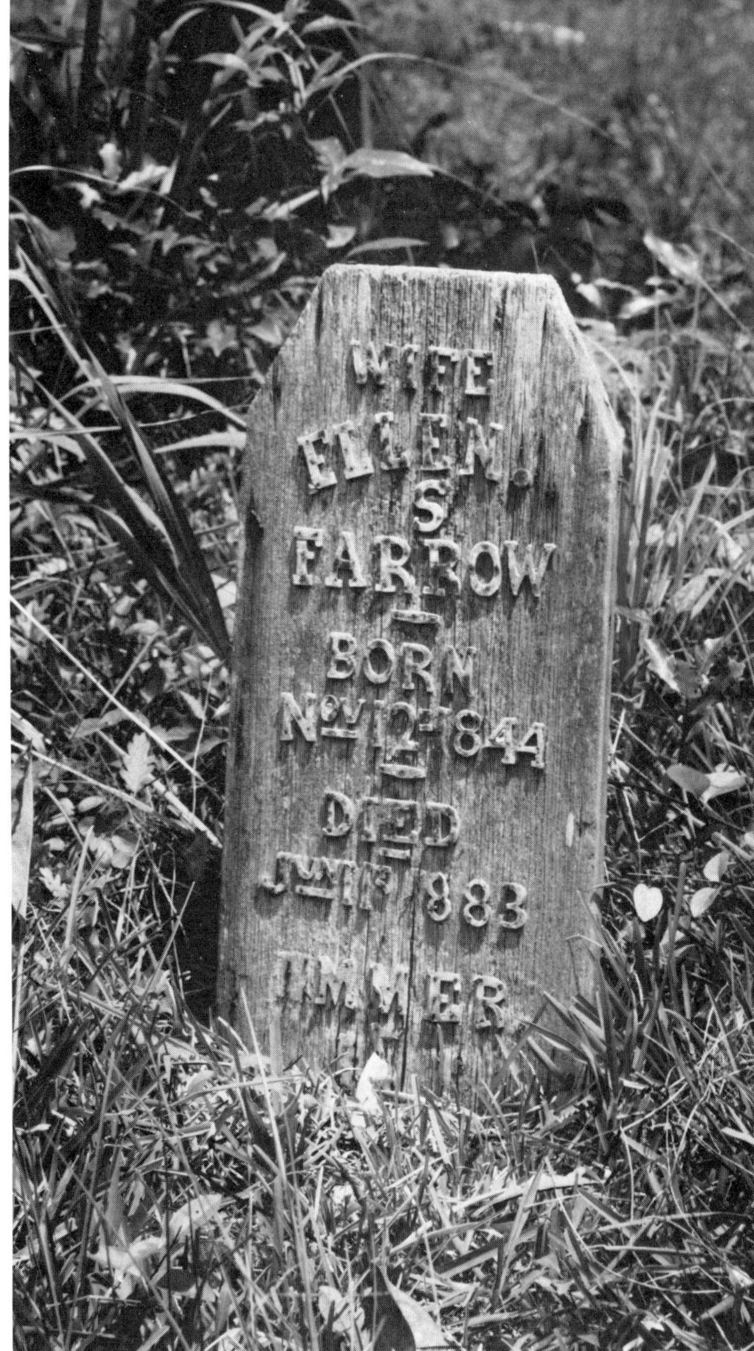

186. Bellevue Cemetery. Farrow marker, 1883.

In the Farrow plot is a wooden slab with shaped head and carefully molded metal letters: "Wife—Ellen S. Farrow, born Nov. 12, 1844, died Jan. 11, 1883—Mother." The Farrow marker (fig 186) is not a purchased marker from an ordinary stonemason, but a tribute of time and artisanship that makes it one of the finest pieces of folk art in the Wilmington cemeteries.

For most Wilmingtonians and for other visitors, Bellevue is unexplored open space. Of those who do discover it, most find it intriguing. Though no longer "properly disclosed" it is "ornamented with shrubbery and evergreens," as stated in the 1872 incorporators' purpose and contains in its collection of markers an impressive sampling of outdoor sculpture and funerary art. Its octagonal cemetery lodge is not only the single survivor of its type in Wilmington, but a rare survivor in any cemetery.

Mary Bridgers Park

Between Chestnut Street and Princess Place Drive, Burnt Mill Creek and North Nineteenth Street
c. 1930

Mary Bridgers Park, adjacent to the Carolina Heights development on the east and northeast, may well have been intended as a park to protect the development from other suburbs and to provide open space. In Burett H. Stephens's 1908 drawing of Carolina Heights, printed in the *Morning Star*, November 8, 1908, the area is shown as wooded and undeveloped. Whether this reflected the actual condition of the area or its intended use is not known. Mary Bridgers did own the land, however, and the Carolina Heights plan stopped short of developing it. Though some of the land is low, marshy, and suitable for limited development at best, much of the area would have been usable for construction.

Whatever Mrs. Bridger's intent, she died in 1910 without having completed her work, and it was not until 1930 that Bridgers' heirs offered the area to the city for park purposes. In that same year the park was surveyed, and the name Mary Bridgers Park was accepted. Additional land was transferred to the city in May of 1938.

Both parcels of land were on the western side of what was known as Green's Mill Pond. The site was one of early mills, one of these was Mr. Green's. Either his mill or some other mill burned, thus giving the creek its later name Burnt Mill Creek. A later steam sawmill erected on the site of the "Burnt Mill" by William Wilson was evidently completed, but the name of the creek or the area was not changed. The *Star* reported on January 9, 1880, that the new steam mill would assume operations on or about February 1.

During the Civil War a series of earthworks and water barriers, intended to protect the city from assault from the east by land, was constructed in the area by Confederate forces.

When the city began clearing and filling in the area c. 1930, Burnt Mill Creek was the eastern boundary of Wilmington. After the city limits were extended east of Burnt Mill Creek on January 1, 1946, negotiation began immediately to secure a dragline for the purpose of deepening and straightening the creek. The intent was both to provide better drainage and to make it possible to improve the area for park usage.

The Mary Bridgers Park area is an irregular-shaped glen of trees, sloping down to and following the bends of Burnt Mill Creek. Massive cypress and other native trees of the area, including sycamore, live and water oak, and yellow pine, have been retained. Spanish moss drapes the trees, pickerel weed and other marsh plants grow in the shallow pools beside the creek, and the grassy slopes are mown but not manicured.

Though in a well-developed residential area, the effect of the park is natural, open, and cared for.

B'nai Israel Cemetery

North Eighteenth Street at Princess Place Drive
1898

On January 18, 1898, a Wilmington newspaper reported: *"A Jewish Society Formed.* The B'nai Israel Society of Wilmington, which yesterday became incorporated by the Secretary of State, has been formed to be a benevolent, religious and charitable institution and to be a non-profit one. Its purposes will be to erect a house of worship, establish and maintain schools, aid its members in distress and to provide a suitable place of burial for its dead." B'nai Israel was an Orthodox Jewish congregation that later constructed its synagogue east of the city.

Almost immediately after its founding, the group began to search for a cemetery site. The newspaper reported on January 21, 1898, that N. Jacobi and M. Levy had been appointed a committee to purchase suitable land. On February 21 it reported that "the B'nai Israel Society has purchased a tract of land southeast of Bellevue Cemetery and will convert it into a Hebrew Cemetery."

The oldest stone in B'nai Israel seems to be dated 1909, though burials may have taken place earlier. Certainly the cemetery was prepared before that time, but B'nai Israel was a small group, and it is possible that a cemetery was not needed during its first decade.

The cemetery is enclosed along North Eighteenth Street by an iron fence with double gates bearing the name of the cemetery. The other sides are walled. The enclosed area is open and well manicured. Stones display extensive use of Hebrew, so that there is a feeling of religious uniqueness and oneness about this burial ground that is not obvious in most cemeteries.

Bulluck Park

Between Chestnut and Market Streets, Burnt Mill Creek and Wilmington National Cemetery
1923–53

The *Dispatch* reported on December 2, 1925, that the city had accepted an offer from the Brookwood Company for land on the east side of Burnt Mill Creek, providing the city would receive the same offer from the owners of a similar strip of land on the west side of the creek adjoining the National Cemetery. Evidently the land to the west of the creek was not obtained at that time, and the land to the east of the creek would have been outside the city limits, so no transfer from Brookwood to the city was accomplished. This marked the beginning of planning for a park in the area, however.

As in the area of Mary Bridgers Park, this land is on the west side of Burnt Mill Creek, which was straightened and deepened during work carried out by the city in 1947–48. Although fill operations had already been going on in the area for some time, the present area of the park was still in private ownership during that period.

In 1943 the city attorney prepared a deed to the

property, then owned by Dr. Ernest S. Bulluck, in which Bulluck would deed the property to the city in exchange for the waiver of street assessments against his property. Elaborate plans were drawn for the proposed park according to the *Star* for May 23, 1944:

The completion of preliminary sketches for the development of Burnt Mill Creek Park, drawn by Ralph W. Snell, Supt. of the Parks Department, have been completed and await action of the city council.

The park which will be built along the design of a sunken garden, will be planted with an abundance of shrubs, flowering trees and flowers of all types. It is to be located adjacent to the National Cemetery property, between Chestnut and Market Streets.

Dr. Bulluck died before executing a deed to the city, and it was not finally signed by his wife Mary H. Bulluck until 1952. At that time Mary Bridgers Park to the north and Wallace Park to the south were already in city ownership, and acquisition of the Bulluck Park area gave the city continuous park along Burnt Mill Creek for some ten blocks from Metts Avenue on the south to Princess Place Drive on the north.

With transfer of the Bulluck property, the name of the proposed park was evidently changed from Burnt Mill Creek Park to Bulluck Park. The area was quite low and swampy, and a continuous program of clearing and filling was carried out by the street department of the city until 1954, when the area was turned over to the parks department.

Between 1954 and 1957 the Chestnut Heights Garden Club accomplished a landscaping project aimed at providing flowering plants for the area and open lawn space, both planned for easy maintenance. Some 1,500 azaleas and a smaller number of other plants, including pittosporum, osmanthus, pilatka holly, gardenia, dogwood, crab apple, redbud, and a variety of bulbs, were planted. The bulbs were concentrated in naturalized plantings along the east bank of the creek, where they serve the dual purpose of erosion control and color. Other plants were set throughout the area in a plan developed by the garden club. Native cypress and other trees remain, as do wild plantings along the creek.

Bulluck is essentially a springtime park of blossom and color best viewed from the Wilmington National Cemetery, whose north and east boundaries the park protects. There is also easy access directly from Chestnut Street.

Wilmington National Cemetery

Market Street at North Twentieth Street
1867

Wilmington National Cemetery is changed remarkably little from its 1868 description in *Roll of Honor*, a Government Printing Office list of national cemeteries and those buried in them.

This national cemetery is situated one mile east of the city of Wilmington, N.C. and one and ½ miles from the Cape Fear River and about the same distance from the depot of the Wilmington and Weldon Railroad.

It embraces about 5 acres of land, which belonged to J. D. Ryttenberg. The land is high and rolling; the site is a good one and well adapted to cemetery purposes.

Interments were made in this cemetery from February to April, 1867.

It contains the remains of those Union soldiers who were originally buried at Fort Fisher, Smithville, Cape Fear river, and at points along the Wilmington & Manchester and the Wilmington & Weldon railroads; and some who were removed from the city cemetery and the Lutheran cemetery at Wilmington.

The cemetery proper is laid out in square lots or blocks having a center avenue 16 feet in width running from the south to the north side of the cemetery and also one of the same width extending around it. These avenues are graded. The lots are separated by walks 5 feet in width.

A flag-staff has been erected in the center of the cemetery, and about 180 live oaks and a quantity of plants, flowers, and shrubbery are now set out, and grass seed has been sown.

A large majority of the graves are marked with suitable head-boards, properly lettered and numbered, the remainder are in the process of being marked.

All other necessary improvements, with a view of ornamenting the cemetery, will soon be made. A superintendent has been appointed to take charge of this cemetery.

The number of soldiers buried here is as follows, viz: Number known 699, number unknown 1,360.

An 1874 inspection report gives a further breakdown of burials. By that time a total of 2,060 burials had taken place. Of these, 1,503 were white, of whom 646 were known and 857 were unknown. Some 557 of those interred here were black. Of these, 55 were known, and 502 were unknown. This was typical of national cemeteries. Bodies were often hastily buried where they fell—sometimes by the opposite force, depending on who advanced, held ground, or retreated. After the armies had passed through, care of graves often ceased, so that even if they were marked, the markers had often disappeared by the time the bodies were disinterred and moved after the end of the war in 1865.

In Wilmington and many other southern cities, there was also an initial problem with public acceptance. Wilmington had been a Confederate city, the last major Atlantic port open to the Confederacy. As the terminus of the train and port facilities that provided a lifeline to Lee's forces in Virginia, the city did not welcome a major Union cemetery in its midst. Though called *national*, the cemetery accepted for burial only bodies idenitfied as those of Union men.

Inspector General Lorenzo Thomas reported on November 4, 1868, in the *Report of The Inspector of National Cemeteries 1869*, located in the files at the University of North Carolina at Wilmington that: "the feeling of the community is not favorable to the cemetery, and shrubbery, though abundant, cannot be obtained except at high prices . . . at one time it was contemplated to discontinue the public road on which the cemetery fronts, and locating it in a different direction, but I judge the people owning land on this highway prevented the measure, if seriously contemplated." There were local charges of grave robbery and persistent whispers that not all the bodies reinterred in the cemetery were those of the Union dead.

As late as November 12, 1881, Col. William Lamb, Confederate commander at Fort Fisher, charged in the *Philadelphia Times* that:

On revisiting Fort Fisher after the war I found that the post burial ground, where my soldiers who died previous to the battle were buried, had been robbed of all its dead, and was told that a contractor for the government had stolen their bodies in order to be paid for supplying them with coffins under an appropriation to bury the dead of the Northern armies. . . .

I had the consolation when contemplating this act, that, although their dust had been disturbed, their memories were none the less precious to the Southern heart, nor their reward for duty done, less complete at the Hands of Him who doeth all things well.

Inasmuch as the hilltop plot in Oakdale had been secured for a Confederate cemetery in 1866—with some four hundred unknown bodies moved there and funds available for a monument—local opposition seems to have faded by the time of Colonel Lamb's 1881 charge. Indeed, his words seem to highlight the possibility that both plots probably contained the dead from both armies.

With the later burial of veterans who had served in the American armed forces after 1865, the cemetery did become truly national and was written about locally with a good deal of pride. Today Wilmington National contains dead from every American conflict from the Civil War to the Southeast Asian involvement in Vietnam.

Except for the fact that the road around the perimeter of the cemetery is now grassed and the plots are fuller, the 1868 description is remarkably accurate. Stones march through the cemetery in military precision, the lines straight from any viewpoint. Most stones are government issue, with only a few private markers interrupting the rhythm of those whose rounded tops indicate known Union burials and whose flat tops indicate unknowns. (Government-issue stones to Confederate soldiers, of which there are none in this cemetery, have pointed tops.)

The brick walls around three sides of the cemetery were constructed from 1875 through 1878. The original cemetery wall along Market Street was built

187. Wilmington National Cemetery. Bandstand, 1887.

of sandstone from Manassas, Virginia, in the area of the famous battleground. On Market Street these walls were replaced in 1934. The 1934 brick walls are low with iron atop, allowing views of the cemetery from the street that were not possible with the earlier wall. The present gate was hung in place in 1956, when the entrance approach was modified. The gatepost plaques are 1976.

Completed soon after the cemetery opened in 1867, the first lodge and keeper's dwelling of frame construction was evidently drafty and unsatisfactory. It was replaced in 1875 by a stone French Second-Empire style structure with mansard roof. When plans were announced in 1933 to replace the 1875 lodge with another structure, there was local protest, and a campaign was mounted to save that structure. The preservation effort was not successful however, and the present Dutch Colonial lodge with gambrel roof, brick first floor, and stucco half-timbered second floor was constructed on a foundation that used the stone of the earlier lodge.

The present flagpole is in the same area as the 1868 one but is a replacement, dedicated on May 15, 1928.

To the southeast of the flagpole is the cemetery bandstand (fig. 187) completed in April 1887 of iron manufactured by the Champion Iron Company, Kent, Ohio. It is the only structure of its type that survives in Wilmington cemeteries, though Oakdale once had similar summerhouses. Originally the National Cemetery bandstand had a canopy roof atop decorated iron columns. The steps, floor, and balustrade were retained when the covering was removed to Greenfield Park.

Live oaks planted in 1874 still thrive, as do several camellias planted either at that time or soon thereafter. One of these—Camellia Japonica, var. Alba Plena—has received considerable notice from time to time because of the tradition surrounding its origin. It is said that the plant was a gift from the emperor of Japan to this country through President U. S. Grant and that Grant ordered it planted here. There were, it is said, other camellia planted in other cemeteries from the same gift, but only this one has survived. From its size and girth, there seems no reason to believe that it is not old enough to have been planted during the Grant administration, 1869–77, and shrubbery is known to have been planted here in 1874. No hard evidence has yet been uncovered to prove the exotic origin of the plant. However it came to be here, the shrub is one of the showiest in the area when it begins its fall blossoming.

In sections 8 and 9, northwest of the flagpole, lie 28 Puerto Rican civilians, victims of the 1918 influenza epidemic, their plight seemingly compounded by mismanagement and neglect. Of the nineteen hundred Puerto Rican laborers who arrived in Wilmington aboard the government ship *City of Savannah* on November 12, 1918, it was reported that at least three hundred men were ill. They had left Puerto Rico while the influenza epidemic was raging there, many without shoes, all with only tropical clothing that ill prepared them for November weather in Wilmington. The voyagers ran into a severe storm at sea and discovered after the illness began to develop that there was not suitable food aboard for those who were ill.

The laborers had been on their way to Fayetteville to help in the construction of Camp Bragg, but shortly after their arrival in Wilmington it was announced that their services would no longer be needed. The ship began to move the sick toward the hospital at Fort Caswell. Nine of the first one hundred fifty men transferred died soon, and their bodies were transported to Wilmington National for burial on November 18. On November 20 four more bodies were buried there. Though the government announced plans to compensate the Puerto Ricans for the time they had spent away from their homes, it was too late for the twenty-eight of them who now rest in the Wilmington National Cemetery, their stones identifying them as "Employee, U.S.A."

A large number of blacks who died in the Civil War were buried here, their stones identifying them as "*U.S.C.T.*" or "*U.S. Col. Inf.*": either U.S. colored troops or infantry.

Among civilians buried at the cemetery is Inglis Fletcher, North Carolina's indefatigable novelist. Her *Roanoke Hundred* and other novels with a North Carolina theme made the seventeenth- and eighteenth-century Carolina coast familiar to millions of readers around the world. Mrs. Fletcher died in 1969, and her funeral was attended by a great number of her literary friends. Her grave is to the northwest of the flag circle where her husband, John G. Fletcher, a Spanish-American War veteran who died in 1960 is buried.

Wallace Park

Along Burnt Mill Creek between Metts Avenue and Market Street
c. 1930

Wallace Park buttresses Carolina Place on the east and Brookwood on the west. Begun simultaneously with Carolina Heights to the north, in the early twentieth century, Carolina Place stretched from boundaries nearer town to a natural boundary—the swamps, marshes, and meander of Burnt Mill Creek. To the east of this natural boundary, the Brookwood suburb developed in the 1920s.

Since the creek marked the official eastern boundary of the city, most early work was to its west—though with dredge and fill operations, the meander of the waterway changed along with the amount of land and the stability of the land along its western, or town, side.

When the city extended its corporate limits west of the creek on January 1, 1946, one immediate result was the city securing a program to deepen and straighten Burnt Mill Creek. This not only provided better drainage and lessened sanitary and insect pest problems, but allowed beautification and public use of the land along the creek. The area between Market Street and Metts Avenue was deeded to the city by O. T. Wallace with the purpose of developing it into a park.

Burnt Mill Creek is now almost straight between Metts Avenue and Market Street, though the eastern boundary of the park gives some idea of its earlier course. Of the three parks along the creek, Wallace alone crosses the creek and secures both banks. The waterway is less natural and more channelized here than in either of the other two parks. Wallace Park is the largest of the three, and vistas and views along the stream are excellent. Cypress trees are sizable, and the collection larger than in either of the other parks. Essentially the park consists of a collection of native trees, the stream, and wide-seeded open spaces that require minimal upkeep.

188. Kenan Memorial Fountain, detail; center of intersection of Market Street and Fifth Avenue.

Appendix A
National Register of Historic Places

The National Register of Historic Places, maintained by the Keeper of the Register in the Office of Archaeology and Historic Preservation, National Park Service, Department of the Interior, Washington, D.C., is a national listing of properties significant in American history, architecture, archaeology, and culture. The register is an index of the remaining three-dimensional evidence of our past. Sites and properties that meet the criteria established by the National Register, that are approved for nomination by the state review board, and that have provable significance after an exhaustive architectural and historical documentation program are nominated to the Register by the director of the Division of Archives and History, North Carolina Department of Cultural Resources, the state historic preservation officer. If the nomination is approved by the register, the property is then entered in the National Register of Historic Places.

In Wilmington the following sites are presently listed in the National Register:

1. *Wilmington Historic District*: Boundaries: Beginning at the juncture of the rear property line of the south side of Wright Street and the east bank of the Cape Fear River; running east along the rear property line of the south side of Wright Street to the rear property line of the east side of South Seventh Street; running north along the rear property line of the east side of South Seventh Street to the rear property line of the south side of Church Street; running east along the rear property line of the south side of Church Street to the rear property line of the east side of South Eighth Street; running north along the rear property line of the east side of South Eighth Street to Dock Street; running east along the north side of Dock Street to the rear property line of the east side of North and South Ninth streets; running north along the rear property line of the east side of North and South Ninth streets to the rear property line of the north side of Grace Street; running west along the rear property line of the north side of Grace Street to the rear property line of the east side of North Eighth Street; running north along the rear property line of the east side of North Eighth Street to the rear property line of the north side of Harnett Street; running west along the rear property line of the north side of Harnett Street; running west along the rear property line of the north side of Harnett Street to the east bank of the Cape Fear River; running west along an imaginary line extended from the above rear property line of the north side of Harnett Street reaching across the Cape Fear River to a point 100 yards west of the west bank of the river; running south parallel to the river bank along this 100-yard line to a point opposite the beginning point; running directly east across the river to the beginning.

2. *Market Street mansions*: Boundaries: 1700 block of Market Street, beginning at the junction of Perry Avenue and South Eighteenth Street, and running west along midline of Perry Avenue to its junction with South Seventeenth Street; thence running north along the midline of South Seventeenth Street, across Market Street and along North Seventeenth Street to the rear property line of the Bridgers-Emerson-Kenan House; thence east along said rear property line to the intersection with the west property line of the Holt-Wise House; thence north along said line to its intersection with the midline of Princess Street; thence east along said line to its intersection with the midline of North Eighteenth Street; thence south along said line, across Market Street, continuing along South Eighteenth Street to the point of beginning.

3. *U.S. Custom House–Alton F. Lennon Federal Building*: Location: North Water Street between Market and Princess streets.

4. *City Hall–Thalian Hall*: Location : northeast corner, North Third and Princess streets.

The following individual sites, most of them located within the Wilmington Historic District, also meet the criteria of the National Register. Those properties marked "(1)" were approved by the State Review Board on September 19, 1969. Those sites marked "(4)" were recommended to the Division of Archives and History by Tony P. Wrenn in September of 1971. On September 1, 1971, the list was presented to representatives of the Division of Archives and History in Wilmington, and they concurred in the recommendations. During that joint on-site survey, several additional sites were added to the list of sites marked "(4)". These were all presented at the review board meeting on April 25, 1972, when all properties marked "(4)" were approved. That list follows:

Cape Fear River
U.S.S. *North Carolina—"The Showboat"* (4) (fig. 14)

North Water Street
North Water Street, between Market and Princess, *U.S. Custom House* (4) (fig. 15) (now listed in the National Register)

North Front Street
25 North Front Street, *McRae Building–Otterbourg's Iron Front Men's Wear Depot* (4) (fig. 25)
116 North Front Street, *George R. French & Sons Building* (4)
201–3 North Front Street, *Murchison Building* (4) (fig. 28)

South Front Street
322 South Front Street, *Honnet House* (4) (fig. 36)
400 South Front Street, *Governor Dudley's Mansion* (4) (fig. 37)
508 South Front Street, *Wessell-Harper House* (4) (fig. 40)

South Second Street
23 South Second Street, *DeRosset House* (4) (fig. 44)
121 South Second Street, *Ballard-Potter-Bellamy House* (4) (fig. 45)

North Third Street
North Third Street at Princess, southeast corner, *New Hanover County Courthouse* (4) (figs. 10, 50)
North Third Street at Princess, northeast corner, *City Hall–Thalian Hall* (1) (figs. 10, 51, 114, 115), (now listed in the National Register.)

South Third Street
1 South Third Street, *St. James Episcopal Church* (4) (figs. 10, 52, 53)
15 South Third Street, *Donald MacRae House* (4) (fig. 55)
100 South Third Street, *Bridgers House* (4) (fig. 57)
120 South Third Street, *Edward and Henry Savage House* (4) (fig. 59)
126 South Third Street, *Zebulon Latimer House* (1) (fig. 62)
202 South Third Street, *Henry Latimer House* (4) (fig. 65)
208 South Third Street, *Edward Latimer House* (4)
302 South Third Street, *Hassell-Parsley-French House* (4)
305 South Third Street, *Murchison House–Diocesan House* (4) (fig. 68)
318 South Third Street, *Burrus House* (4) (fig. 69)
402 South Third Street, *McKoy House* (4) (fig. 72)

North Fourth Street
602–6 North Fourth Street, *Consolidated Market and Fire Engine House no. 3* (4) (fig. 74)

South Fourth Street
1 South Fourth Street, *Temple of Israel* (4) (fig. 75)
116 South Fourth Street, *Wilkinson-Belden House* (4) (fig. 79)
306 South Fourth Street, *Bell House* (4) (fig. 82)

North Fifth Avenue
15 North Fifth Avenue, *Conoley-Hanby-Sidbury House* (4) (fig.84)
19 North Fifth Avenue, *Von Glahn House* (4) (fig. 85)
502 North Fifth Avenue, *St. Stephen AME Church* (4) (figs. 86, 87, 88)

South Fifth Avenue
10 South Fifth Avenue, *Williams House* (4)
20 South Fifth Avenue, *Costin House* (4) (frontispiece)
120 South Fifth Avenue, *Wessell-Hathaway House* (4) (fig. 89)
124 South Fifth Avenue, *H. B. Eilers House* (4) (fig. 90)
220 South Fifth Avenue, *the St. Mary Church* (4) (figs. 92, 93, 94)

Chestnut Street
710½ Chestnut Street, *Chestnut Street United Presbyterian Church* (4) (fig. 109)

Princess Street
516 Princess Street, *Manning-Cobb-Toon House* (4) (fig. 117)

Market Street
224 Market Street, *Burgwin-Wright House* (1) (fig. 120)
409–11 Market Street, *John A. Taylor House* (1) (fig. 123)
412 Market Street, *Martin-Huggins House* (4) (fig. 124)
421 Market Street, *First Baptist Church* (4) (fig. 126)
503 Market Street, *Bellamy Mansion* (1) (figs. 130, 131, 132)
514 Market Street, *William Jones Price House* (4) (fig. 133)
602–8 Market Street, Bellamy Mansion II (4), "demolished"
603 Market Street, *St. Paul's Evangelical Lutheran Church* (4) (fig. 134)

Dock Street
207–9 Dock Street, *DeRosset House* (4) (fig. 44) (see 23 South Second Street for description)
208 Dock Street, *the St. Thomas the Apostle Church* (4) (fig. 137)

Orange Street
102 Orange Street, *Smith-Anderson House* (4) (figs. 142, 143)
104 Orange Street, *Dr. Edwin A. Anderson's Office* (4)
110 Orange Street, *Hogg-Anderson House* (4)
114 Orange Street, *St. John's Masonic Lodge–St. John's Art Gallery* (4) (fig. 144)
318 Orange Street, *Rankin-Orrell House* (4) (fig. 147)
520 Orange Street, *Willard House* (4) (fig. 149)

Nun Street
202 Nun Street, *Beery House* (4) (fig. 12)

Church Street
6 Church Street, *Georgian-style coastal cottage* (4) (fig. 164)

Also recommended in the September 1971 memorandum and subsequently approved on April 25, 1972, were:

Market Street Mansion, 1700 block of Market Street (4) (figs. 169, 170, 171, 172) (now listed in the National Register)
Oakdale Cemetery (4) (figs. 177, 178, 179, 180, 181, 182)
Wilmington Historic District (4) (now listed in the National Register)

Were the list being evolved today, a number of additional sites and historic districts would be added to those recommended above, and the list should not be considered final or all-inclusive.

Appendix B Paving Materials

This brief history of paving materials in the townscape covers the late nineteenth and early twentieth centuries. Most cities had little paving until early in the twentieth century. Typical turn-of-the-century paving materials—brick, paving block, and cobblestone—may be seen scattered throughout the Historic District of Wilmington.

Paving brick was dense, hard-fired brick, different from the brick used for standard construction; each brick measured a uniform eight and one-half inches in length. Processed clay or shale, pressed into a mold to give dimensional stability, was heated and was baked (vitrified) in kilns to form paving brick. Many manufacturers produced miscellaneous paving brick under various names during the early twentieth century. Often the manufacturer imprinted the name of the company on one broad surface of the brick; for example: "Augusta Block," "Catskill Block," "Southern Clay Mfg. Co.," "Peebles Block," "Reynold Block," "Ragland Block." This practice not only advertised the maker, but improved traction by offering a varied surface. The predominate producers of paving brick were located in the areas surrounding Atlanta and Richmond, where an ample supply of raw materials was available. Locally produced brick was supplied by Roger Moore of Wilmington, Manufacturer of Brick. In 1910 Roger Moore's Sons Company produced one million bricks per month, which were shipped out of the city by rail and were delivered locally by teams of horses.

Paving block consisted of quarried stone or granite cut into rectangular shape. Paving block were shipped by rail from quarries near Richmond, as well as from quarries near Petersburg, Virginia which were owned by the Atlantic Coast Line Railroad, whose main offices were located in Wilmington. Schooners from Europe used stone paving or cobblestone as ballast during the late nineteenth century. Some blocks, actually a type of brick, were pressed into molds and shaped into blocks from raw material clay, macadam, or cement. At the turn of the century a machine named "The Wizzard" produced block from brick. This machine was used to cast brick that resembled block by shaping the clay with selected tin dies. As with brick, paving blocks arranged in a variety of linear, crisscross, or serpentine patterns and graded to facilitate water drainage can still be found in many Wilmington streets.

A PARTIAL LIST OF EARLY PAVING MATERIALS

Augusta Block—Paving brick, characteristically dark gray, containing raised lettering "Augusta Block" imprinted on one broad surface; supplied by Augusta Block Company of Georgia, c. 1909.

Asphalt Paving Block—A type of macadam, or composition material, of uniformly rough surface texture and dark gray color; supplied by Hastings-on-the-Hudson, c. 1912. (Not true asphalt as known today.)

Belgian Paving Stone—Small rectangular blocks of quarried stone or granite, commonly used paving material of late nineteenth and early twentieth centuries; also called "Washington Block;" supplied from quarries in Richmond, and Petersburg, Virginia, owned by The Atlantic Coast Line Railroad, c. 1880s—early 1900s.

Catskill Block—Paving brick, characteristically dark red, containing raised lettering "Catskill Block;" unusually long, nine and one-half inches in length; source of supplier unknown; in use, c. 1901.

Cobblestone—Smooth pavers of stone or granite; transported from Europe as ballast on sailing ships; supplied by Grey Stone Granite Company, c. 1892.

Octagonal Cement Block—Typical sidewalk paving material of early twentieth century; supplied by W. E. Glenn of Wilmington, c. 1904.

Peebles Block—Paving brick, red-gray, or blue-gray, containing prominent raised lettering "Peebles Block" and small indented lettering "Portsmouth, Ohio"; source and date of supplier unknown.

Ragland Block—Paving brick, gray-brown or red, containing raised lettering "Ragland Block"; source and date of supplier unknown.

Reynolds Block—Paving brick, gray-brown or ochre, containing indented lettering "Reynold Block"; supplied by Tennessee Paving Brick Company, Chattanooga, Tennessee, c. 1900.

Southern Clay Mfg. Co.—Paving brick, blue-gray, red or ochre, containing raised lettering "Southern Clay Mfg. Co." within diamond-shaped border; supplied by Southern Clay Manufacturing Company of Alabama; date unknown. (See fig. 155.)

SOURCES

National Register of Historic Places.

Mr. David Black, North Carolina Archives and History, Raleigh.

Mr. Marion R. Cochran, Chief Engineer, Brick Association of North Carolina, Greensboro.

Mr. Gene Long, Merry Brothers Brick and Research Company, Atlanta, Georgia.

Mr. Augustus B. Moore, Jr., Wilmington, North Carolina.

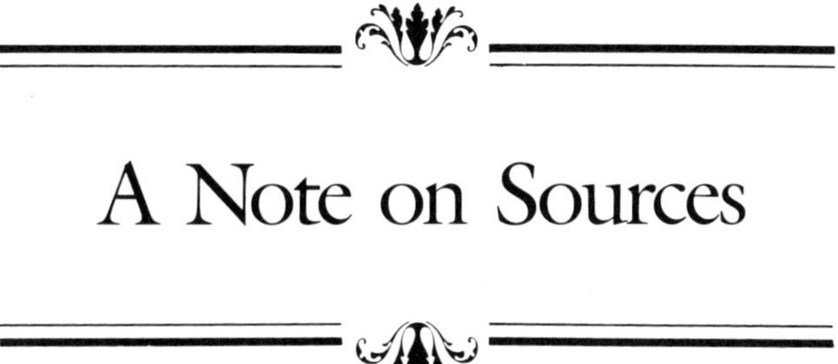

A Note on Sources

An effort has been made to integrate footnotes into the text; newspaper and published titles and dates are normally included there when material is used from such sources. When cartographic or directory material is used, these sources too are normally identified in the text. In the case of legal material, the parties to a legal document—deed, will, insurance policy, etc.—and the date are normally given. While this is not the context in which footnote material is usually given, it did allow space in the published work to be used for additional text and graphics. "An appendix on Architects, Builders, Artisans, Sculptors, and Others" has also been prepared. This appendix consists entirely of documentary material. It is a source book, which details much of the information gathered on artisans while this volume was being prepared. It is also, to my knowledge, the first effort in North Carolina to identify local artisans or those who have accomplished local work, giving both source material on their lives and on their work, both in North Carolina and elsewhere and containing information on the location of the work. It is believed that the appendix will be a major source of information for architectural historians and other scholars. Anyone wishing to have a copy of this appendix may write the Junior League of Wilmington, N.C., The Carriage House, Cottage Lane, Wilmington, N.C., 28401.

Once it was decided which structures would be covered for this work, we made an attempt in our work in Wilmington to do a chain of title, check the Sanborn and other maps, check city directories, check newspapers, and check private papers on each property and its owners. As the material was amassed, a file was formed on each structure included. These files have been put in order and a complete copy has been deposited in the William Randall Library at The University of North Carolina at Wilmington, where they are available for public use. There are also a number of files on structures not in this work, since several buildings we wished to include were destroyed during the period of the study, and the decision was ultimately made to include only standing buildings. Included in the Wilmingtoniana Collection at the Wilmington Public Library are the various drafts of this work. Some drafts contain information that others do not, for space or other reasons. Included in this material is a survey list of structures and sites in the historic-district and streetcar-suburb areas. The list includes address, whether the structure is a dwelling or has commercial or some other use, whether or not photographs and other material exist in the survey files, and frequently a name. Source for the name is given where known. Dates, architects, and other artisans are also listed. The survey list includes an area list covering paving material, street furniture, and amenities. It is the most complete inventory yet developed of the areas covered, containing over 1,400 entries—buildings and sites the author looked at and felt to have value. Many are now gone, and the list serves as a record; others deserve fuller treatment. The list, essentially completed in 1976, serves as a picture of the city at that time, though it covers only a small part of the urban area. It makes recommendations on other areas that ought to be covered. The Wilmingtoniana Collection also contains most of the publications used in this work, plus a great amount of additional material.

Another major source of material was the Archives of the Lower Cape Fear Historical Society, housed in the Zebulon Latimer House, headquarters of the society. These files contain copies of the Sanborn Insurance maps, other cartographic material, and a mass of original material concerning the city and the surrounding area. Private papers, diaries, published works, architectural renderings, and a great many documentary photographs are included in the collection.

Both St. John's Museum of Art, Inc., and the New Hanover County Museum also contain local material. These range from paintings by local artists, sometimes showing local buildings or views, to examples of locally produced ironwork.

Material in the survey files of the Division of Archives and History Department of Cultural Resources in Raleigh, contains a good deal of information not included in the Wilmington files. This included architectural descriptions on a very large number of buildings or sites not included here, and thousands of photographs, many of them buildings that no longer stand. These photographs are a prime collection of the Wilmington that existed in 1973, when most were taken. The files, especially on National Register properties, also contain a great amount of historical data and additional architectural analysis. They are prime files for the researcher.

There are also many private collections of interest to the researcher. A number of churches have archives and/or published histories, and there are several local collections that are notable. The collections of Bill Reaves and of Ida Brooks Kellam are among these. The Historic Wilmington Foundation files contain information on houses that have foundation plaques. This material is updated as new research is accomplished and includes documented historical and architectural analyses of a number of houses.

All deed information and all insurance records prior to 1856 can be found at the Register of Deeds in the New Hanover County Court House.

The North Carolina Room at the New Hanover County Public Library has a microfilm of the seven Sanborn maps of Wilmington. The originals, contained within the complete set of Sanborn maps, are to be found at the Library of Congress. The Sanborn maps were made as insurance maps that bank and insurance companies and their agents could lease. The Sanborn Map Company still exists today in New York.

The maps of Wilmington cited in the text were published in 1884, 1889, 1893, 1898, 1904, 1910, and 1915. The Sanborn maps are of heavy-density sections of towns, and the earliest Sanborn map of Wilmington (1884) deals only with certain sections of Wilmington that were mainly industrial.

The map referred to in the text as the Gray map is actually one of the many maps contained within the atlas entitled *The National Atlas, containing elaborate topographical maps of the United States and the Dominion of Canada, with plans of cities and general maps of the world; also, descriptions and tables, historical and statistical, with a reference list* (Philadelphia: O. W. Gray and Son, 1882). The map of Wilmington in that volume represents the city as drawn in 1881. The North Carolina Room at the New Hanover County Library has a copy of the Wilmington map, but not the complete atlas. The atlas can be found in the Map Collections, University of North Carolina at Chapel Hill.

Among the printed works, the following were the most useful:

General

Chamber of Commerce, *Wilmington: The Metropolis and Port of North Carolina: Its Advantages and Interests.* I. J. Issacs, comp. Wilmington: Wilmington Stamp and Printing Company., 1912.

Chamber of Commerce, *Wilmington, North Carolina, Past, Present, and Future. . . .* Wilmington: J. A. Engelhard, 1872.

Hewlett, Crockett W., *Two Centuries of Art in New Hanover County.* Durham, N.C.: Moore Publishing Company, 1976.

Isaacs, I. J., comp. *Wilmington Up-to-Date, the Metropolis of North Carolina Graphically Portrayed.* Wilmington: W. L. DeRosset, for the chamber of commerce, 1902. (Contains many fine illustrations.)

Donald Jackson and Dorothy Twohig, eds. *The Diaries of George Washington*, vol. 6, *January 1790–December 1799.* Charlottesville: University Press of Virginia, 1979.

Reiley, J. S. *Wilmington, Past, Present and Future. . . .* N.p: n.p., [c. 1884]. (Contains extremely fine cuts of Saint Paul's Church, frontispiece; Tileston Normal School, frontispiece; City Hall and Opera House, p. 61; St. James Church, p. 71; First Baptist Church, p. 75; view of the city, p. 77; Bank of New Hanover, p. 91; T. J. Southerland Livery Stable, 108–10 Second Street, p. 101; Otterbourg Building, 22–28 North Front Street, p. 110; W. H. Green Iron Front, 117 Market Street, p. 122.)

Sprunt, James. *Chronicles of the Cape Fear River, Being Some Accounts of Historic Events on the Cape Fear River.* Raleigh, N.C.: Edwards & Broughton, 1914.

Information and Statistics Respecting Wilmington, North Carolina. Wilmington: Jackson & Bell, 1883.

Tales and Traditions of the Lower Cape Fear, 1661–1896. Wilmington: Le Gwin Bros, 1896. (Includes some fifty-seven pages of business listings.)

City Directories

Frank D. Smaw, Jr. *Smaw's Wilmington Directory Comprising a General and City Business Directory and a Directory of Colored Persons to which is added a complete Historical and Commercial Sketch of the City* [by J. T. James]. Wilmington: Frank D. Smaw, Jr., 1867.

Sheriff's Wilmington, N.C., Directory and General Advertiser, 1879–80. Wilmington: P. Heinsberger, 1879.

Boyd's Wilmington, N.C. Directory and General Advertiser, 1881–82. Wilmington: P. Heinsberger, 1881.

Directory of the City of Wilmington North Carolina, 1889. Wilmington: Julius A. Bonitz, 1889. (Contains a fine cut of Geo. R. French and Sons store, 108 North Front Street, in French advertisement, frontispiece.)

J. L. Hill Printing Co.'s Directory of Wilmington, N.C., 1897. Richmond: J. L. Hill, 1897.

J. L. Hill Printing Co.'s Directory of Wilmington, N.C., 1900. Richmond: J. L. Hill Printing Co., 1900.

Hill Directory Co.'s Directory of Wilmington, N.C. 1902. Richmond: Hill Directory Co., 1902.

Wilmington, N.C., Directory, 1903. Richmond: Hill Directory Co.

Wilmington, N.C., Directory, 1907. Richmond: Hill Directory Co., 1907.

Wilmington, N.C., Directory, 1909–10. Richmond: Hill Directory Co., 1909.

Wilmington, N.C., Directory, 1911–12. Richmond: Hill Directory Co., 1911.

Wilmington, N.C., Directory, 1915–16. Richmond: Hill Directory Co., 1915. (Contains a fine cut of Citizens National Bank Building, Market and North Front streets, on inside front cover).

Wilmington, N.C., Directory, 1918. Richmond: Hill Directory Co., 1918. (Includes fine cuts of The Orton in advertisement, frontispiece, and of the Hotel Wilmington in their advertisement opposite p. 356).

Wilmington, N.C., Directory, 1919–20. Richmond: Hill Directory Co., 1919.

NEWSPAPERS

Newspaper[1]	*Publication dates*	*Weekly or daily*
Cape Fear Recorder	1816–32	weekly
Daily Dispatch	1865–67	daily
Daily Herald	1854–63?	daily
Daily Journal	1851–78?	daily
Evening Dispatch	1894–1923	daily
Hillsborough Recorder (Hillsboro, N.C.)	1820–79	weekly
Messenger	1867–1900+	daily
Morning Herald (New Bern, N.C.)	1807–10	weekly
Morning Star	1867*	daily
The Occident (Cincinnati, Ohio)	1843–67	
Philadelphia Times (Philadelphia, Pa.)	1876–1902	weekly
Raleigh (Raleigh, N.C.)	1799–1821	weekly
The South (New York)	unknown	unknown
Star-News	1929	weekly
Tri-Weekly Commercial	1846–58?	tri-weekly
Weekly Chronicle	1839?–51?	weekly
Weekly Star	1870?–1913	weekly
Wilmington Advertiser	1837–41	weekly
Wilmington Gazette	1797–1816	weekly
Wilmington News	1923–	daily
Wilmington New-Dispatch	1923–29	daily

[1]Unless otherwise noted, all newspapers listed above are Wilmington publications.

? = Firm dates cannot be established.

\+ = paper began publication in 1867 and continued after 1900, but is not now being published.

* = paper began publication in year mentioned and is still being published.

Sources:

Newspapers in Microform: United States, 1948–1972. Washington, D.C.: Library of Congress, 1973.

Newspapers in Microform: United States, 1973–1977. Washington, D.C.: Library of Congress, 1978.

North Carolina Newspapers on Microfilm: A Checklist of Early North Carolina Newspapers Available on Microfilm from the State Department of Archives and History. Raleigh, N.C.: State Department of Archives and History, 1971.

Publications on Microfilm. Wooster, Ohio: Bell and Howell, 1981.

Union List of North Carolina Newspapers: 1751–1900. Raleigh, N.C.: State Department of Archives and History, 1963.

Index

Italic numbers refer to page numbers of illustrations.

TONY P. WRENN is Archivist, American Institute of Architects, Washington, D.C.

WM. EDMUND BARRETT is a free-lance architectural photographer in Centreville, Virginia.

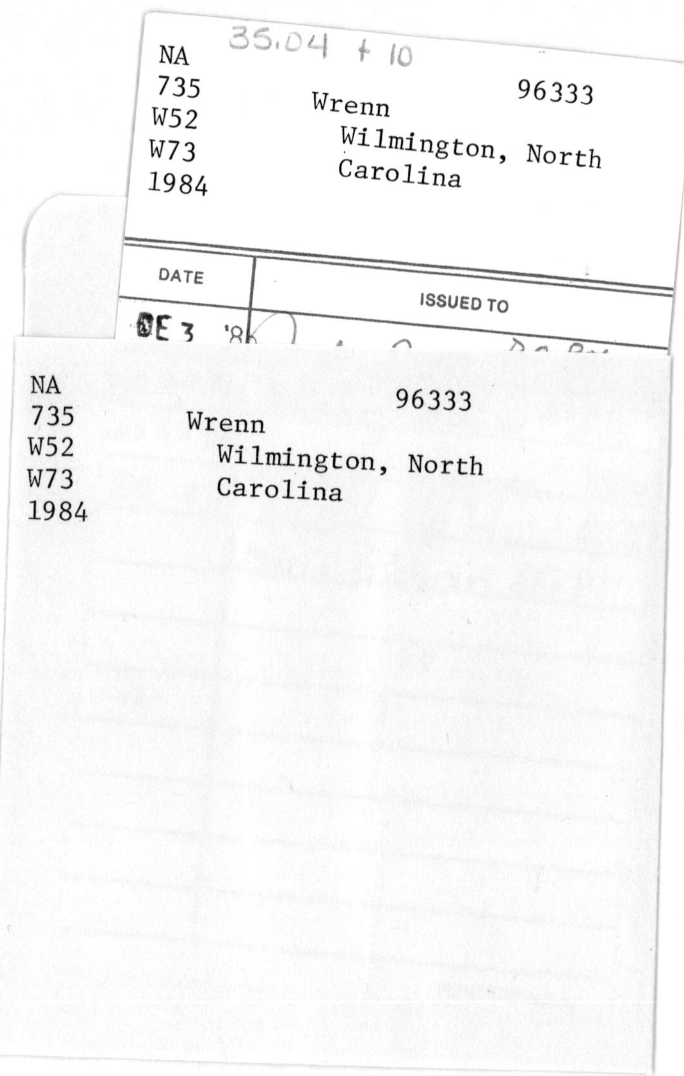

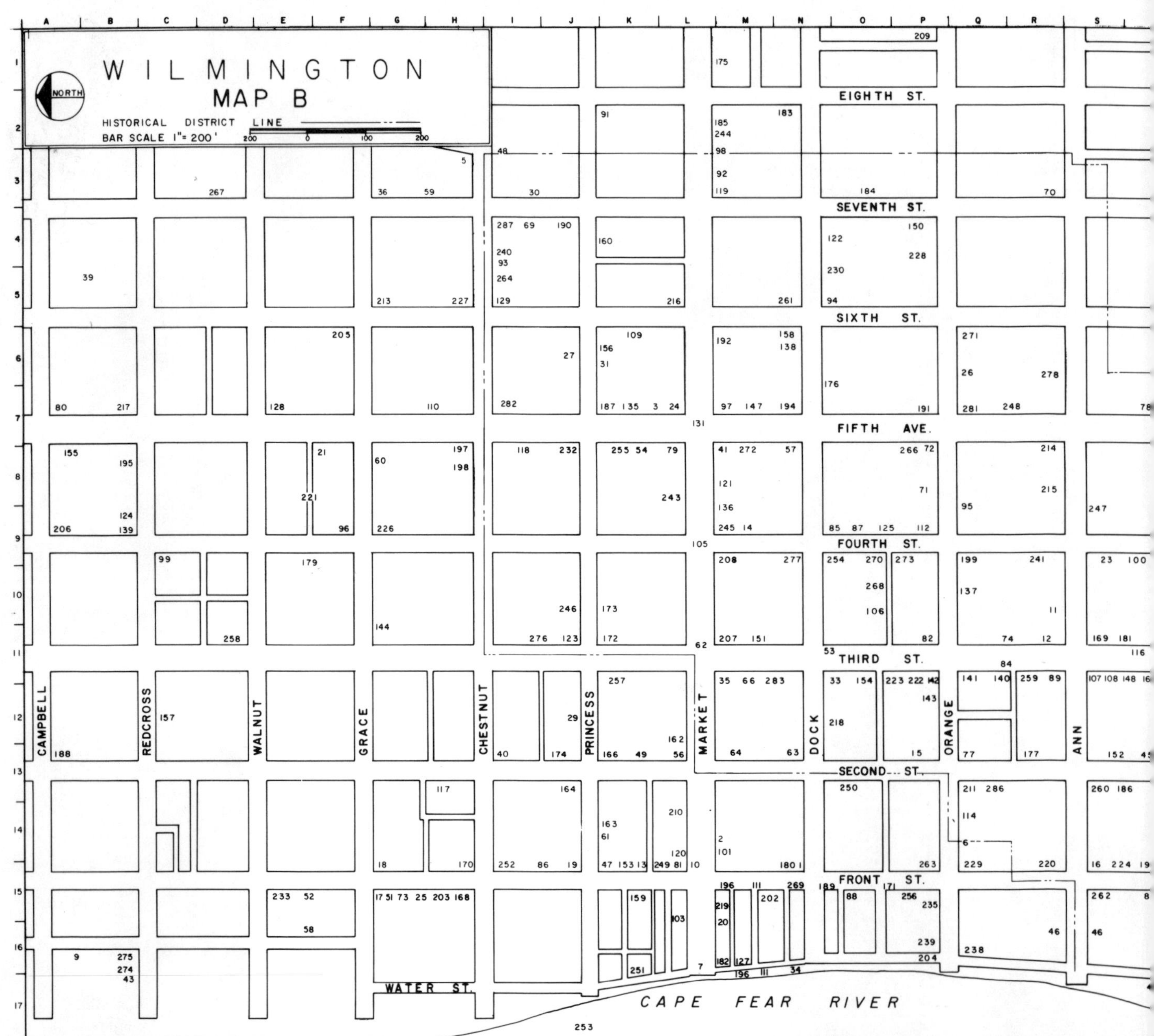
WILMINGTON
MAP B
NORTH
HISTORICAL DISTRICT LINE
BAR SCALE 1" = 200'
EIGHTH ST.
SEVENTH ST.
SIXTH ST.
FIFTH AVE.
FOURTH ST.
THIRD ST.
SECOND ST.
FRONT ST.
WATER ST.
CAMPBELL
REDCROSS
WALNUT
GRACE
CHESTNUT
PRINCESS
MARKET
DOCK
ORANGE
ANN
CAPE FEAR RIVER